PERSPECTIVES ON PLACE

THEORY AND PRACTICE IN LANDSCAPE PHOTOGRAPHY

First published 2015 by Bloomsbury Academic

Published 2020 by Routledge
2 Park Square, Milton Park, Abingdon, Oxon OX14 4RN
605 Third Avenue, New York, NY 10017

Routledge is an imprint of the Taylor & Francis Group, an informa business

British Library Cataloguing-in-Publication Data
A catalogue record for this book is available from the British Library.

Library of Congress Cataloging-in-Publication Data
Alexander, Jesse.
Perspectives on place : theory and practice in landscape photography / Jesse Alexander.
pages cm
Includes bibliographical references and index.
1. Landscape photography. 2. Composition (Photography) I. Title.
TR660.A54 2015
778.9'36--dc23
2014006883

Design: Hoop Design
Cover: *Hong Kong, Back Door 02*, 2003 - Photograph by Michael Wolf / Laif, Camera Press London
Printed and bound in China

ISBN 13: 978-1-4725-2409-6 (hbk)
ISBN 13: 978-1-4725-3389-0 (pbk)

PERSPECTIVES ON PLACE

THEORY AND PRACTICE IN LANDSCAPE PHOTOGRAPHY

J.A.P. ALEXANDER

Routledge
Taylor & Francis Group
www.routledge.com

FOREWORD

The camera can anchor us to a specific place or to an idea that enables us to explore, observe, and re-present both the external world and our internal reactions to it. So why is it that most camera owners seem to select the same "scenes"—waterfalls, sunsets, towering mountains, and sylvan glades?

Our social, educational, and cultural background establishes our visual literacy and how we interpret photographs. We inevitably see in them what we want to see. In my opinion, the majority of landscape photographs I see rarely challenge or surprise. They are predictable and formulaic and pose few philosophical or visual questions. They often appear to be conservative artifacts celebrating the status quo.

Half the population of Britain lives within one hour's drive of the borders of the first national park in this country, the Peak District National Park (established in 1951). I live only one mile away from it. Tourism is our area's biggest employer and reliant on the partial and persuasive use of photography to attract visitors in order to maintain economic stability for the inhabitants of this mostly rural community. While enjoying being among the hills and dales, visitors indulge in the largest creative pastime in the world—photography. And they nearly always attempt to recreate the images that persuaded them to visit the area in the first place. To do "something different" is rarely a considered option. Why? Just look at the photographic magazines at your newsagents and online at photography holiday websites. They nearly all unashamedly offer advice on how to make "good" landscape photographs, based on unchallenged compositional templates and stylistic gimmicks, with illustrations that are so similar they could almost have all been made by the same photographer.

But photography can offer so much more, even to the novice, than that. Photography can be a formidable tool of investigation for the curious and adventuresome, as it offers firsthand experience of the many mysteries around us: the mysteries of nature and society—and of ourselves. It combines the real world and the world of the imagination.

Despite what the "experts" say, you don't have to go to remote or exotic places, national parks, or mountain ranges to make landscape photographs. The land is the stuff under your feet and is everywhere—in your backyard and garden, in retail parks and industrial estates, as well as in picturesque dingles and glens. It is also not about the conjunction of the horizon with the azure blue sky or sunsets or grand vistas. It is about *you*, dear reader, and the fact that you are reading this means that you probably have a passion for photographing the land and nature, or you have been asked to do a project or write an essay on landscape photography. Either way, you are in good hands because Alexander is an excellent guide and advocate. He has set stimulating and appropriate assignments that challenge as well as educate. The book is designed to inspire and intrigue rather than just be informative, which, of course, it is too. What the author has done in this book is expose the reader to the wide ranges of different, and sometimes contentious, approaches to the genre and analyzed how a variety of practitioners "see" more in the genre than just the clichéd view. He also explains, in detail, the techniques they have employed to realize their diverse visions, whether they are driven by aesthetics or social, and even scientific, documentation.

He also reveals how photography, which is still really a new medium in comparison to painting and sculpture, has engaged with the landscape as a vehicle for making art, historically as well as in the new millennium.

Commentators frequently question whether photography is a stand-alone art form, but the quest for an acceptable definition of Art "will only lead us into a philosophical tar pit," as Edward Weston, a seminal figure in landscape photography, put it. So let us instead consider, as Alexander does in this book, the application of creative photography that does not seek to illustrate text or sell merchandise—photography for its own sake, if you like. It is obvious he knows his tools, and their creative potential, as much as a painter or sculptor does. He is, after all, an accomplished and experienced photographer. The tactile aspects inherent in the use of brush or chisel, pencil or blowtorch may be absent, but these are surely only agents used by the maker to transform one thing into another. Paint, carve, draw, weld—photograph. What matters is the practical skill and imagination applied to the task.

> *I think one's sense of appearance is assaulted all the time by photography . . . 99 percent of the time I find that photographs are very much more interesting than either abstract or figurative painting. I've always been haunted by them.*
> Francis Bacon, painter

Photography has become the preferred medium for so many artists today that the boundaries between fine art and photography seem to have been irrevocably blurred. But that does not diminish the importance of learning about its unique history, practices, and techniques. In fact, photography's popularity makes it even more relevant today than ever, with as many photographs being taken every two minutes than in the whole of the nineteenth century!

It is *not* just another medium to be vicariously taken off the art room shelf, as Alexander so eloquently demonstrates in this book. This book is also not just about landscape photography and how to engage with it. It is a celebration of *camera vision*—the practice of seeing, thinking, and creating photographically—and the individuals who pursue it passionately.

PROFESSOR PAUL HILL
www.hillonphotography.co.uk

INTRODUCTION: WHERE IS THE LANDSCAPE?

Although the landscape as subject matter for professional artists—within its own distinct category—is a relatively recent pursuit, humans have depicted their environments and the things within them for as long as they have had the means to do so. The earliest cave paintings that we are currently aware of, at Chauvet in France and dated back 30,000 years, depict with uncanny realism hunting scenes sketched out in charcoal. It would, perhaps, appear that the urge to represent our surroundings is so deep rooted that we might suppose such activity is a kind of base instinct. We may already seem a long way from landscape photography. However, consider the great volumes of pretty views that fill calendars and coffee-table books, that are used to market tourism to exotic destinations and sell a plethora of other commodities, and that decorate the walls of our homes, offices, libraries, and hospitals. Landscape pictures are everywhere.

These kinds of landscapes, as generic pictures of nature, are usually in the company of more detailed pictures of things that can be found in the landscape, such as flowers and insects—at least the pretty and nonbiting ones like butterflies. Department stores have plenty of this kind of ready-to-go wall art to spruce up the home, although much of it looks very alike. Intriguingly however, the same department store is now just as likely to offer you a not-so-calming image of nature's antithesis—the city. New York is arguably the conurbation of choice, and what could make a bolder statement about someone's personal taste than a giant canvas of the metropolis at night illuminated with the streaks of car headlamps whooshing through a long exposure and lots and lots of neon?

The history of landscape photography is full of practitioners who have studied both the town and the country as their subjects, and every conceivable kind of terrain between the two, as well as beyond. We still, however, tend to think about landscape in predominantly rural terms, and when subject matter veers away from these motifs, we feel the urge to ascribe a different label to it, such as "seascape," "urban landscape," or "industrial landscape."

Many students are put off exploring landscape photography by a misconception that the places they have access to are not deemed worthy of being decent landscape material. Such an idea is, ironically, likely to be due to the power that the most celebrated landscape photographs have exerted upon our notion of what encompasses a "good" landscape picture. As we shall see, it is not necessarily the *land* that makes the landscape, but how the photographer approaches, works with, and presents the finished photograph wherein the artistry lies. Wherever you are, and whoever you are, you have got a different voice to be heard, or rather, a vision to be seen.

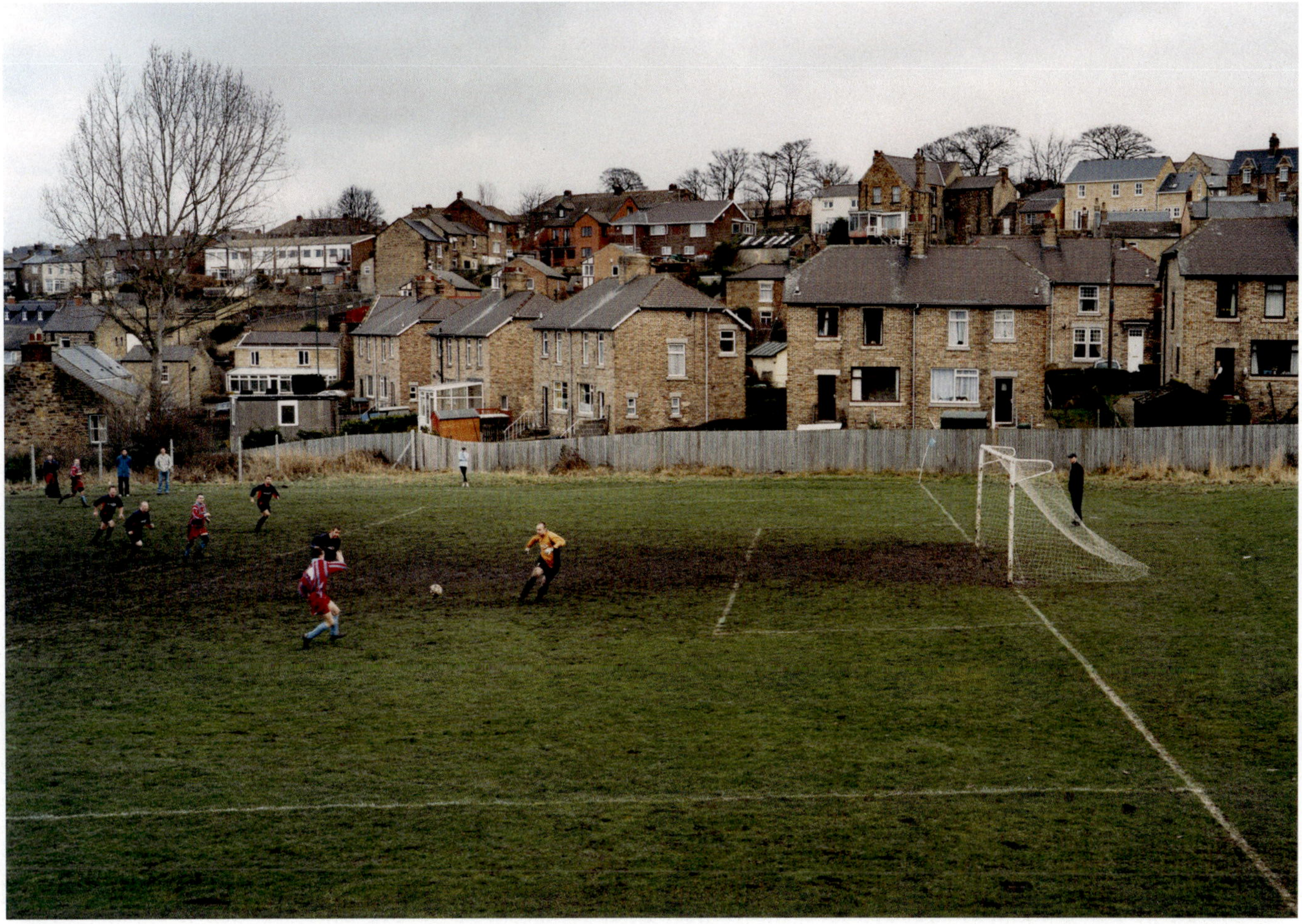

Fig. 0.1

Fig. 0.1
HANS VAN DER MEER
Consett, England, 2004* from the series *European Fields
In 1988, Hans van der Meer had a chance encounter with a photo archive in the Netherlands and was struck by a collection of vintage press photographs of football matches. Some of these pictures were taken from the kind of high vantage point that van der Meer adopted for his own later investigations. These kinds of elevated views seemed remarkable to the photographer who, like the rest of us, is mainly familiar with sports photography in terms of the significant details of the match or tournament (close-ups and action shots), rather than imagery that gives a sense of the event itself. Van der Meer's project, which has expanded considerably over the years, reclaims the significance of the actual locations in which these amateur league football matches take place. Such an approach has led to a unique body of photographic work in relation to both sports and landscape photography. The photographer has provided us with records of these matches, which are completely eclipsed by the sport's more glamorous leagues and show the games in the context of the landscapes and the communities that the players are connected to.

LANDSCAPE AS GENRE

> *Landscape . . . can be seen, as it was in nineteenth-century debates, as a general name for substances—it can mean bricks and mortar, leaves and fields, the desert, automobiles on a street, overcast or sunny skies, rural and suburban trees, concrete architecture, ghettos, a seascape at night, a seaside resort, the post-conflict rubble of a war-torn city, a tourist resort, industrial spaces, interiors or panoramic views. "Landscape" is not all things to all people, but a highly differentiated discourse on representing space.*
> David Bate[1]

Genres help us to define and compartmentalize things. They allow us to distinguish, for instance, between one book that mainly discusses the representation of people and another that discusses the representation of place. If not confusing, at times, they can also be problematic: the repeated identification of a style of picture or certain subject matter with a particular genre inevitably leads to the formation of preoccupations about exactly what types of pictures *should* look like, what purpose they *should* serve, even what shape they *should* be. Would a photograph of a person standing within a rural setting be classed as a portrait or a landscape? Can it be both?

Like other well-established fields of photography (still life, tableaux, portraiture), genres of photography have appropriated the terminology of traditions in other disciplines—notably painting. Strictly speaking, the landscape as a specific area of painting was not defined until the late sixteenth century, with the Dutch word *landschap*.[2] Although the land was depicted in a variety of contexts (frescos, theater scenery, maps, and illuminated manuscripts), it performed a supporting role, providing a setting for allegorical narratives rather than taking center stage as the primary subject matter. The popularity of landscape painting reached its height in the paintings of eighteenth- and early-nineteenth-century romanticists. The legacy of their idealized depictions of the land has persisted over the centuries and has extended into popular stereotypes and misconceptions of what landscape art looks like.

Perhaps the most useful way of understanding the nature of landscape is through W.J.T. Mitchell's assertion that "landscape" is more usefully understood through its form as a verb (*to* landscape) than as a noun (*a* landscape or *the* landscape).[3] "To landscape" clearly implies an intervention with a terrain or a space within it. Historically, this kind of "landscape gardening" and "landscape architecture" has been celebrated in the grand parks and gardens of the aristocracy. Built into the gardens of designers such as Capability Brown were specific places from which certain aspects of the garden were to be optimally viewed. Although

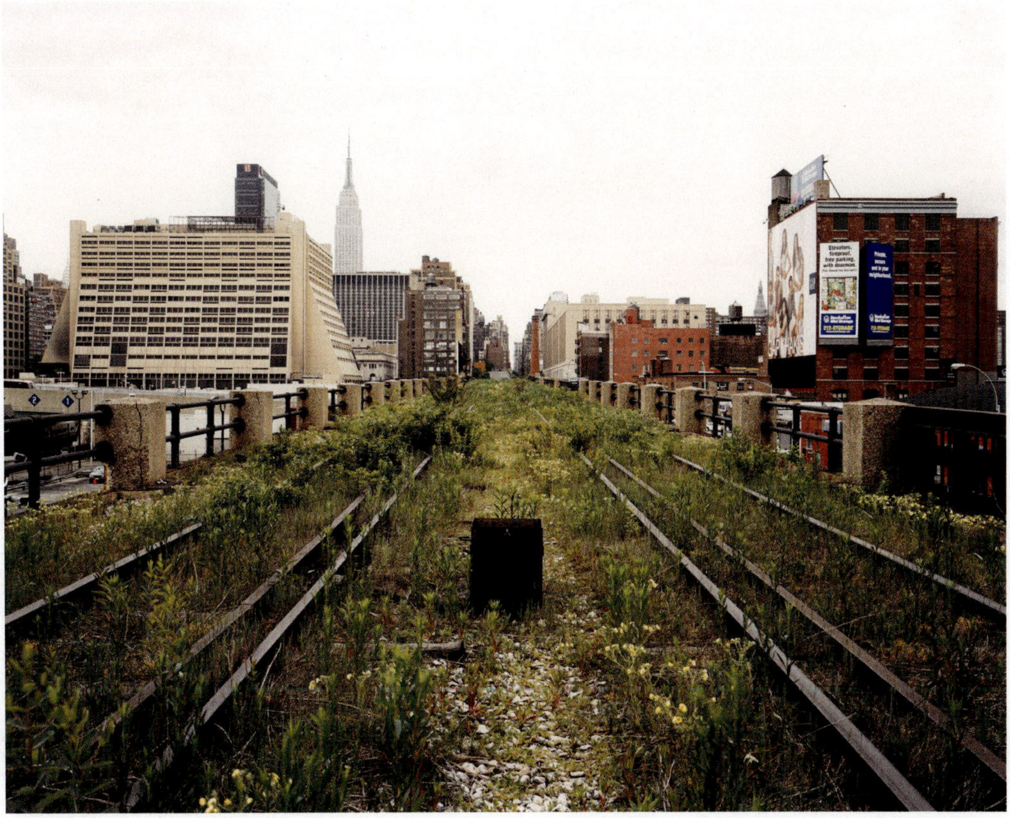

Fig. 0.2

Fig. 0.2
JOEL STERNFELD
A Railroad Artifact, 30th Street, May 2000* from *The High Line
Since the 1970s, Joel Sternfeld has photographed the American landscape, exploring the ordinary as well as revealing the incongruous details of everyday life. He was drawn to the abandoned High Line, an elevated section of railway that remains on part of Manhattan's West Side. Although the High Line is now a public park, for many years its future was uncertain. In this time, Sternfeld documented the industrial relic and the changes that affected it throughout the seasons. Unbeknownst to many who wandered beneath it, during its neglect vegetation took hold and claimed the rusting track, transforming the High Line into an unkempt garden suspended above the city.

they were designed in three dimensions, they were intended to be consumed almost like pictures.

The image of bulldozers and heavy machinery excavating minerals or making way for housing perhaps most vividly illustrates the degree to which we *landscape* the topography of our environment. However, this dramatic intervention is replicated more subtly when we press our eye to the viewfinder and decide where to position the various subjects in relation to one another, as well as decide on the many other technical decisions that affect the appearance of the final *landscape* picture. Landscape is therefore not *the* land or *the* space or *the* topography but rather the processes involved in its representation.

Throughout this book we will encounter different ways of responding to or exploring the parameters of the landscape genre, but other definitions of the word might also facilitate our point of departure. "Landscape" is often used metaphorically in conjunction with adjectives such as "the economic landscape" or "the cultural landscape." In these examples (in which we might actually have substituted "landscape" for "climate"), the word "landscape" is used to suggest a kind of all-encompassing overview of a topic or the same distanced point of view that we have popularly come to expect from the composition of landscape pictures. These phrases allude to the current state of affairs or broader context of a certain topic. Perhaps, therefore, photography, which has always been employed as a means by which to communicate the here and now is particularly well suited to explore the many and varied ways that we engage with our environments.

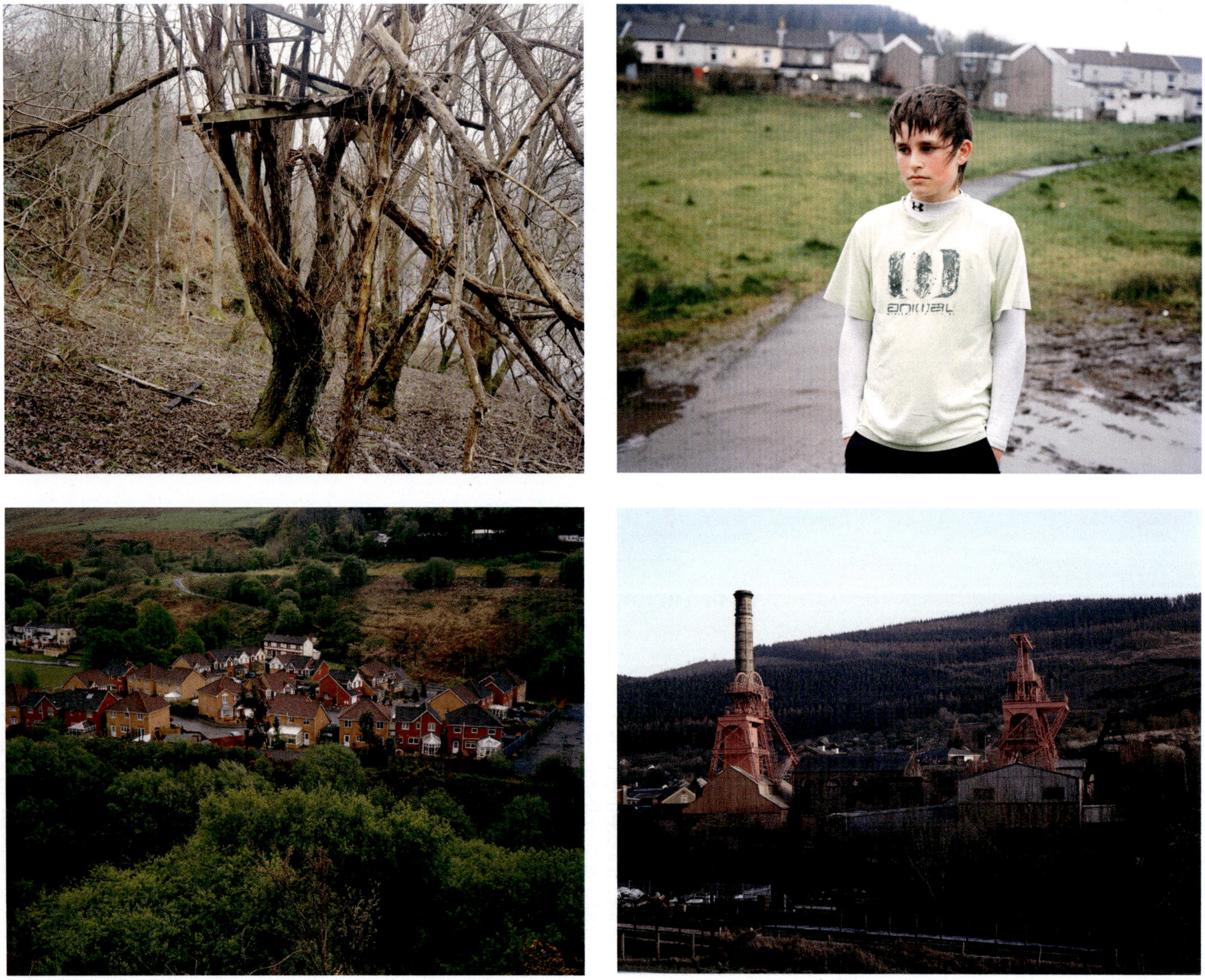

Fig. 0.3

Fig. 0.3.i–0.3.iv
GAWAIN BARNARD
Maybe We'll Be Soldiers, 2011

Maybe We'll Be Soldiers *is an ongoing project that explores the transition of youth in the place I grew up, the South Wales Valleys. The work is partly autobiographical with quiet portraits and precise landscapes depicting a former industrialized area while the transition of youth is against the altered hillside topography. The uncertainty of adolescence is confronted by a combination of forthright landscapes looking to the industrialized past, and verdant foliage and dark walls of color landscapes seem to come between the young and their future. While the project sits across the genres of portrait and landscape the region's future tries to shrug off the economic hardships of the past.*
Gawain Barnard

WHY EXPLORE LANDSCAPE ART?

Our environments are constantly changing and evolving. The topicality of issues around the planet's changing ecology and climate has been reflected in the popularity of landscape as subject matter in contemporary photography over recent decades. What once belonged firmly within the realm of noble fine art photography has expanded in recent years into documentary territories as well, becoming an object of social concern rather than predominantly poetic subject matter. In addition to the environment, landscape photography crosses into other areas of discourse, such as national identity, historical narratives, and myriad social and political issues. Landscape does not simply examine how we relate to our environment but also how we relate to one another. It is a field of research that is current, and it is urgent.

The breadth of possibility in terms of subject matter for landscape projects is as rich as the depth of philosophical discussions around how we choose to represent our surroundings. These discourses will stray into the territories of other media, such as literature and film, and other disciplines, including history, ecology, and psychology. Not only can landscape projects be developed around any geographic location but they also can be used to discuss remarkably diverse topics and subject matter. Despite its popularity, practitioners continue to explore the photographic potential of landscape in innovative and challenging ways. The selection of works discussed within this book reflect the diversity of the technical and conceptual approaches of its practitioners.

Landscape photography is a popular activity. The plethora of magazines, books, websites, workshops, and courses dedicated to the mastery of techniques of landscape photography is remarkable. However, landscape imagery is equally relevant to those who do not consider themselves to be *makers* of landscape pictures. Most of the titles on landscape photography tend to address technique and practice independently from theoretical and contextual discussions of the subject. This book is designed to deliberately blur those false boundaries and functions as a primer for those wishing to develop this aspect of their practice or who are intrigued to find out what themes underpin contemporary landscape photography. If you are currently engaged in formal study, then this book will help you to develop projects that are both technically accomplished and conceptually robust. Endnotes have been included at the end of each chapter to indicate sources for further reading if you wish to find out more.

YOUR HEALTH AND SAFETY AND THE LAW

Exploring the landscape can be immensely rewarding, particularly if you are inclined toward working outdoors and you enjoy the associated challenges. Landscape photography is not a hazardous activity and, generally speaking, no more or less dangerous than other kinds of photography. However, if you are working in more remote or exposed locations, you should always take extra time to consider any potential risks. Make sure you check the weather forecast and know when it will get dark and, if working around the seashore or estuaries, the tide times. This information will also be useful for planning your shoots and your photographs. Consider what additional equipment or supplies might be useful. Landscape photography is often considered a solitary pursuit, although in practice this is not always the case. Recruiting the assistance of a peer can help lighten the burden of carrying camera equipment if you need to walk any distance and also offer moral support if any unforeseen problems arise in the field. If you are working in remote or hazardous places, it is a good idea to tell a reliable person where you are going and how to raise the alarm if you are not back according to schedule. Take risks with your creativity, not your safety or that of your helpers.

In recent years, there have been well-documented accounts of photographers being unjustly challenged by officials while taking pictures in public. Legalities vary from country to country. Generally speaking, however, the law does not prohibit you from photographing most things, provided you are on public property. But in terms of what may or may not be published and in what context, matters are more complicated. If you are photographing on private property—even if it is publically accessible—to negate the possibility of problems arising during the shoot or at a later date, it is prudent to obtain permission from the landowner or property owner first. This is particularly important when working within a commercial context. You should familiarize yourself with the laws in your area and respect them. If you are traveling farther afield, you should pay even greater attention to legal restrictions and also respect local etiquette and customs. If you anticipate that you will be challenged while working and will be within the law, you should take evidence with you that confirms your right to photograph at that place, such as a copy of the legislation or written permission from the property owner or landowner. Understanding your rights, as well as your responsibilities, as a photographer is a key component of professional practice.

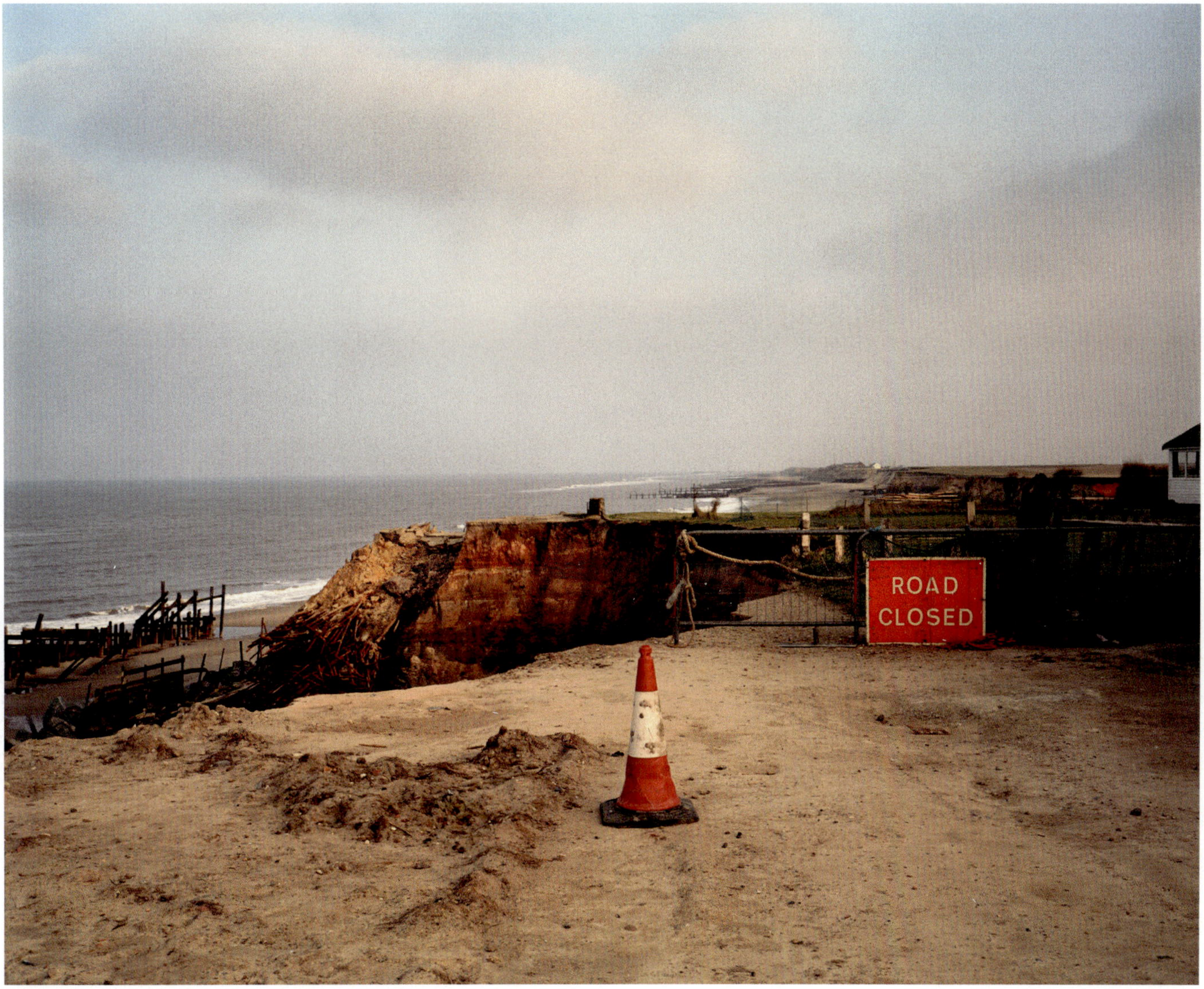

Fig. 0.4

Fig. 0.4
JONATHAN OLLEY
Road Collapse, Happisburgh, Norfolk, England, UK, 2003* from the series *The Sea Wall

Jonathan Olley is often drawn to sites of conflict and marks of man's foolishness. *The Sea Wall* is an investigation of coastal erosion and the effects of flooding in the UK. The dramatic effects of climate change upon our landscapes are understandably a prominent theme within contemporary photography (see p. 131). Some environments and types of terrain are more hazardous than others. Understanding how to operate safely and effectively within them is just as important as understanding how to operate your camera.

Fig. 0.5
JO METSON SCOTT and NICOLA YEOMAN
***Formations, 2010* from the series**
And Then
For the ongoing project *And Then*, Jo Metson Scott and set designer and artist Nicola Yeoman perform a series of carefully planned interventions within the landscape. Using temporary structures and often makeshift resources, they recreate playful scenarios that evoke fairy tales and other cultural references. The dreamlike visual qualities make an explicit connection to childhood and imagination, and the narratives that the pictures depict are deliberately open ended, allowing viewers to make up their own minds about what happened before or after the moment depicted—to complete the phrase *and then* . . .

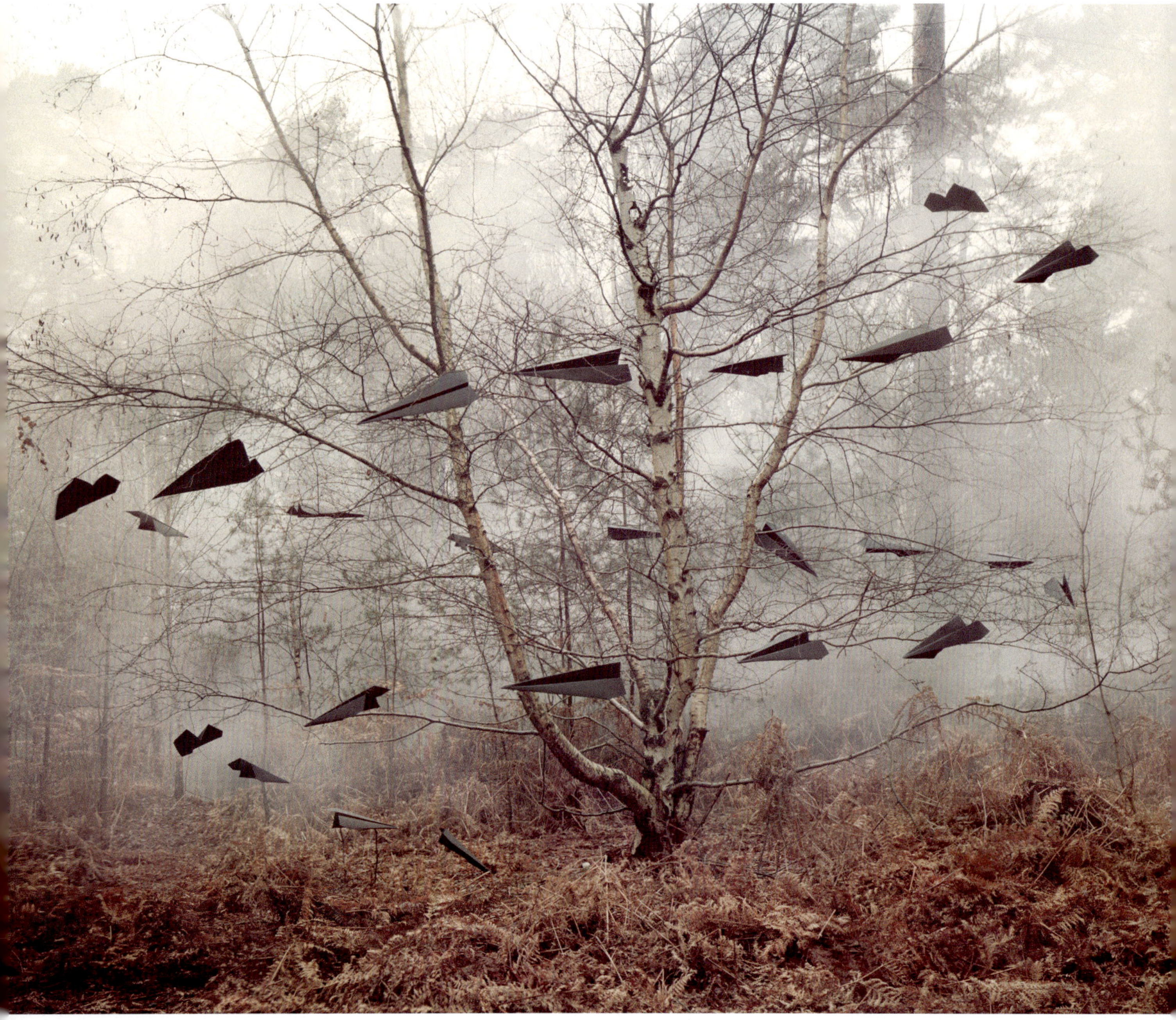

Fig. 0.5

GIVING AND RECEIVING FEEDBACK

Whether studying within an academic context or for your own personal development, exchanging ideas and feedback on your work is a vital component of your learning. In addition to expanding your skills base, intellect, and level of discernment, precisely the same kinds of discussions around your own practice (such as influences, technical and creative choices) take place in contemporary practice at more advanced critical levels.

Although you are ultimately responsible for the creative choices in your practice, in order to expand and develop your photography, you need to be open to the interpretations of others. This is as true for academic and contemporary art contexts as it is for commercial spheres. It is important to develop the communication skills to relay feedback appropriately as well as incorporate the perspectives of others into your own assessment of your work.

If you do not yet have a peer group established, then you should try to set one up either locally or virtually, or both. Peers are important because they test your ideas and assertions—they are not competitors but collaborators within the creative process. Five practical projects have been written into this book, and there are discussion questions at the end of each chapter. If you don't already have one, consider setting up your own blog or Flickr account to publish your projects, and use it to collect feedback from your peers and generate discussions. Even if you are not in a position to discuss the points suggested, use them as opportunities to reflect upon what you have read.

When offering feedback, always be constructive. That is not to say that feedback should always be glowing, but don't make a negative comment about an aspect of someone's work without also offering a suggestion of how to enhance or develop it. Likewise, if the work appeals to you, try to explain why it does. When people do give you feedback, absorb their comments in their entirety; don't dwell on the more obviously positive or negative details alone, and never take feedback on your photography personally.

Remember that some people are more polite than others and some appear to be rude although they are well meaning. It is important to respect the sensitivity of some individuals, particularly those who are less familiar with photography or able to articulate their thoughts as fluently. Always conduct yourself as you would expect someone else to behave toward you or as you would have expected them to behave toward you at an earlier point in your studies.

1 David Bate, *Photography: The Key Concepts* (London: Berg, 2009), 93.

2 Simon Schama, *Landscape and Memory* (London: HarperCollins, 1995), 10.

3 W.J.T. Mitchell, *Landscape and Power* (2nd ed.) (Chicago: University of Chicago Press, 2002), 1.

Chapter 1
TAMING THE VIEW

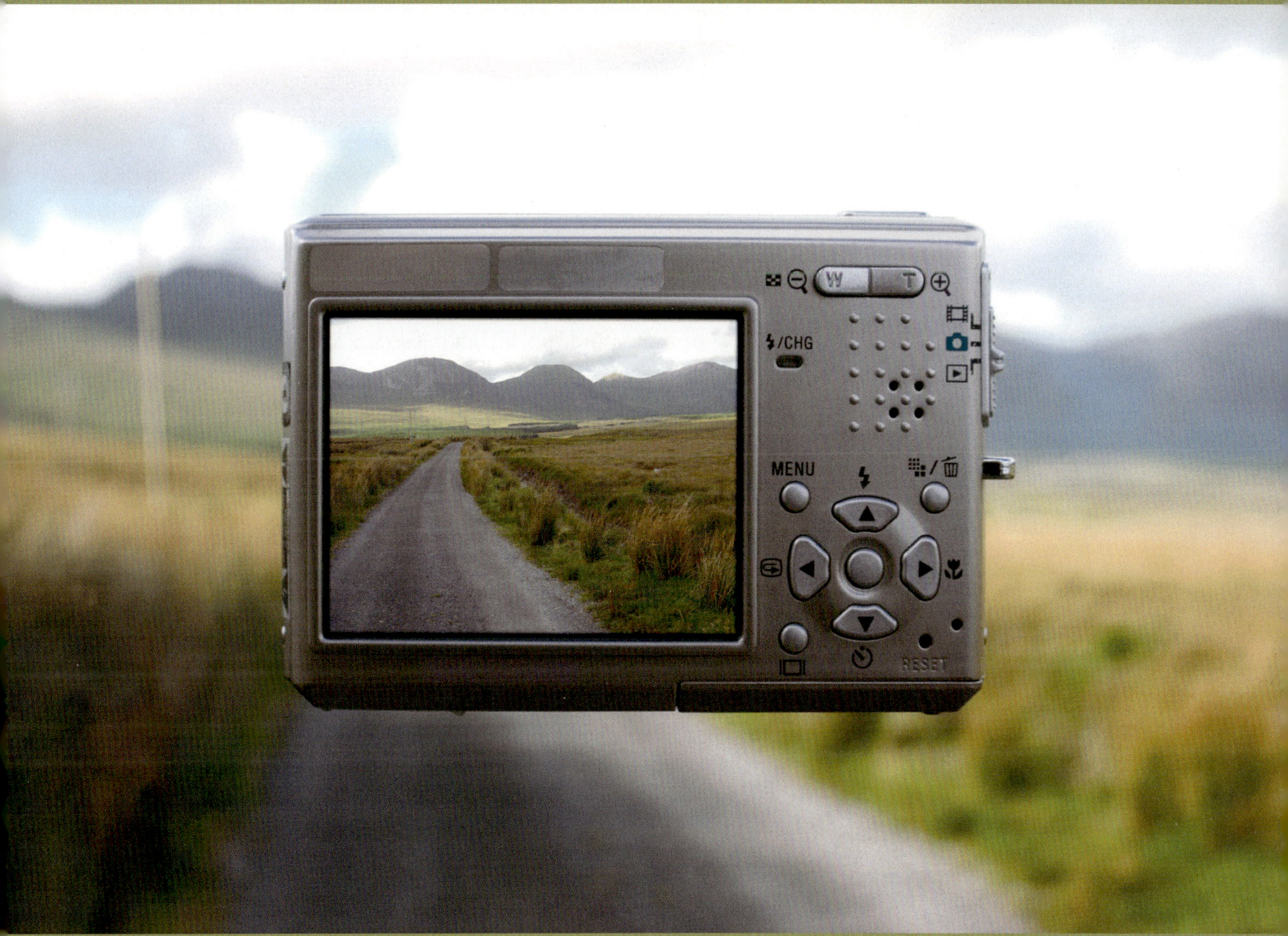

Fig. 1.1

Fig. 1.1
SUZANNE MOONEY
Benna Beola from the series *Behind the Scenes, 2006*

In spite of the diversity of technical and conceptual approaches of landscape photographers, they all have these two things in common: an appreciation of the importance of the fundamental processes of photography and an understanding of how these can be controlled or manipulated to create the series of images that they want a wider audience to see. As well as strengthening your understanding of these principles, it is important to consider how technical decisions—the selection of a particular camera or lens or the decision to work in black and white rather than in color—can have a bearing not just upon how someone's photographs *look* but also on how he or she might go about making them.

Like other areas of art and design, the composition of the photograph is fundamental to its appearance and appeal, but it also has a great effect on how it is read, in other words, the order in which we process the visual information within a photograph and interpret a message or meaning. This chapter examines how materials and techniques influence the creative process from the perspective of both maker and consumer of landscape photographs. It also considers *why* we might feel the urge to capture the landscape and reflects on some of the varied ways that narratives are expressed in landscape practice.

Fig. 1.2
TIMOTHY O'SULLIVAN
Vermillion Creek Cañon, 1872
Timothy O'Sullivan was one of several photographers who were commissioned to accompany geologic expeditions as well as document the construction of major infrastructure. Like the medium of photography itself, O'Sullivan's pictures from these trips sit between a functional, scientific use and something much more enigmatic. O'Sullivan was also one of the most celebrated battlefield photographers of the American Civil War (see p. 164).

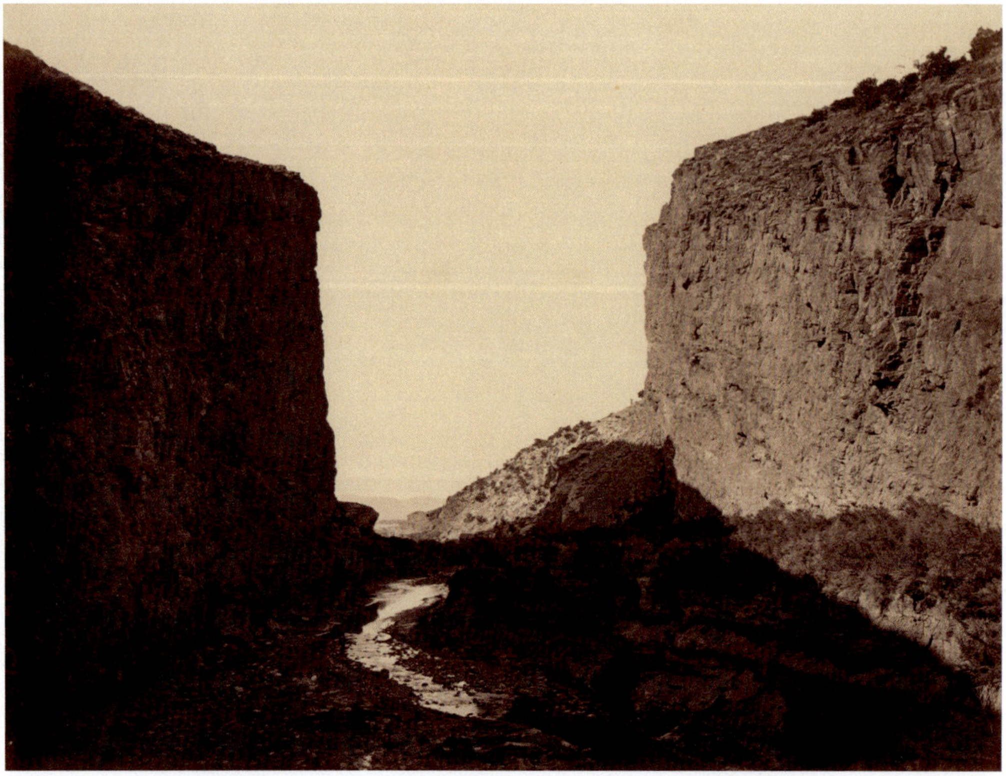

Fig. 1.2

Landscape pictures can offer us, I think, three varieties—geography, autobiography, and metaphor. Geography is, if taken alone, sometimes boring, autobiography is frequently trivial, and metaphor can be dubious. But taken together . . . the three kinds of information strengthen each other and reinforce what we all work to keep intact—an affection for life. ROBERT ADAMS[1]

GEOGRAPHY, AUTOBIOGRAPHY, METAPHOR

Before we begin thinking about how landscape pictures can be made, it is pertinent to consider a little of the potential of what landscape images can be or do. There are many philosophies of landscape, boldly defining what demarks it from other genres; however, Robert Adams's description of three varieties of landscape pictures seems a particularly pertinent point of departure. Adams is one of the world's most celebrated contemporary landscape photographers and has also written extensively about photography. Each of these varieties touches upon the intent of the photographer, but as we shall see, it is seldom possible to keep each one exclusive from the other.

GEOGRAPHY

Adams's first category of landscape photography addresses landscape in its most basic state: as an authoritative visual record of a place. It might describe the physical geography—the topography, as well as the weather conditions a place was under at the time—or it may well begin to describe some of the human interactions that take place within the frame. The efforts of the American survey photographers working in the late 1800s offer some interesting historical examples of photographs as geographic records. Timothy O'Sullivan (1840–1882) was one such photographer who joined the geologic survey expeditions of Clarence King to explore and map uncharted areas of the U.S. interior. One of the most famous expeditions was the Fortieth Parallel Survey, which investigated the Great Basin region between 1867 and 1874. O'Sullivan was tasked with creating a photographic record of the expedition and the territories that were surveyed. Intriguingly, King simply asked O'Sullivan to take photographs that "gave a sense of the area," not necessarily to function as evidential or scientific documents.[2]

O'Sullivan's contemporaries included Carleton Watkins (1829–1916), William Henry Jackson (1843–1942), and Andrew Joseph Russell (1829–1902), and they all worked on similar projects as well as on the construction of major infrastructure, such as the Union Pacific Railroad and other industrial enterprises. O'Sullivan's photographs from the Fortieth Parallel Survey, however, have been recognized as particularly remarkable contributions to landscape practice.[3] Unlike the pictures of many of his contemporaries, who tended to compose pictures with the conventions of the picturesque frame, O'Sullivan's exaggerated and aggressive compositions revealed a relationship to the land that was perhaps a little closer to the truth of it being inhospitable and unwelcoming to the trespassing expeditionaries. Even with modest ambitions, this illustrates the potential of landscape photographs to transcend their purely evidential value.

Thomas Joshua Cooper's ongoing major body of work, *The Atlantic Basin Project,* also has a distinctly *geographic* methodology behind it. For his landscape work, Cooper uses photography to map very precise geographic points and boundaries. For *The Atlantic Basin Project*, he is assembling pictures from the coastlines and islands around the whole of the Atlantic Ocean, which touches the five continents of the world.

AUTOBIOGRAPHY

Cooper is conscious of the similarity in the appearance of many of his pictures.[4] By the nature of the project, they include the sea and the land. They tend to show movement of the water due to the slow shutter of his vintage camera, and despite the importance of location to their making, the tightness of the frame leaves little of topographic significance to the viewer in terms of what is actually there. However, this deliberate homogenization reveals the photographer's personal intention to use the project to reflect upon the globalized nature of contemporary life: the Atlantic Ocean touches and connects all of us, but perhaps there is a danger that the breaking waves will smother cultural intricacies and differences to the extent that we all become one giant swirling pool. As the title of Fig. 1.3 demonstrates, Cooper's visual homogenization is deceptive, as each of his photographs—like each of the lives of the citizens who touch the Atlantic Basin—is distinct and unique.

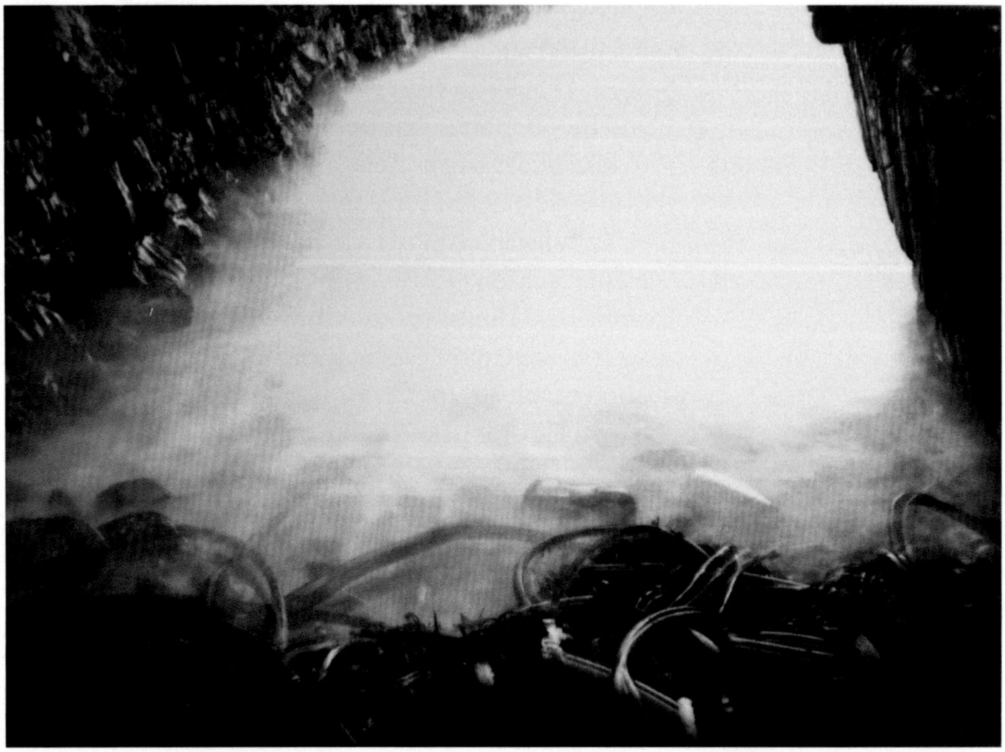

Fig. 1.3

Fig. 1.3
THOMAS JOSHUA COOPER
Freedom Day—Southwest—Table Bay Looking Towards Cape Town and Remembering

Robben Island, Cape Town South Africa, 2004
Thomas Joshua Cooper takes a distinctly geographic starting point for his projects, including his ongoing *The World's Edge: The Atlantic Basin Project*, to which this photograph contributes. This simple yet extremely ambitious strategy demonstrates the potential to address more complex themes and offers a personal insight into the mindset of the photographer at the time of exposure. Cooper always works with a 5" × 7" large-format camera, built in 1898.

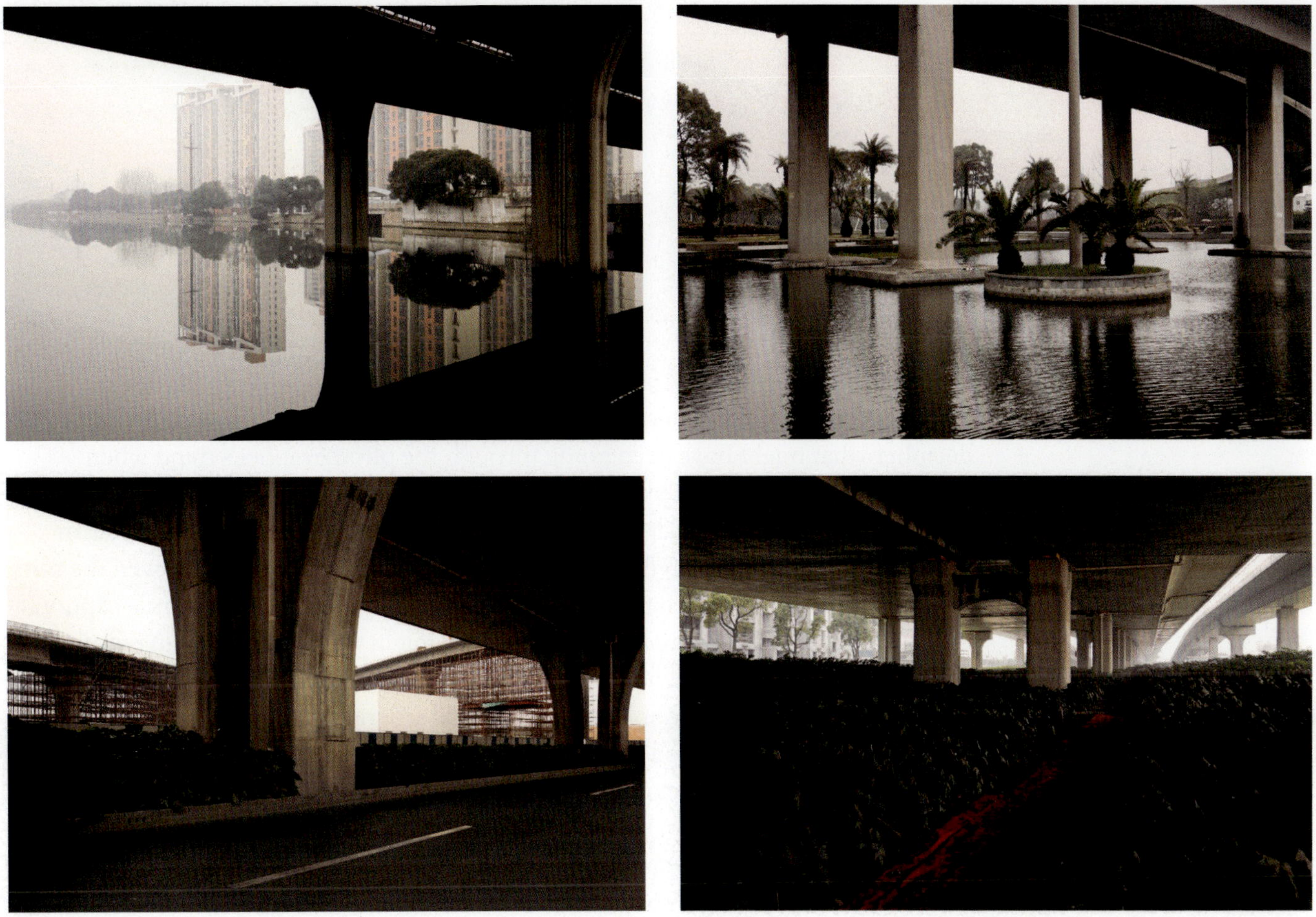

Fig. 1.4

Fig. 1.4.i–1.4.iv
Dewald Botha
Suzhou Ring Road, 2013
Dewald Botha's *Ring Road* project illustrates Adams's three varieties of landscape photography. As well as being a transport system, we could envisage a ring road as being a kind of enclosure: a bird's-eye view might reveal it as a giant defensive wall. For Botha, the ring roads became a metaphor for the barrier he felt between himself and the people around him.

The element of personal expression is present in almost every photographic act. Most of us use photography to record the things, people, and places that we are fond of or that just grab our attention. While geography and metaphor are also important aspects of Dewald Botha's *Suzhou Ring Road Project*, it has a distinctly autobiographical element as well. For Botha, a South African living and working in China, the two ring roads in Suzhou began to signify something far more personal. The roads served as a physical representation of a cultural barrier that placed the native people around him on the "inside," leaving him on the "outside." This sense of isolation is communicated in Botha's photographic strategy. In many of his images, the roads themselves dominate the top section of the frame and cast ominous shadows on the foreground, revealing detail predominantly in the center strip of the frame. This prompts a sense of a constrained view of his surroundings, of myopically looking *through* the landscape rather than looking *at* it. This restriction of information might provide a visual translation of Botha's personal response to this environment, of being able to engage with and participate within it only partially. Botha uses the ring road strategically, as a metaphor for a cultural barrier.

METAPHOR

Adams's third variety of landscape photography is the means by which we can decipher what might have been going through the photographer's mind when he or she took a particular photograph. A metaphoric message might be very literal; a photograph that depicts a beach full of holidaymakers is another way of communicating the written description "an overcrowded beach." However, the same photograph, especially with the aid of a sequence of other photographs, a caption, or the specific context in which it is presented, might allude to something far more interesting. Massimo Vitali has spent much of his artistic career photographing beaches, resorts, and other holiday destinations around Europe. From a casual glance, we could be forgiven for thinking that his photograph *Calafuria* is just another holiday snap or perhaps belongs to another vernacular context, such as a tourist brochure. Vitali's approach, however, could not be further from this. He makes his photographs from a customized platform to allow him an elevated vantage point and uses a 10" × 8" view camera, which is equally conspicuous. As the title of Vitali's series—*Natural Habitats*—alludes, the photographer's preoccupation is the study of Europeans at play and, in particular, how this notion of recreation is associated with types of spaces and certain parts of our landscape. Overcrowded Mediterranean beach resorts feature prominently in Vitali's work, and in this respect, *Calafuria* is unusual. In fact, strewn across the rocks of this part of the Adriatic coastline, rather than being *on the beach*, the figures appear to be *beached*. If images of unfortunate sea mammals or colonies of penguins or other sea birds spring to mind, then metaphor is at work. Without the potential for metaphor, in many instances it wouldn't be possible to make sense of somebody else's pictures; they would have little relevance to anyone other than the photographer.

As Adams says, each of these varieties is potentially stagnant without the others. His ethos also touches upon something that the majority of landscape practitioners have in common, from conservative pictorialists to the more inventive: that landscape pictures will fail without an attempt to express a sense of the maker's perception of it. Adams's three varieties are useful to bear in mind when developing ideas for projects: *Geography*—what is unique about the place in the viewfinder? *Autobiography*—why have you chosen to photograph it? *Metaphor*—what can you *say* with this landscape picture?

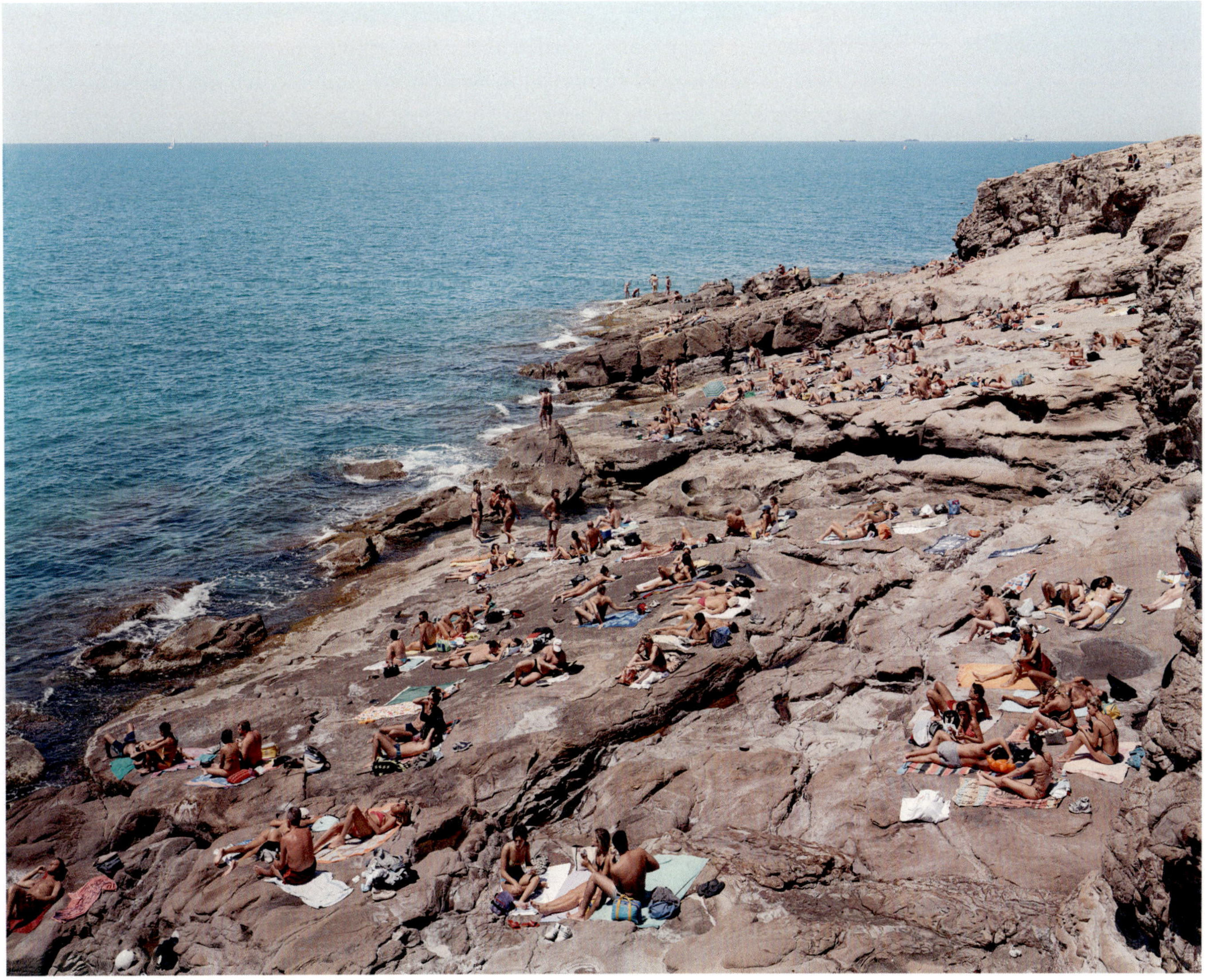

Fig. 1.5

Fig. 1.5
MASSIMO VITALI
Calafuria, 2003 **from the series**
Natural Habitats
As well as addressing themes of leisure and play, Vitali's work directly addresses ideas that underpin photography, such as the voyeuristic gaze of the camera and the pleasure of looking.

If a photograph is to communicate its subject in all its intensity, the relationship of form must be rigorously established. Photography implies the recognition of a rhythm in the world of real things. What the eye does is to find and focus on the particular subject within the mass of reality; what the camera does is simply to register upon film the decision made by the eye. . . . One does not add composition as though it were an afterthought superimposed on the basic subject material, since it is impossible to separate content from form. Composition must have its own inevitability about it.
HENRI CARTIER-BRESSON[5]

CONSIDERING COMPOSITION

Composition is commonly regarded as the determining factor in the success of a photograph. The formal composition of a photograph is often the first thing that we describe in an analysis of a picture; however, there are several ways to approach this term. Broadly speaking, we can address composition from three perspectives: *what* the photographer chose to put in the viewfinder, *how* the photographer composed it, and the moment *when* the photographer chose to make the exposure.

THE WHAT

The pictorial layout of the frame aside, it is important to consider *what* is actually contained in the viewfinder, the content rather than the form. This may sound obvious, but it is easy to become preoccupied with the design of the image without actually thinking about the relationship between the elements within the frame, not just in terms of their graphic arrangement but what the juxtaposition of these particular things might suggest to the viewer. The organization of different subjects in the viewfinder can influence the order in which a viewer looks at a picture and processes the visual information, and hence the order of importance ascribed to the subjects is determined. The relationship between the elements within the frame has implications for how a message or meaning can be constructed or suggested. The message or meaning may be something very candid or something oblique, even poetic. The actual subject matter might be something the photographer seeks out or perhaps something that stops him in his tracks; these kinds of observational skills are as important to nurture as are graphic compositional skills. While composition in terms of design can be refined systematically to a degree, there is no formula for noticing things like unusual details, peculiar relationships, or incongruous objects: in short, seeing things differently. The ability of the camera to combine all sorts of objects within a frame at one moment is something that makes photographs intriguing to look at and rewarding to create.

THE HOW

How the different elements in a picture interrelate in terms of shape, texture, color, or tonal balance largely defines the picture's visual qualities. To use an analogy, do the separate parts of the picture synergize like a well-disciplined chorus or do the untrained individual voices attempt to outcompete each other, resulting in a hideous racket? How the visual elements are designed in a picture is probably the most common discussion around pictorial landscape photography, and there are several rules to which traditionalists adhere to consistently offer a pleasurable experience for the viewer. Manuals of landscape photography encourage readers to exploit how linear perspective

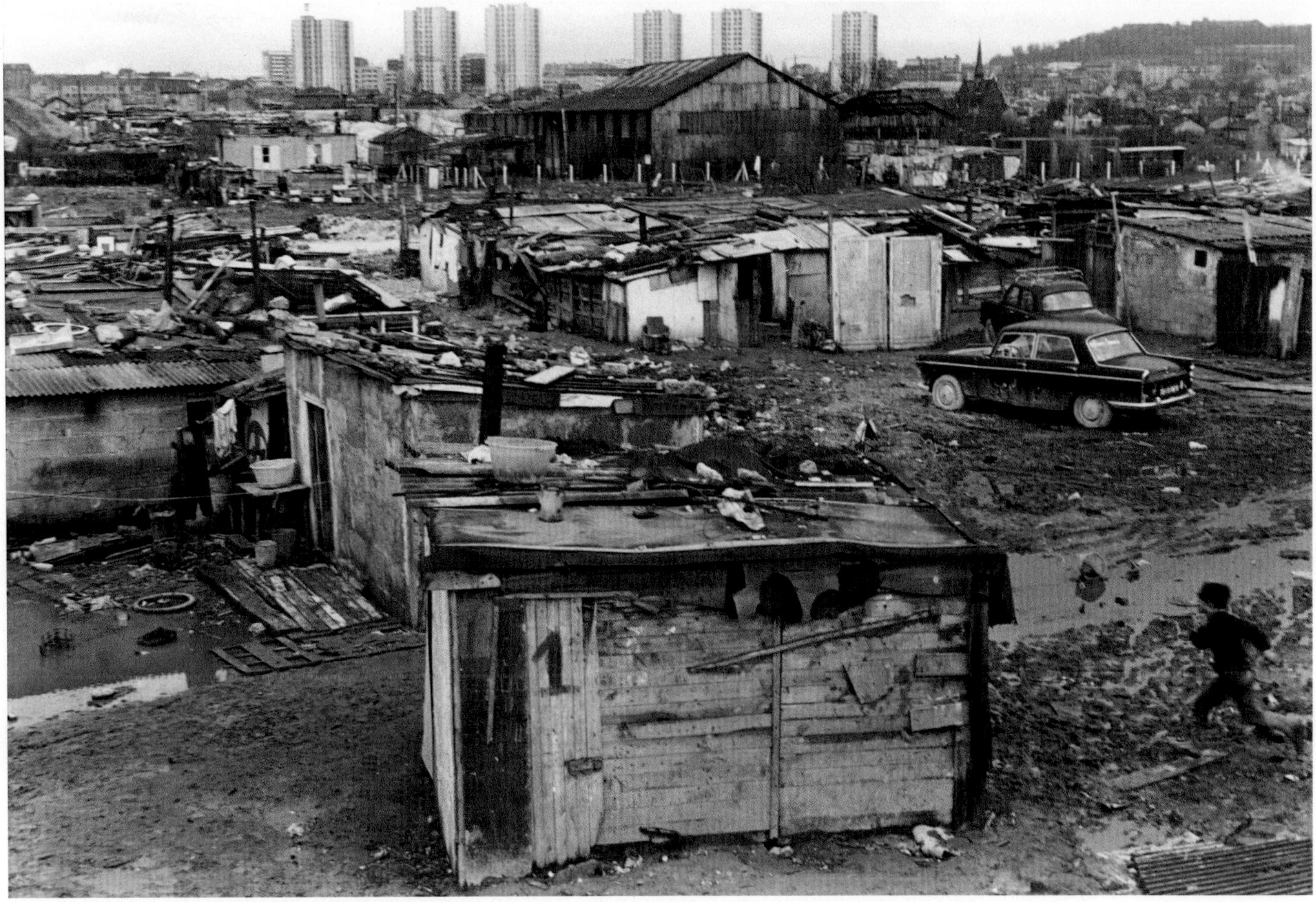

Fig. 1.6

Fig. 1.6
HENRI CARTIER-BRESSON
The Hauts-de-Seine "department." Town of Nanterre, France, 1968
Henri Cartier-Bresson is best known for his reportage work and for his part in establishing the famous Magnum photography agency, which sought to put photographers in greater control over the editorial use of their pictures. Unlike many of the photographers discussed in this book, Cartier-Bresson always worked with a 35-mm rangefinder camera, which allowed him to quickly compose dynamic imagery and helped define the style for which he is famous.

contributes to how our eyes explore an image and reiterate the importance of staggering objects along invisible lines leading from the outside edges of the frame toward the central vanishing point.

Other principles of composition include the famous rule of thirds.[6] The principle says that by dividing the frame into a grid of nine equal squares or oblongs, visually harmonious compositions can be achieved through separating key pictorial elements in either one or two of the three portions of the frame, for instance, framing a foreground in the bottom two-thirds and the horizon in the top third. Furthermore, placing points of the subject or other details on any of the four central power points, where the corners of the squares join, is said to consistently add balance and order to the frame. The rule of thirds is so ingrained within the culture of photography that many cameras have this grid overlaid on the focusing screen or viewfinder. Adhering to such a formulaic approach for one's own picture making is not conducive to a progressive approach to one's practice. We shall explore further the implications of visually harmonious pictures in Chapter 2.

THE WHEN

The final element of photographic composition is crucial to how still photography is distinguished from other media, such as painting and video. In 1952, Henri Cartier-Bresson (1908–2004) famously articulated the phrase "the decisive moment" in relation to photography. This was the title of his monograph, within which he elaborated on this: "To me, photography is the simultaneous recognition, in a fraction of a second, of the significance of an event as well as of a precise organization of forms which give that event its proper expression."[7] The decisive moment has quite literally become photography's unique selling point. Photographic manufacturers have been keen to use the decisive moment to market their products, making a distinct relationship between the photographic split-second moment and our personal memories. For instance, "Share Moments. Share Life" was Kodak's strapline in 2001. The ability to discern between the decisive moments and indecisive or insignificant ones has become one of the defining characteristics of the accomplished photographer. It is therefore perhaps disappointing that currently, manufacturers of both professional and consumer cameras devote so much attention to innovations that undermine this skill. These innovations include

Fig. 1.7
CARLETON WATKINS
Kern River Canyon, Sierra Nevada Mountains, California, 1888
Carleton Watkins's picture is a typical example of a classically framed landscape. The line of the hill on the left of the frame extends toward the central vanishing point, which is where the foreground river also leads. The image exhibits the linear perspective that is intrinsic to photographic representation. Compositions that adhere to perspectival representation supposedly offer a more pleasurable image because they simulate a more realistic viewing experience and draw you in to the picture, contributing to a more immersive experience.

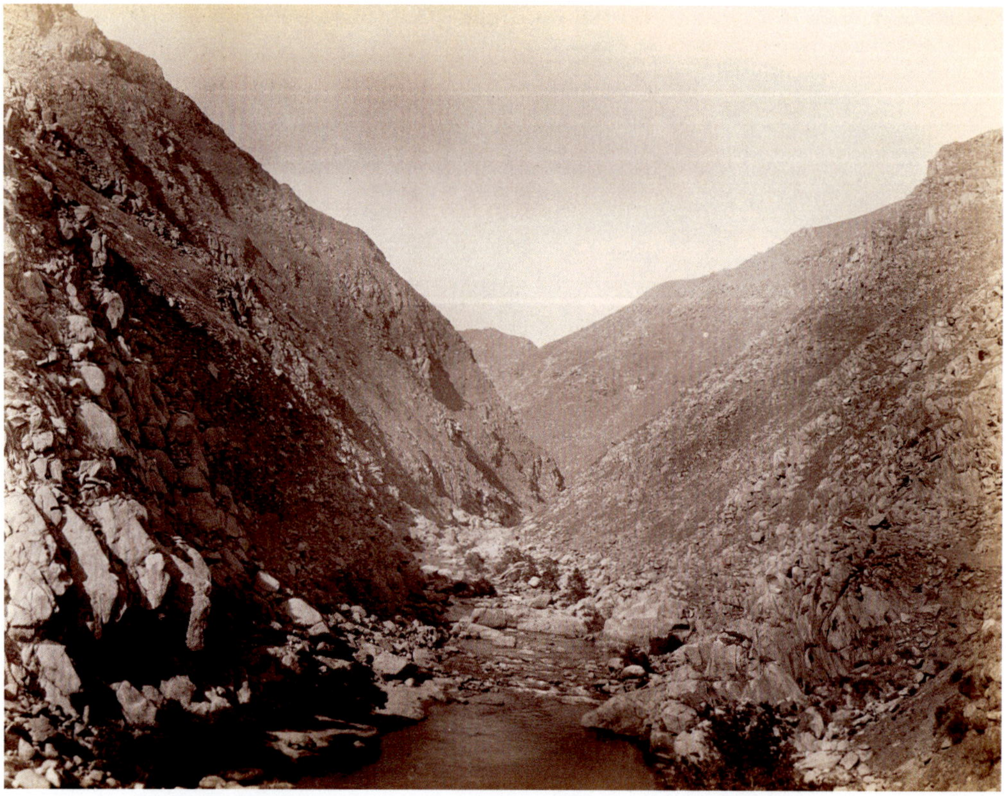

Fig. 1.7

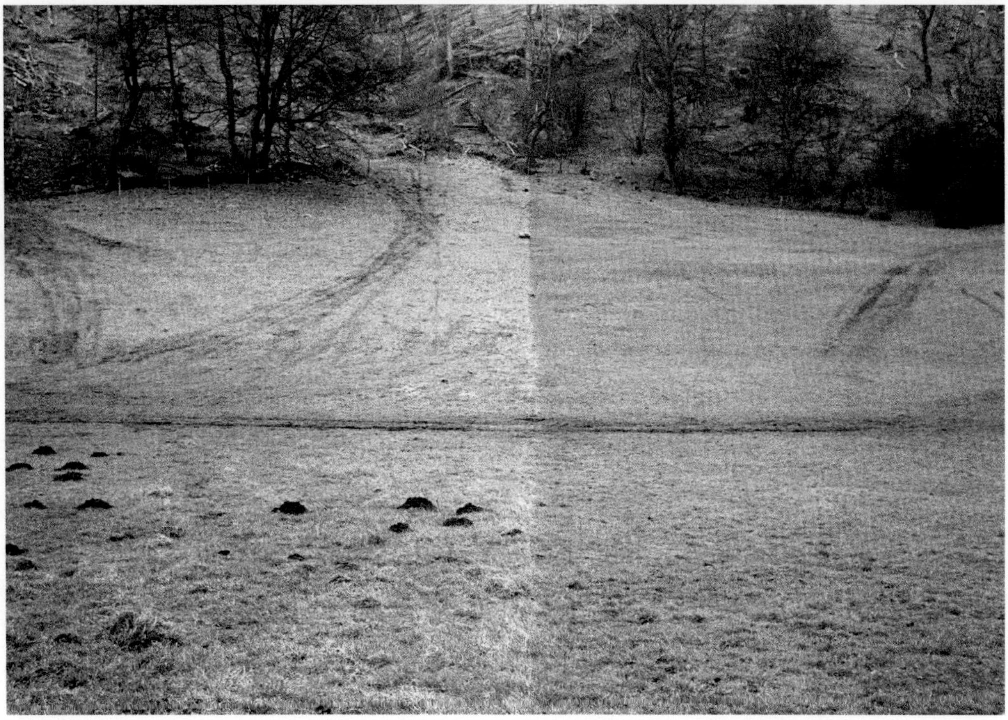

Fig. 1.8

Fig. 1.8
PAUL HILL
Divided Field, Ilam, 1988* from the series *White Peak Dark Peak
Hill's photograph demonstrates an unorthodox composition that is typical of his *White Peak Dark Peak* series (see p. 62). The image defies the rules in terms of composition and excludes a horizon to help anchor the viewer to the picture. Hill employs rigid geometry, with a distinctive vertical divide between the two fields, cutting the frame in half rather than thirds. The severity of this framing might seem incongruous to a visual depiction of this particular landscape—one that is celebrated for its rugged beauty. This is perhaps exactly the intention of this photograph: we see an unfamiliar impression with harsh straight edges as opposed to organic curves. It is a landscape with distinct boundaries. The strict organization of Hill's frame references the kind of order that is imposed upon the rural landscape and has defined conceptions of the countryside.

Sony's Smile Shutter feature which, according to its marketing copy, "ensures you snap people looking their best," and Nikon's Slow View, which allows you to select a decisive moment retrospectively from a replayed slow motion sequence so that "once you see an image you like . . . the precise moment is yours!"

Typically, landscapes tend not to be as mobile as other subjects. However, this does not mean that timing of exposures is any less significant. Users of an area of land move about within it with as much unpredictability as any other subject, and this can influence the composition in terms of design as well as the relationships between different pictorial elements. Indeed, this coalescence of form and subject matter is at the heart of Cartier-Bresson's decisive moment, not just the timely release of the shutter. The actual duration of the shutter's release also contributes to the misconception of the significance of timing in landscape practice. Due to the combination of several factors (the importance of smaller apertures with larger camera formats and working in low light situations such as early morning and late evening), shutter speeds tend to be slow within landscape photography.[8] But that does not mean that timing is less important: landscapes are always changing and have stories to reveal.[9]

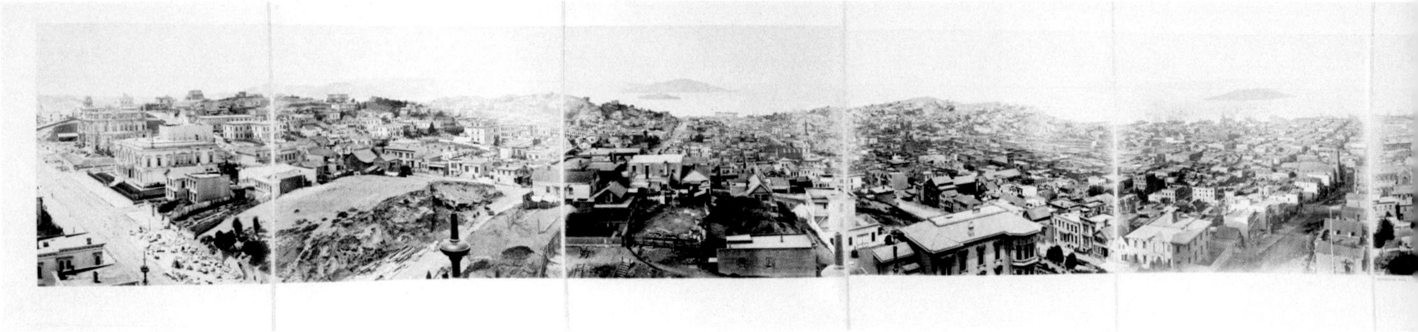

Fig. 1.9

FRAMES AND FORMATS

Different types of cameras are engineered to create differently proportioned photographs, that is, the difference between the longest and shortest edges of the picture that a particular camera makes. As shown in Fig. 1.11, in analog photography, the size of the film that the camera is designed to use is significant as well. Before negatives were enlarged in the darkroom to make prints larger than the original negative, they were used to make contact prints, which were the same size. Therefore, if you required a bigger print, it was necessary to acquire a larger camera that could accommodate a bigger negative, or plate. This was taken to extremes by J.A. Anderson Company's Mammoth Plate camera, which took an eight-foot-long negative.

Whether printing from negatives in the darkroom or scanning film digitally, the choice of film format—35 mm, 120 (medium format), 5" × 4", or 10" × 8" (large format)—has a significant impact upon the visual quality of the resulting photographs, particularly when printed at larger sizes. All types of film are made up of a particular recipe of silver halide crystals, which form a light-sensitive emulsion. These crystals vary in size according to their sensitivity to light. The more sensitive the emulsion, the larger and potentially more visible the crystals, or grains. Films with larger grains have a higher ISO rating than those with smaller grains, which are less sensitive to light. To achieve a print with the least visible appearance of film grain it is necessary to reduce the factor by which the negative is enlarged (as well as shooting at as low an ISO setting as possible).

This is not meant to imply that landscape photographs *should* necessarily be free of film grain (or noise, which is the digital equivalent); however, it is reasonable to generalize that landscape photographers tend to prefer continuous tone and fine detail over grainy images. In digital photography, we know that the number of pixels within the camera's image sensor limits the size to which an image can be enlarged before it appears pixilated. The astonishing degree of detail that large-format cameras are able to record can lend a remarkable presence to prints when installed within a gallery context and represents one reason for the continued popularity of large-format cameras, the designs of which have remained relatively unchanged since the 1840s.

NATURALISTIC VIEWS

Most cameras produce an image that is oblong. While there are many exceptions to this rule, in photography as well as in other visual media (such as painting, drawing, and cinema), the shape of landscape images tends to be horizontally oblong, literally in what we commonly refer to as "landscape" orientation. Because

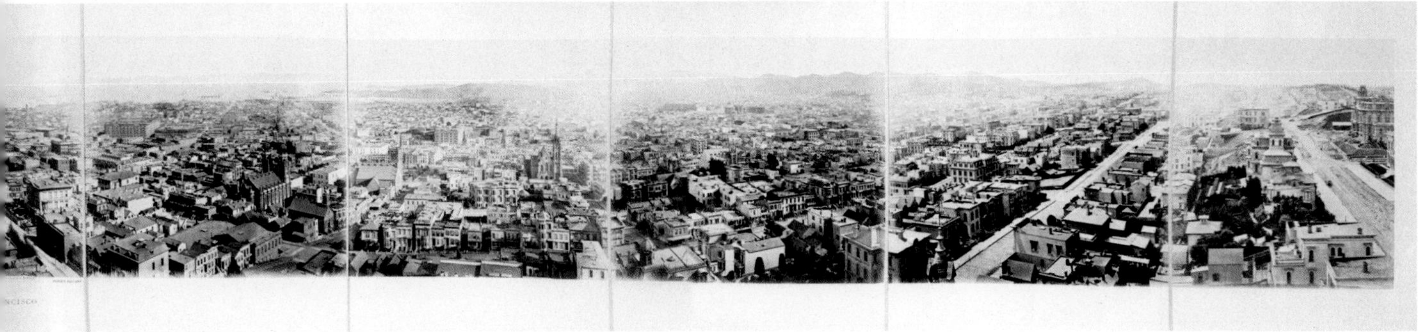

Fig. 1.9
EADWEARD MUYBRIDGE
Panorama of San Francisco from California Street, 1877
Muybridge was an innovative photographer who led a colorful life. He is best known for developing a high-speed camera shutter that enabled him to produce his "motion studies." The visual deconstruction of animal and human locomotion that this revealed was the precursor to the moving image.

of the way that cameras have historically been designed and landscape pictures are traditionally shaped, one could almost be forgiven for believing that in order for a picture to be considered as belonging to the landscape genre, it *must* be shaped and oriented accordingly. The horizontal frame is however, closer to naturalistic, ocular vision than is a square or vertical frame. Creating a vignette, either through an elliptical window mount (a *passe-partout*) to mask the sharp corners of a photograph or dodging or burning the edges of the print in the darkroom, was an approach adopted by some nineteenth-century pictorialist photographers to create the illusion of an appearance as someone might experience it for himself. Since much landscape imagery has served to simulate (albeit an idealized) experience of a view, the close relationship between picture shape and the genre is understandable.

The moving image is another example of a powerfully conventionalized frame. We also associate the moving image with a horizontally oblong frame. This wasn't always the case however, and until the mid-1950s, cinemas projected movies in Academy ratio, which was much squarer, at 1.375:1. The importance of the ergonomics of the camera in terms of how we use them is exemplified by the popularity of smartphones in lieu of personal cameras. The design of smartphones lends them to vertical, or "portrait," orientation for taking photographs and recording videos, which is subverting the established convention of the moving image as a wide screen, turning it—within current domestic photography at least—into a "tall screen."

As we can see in the work of Eadweard Muybridge (1830–1904) (Fig. 1.9), the panoramic photograph takes the preoccupation with horizontal orientation in landscape photography to an extreme degree. The word "panorama" has Greek etymology and translates roughly as "all-encompassing view." But in recent years, the term has evolved to refer to any photograph that is considerably wider than it is tall, irrespective of the subject matter or angle of view. Muybridge's segmented panoramic view of San Francisco has an almost quaint appearance today, and it is difficult to imagine how novel such a representation would have seemed at the time. Compared to modern processes,[10] Muybridge's technology was rudimentary and the process labored. The exercise would have taken as long as a whole day to complete and required multiple versions of each frame to ensure a tonally consistent end result. Muybridge was probably the first person to photograph a 360° panoramic landscape view. Rebecca Solnit observes, "It is conceptually dizzying to realize that several hours of the day are on view at once, and that the hours are not necessarily in order. . . . Just as the viewers are seeing in several directions at once, so they are looking at several separate moments at once."[11]

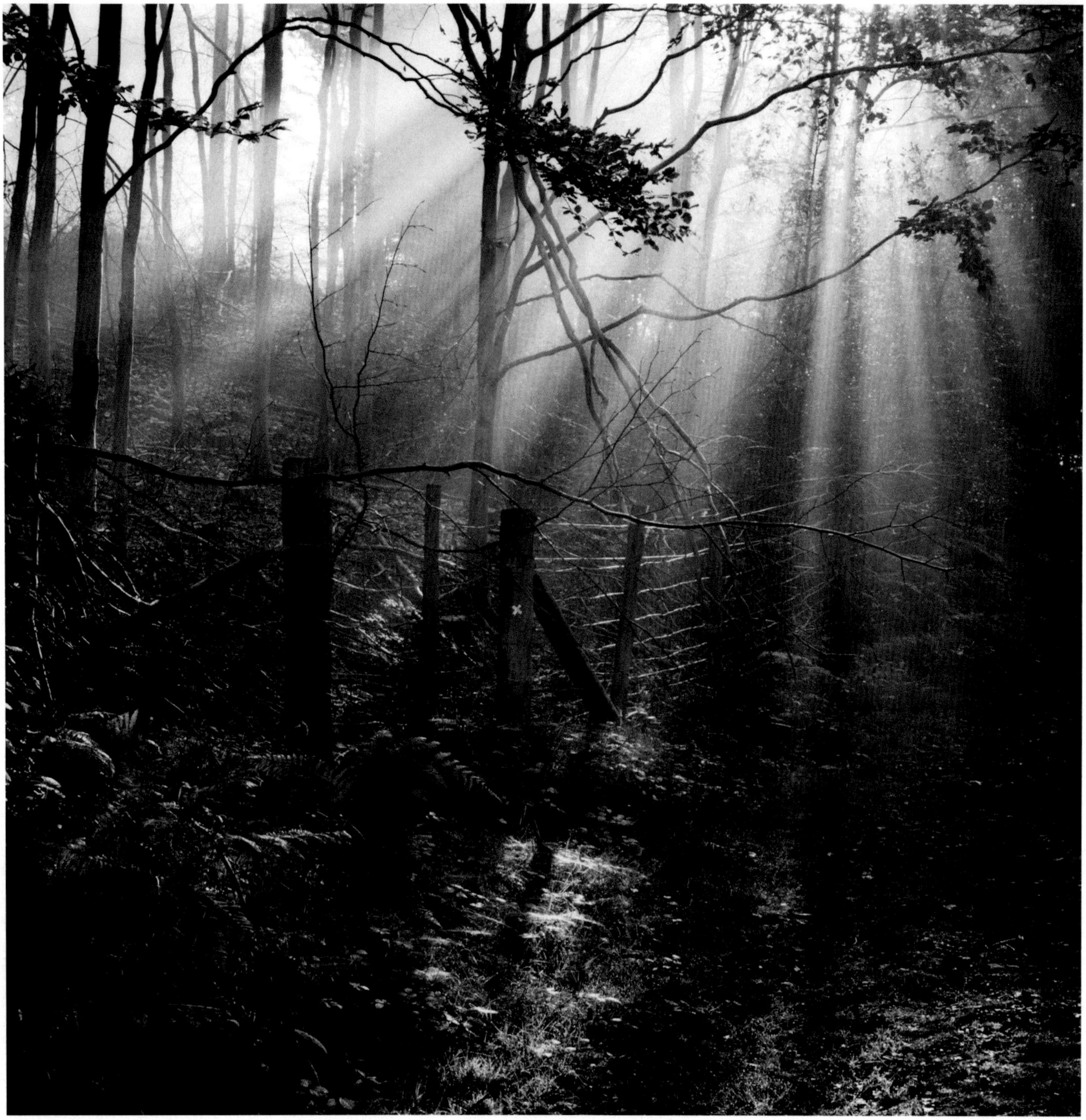

Fig. 1.10

Fig. 1.10
FAY GODWIN
Fence, Parkend Woods, Forest of Dean, 1985* from the monograph *Landmarks, 2001

Fay Godwin (1931–2005) was well known for often working with a square-frame camera, more common to portrait and fashion photography than to landscape. Her 6 × 6 cm medium-format camera offered Godwin a reasonable alternative to the cumbersome large-format camera (which can be physically demanding for excursions on foot) without compromising too much on image quality. The square frame lent itself well to Godwin's progressive approach to landscape photography. Her resulting images display a conspicuously photographic *containing* of the view, with the different elements tightly arranged and meticulously balanced. This aesthetic echoed her subject matter and philosophy toward landscape through which, among other issues, she sought to address concerns around public access to the British landscape.

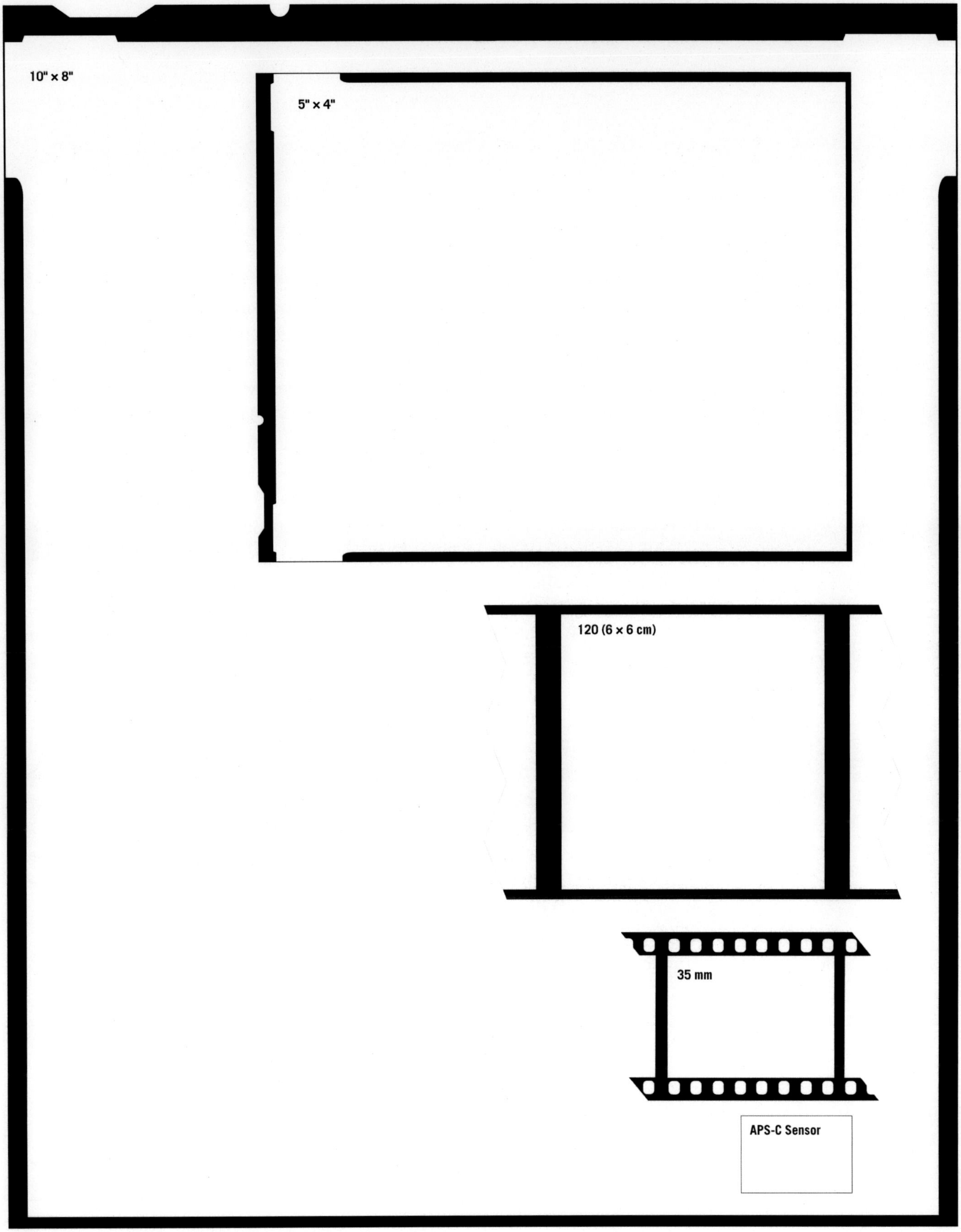

Fig. 1.11

Fig. 1.11
Scale illustration of the range of camera formats

LENSES FOR LANDSCAPES

The lens that you select to work with will have a profound impact upon your photography: it will affect how your photographs are rendered optically, but to an extent, it can define the relationship between you and your subject. Camera lenses can be classed roughly within one of three categories: wide angle (a focal length around 17–35 mm), standard or portrait lenses (50–100 mm), and telephoto lenses (100 mm and up). The focal lengths indicated here are for lenses designed for 35-mm analog cameras and full-frame digital single-lens reflex cameras (DSLRs). Fig. 1.12 describes the standard lens of each camera format. As you can see, different camera formats will require a lens of a particular focal length in order to display the equivalent angle of view. A standard lens describes the focal length that is roughly equal to the diagonal measurement of the image format of the camera. In terms of magnification of the subject, this happens to create an image that is similar to ocular vision. But this should not be confused with the equivalent angle of view to human sight.[12]

Traditionally, landscape photographers have favored lenses within a wide-angle to standard focal length bracket. These lenses lend themselves to more naturalistic subject magnification and the synthesis of foreground to background objects, which facilitates the movement of the viewer's gaze *through* the picture. Wide-angle lenses also have greater depth of field than do longer lenses, allowing photographers to keep more of a scene in sharp focus, even at larger aperture settings. Telephoto lenses by contrast have a narrower depth of field but, more significantly, tend to give the appearance of flattened perspective, that is, they can make the distance between subjects at different distances from the camera appear unnaturally smaller. But as with any piece of equipment or process, these lenses of course have the potential to be put to creative effect.

Fig. 1.12
Standard lens focal lengths

Format	10" x 8"	5" x 4"	6 x 6 cm	35 mm (film or full-frame DSLR)	APS-C (consumer compact cameras and DSLRs)
Focal length of standard lens	300 mm	150 mm	80 mm	50 mm	25–38 mm (according to manufacturer and model)

Fig. 1.12

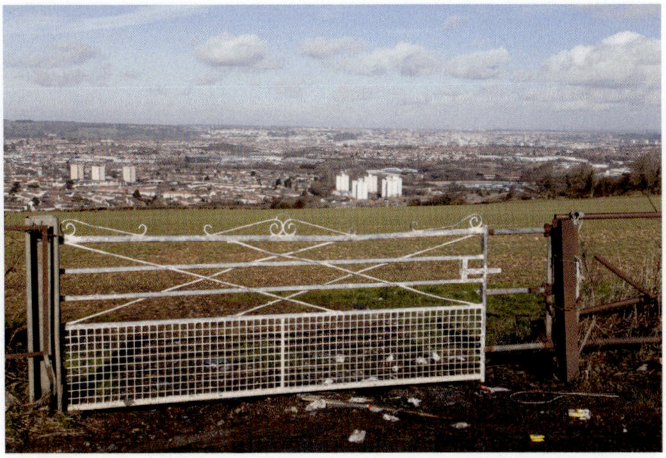

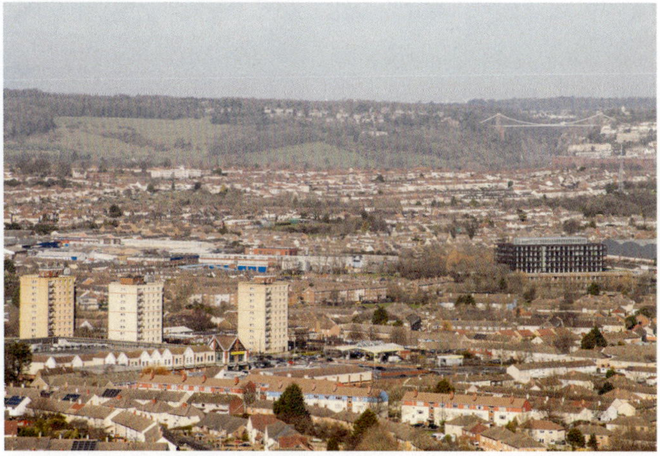

Fig. 1.13

Fig. 1.13.i and 1.13.ii
Two shots from the same position with different focal lengths showing very different views
These two photographs demonstrate the different visual possibilities presented by the same situation. Both shot on a 35-mm format, the left image used a 35-mm lens and the right, a telephoto lens at 190 mm. The telephoto lens can often create satisfactory images by compressing several subjects together within the frame. The wide-angle lens, on the other hand, requires a different negotiation between the distant elements and whatever occupies the foreground. Working effectively with these near and far components can show the "background" subject matter in the context of the ground directly in front of the photographer. Telephoto lenses literally overlook these kinds of juxtapositions and emphasize not just the physical distance between the photographer and subject but sometimes even suggest the photographer's lack of engagement with the subject.

Zoom lenses are practical to use, allowing the photographer to minimize the burden of carrying equipment and not have the inconvenience of changing lenses. However, fixed focal length, or prime, lenses have many benefits too: because their optical engineering is simpler they can generally offer visual superiority within a given price bracket. Also, prime lenses usually have greater maximum apertures than do zoom lenses, allowing the photographer to work in dimmer conditions or with a faster shutter speed.

An even greater difference between the two types of lens, however, is how they influence a photographer's behavior. Two photographers working on the same subject, one using a zoom lens and the other a prime lens, will reveal distinctly different approaches to how they work. It is likely that the one working with the zoom lens would be fairly static, using the zoom function to scrutinize the subject. The one working with the prime lens, however, would be more likely to be proactive in approach, working *around* the subject and experimenting with angles, perspective, and distance. Photographers who work with prime lenses become accustomed to the angle of view of their equipment and are more adept at "previsualizing" their images. This means that they can calculate where they need to be in relation to the subject or group of subjects even before looking through the viewfinder. As well as previsualizing your photographs, this kind of methodology is conducive to conceptualizing your work, liberating your vision from the confines of the viewfinder and allowing not just your eyes to do the framing but also your *mind*.

Fig. 1.14
JUSTIN QUINNELL
Bridge View. Six-month exposure taken from the winter solstice 2007 to the summer solstice 2008
Justin Quinnell takes a highly experimental approach to his practice and builds rudimentary, yet effective, pinhole cameras out of unusual objects. The pinhole camera, which renders an image through the selection of light waves through a small aperture, allows Quinnell to make very long photographic exposures. In the case of this image, he made a pinhole camera from an old aluminum beer can and taped it down to record the sun's movement across the southern sky over the course of half a year. Quinnell uses a piece of photographic paper without developing it and then a flatbed scanner to directly copy the latent image on the paper. As well as revealing an extraordinary view, this photograph reminds us that the precise position of the sun in the sky is different on each day of the year, which has implications on how it casts daylight on objects on the ground, confirming P. H. Emerson's assertion that a scene will never look exactly the same from one day to the next.

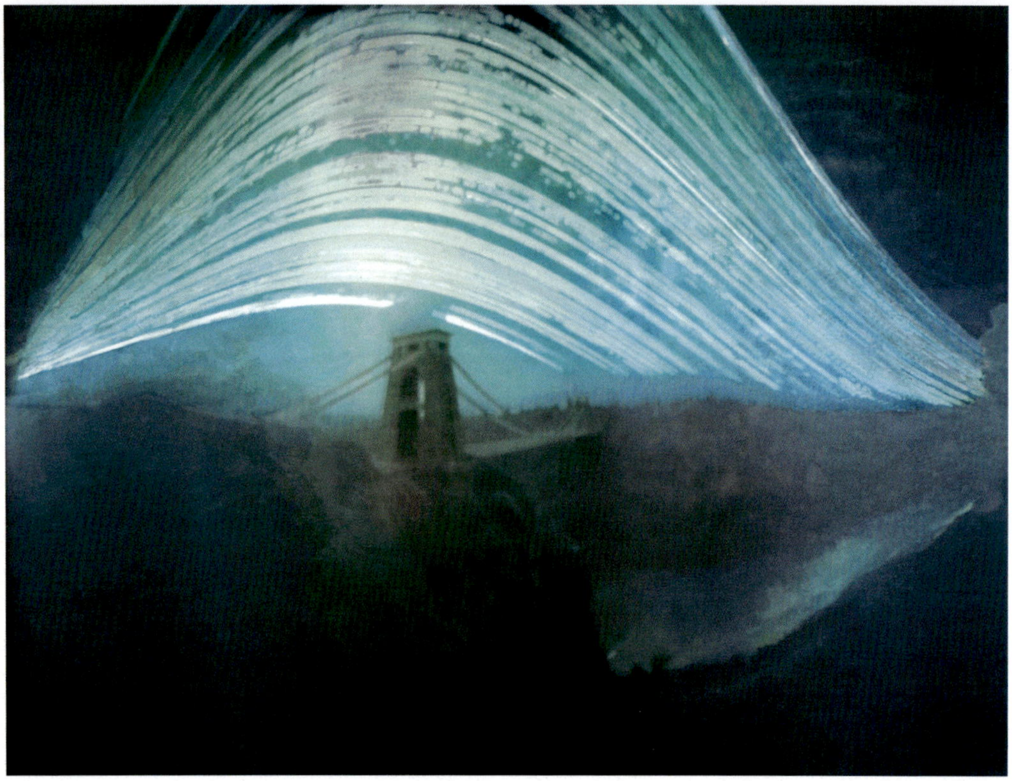

Fig. 1.14

PROPERTIES OF LIGHT

As its Greek etymology suggests, light is the key ingredient of photography. From the rudimentary photogram to the most sophisticated digital cameras, without the electron-releasing power of light, it would not be possible to record photographic images. In all spheres of photography, the particular properties of a light source are integral to how the subject looks. These properties include its temperature (see p. 94), direction, source type (single point or diffused), and brightness in relation to other light sources. Particular attention to lighting is sometimes considered a defining characteristic of the genre, and since landscape photography tends to involve working outside and with available light alone, there is some truth in this assertion. In many situations, the weather and lighting conditions appear to be the most dynamic part of a picture, so it is natural for the viewer to question why the photographer made an exposure at a particular time on a certain day: What was it about *that* moment—or those conditions—that compelled the photographer to make an exposure? It often seems that being part of the canon of great landscape photographers requires if not an innate sensitivity to the properties of light, then an almost supernatural alliance with it. This may be attributed to deliberate mystification by photographers and their publicists or perhaps because critics have been at a loss as to how to make sense of certain practitioners who consistently arrest them with spectacular imagery.

Do not put off doing a coveted picture until another year, for next year the scene will look very different. You will never be able twice to get exactly the same thing. P.H. EMERSON[13]

Fig. 1.15
JESSE ALEXANDER
La Grande, Oregon, 2004
The seductive quality of light in the "golden hour" (the time after sunrise or before sunset) rarely fails to enhance any picture. The vivid colors that we see when the sun is closer to the horizon are caused by moisture in the atmosphere that scatters the shorter lengths of light, leaving the longer yellows and reds. The extended shadows that are caused by the sun's position closer to the horizon can also add shapes and dynamism to a composition. For this picture, the camera was turned away from the setting sun as it passed behind a hill to exploit the color of the light and enrich the subject and the darker sky in the distance.

Fig. 1.15

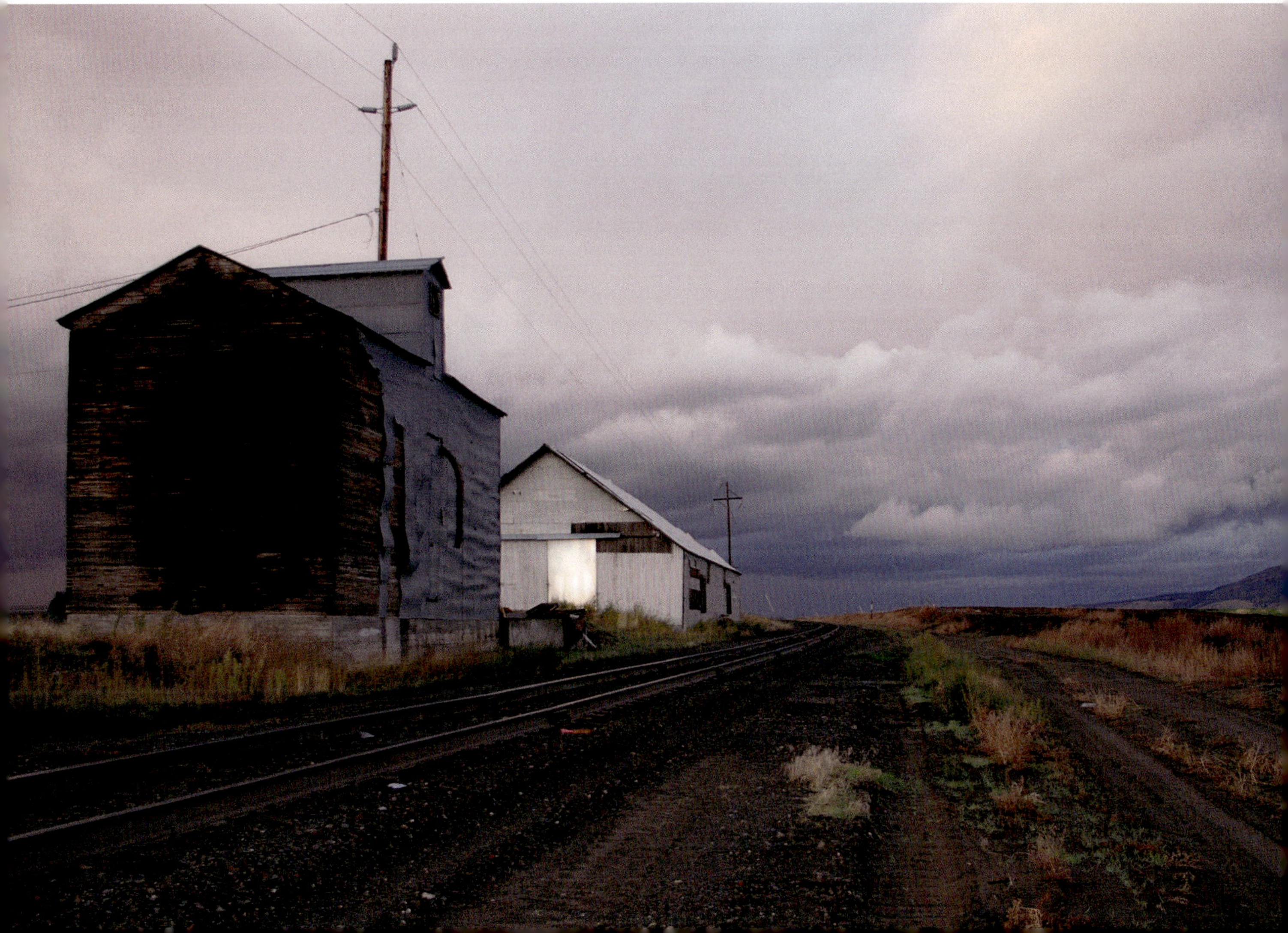

PHYSICAL PROPERTIES OF LIGHT

Light is an electromagnetic wave and just like other forms of energy, it travels in waves and behaves accordingly. At the *longer* end of the electromagnetic spectrum are radio waves and at the other extreme, radioactive gamma rays. A relatively narrow range of electromagnetic waves is perceptible to the human eye, which is referred to as the "visible spectrum" or "visible light."[14] These electromagnetic waves are the familiar colors of the rainbow, which when mixed produce white light. When light passes through a prism, it is refracted and separated into its component parts and identifiable as different colors, violet being of shorter wavelengths and red being of longer within the spectrum of visible light. When we identify the color of a particular subject—green leaves for instance—we do so because the chemical composition of that object (in this case chlorophyll) reflects green light but absorbs other lengths of visible light. In the same way that the green receptors in a digital camera's sensor release an electrical charge from these reflected green light waves, which build up an image, the retina of the human eye has photoreceptor cells, which are sensitive to the three primary colors—red, green, and blue.

Infrared imaging technologies have enabled us to visualize some of the far red waves that are longer than those in the visible spectrum. Color and monochrome infrared photography both have industrial applications, such as forensic use, military intelligence, and conservation, although these processes and materials have been used extensively by practitioners with expressive intentions.[15] The imagery that is produced by infrared technology can be visually striking, for instance making green foliage shimmer when captured with monochrome film, because healthy plant cell walls reflect infrared light. The surreal aesthetic of infrared understandably entices many photographers to experiment with it. It is of course possible to imitate the effect of infrared imaging with photo editing software by selectively adjusting the levels of individual color channels (see Fig. 3.8). However, devotees of analog infrared photography are often keen to point out that such techniques are merely visual simulations and have little in common with *real* infrared photography.
The unpredictability of infrared photography means that those who manage to consistently produce successfully exposed photographs do so through a dedication to the materials and techniques that generally transcend a mere enchantment with the aesthetic effects that can be produced. Practitioners working with infrared light are often drawn to it because of its capacity to visualize what we cannot see with our own eyes. This matter of our biological limitations parallels with the philosophical matter of human understanding: the spiritual question of what else might be around us that we are unable to see.

The refractive properties of light are also important to photographers, as they allow light waves to be diffused. When light strikes an opaque substance, such as

Fig. 1.16
SUSAN DERGES
Full Moon Briars, 2006* from *Cloud Series

Susan Derges produces one-off photograms created within the landscape or the darkroom or a combination of the two. Water, which like light is another fundamental element of life, is a recurring subject within her practice. Derges places sheets of photographic paper beneath the surface of water and exposes it to the light from a handheld flash unit to record the image transmitted from the surface of the water. In this piece, the artist has combined a photographic transparency of the sky and the moon that was taken through a telescope and the lens-less photogram process to render these two elements—the near and the far—within a single exposure. Her works often simulate a peculiar viewing position, simultaneously giving a sense of looking down onto the water and seeing the reflected image of the sky above and feeling that you are below the surface looking up at the sky and the shadows of the foliage that surrounds the pool or river. The artist's work recalls the early experiments of William Henry Fox Talbot and speaks of photography and its raw physical properties.

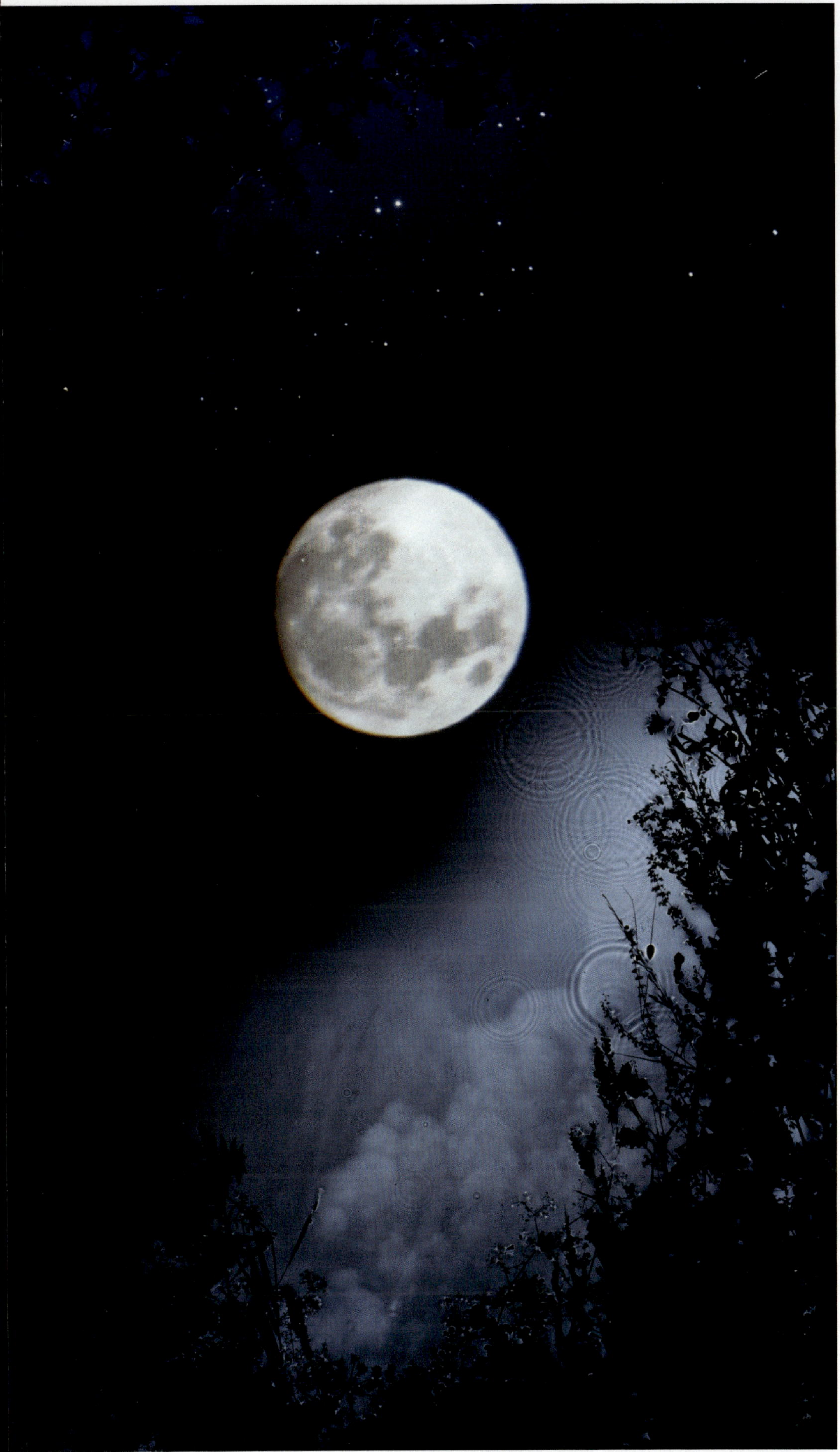

Fig. 1.16

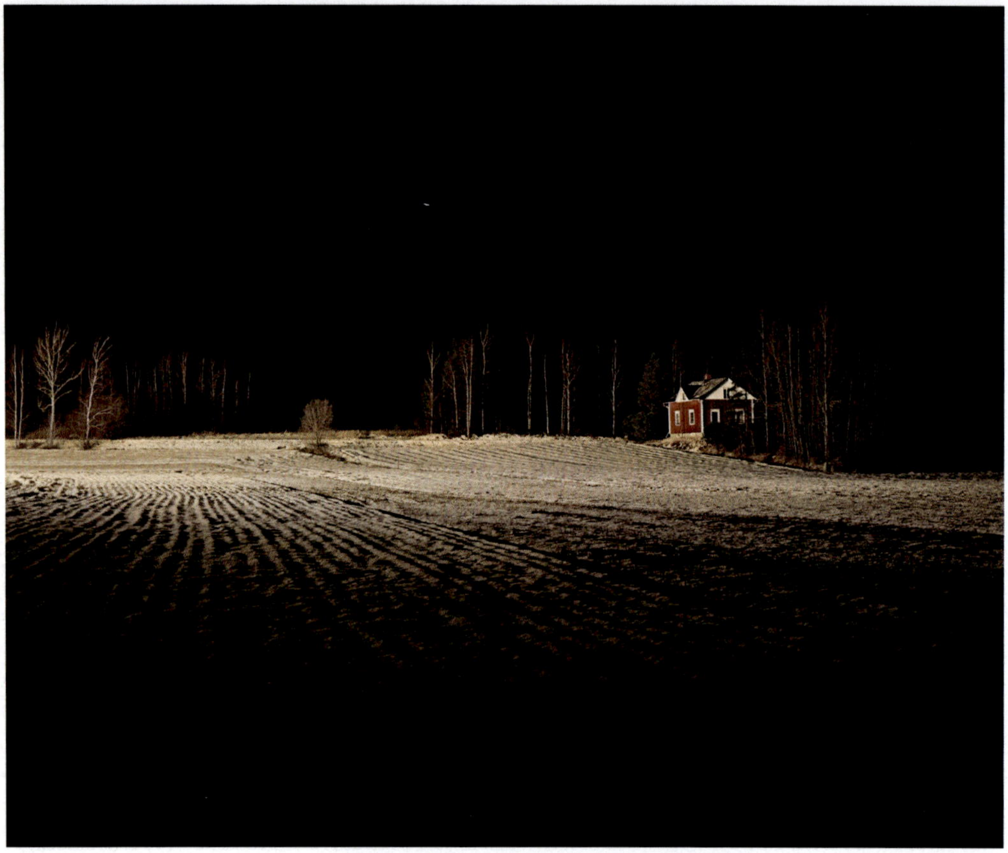

Fig. 1.17
MARTINA LINDQVIST
Untitled 05* from *A Thousand Little Suns*, *2010
In Martina Lindqvist's series, we can see how light rather than standing as a metaphor for hope or positivity can instead create an uneasy presence. The visible effects of light pollution in the series address environmental concerns and also confront the culture/nature binary. (See also *Forest* by Paul Seawright, p. 166.)

Fig. 1.17

a piece of tracing paper, some light fabric, or a layer of cloud, most of the light transmits through it, but its straight line of travel is interrupted and some waves emerge on the other side on a slightly different trajectory. When a single light source such as the sun or a lightbulb is diffused, it also loses intensity because some of the light is reflected back toward the light source or is absorbed by the diffusing material. This interrupted light strikes the subject from many different directions and softens the appearance of shadows cast onto or by the subject. Typically, although by no means universally, photographs that are lit by a diffused light source can appear to have a lot of middle tones (see p. 44) and might be less contrasting in appearance to one made with a harder or more pointed light source. On the other hand, a photograph lit by an undiffused light source is likely to appear more contrasting because there will be more shaded areas. In practice however, because a subject and its environment will reflect light onto itself, how hard or soft a light source is depends upon the proximity of the light source to the subject. For instance, a large, diffused light may throw soft light onto an object close to it, but the farther apart the subject and light become, the smaller, more pointed and harder the light source will be.

MOOD AND LIGHT

Developing an understanding of the physical properties of light is useful for taking greater ownership of how your photographs look, for instance using light to model a subject as you choose or convey a sense of the subject's physical properties through chiaroscuro. But it is just as important to come to terms with the symbolic potential of light, if not more so, because light is integral to conveying meaning in pictures by suggesting mood, emotion, and narrative. Light—and its binary opposite, darkness—acts powerfully upon the human psyche. On a theological level, we see the dichotomy between light and darkness—good and evil—in creation narratives across all cultures. This light/dark binary appears in our verbal as well as visual language: light is always used positively (such as a "lighthearted" or an "enlightened" person), whereas darkness invariably has negative, even malevolent, connotations, such as a "dark mood," "dark days," or the "dark arts."

Lack of tonal contrast can be used to equal effect. Many of the photographs in the *New Topographics* exhibition in 1975 (see p. 126) were taken on overcast days when the sunlight was diffused, casting minimal shadows, or were taken during the middle of the day when shadows cast by the sun were shorter and less conspicuous. For some of these practitioners, this was an attempt to strip the images of emotion or artistic expression, reducing them to a deadpan, factual state. Conversely, tonal flatness can lend an eerie "otherness" to images, such as in Nadav Kander's photograph from *The Long River* (Fig. 2.13). Perhaps a tension arises here from the ambiguity of the light source that exposes the scene: with extreme diffusion, the light appears not to come from one particular direction but from everywhere. This might also be the case with the extensively artificially lit photographs by Tim Simmons, where the eye and the mind struggle to make sense of how the scene is illuminated (see p. 107).[16]

Light appearing where it shouldn't is an important feature of Martina Lindqvist's series *A Thousand Little Suns*. Lindqvist's nighttime images of rural dwellings and farm buildings in central Finland are illuminated by incongruous, dirty tones. This remote landscape *should* be shrouded in darkness during winter months; however, the landscape is revealed during the camera's long exposure by the light pollution from the distant towns and cities. In Lindqvist's photographs, the light seems out of place, even invasive. And unlike euphoric, sun-drenched images of daybreak, this muddy warmth is neither soothing nor reassuring, but unnerving—the effect, perhaps, of an encroaching, apocalyptic inferno? The topography within Lindqvist's photographs is significant also, as this relates to a duality in addition to that of darkness versus light. The spaces in her series are at the edges of forests, which are, as she asserts in her artist's statement, "the most natural of spaces" but which "are truly unnatural for the cultured human being." In this sense, the artificial light encroaching on the forest might be seen as a metaphor of a nature/culture dichotomy. Located by the photographer at a threshold between culture and nature, do we dare take a few steps farther into the forest—into the unknown?

Fig. 1.18
JESSE ALEXANDER
Hardbrüke, Zürich, Switzerland, 2012
The photographer used a tripod to capture this image taken at night using a 5" × 4" camera. In this 10-second exposure, the static objects such as the architecture are sharp, although the movement of the figures is visible. Working with a tripod in a busy public place can be difficult and is also a tripping hazard. Nonetheless, tripods are excellent at drawing unnecessary attention to the photographer. Institutions and officials are generally less tolerant of professional photographers than of amateurs and often differentiate between the two by whether or not they use a tripod.

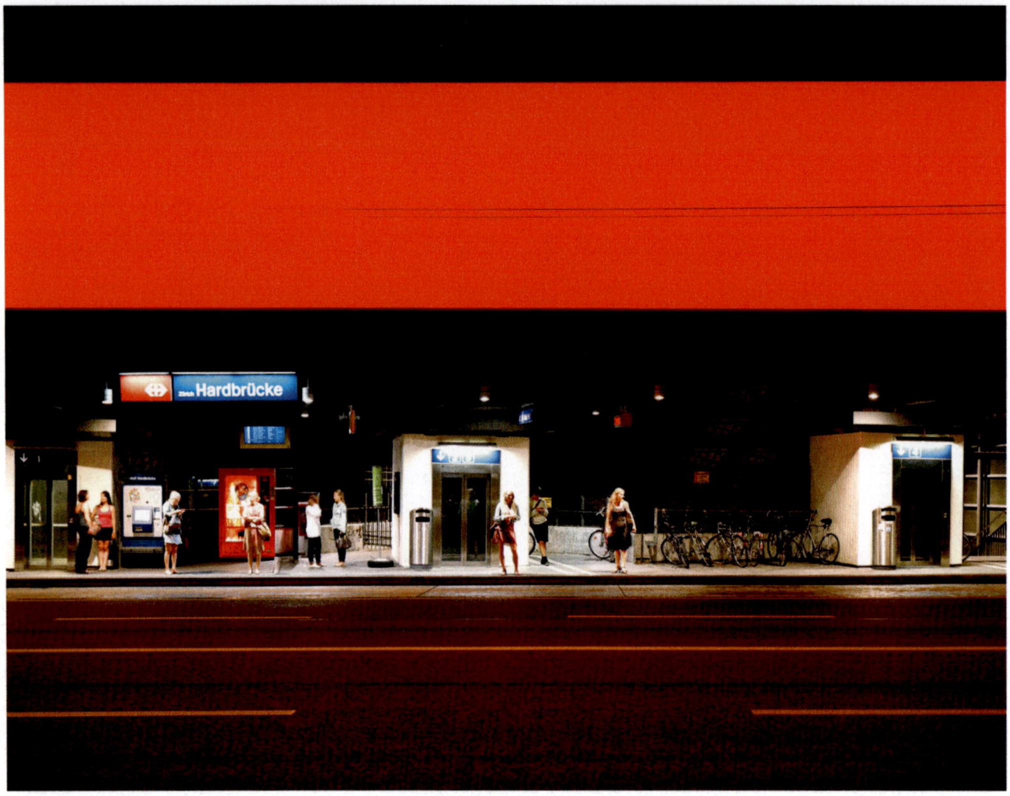

Fig. 1.18

TRIPOD OR HANDHELD?

Certain situations and scenarios will dictate whether you will have to use a tripod to support your camera to render a sharp image. It is practically impossible to operate large-format cameras without one. Whatever camera format you use, low light situations will demand a slower shutter speed, and you will have to utilize some sort of support if you wish to avoid camera shake. There are other practical reasons for working with a tripod, such as being able to hold filters over the lens (see p. 96) or perhaps to maintain a consistent frame if you are bracketing an exposure or creating a montage of multiple frames (see p. 102). Although manufacturers are constantly developing novel functions, the basic tripod design is rudimentary. Tripods are worth investing in, as they will not be outdated as quickly as other pieces of equipment. The size and weight of a tripod should match the weight of the camera that it is supposed to support, but it is advisable to err on the side of caution and use as sturdy a tripod as you are prepared to pay for—and carry!

There are of course plenty of situations for which a tripod is unnecessary and more likely to hinder spontaneity. However, working with a tripod can help develop a greater degree of discernment in terms of composing images. Mounting the camera on the tripod temporarily fixes the camera's point of view within a scene in a way different from having it hanging around your neck or in your hands. Divorcing you from your tool can also liberate your other senses so that you may be more attuned to the nuances of your environment. Affixing the camera to a point allows you to reflect, consider, and adjust the frame incrementally rather than by strides. This process of slowing down your approach is sensible, even in scenarios where a tripod isn't strictly necessary, such as in bright conditions with smaller camera formats. Using a tripod can be conducive to a methodology that aspires toward *making* pictures rather than simply *taking* them.

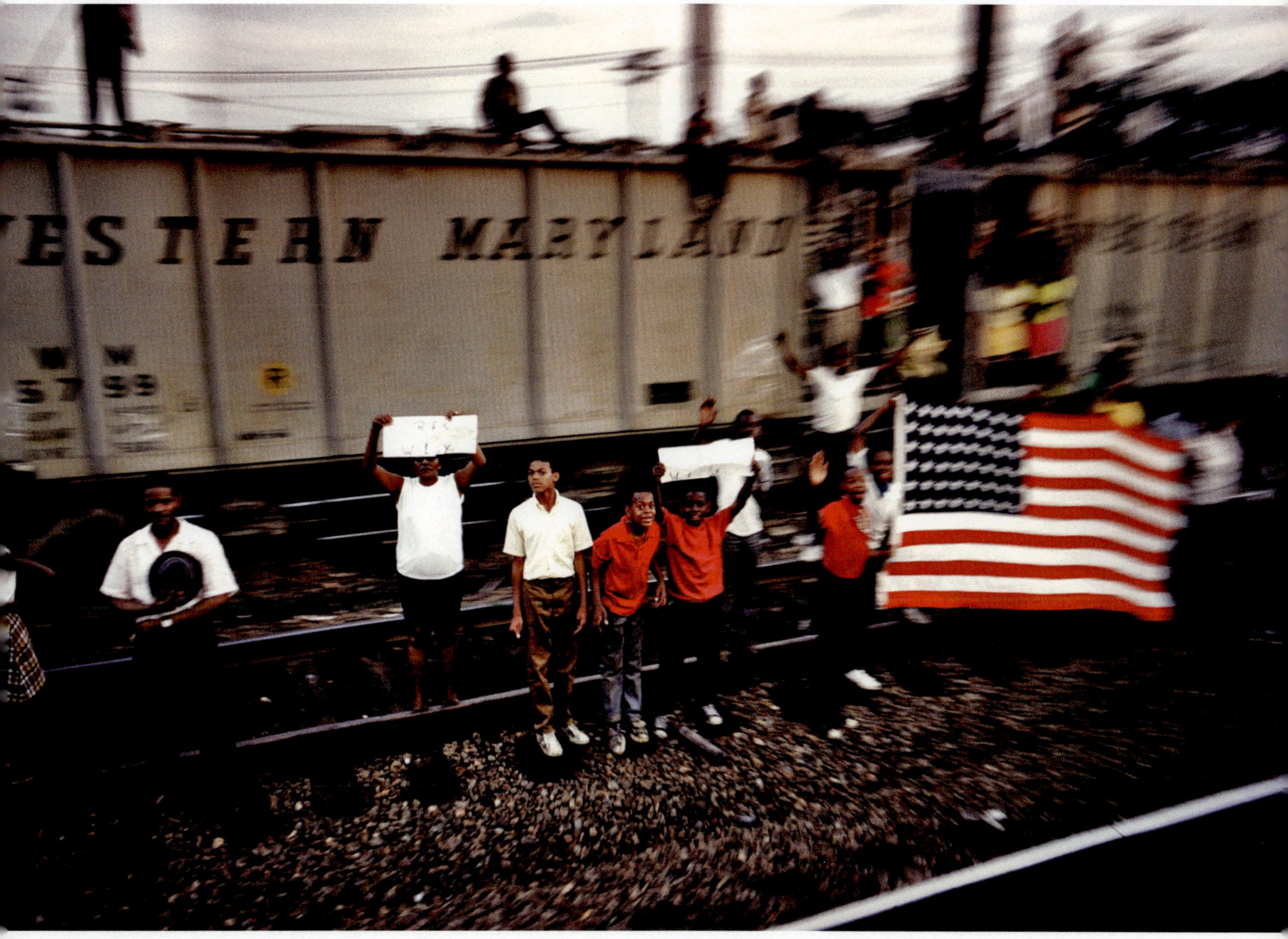

Fig. 1.19

Fig. 1.19
PAUL FUSCO
Robert F. Kennedy Funeral Train, 1968
Paul Fusco rode Robert Kennedy's funeral train as it traversed from New York City to Arlington Cemetery following his assassination. Although this work might not seem to sit comfortably within a discussion of landscape photography, Fusco's physical transect through the country also revealed a societal cross section of a grieving nation. Far from the pensive composure of much expressive landscape work, the conspicuously poor technical quality of Fusco's images (shot on 35 mm from the open door of the moving train) ascribes authenticity to the series and reflects the emotion of the crowds as they gathered to pay their respects to the passing cortège.

THE ZONE SYSTEM

Both digital and analog processes are limited in terms of the range of tones that can be rendered in a single exposure by either the image sensor or on film. Monochrome film can generally register a greater range of light intensities than color negatives can, and until recently, digital cameras were even more limited in this respect. To illustrate the problem of this limitation, take the classic faux pas that most manuals of photography caution against—photographing a figure in front of a brightly lit background, such as a sunset. The resulting silhouettes demonstrate the camera's inability to record detail in the brightest tones and the relative darkness of the shadows elsewhere in the picture. In reality, the human eye also suffers from the same problem, although, comparatively speaking, it is far superior to most cameras.

This kind of high-contrast lighting situation has always been challenging for photographers wishing to capture a naturalistic image. High-contrast scenarios will present themselves in almost every field of photographic practice, although they are particularly common in landscape photography. Failure to expose adequately, whether using film or working digitally, will result in a negative or image file that is challenging to work with, the print of which will ultimately be of inferior quality to one made with greater attention to exposure settings. Tricks can be performed in postproduction to rectify poor exposure (within the darkroom as well as with imaging software), but there is no substitute for a correctly exposed photograph to begin with. A little extra effort before the shutter is released can mean a lot less hassle afterward and generally speaking, better image quality.

For Ansel Adams (1902–1984)—one of the most iconic practitioners of landscape photography—the principal artistry in photography lay in the attention that was invested in the photographic act itself. The production of prints in the darkroom was certainly an important part of the creative process. However, crafting

Fig. 1.20
Eleven-point Zone System

Zone 0	**Zone I**	**Zone II**	**Zone III**	**Zone IV**	**Zone V Middle Gray**	**Zone VI**	**Zone VII**	**Zone VIII**	**Zone IX**	**Zone X**
Darkest part of negative; no detail	Very slight tonality –4 stops	–3 stops	–2 stops	–1 stop	0 ev	+1 stop	+2 stops	+3 stops	Highlight tones with some texture +4 stops	Pure white; no detail

Fig. 1.20

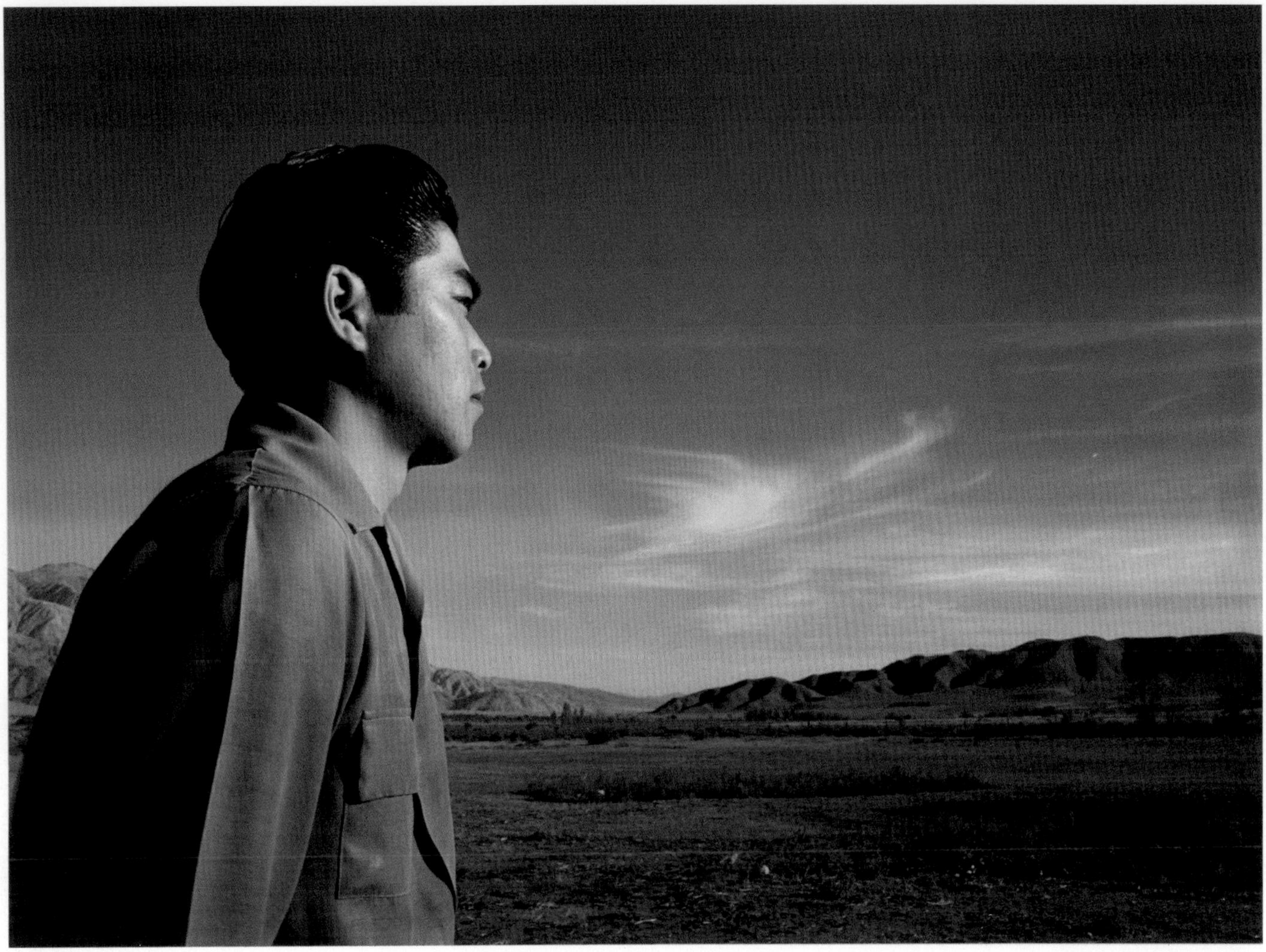

Fig. 1.21

Fig. 1.21
ANSEL ADAMS
Tom Kobayashi, Landscape, South Fields, Manzanar Relocation Center, 1943
Following the attack on Pearl Harbor in 1941, the U.S. government incarcerated Japanese Americans living along the Pacific Coast. In total, around 110,000 people of Japanese heritage were interned in camps like the Manzanar Relocation Center, north of Los Angeles. Ansel Adams was unhappy with this policy and wanted to visit the camp and photograph the people living there. Many of Adams's photographs from this project depict the internees within the context of their environment, establishing a visual connection between the Japanese Americans and the country from which they were ostracized.

the image beforehand—"in camera"—was one way that Adams and his secessionist predecessors distinguished themselves from earlier generations of pictorialist landscape photographers, for whom manipulation of the print *after* the exposure was the critical aspect of photographic artistry (see p. 112). In addition to meticulous framing, careful timing, and the selection of special-effect filters (see p. 96), choosing the precise exposure settings was a principal consideration. The Zone System, which Adams developed with Fred Archer from the 1930s to the 1980s, was a means to more consistently control the tonal density of a negative to more accurately previsualize the appearance of the final photograph. The Zone System separates the total tonal sensitivity of a negative and establishes discrete segments, or zones, within that range, each of which represents a full *f*-stop's difference in terms of exposure. The total number of zones that a brand of film or particular model of camera can accommodate within a single exposure is referred to as its "dynamic range."

It is important to consider Zone V, as this middle gray is the tone that the photographic light meter (whether handheld or built into the camera) identifies when it indicates that a subject (*any* subject) is correctly exposed. As far as the light meter is concerned, this is the best way to ensure that the greatest number of tones will be rendered. Zone V presents the photographer with two problems. First, not all objects are gray or have an equivalent "average" density of color tones. Second, deciding exactly where or what within a scene is middle gray is largely subjective. In

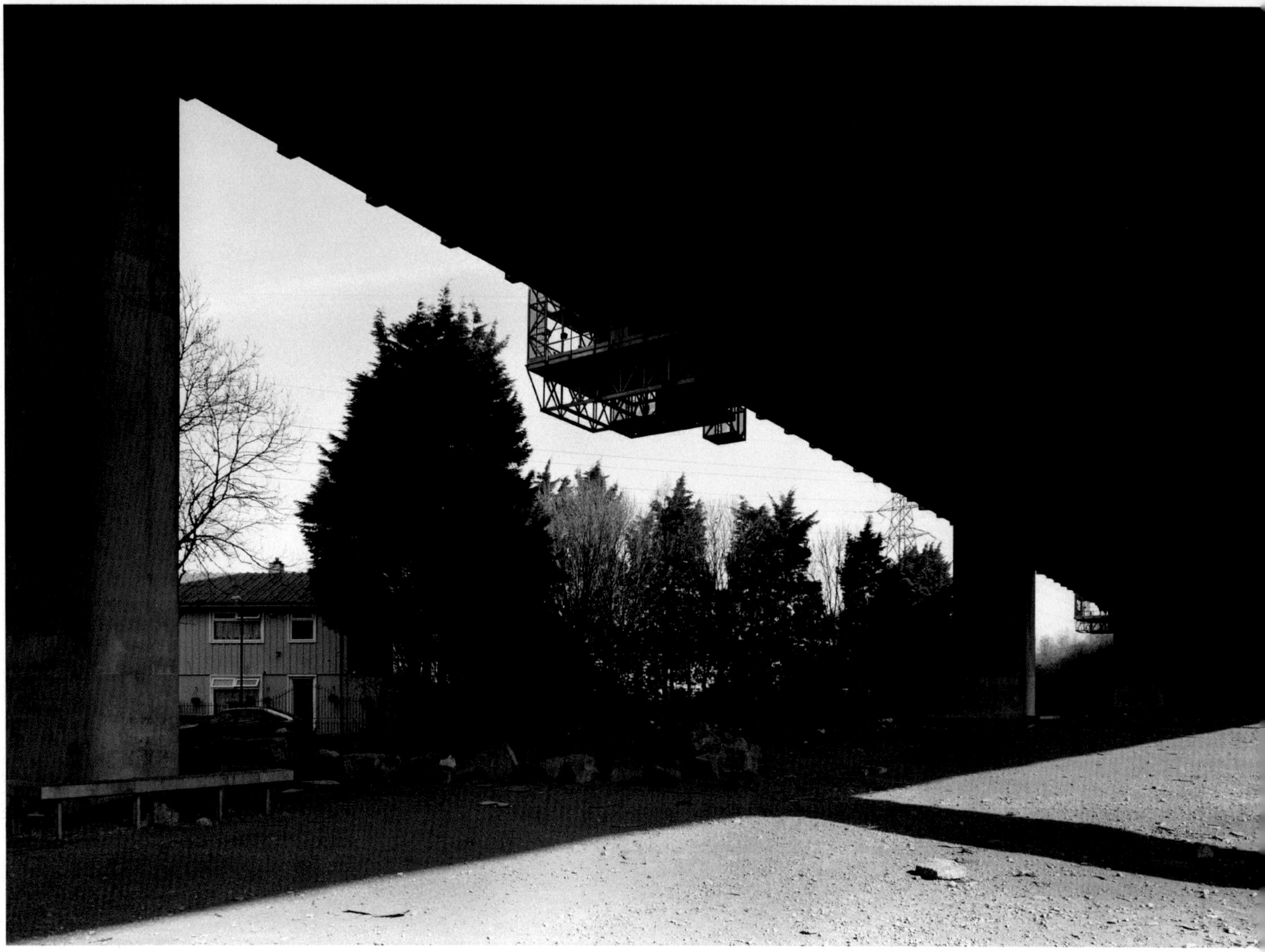

Fig. 1.22

fact, placing a purpose-made gray card next to a subject and taking a light reading from it before removing it from view and taking the shot is one method of achieving the maximum possible tonal range for a particular lighting scenario.

COMPENSATING FOR THE CONDITIONS

The card method, however, will not necessarily yield an image that resembles the scene as the photographer saw it or indeed how she might prefer to represent it. For instance, the method described would work to reproduce a naturalistic image of an evenly lit scene, but when there is a contrasting mix of tones and light or a scene is particularly dark or bright, it is necessary to adjust exposure settings accordingly. There are many methods for taking light readings. These methods will vary according to scenario and equipment, but in almost every situation it is necessary to adjust the camera light meter to compensate for darker or brighter subjects and lighting conditions.

As well as the key variables of exposure time, light intensity, and ISO sensitivity, in analog photography other minor factors can influence the density of the final negative, which can have slight but not insignificant effects upon the tonal range of the final print. Ansel Adams sought to refine and better manage some of these variables that affected exposure, such as developer formula and development times. The Zone System is a systematic procedure whereby photographers' personal choice

Fig. 1.22
JESSE ALEXANDER
Avonmouth Bridge, UK, 2009
The composition and lighting of this photograph illustrate a highly contrasting situation, whereby a very dominant element of the frame is much darker than the rest of the image. If a center-weight light meter had been used in this situation without making any compensation for exposure, the underside of the bridge would have appeared much lighter, rendering more detail throughout the architecture of the bridge, but the foreground and the other brighter elements would have been overexposed, losing detail and appearing "washed out." Another metering technique is to simply take light meter readings from the brightest and darkest parts of the scene and then calculate a medium.

Fig. 1.23
MICHAL IWANOWSKI
Rioviniu Gatve, Vilnius, Lithuania, 2013
from *Clear of People*
Iwanowski's photograph from *Clear of People* (see p. 161) exemplifies another frequently challenging technical scenario in terms of exposure. Without compensation for exposure, the snow-covered scene would have been rendered much darker than it actually appeared, because instead of "seeing" bright white snow, the camera light meter sees average, Zone V *gray* snow. In a similar situation, it would be necessary to either take a light meter reading of the snow in the foreground and then overexpose by 3 or 4 *f*-stops or set the camera light meter to 3 or 4 stops above exposure value (+3 or +4 EV). The image is also a useful reminder that a technically sound photograph does not necessarily have to contain a broad or evenly distributed range of tones. In fact, the contrast between the snow and the darker details creates tonal contrast, which is generally pleasing to the eye.

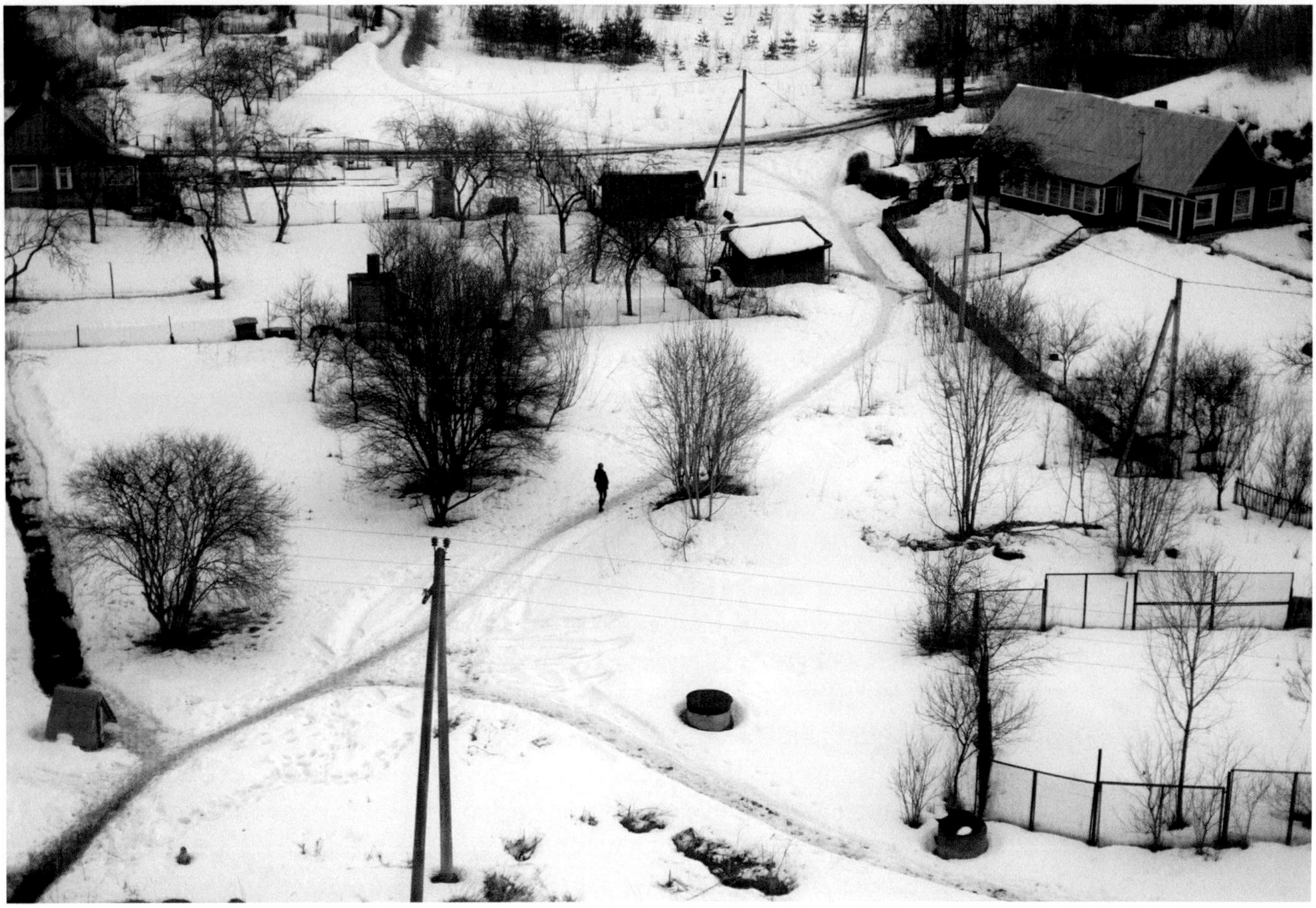

Fig. 1.23

of film stock and processing chemistry is aligned with their light meters, enabling them to consistently achieve as great a tonal range as possible. To explore this comprehensively is beyond the scope of this discussion. However, it is important to bear in mind that while principles and technical processes in analog and digital photography are standardized, it is worth testing the manufacturer's specifications and exploring the limits of your own equipment.

BEHIND THE VIEW

Generally speaking, the most fundamental level on which any artwork will be judged is its aesthetic level: whether a piece of art is arresting, seductive, or repulsive to look at or however else a work might interact with a viewer's other senses. However, after we assess its appearance, we tend to look for something else within a work of art—clues about the maker's intention or what else the work might comment upon. To use a musical analogy, do the lyrics just *sound* nice or do they actually *say* something intelligent or poetic?

It is difficult to give a name to that which lies beyond the purely visual qualities of the photograph's thin surface, what we can humbly call the deeper, potentially infinite expanse of interpretation and discussion. Artists and critics often talk about layers or levels of meaning when it comes to a single work, a project, or a series of photographs. To appropriate the terminology of semiotics (a division of linguistics that has contributed much to the discourse of contemporary art), we can separate the "denotation" of a picture, or its appearance—what is inside the frame and how it is rendered technically—from its "connotation"—what these things communicate, or rather how they are interpreted. Or to put it another way, what does a picture describe, and what does it imply?[17]

"Narrative" is often used to describe this interpretive aspect of photography. In its simplest sense, narrative refers to the recounting of information. In a legal context, this could be a witness supplying a prosaic narrative of a linear sequence of events. For instance, investigators use forensic photographs in conjunction with other evidence to piece together an accurate narrative of a crime. Text is often used to "anchor"[18] the narrative of press and reportage photographs, to reinforce or clarify what appears to be going on in the scene depicted. Narrative within pictures should not be confused with the relationship between image and text: a photograph's caption (whether written by the photographer, newspaper editor, or copywriter) is not *the* narrative. It may offer a commentary of the picture; however, the two things offer different "truths," which coalesce as *a particular* narrative when they are combined.

These cases, however, address narrative in terms of something tangible—versions of an event that apparently took place. Often in contemporary photography, narratives are nonlinear[19] but might be conceptual or intertextual—relating to other stories (real or imagined) or engaging with works of art made by earlier practitioners.[20] These narratives are potentially harder to make sense of in the first instance and won't necessarily have a *definitive* message, but rather are a complex web of ideas, themes, and stories.

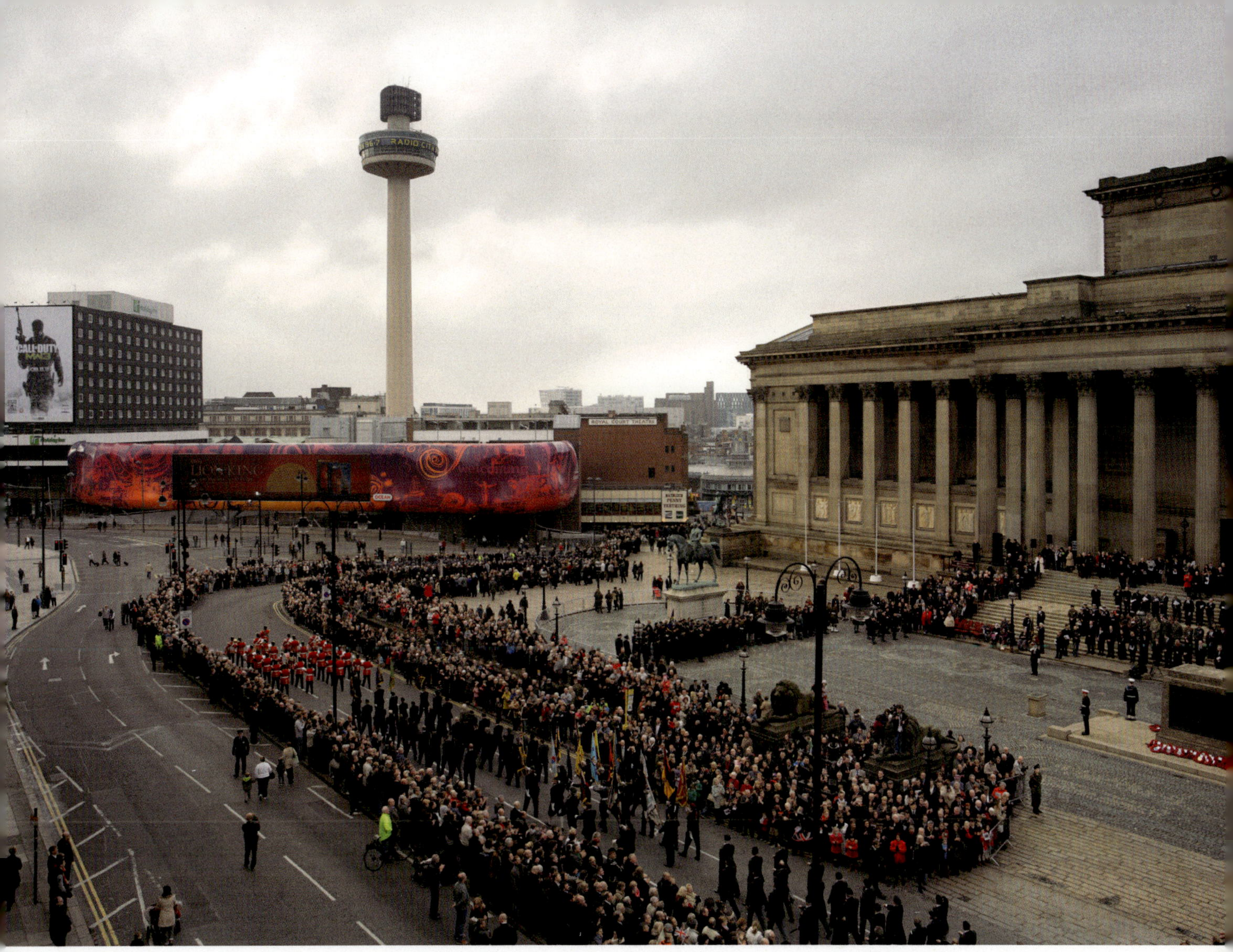

Fig. 1.24

Fig. 1.24
JOHN DAVIES
Call of Duty, Remembrance Sunday, Liverpool—November 13, 2011 **from the ongoing series** ***Signs of War***

Call of Duty is a typical example of John Davies's strategy, whereby from an elevated position, he shoots urban and rural landscapes that are rich in detail. History is a prominent feature of Davies's work. He is drawn to places that have a particular socio-industrial significance. The high vantage point adds to a sense of *overview*, a distanced, reflective commentary on a subject rather than a dispatch from ground level—from *within* it. In this series, Davies investigates the conspicuous traces of the culture of war across the British landscape. An accusing relationship is revealed here between the annual memorial event, which serves to remember and reflect upon those who gave their lives answering a call of duty, and the poster in the top left of the scene advertising the launch of the latest edition of the video game *Call of Duty*. The juxtaposition of the memorial procession, solemnly revering those who have been killed in action and giving thanks for the armed forces more generally, confronts the seduction of war as represented through popular culture. The fantasy of killing and the reality of dying collide.

Photography isn't looking; it's feeling. If you can't feel what you're looking at, then you're never going to get others to feel anything when they look at your pictures. DON McCULLIN[21]

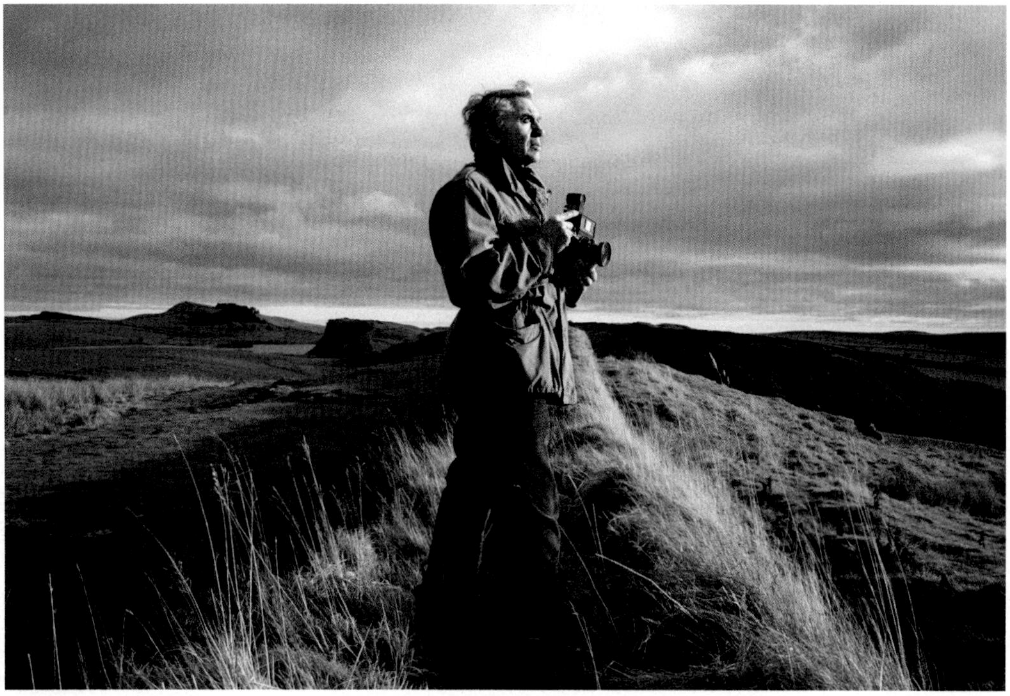

Fig. 1.25

Fig. 1.25
TOM STODDART
Don McCullin
The visual sensibilities of Don McCullin's landscapes of England are reflected in his portrait taken by Tom Stoddard. McCullin's pictures of the English countryside have a kind of paradox: they simultaneously portray the land as bleak and visually appealing. His work conveys something of the anguish that resides within him and the ghosts that haunt him from his frequently harrowing career as a photojournalist and combat photographer.

PERSONAL STORIES

Critics of landscape photographs often debase practitioners whose heightened aesthetics amounts to either a distraction or a barrier to more thoughtful narratives that the artist might be trying to express. The landscape work of Don McCullin makes an interesting reference point in this regard, as an example of where aesthetic qualities are inextricably linked to real-life narratives behind his work. Although perhaps heightened through tonal control and contrast, his photographs of rural England present images that are far removed from idyllic representations of the countryside. McCullin's landscapes are dark, both in terms of their denoted formal qualities and the kinds of feelings that are connoted. His landscapes have been likened to images of war zones: contrasting winter skies that resemble thick, acrid smoke and flooded fields reminiscent of waterlogged shell holes. On one level, we could see McCullin's landscapes as autobiographical diary entries—momentary reflective expressions. However, with the knowledge of McCullin's history, such an explanation seems superficial.

McCullin is one of the most celebrated photographers of his generation, having gained particular acclaim for his combat photography. Throughout his long career, the photographer has always been candid about his decisions to photograph war, famine, and other scenes of human atrocity and barbarity, which have taken their psychological toll on him. Although McCullin's social documentary and landscape projects also are very well received, it is his combat photography that he is most revered for. A remarkable feature of McCullin's landscapes is the palpable sense of personal trauma that they carry. His combat photography, which he has attempted to emancipate himself from both professionally and emotionally, maintains a presence in his pictures. To consider McCullin's landscapes in relation to a textual narrative, captioning his pictures would seem pointless: composed contemplatively, captured in a field, and reflecting an inner pain, they have little to say about the place within the picture but much about the space behind the photographer's eyes, which is overlaid on the picture. McCullin himself has related this practice to both emotional closure on the ghosts of his past and coming to terms with his own mortality. "I'm becoming more poetical; and of course, it's got something to do with the fact that I'm looking at the horizon of the end of my journey. I'm looking at the infinity mark where I will finally wind up."[22]

EXTENDED NARRATIVES

The vast majority of Don McCullin's reportage work between the 1950s and the 1980s was published in the form of photo-essays (predominantly in newspaper supplement magazines), which have particular relevance to a discussion of narrative in photography. These kinds of publications have evolved from the illustrated magazines that were extremely widely read and were most popular around the 1940s. The photo-essay is an effective means of communicating narrative through an extended sequence of images in print media, often enhanced by reproducing images at various sizes and combining different styles of photographs, such as portraits, close-ups, and landscapes, along with pictures of the actual news story.[23]

The picture essay isn't strictly something that is confined to reportage photography and current newsworthy events. Fashion shoots for magazines (the ones taken on location as opposed to photographs taken against a plain backdrop in the studio) are referred to as "stories." Any kind of magazine feature will, of course, incorporate photographs. It is important though to be able to distinguish between when photographs are used merely to illustrate a story that is mostly conveyed through text and when the photographs are doing most, if not all, of the talking. The photo-essay is perhaps one possible source of the popularity of the photographic series over the singular image, in contemporary photography at least. Certainly, for a long time artists have produced work in particular sets or individual pieces that could be seen in the context of their wider practice, or oeuvre.[24] It is also difficult to entirely separate still photography from a discussion of the moving image, to which sequencing is of course an integral component. But the ability to compose a *collection* of photographs, carefully considered in relation to

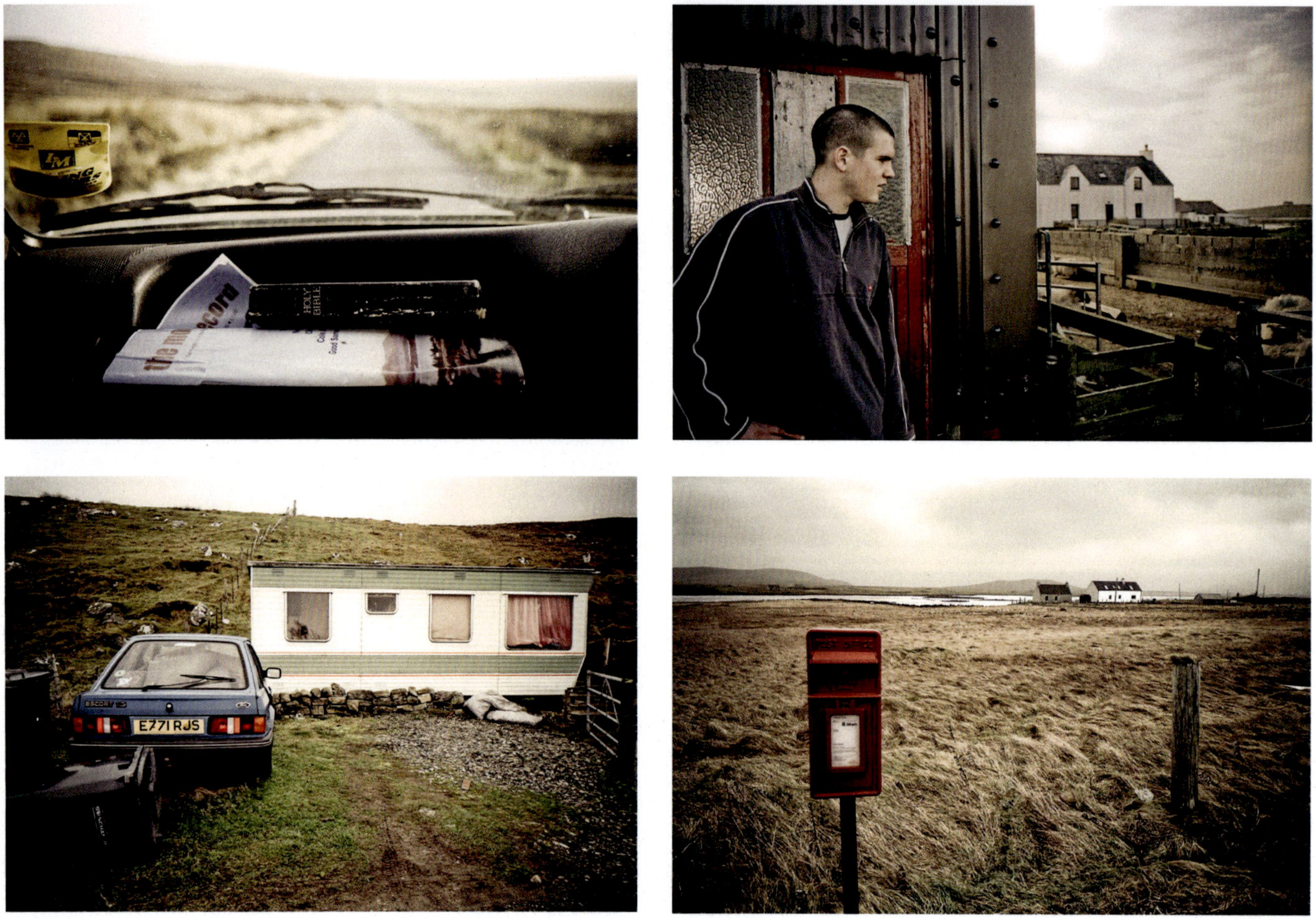

Fig. 1.26

Fig. 1.26.i–1.26.iv
JOSÉ NAVARRO
Passing Place

When working on a long-term project like Jose Navarro's *Passing Place*, which took him on multiple trips to the island of North Uist in the Scottish Outer Hebrides, at some point it will be necessary to stop and make sense of the many photographs that soon build up. Navarro used photography to explore and document the lives of the remote community, which is sustained through the land management system of crofting, which in the context of the British Isles is particular to the Scottish landscape. Navarro embedded himself within the community to gain an insight and ultimately communicate a sense of what the place and the people are like. On a practical level, there is a mix of imagery, which as well as providing a range of information, gives a sense of rhythm to the sequence, denying the possibility of repetition or tedium. In terms of what the work communicates, there is no particular linear narrative. We are not presented with a simplistic "day in the life of a crofter" or a polemic statement about this endangered way of life. However, the photographs offer a glimpse into an unusual location and the community that has adapted to it, a community whose day-to-day life is perhaps more intimately linked to the elements than are most communities in the rest of the British Isles. The narrative is open ended, and there is plenty of opportunity for viewers to engage with the work and interpret what they see.

one another to communicate a narrative, is as important as having a good eye for a single photograph.

Opportunities for having photo-essays published are very different now. Television and in turn the Internet have limited the traditional photo-essay to relatively few publications. While some broadsheet weekend supplements do publish illustrated stories, much of what resembles a photo-essay is actually more likely to be a preview of a forthcoming exhibition or coffee-table book. Nonetheless, the Internet is an exciting platform to publish photographs and experiment with different ways of sequencing, timing, and juxtaposing photographs with other media, such as text and sound (including music, verbal commentary, interviews, and more abstract soundscapes). With new platforms also comes the potential for new, more complex narratives and features like rollovers and hyperlinks, which can allow viewers to find out more information about the subject matter or issues discussed within the photographic project.[25]

1 Robert Adams, *Beauty in Photography* (New York: Aperture, 1996), 14.

2 Joel Snyder in W.J.T. Mitchell, *Landscape and Power* (2nd ed.) (Chicago: University of Chicago Press, 2002), 192.

3 Identification of the artistic credibility of O'Sullivan's survey photographs, as well as his images of the American Civil War (see p. 164), is predominantly owed to John Szarkowski, who as curator of photography at the New York Museum of Modern Art, extolled the merits and significance of these works. See John Szarkowski, *American Landscapes* (New York: Museum of Modern Art, 1981).

4 See interview with the photographer in T.J. Cooper, *Point of No Return* (London: Haunch of Venison, 2004).

5 Reproduced in Henri Cartier-Bresson, *The Mind's Eye* (New York: Aperture, 1999), 32.

6 The rule of thirds dates back to antiquity, although it was attributed in the contemporary discourse of aesthetics to John Thomas Smith, who described it in 1797 in his book *Remarks on Rural Scenery*.

7 Cartier-Bresson, *The Mind's Eye,* 42.

8 For certain practitioners these can be exceptionally long. See for instance Michael Wesely, *Open Shutter Project* (New York: Museum of Modern Art, 2004).

9 We also can consider timing in more abstract terms. See p. 168 for a discussion of how time becomes particulalry important to the making and understanding of certain bodies of landscape work.

10 Many consumer cameras and smartphones have the capacity to "stitch" together multiple frames or render a video sequence into a single panoramic image.

11 Rebecca Solnit, *Motion Studies* (London: Bloomsbury, 2003), 160–61.

12 The angle of view of human sight is approximately 160° × 75°. Standard lenses show an angle of view of around 27° × 40° [diagonal *c.* 45°]. Even super-wide fisheye lenses do not approximate the extent of human vision, which in terms of angle of view is eclipsed by the capabilities of other animals.

13 P.H. Emerson, "Naturalistic Photography for Students of the Art" (1889), in Alan Trachtenberg, *Classic Essays on Photography* (New Haven, CT: Leete's Island Books, 1980), 101.

14 See M. Langford, A. Fox, and R. Sawdon Smith, *Langford's Basic Photography* (9th ed.) (Oxford: Focal Press, 2010), 32.

15 See Richard Mosse's book, *Infra* (New York: Aperture, 2011), in which the photographer used Kodak Aerochrome film, a material used for military surveillance, to document the people and landscape of the Democratic Republic of the Congo.

16 This touches upon what Sigmund Freud called the "uncanny," whereby something appears familiar (in this case, the picture is identifiable as a photographic image of a landscape) and yet isn't *right* somehow, leading to a feeling of displacement and unease. See p. 74.

17 See "The Photographic Message," in Roland Barthes, *Image-Music-Text* (London: Fontana Press, 1977).

18 Ibid.

19 See, for instance, Taryn Simon's project *A Living Man Found Dead and Other Chapters I–XVII* (2008–2011).

20 This particular idea of intertextuality (re-engaging with previously made "texts") is particulalry symptomatic of postmodernism.

21 McCullin, interview by John Tusa, BBC Radio 3, Aug. 15, 2002.

22 McCullin, BBC Radio 3.

23 For a comprehensively illustrated summary of the evolution of these kinds of publications, see Robert Lebeck, *Kiosk: A History of Photojournalism, 1839–1973* (Göttingen, Germany: Steidl, 2001).

24 William Hogarth (1697–1764) was an artist and satirist who used the idea of a sequence of pictures particularly effectively to recount allegorical stories of London society in the 1700s, including *A Rakes Progress* (1735).

25 See Fred Ritchin's theory of hyperphotography, which is discussed in *After Photography* (New York: W.W. Norton & Company, 2009).

ASSIGNMENT 1

SURROUNDINGS

PROJECT Create a series of photographs that describe the place where you live. You might wish to use this opportunity to turn your camera on the different places that you visit every day and try to make some interesting compositions with familiar subjects, or you may wish to explore some parts of your town or neighborhood that you do not yet know well.

While you are out shooting, try to think about how you feel about these places: Do they feel comforting and reassuring or do you find them foreboding? Make brief written notes of any thoughts you have as you work. Can you come up with any visual strategies to communicate how you personally feel toward these places?

If you have a zoom lens, fix it at different focal lengths. For instance, try working for a while just at the widest angle, and later, do the same with the lens zoomed in to its closest. Do the different focal lengths influence your approach? Do you have a preference for a particular focal length? Try to explain this in your reflective learning journal or on your blog.

Also (if working digitally) use tape to mask off your LCD screen and try working with square and panoramic frames, as well as the frame native to your camera. Set yourself the goal of *not* cropping your photographs in postproduction. Again, note down how this frame influences your approach.

When you have photographed a few different locations over several shoots, make a contact sheet of your photographs and try to piece together a sequence of up to 12 images. Consider how your editing choice and the order of your sequence contributes to the narrative of your series. Print these out or upload them to your blog, and write a sentence or two under each one describing why you selected it for your series.

RESEARCH AND DISCUSSION Consider the following tasks and write down your thoughts in your reflective learning journal or on your blog. Then discuss them with peers in a group or use them to start a thread on an online forum.

- Try to find a photograph or series of photographs that simultaneously exhibit Robert Adams's three varieties of landscape photography: geography, autobiography, and metaphor. Explain why you think it does.
- Use the Internet and any newspapers or magazines to identify three photographs that you think the photographer *deliberately* under- or overexposed for a creative effect. Why do you think the photographer chose to do this and how has the exposure influenced the way you read the photographs?
- Find some photographs that upon first impression, you believe exhibit strong compositional qualities. Draw a rule-of-thirds grid over the top and see whether these pictures exhibit to the rules.
- Use the Internet and any newspapers or magazines and present three *single* images in which you can identify a narrative.

Chapter 2
DEFINING NATURE

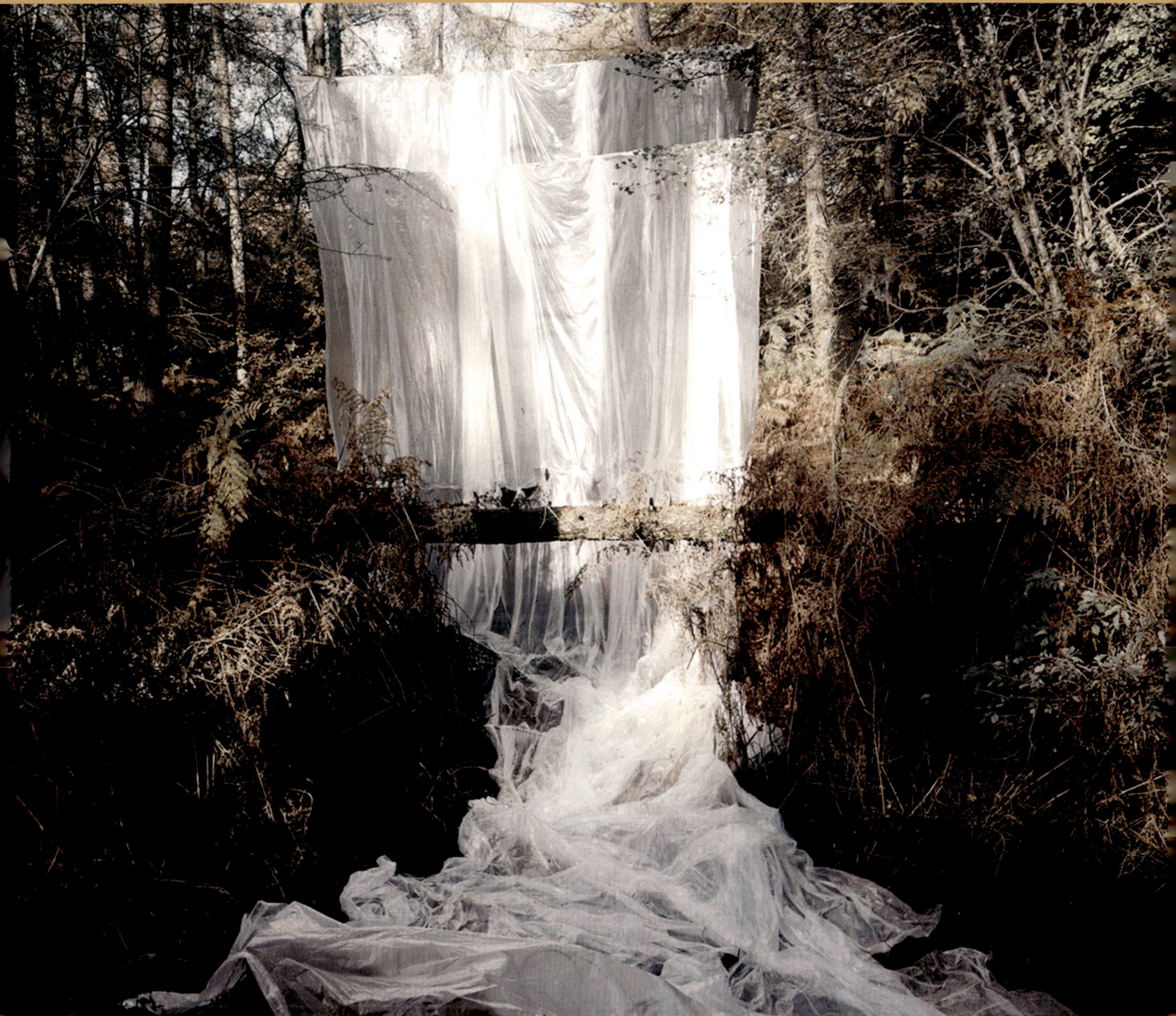

Fig. 2.1

Fig. 2.1
NOÉMIE GOUDAL
Cascade, 2009 from the series
Les Amants

In this chapter, we will discuss some of the ways in which the land has traditionally been—and to a certain extent, continues to be—represented. Much of this discussion will orbit around the themes of the sublime and picturesque values. These ideas underpin both the making and appreciation of much contemporary landscape photography, whose practitioners often scrutinize and critique traditional aesthetic values. Although the sublime and the picturesque are ubiquitous terms, we shall look back at their origins in eighteenth-century philosophy and romantic painting. As we shall see, these principles have played a major role in shaping the landscape genre, but they have also had an impact upon our understanding of what constitutes nature. To conclude this chapter, we will consider how the sublime relates to exploration and look at how photography has been used to map out new territories as well as re-examine more familiar places.

NATURE AND CULTURE

We often think of nature in terms of natural history, the abiotic (nonliving) and biotic (living) features and creatures that make up our planet and are indigenous to it—that is, anything *not* man-made. This extends to other fields of science, such as chemistry and physics, that are concerned with understanding the laws of nature, that interlace life forms with their environment. The man-made environment, perhaps epitomized by the urban metropolis, is often seen as nature's antithesis and, as many Hollywood narratives would have it, the root of social ills: A temporary retreat back to nature is often portrayed as the best antidote to modern living. "Nature" can refer to the elemental, raw characteristics of something: for instance, Stephen Shore's primer, which discusses the fundamental qualities of the photographic image, is titled *The Nature of Photographs*.[1]

Nature is an important theme in the work of Noémie Goudal, and her photograph *Cascade* (Fig. 2.1) engages with it in several ways. Goudal plays with our natural, ocular senses, as well as our ability to process the information. Her photograph is an elaborate trompe l'oeil whereby she introduces a waterfall that cuts through a woodland. Goudal's illusion might convince us for just a short time, until we realize that the water is in fact polyethylene draped over taut wires and staggered as if filling a couple of pools before creating a foaming torrent in the foreground. There is no question that waterfalls are photogenic subjects; the droves of calendars and postcards depicting misty, ethereal substances drifting and swirling enigmatically over rocks attest to this. Goudal's intervention might be seen as a parody of the kind of subject matter that we have come to *naturally* expect from a photograph of a pretty woodland scene. In addition to its formal similarity to water when rendered photographically, polyethylene's bad environmental credentials make it a particularly apposite choice of material to work with. Its poor biodegradability means it has a

Fig. 2.2
TAIYO ONORATO & NICO KREBS (AKA TONK)
Construction Basilicata (Education Department), 2011* from the series *Un Espressione Geografica
Taiyo Onorato and Nico Krebs work in collaboration, often creating playful and quizzical imagery that has its roots in performance art of the 1970s. Much of their work engages with photography as subject matter and not just as the medium of production. In this image, a view of a municipal building is interrupted by a crude timber construction that extends the architecture of the building. This intervention, whereby a background object is combined with something in the foreground carefully arranged from the fixed viewpoint of the camera, plays upon the artificiality of the two-dimensional photographic image, reminding us of its particular kind of mechanical, monocular perspective.

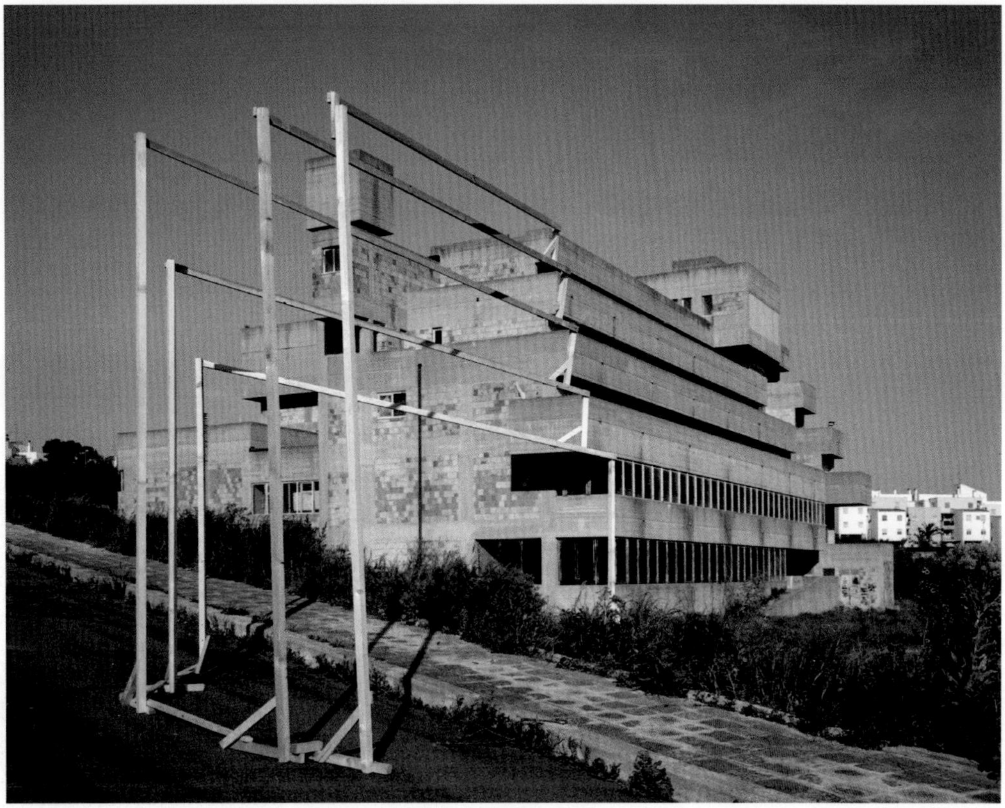

Fig. 2.2

tendency to linger when its usefulness has expired. Rather than conveying a sense of bracing freshness, the choppy water that accumulates at the bottom of Goudal's frame chokes the viewer, in the same way that it smothers this peaceful woodland. We see the aftermath of a battle between nature and culture, represented by the man-made and mass-produced plastic.

Until postmodern discourses in the 1960s and 1970s, which coincided with the environmental movement, it was considered that nature and culture—the way in which humans civilize themselves—were seen in binary opposition.[2] However, culture tends to be the means by which the idea of nature is transmitted, such as in literary narratives, artworks, and other performances. The concept, or rather the culture, of nature[3] is pertinent to a discussion of landscape in all media but perhaps deserves greater importance in photography—an essentially mechanical craft—where "there is always a tension in the camera's relationship to its natural 'other.'"[4]

Beauty and art were once thought of as belonging together, with beauty as among art's principal aims and art as beauty's highest calling. DAVE BEECH[5]

BEAUTY

Throughout the history of art and philosophy, various scholars have articulated their ideas about what, and more importantly *why*, our senses (as well as our minds) receive pleasure from different kinds of stimuli. Edmund Burke was one figure who wrote an influential thesis on beauty, distinguishing it from the sublime, which we shall discuss later in this chapter. Much has been written about the geometry of beauty, about which Burke was completely dismissive. Both historic and contemporary studies support the idea that we recognize beauty in harmonious proportions that exhibit the golden ratio, or pi, rather than, as the popular cliché would lead us to believe, more subjectively within the eye of the beholder. In *A Philosophical Enquiry*, Burke actually relates universal attitudes toward things as a matter of taste, rather than beauty: "The principle of pleasure derived from sight is the same in all." For instance, "Light is more pleasing than darkness."[6]

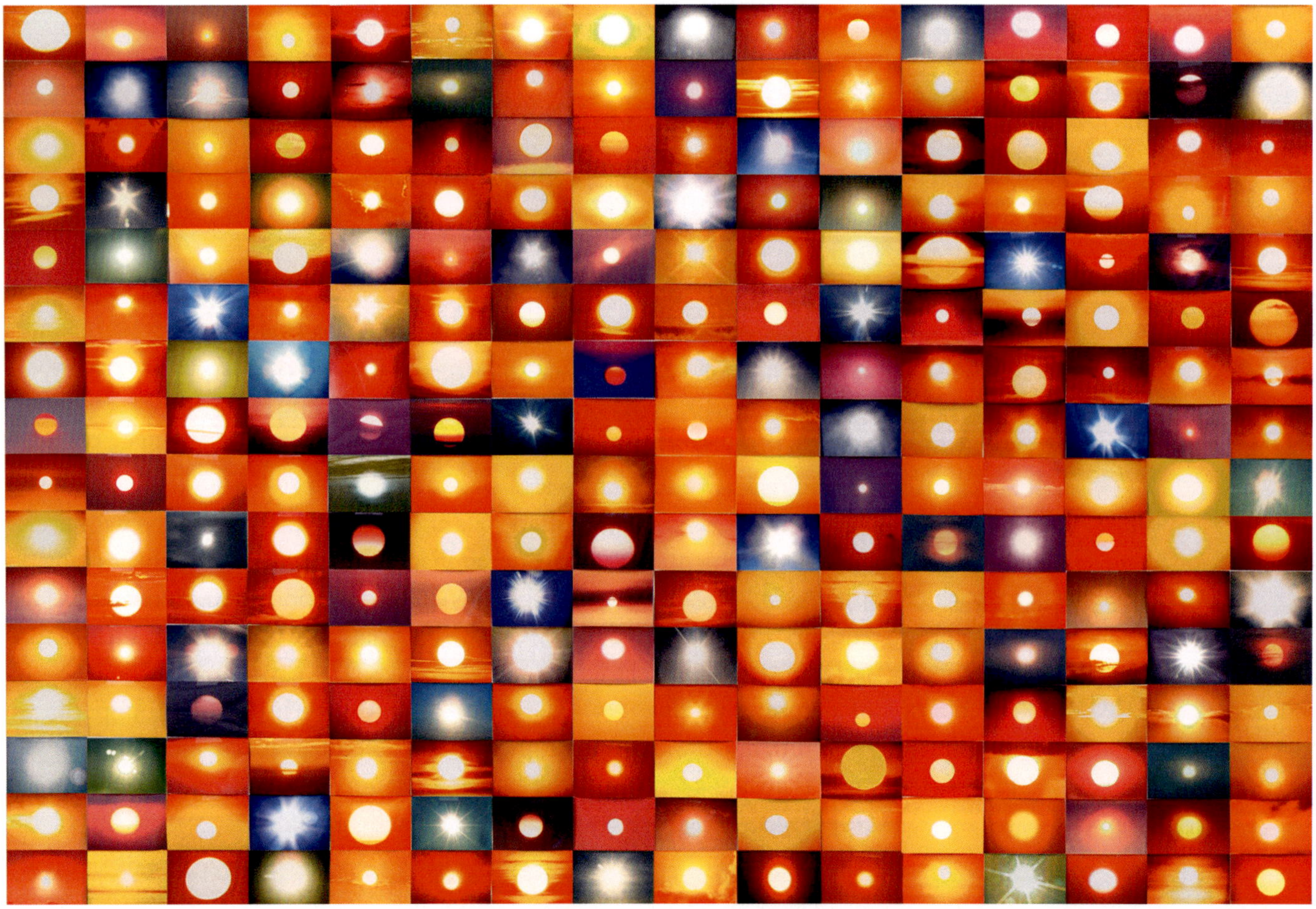

Fig. 2.3

If some sort of evidence could be offered in support of the idea that certain things are universally perceived as beautiful, then perhaps the work of Penelope Umbrico makes a useful point of discussion. Elements of Umbrico's practice involve the appropriation of other people's photographs, which she sources from Flickr. The artist's preoccupation with photography lies in the idea of the medium as a collective practice, something that we all contribute to and to which individual authorship has no relevance.[7] While the image of a fine art photographer exhibiting and marketing prints through a gallery might be at odds with this idea, Umbrico relates collective practice to domestic photography in a digital age and in particular, the context of social networking and image sharing websites that promote photography as a collective activity. In this sense, Flickr acts as a great repository for both our mundane and our significant personal moments—an immense archive that future generations will have infinite ways of engaging with.

Umbrico's ongoing project, *Suns (From Sunsets) from Flickr,* started in 2006 when she used Flickr to find an answer to what the most commonly photographed subject might be. For her installations, Umbrico prints off a selection of the images that are listed in a search result for the word "sunset" on a particular day. For Fig. 2.3, for instance, there were more than half a million images uploaded and tagged with "sunset." In December 2012, there were more than 10 million. For Umbrico, the sunset is particularly significant as a photographic subject because, like other stars and the moon and constellations, a vast number of people are able to photograph it simultaneously. Therefore, although divided by thousands of miles and time zones, the experience of a single setting moment of the sun can be shared and fixed by many.

Fig. 2.3
PENELOPE UMBRICO
541,795 Suns (From Sunsets) from Flickr
(partial) 01/26/06
While the intent of photographing a sunset may be to capture something ephemeral or to assert an individual subjective point of view—the result is quite the opposite—through the technology of our common cameras we experience the power of millions of synoptic views, all shared the same way, at the same moment. To claim individual authorship while photographing a sunset is to disengage from this collective practice and therefore negate a large part of why capturing a sunset is so irresistible in the first place.
Penelope Umbrico

The sun is a particularly extreme example of—to put it in more prosaic terms—something within which we identify exceptional values. The sun is of course fundamental to sustaining life; consequentially it has been celebrated and symbolized in philosophical and spiritual narratives and iconography throughout the history of mankind. Perhaps this cultural heritage—or maybe some primeval force that exerts itself on our subconscious—might have something to do with what prompts us to reach for the camera at the sight of the setting sun.

Fig. 2.5
KEITH ARNATT
From the series *A.O.N.B. (Area of Outstanding Natural Beauty), 1982–1984*
The classification of "AONB" arrived with the same legislation that created the national parks in 1949. AONBs are smaller, more numerous, and dispersed throughout the country in smaller pockets than are the larger, more defined national parks. Keith Arnatt's studies of the Wye Valley, which was designated an AONB in 1971 and which forms part of the border between England and Wales, appear to be a somewhat ironic response to this title. Taken in monochrome under fairly ordinary lighting conditions and showing mundane and unspectacular subject matter, Arnatt's photographs stubbornly resist conventional notions of beauty and representations of this part of the country. On one hand, we could take the work as a lament to this celebrated land, which has been vandalized through man-made interventions. On the other, we might look upon Arnatt's imagery as mocking the notion of ascribing importance to particular bits of the country and giving them greater status over less fortunate parts of the landscape.

POLITICIZING BEAUTY

We may feel that such questions around the human condition are reserved for philosophers and theologians alone. However, in terms of the values that we ascribe to geographic areas, the concept of beauty frequently veers into the discourse of politics and national identity. Factors such as biodiversity and topographical distinction contribute to whether one area of land is considered more or less important than another. Historically, photography has played a supporting role in attributing elevated status to particular zones within a landscape. Upon the completion of his expedition, geologist Ferdinand Hayden (accompanied by photographer William Henry Jackson) managed to convince the U.S. Congress to pass a bill that established the Yellowstone National Park in 1872. Since then, other territories in the United States have acquired similar significance, which has

Fig. 2.4
PAUL HILL
Hall Dale, Stanshope* from *White Peak Dark Peak, 1989
The Peak District in the north of England was established as a national park following legislation in 1949. Many had campaigned for widening access to open land since the 1930s, but it wasn't until after the Second World War that parliament unanimously supported legislation to democratize access to the rural landscape. Unlike in other countries, the national parks in the British Isles tend to include populated hamlets, villages, and even towns. Like other parks, the Peak District was identified as significant because of its particular geology as well as its expansive uninhabited areas.

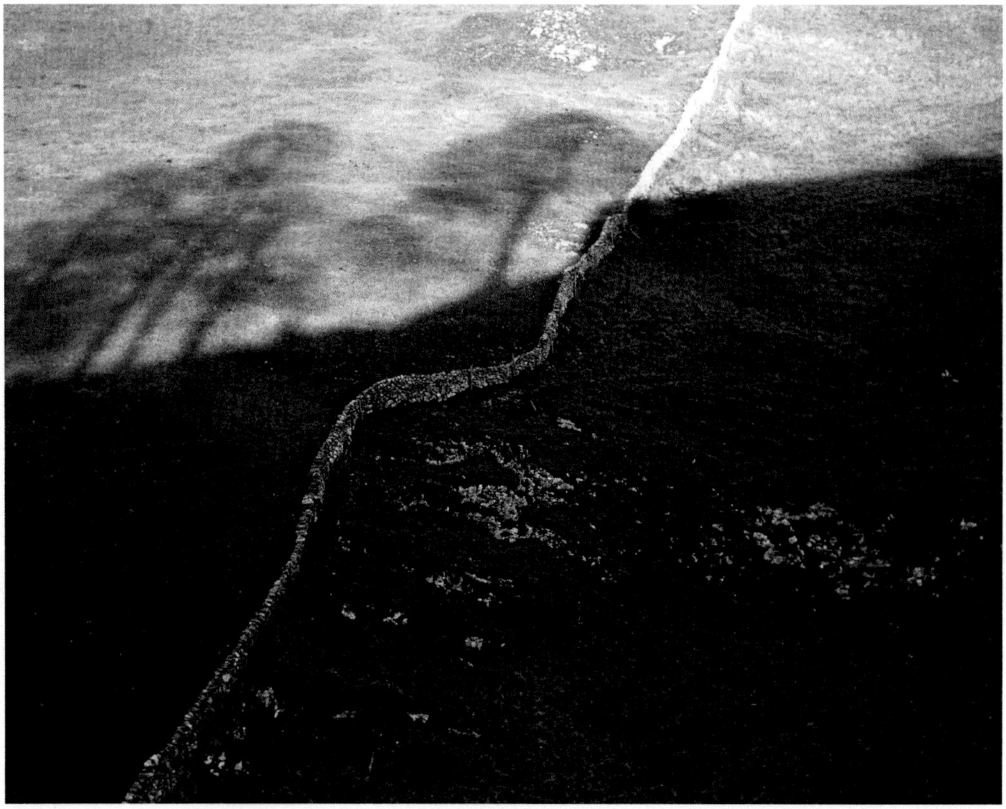

Fig. 2.4

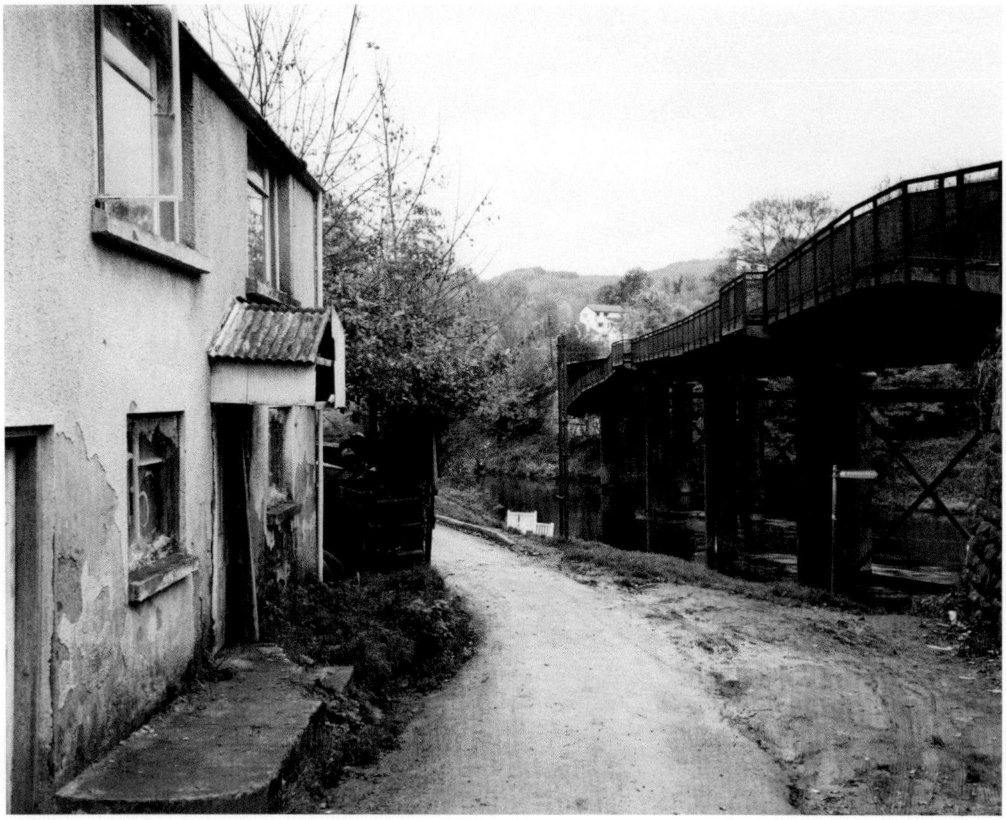

Fig. 2.5

restricted public access to them and afforded them a greater degree of protection from development than other parts of the country. Yosemite National Park in California has become synonymous with the photography of Ansel Adams, who was a stalwart activist for the conservation of the park, which is expressed within his highly celebratory imagery of that area.[8]

Compared to that of the United States, British governments were considerably slower to adopt the idea of national parks. In 1949, legislation was passed to create the first ten sites, which were established in the early 1950s, one of which included the Peak National Park in the north of England. Paul Hill's project *White Peak Dark Peak* is a compelling portrait of parts of that territory, which he studied meticulously between 1978 and 1990. Hill's photographs do not exhibit the drama of an Ansel Adams view but are instead a more pensive and intimate examination of the place, often very specific views and locations returned to over the course of a year or more. The perspective in Hill's images are unconventional for landscape views, looking down on or across a valley, often excluding a horizon and completely immersing the viewer in the scene (see Figs. 1.8 and 2.4). Various types of lines dominate the compositions of many of these images: traditional dry-stone walls, footpaths and tracks, and the marks in the grass from badger runs. As well as strengthening the formal qualities of the photographs, these lines perhaps allude to the ecology of the landscape and its interactions, the complex cycles and synapses where different species and interests overlap and conflict. Hill reveals a landscape that is much more than just a place to be respected for its austere beauty.

THE PICTURESQUE

During a sequence in a television documentary on Fay Godwin (1931–2005), the celebrated photographer, overlooking Ardvreck Castle in Scotland, leafs through a collection of postcards depicting the ruin:

> *I am wary of picturesque pictures. I get satiated with looking at postcards in local newsagents and at the picture books that are on sale, many of which don't bear any relation to my own experience of the place. . . . The problem for me about these picturesque pictures, which proliferate all over the place, is that they are a very soft, warm blanket of sentiment, which covers everybody's idea about the countryside. . . . It idealizes the country in a very unreal way.*
> Fay Godwin[9]

We have all heard of the word "picturesque" and are probably familiar with the kinds of pictures to which Godwin refers, technically sound and aesthetically pleasing photographs that many aspire to make. However, it is worth considering the origins of this term in a little more depth. We might initially imagine "picturesque" to refer to a visual style or artistic movement. Although both of these things are relevant, the picturesque actually has to do more with perceiving the land with a very particular subjectivity, which is, as Malcolm Andrews puts it, to "depoliticize" the landscape.[10] Expunged from the picturesque vision is evidence of the intricacies of the relationship between the land and the social, political, or economic conflicts of interest of those who use it. That is not to say that picturesque images are free of people or man-made structures; on the contrary, we see all of these components. Everything is not only visually balanced in terms of composition of the picture, but there is an allusion toward social harmony as well.

The concept of the picturesque, attributed to William Gilpin, who articulated it in the 1780s, was partly seen as an attempt to bridge Edmund Burke's ideas about the sublime and the beautiful. While we understandably associate the picturesque with *pictures*, it heavily influenced garden design of the time and led to landscape architects introducing more organic shapes and novel structures into their designs, such as follies and grottos. The picturesque was also entwined with travel, or more accurately, tourism. The increasing accessibility of travel—for the upper classes, at least—coincided with Gilpin's ideas of picturesque consumption. His treatise took the form of a guide to the Wye Valley, which Keith Arnatt photographed two hundred years later (Fig. 2.5). In the introduction to Gilpin's guide, he outlines the distinction between picturesque consumption and other types of travel:

Fig. 2.6
JOHN INIGO RICHARDS
Chepstow Castle, c.1755–1775
Perplexingly, Chepstow Castle, which stands impressively at the foot of the Wye Valley and has an equally interesting history, barely receives a mention in Gilpin's *Observations*. Nevertheless, John Richards's (1731–1810) painting of the castle displays some of the typical aspects of a picturesque image: the pleasant weather conditions evoke a calm atmosphere and mirror the benign exchange between the two figures in the foreground. These figures, along with the boats on the river, gently animate the scene. The painter employs a classic *repoussoir* effect of denser tones to the sides of the canvas to contain the scene and focus the viewer inward toward the castle, illuminated by afternoon sun across the center of the picture.

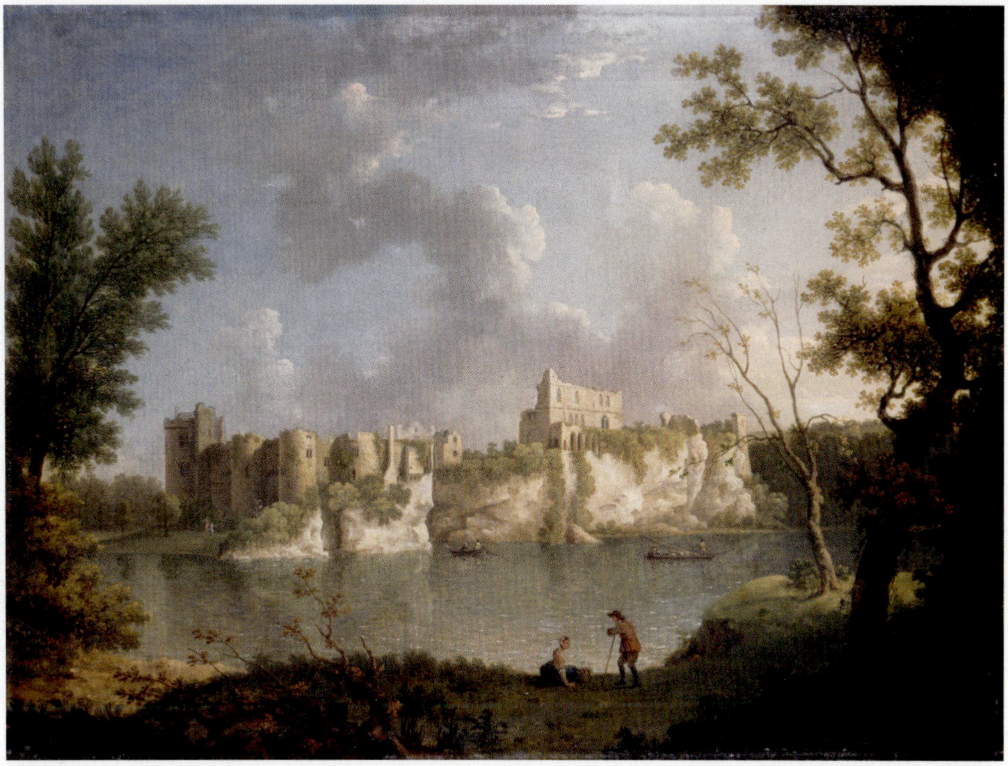

Fig. 2.6

> *We travel for various purposes—to explore the culture of soils, to view the curiosities of art, to survey the beauties of nature, and to learn the manners of men, their different politics and modes of life.*
>
> *The following little work proposes a new object of pursuit, that of examining the face of the country* by the rules of picturesque beauty*; opening the sources of those pleasures which are derived from the comparison.*
>
> Revd. William Gilpin[11]

Gilpin's guide to the Wye Valley and his subsequent publications about other parts of Britain did not just contain a route map to places he felt were worthy of visiting. Indeed, when he made his tour, the River Wye was already an established destination for travelers. The unique abundance of the ruins of fortifications in this is part of Britain clearly appealed to Gilpin, who illustrated his book with his own sketches. Gilpin's descriptions directed travelers toward a particular way of appreciating the scene, and he described ways that the scenes could be improved upon according to his vision of picturesque beauty. He dismissed and steered readers away from places that didn't afford such views. The topographical inaccuracies of Gilpin's sketches hint toward his "rules of picturesque beauty." Rebutting a criticism of this approach, Gilpin responded with, "I am so attached to my picturesque rules, that if nature gets wrong, I cannot help putting her right."[12]

Gilpin's work had a profound influence on not just British tourism but also on tourism throughout the rest of Europe. His guides were popular, and many travelers were inspired to retrace his footsteps. Some respond to Gilpin's picturesque descriptions by observing a scene with a pocket watch–sized device called a Claude glass, which reveals a slightly distorted "painterly" image on a mirror or employed the *camera obscura* to aid a sketch of a notable view.[13] What is worth contemplating here is how the acquisition of personal visual records became synonymous with

Fig. 2.7
PETER KENNARD
The Haywain with Cruise Missiles, 1980
Peter Kennard's picture exhibits the Dadaist irreverence of John Heartfield's political photomontages made in the 1930s. The apparent abuse of such an iconic representation of the southern English landscape aptly mirrored the sense of violation that many felt at having U.S. cruise missiles on British soil during the Cold War.

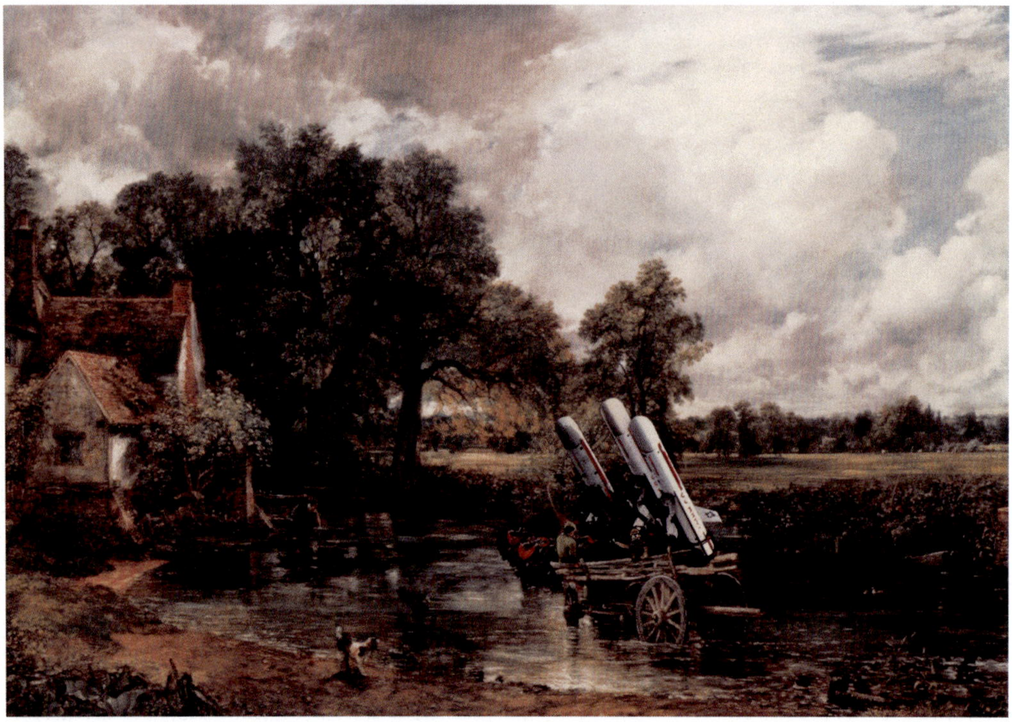

Fig. 2.7

tourism, a device perhaps for affirming the experience of travel.[14] As well as the numerous viewpoints that are defined on maps and road signs across the world, the contemporary postcard, which is an echo of Gilpin's ideas, continues to be consumed and collected and to proliferate idealized landscapes of the countryside.

SUBVERTING THE PICTURESQUE

John Constable's (1776–1837) painting of farm workers in Suffolk has become one of the most iconic images of the British Isles. *The Hay Wain*, painted in 1821, is a typical example of picturesque ideology and aesthetics. It is difficult to resist being seduced by this peaceful scene. One can imagine the shire horse gently plodding past, its leisurely pace of no consequence to the driver, while the jolly banter of the reapers reverberates across the field on the other side of the stream.

Constable depicted the topography accurately with the aid of field sketches; however, the painting was produced at a distance, within the confines of his London studio, with the aim of recreating a romanticized image from his childhood memories and a more contented climate. As close to the nation's heart as *The Hay Wain* may be, it is a dreamy scene in urgent need of waking up. The reality at the time in the Suffolk countryside was not in fact the serenity that Constable's painting describes but rather one of economic hardship and discontent among rural workers, the anxiety of which was expressed to Constable by Fisher, who had the first refusal to purchase the painting.[15]

In recent years, Constable's art has been re-examined by numerous practitioners, including Paul Reas (see Fig. 5.16), Daren Almond, and Richard Billingham. Constable's paintings of Suffolk have been credited for putting previously thought of as unremarkable parts of the country on the picturesque "map." However, Peter Kennard's *Haywain with Cruise Missiles* is a particularly striking take on Constable's painting, which abruptly awakens the scene from its benign slumber. It was first published in 1980 to illustrate an essay in *Camerawork*; however, it has been reprinted in many books and ironically on postcards. Unsurprisingly, the image was adopted by the Campaign for Nuclear Disarmament, with whom Kennard has collaborated extensively over the years. The—symbolic—violation of one of the nation's most cherished artifacts with American missiles stood for the sentiment felt by many toward the installation of cruise missiles at air bases across the UK at the time, such as at Greenham Common. As such an identifiable and cherished image within the British consciousness, *The Hay Wain* was a pertinent and effective image for Kennard to appropriate. Kennard rips Constable's painting from the comfortable realm of the picturesque by imposing a position upon it in relation to British and American foreign policy, rendering it a highly charged, *politicized* image.

RETHINKING THE PICTURESQUE

Kennard's photomontage is just one example of how the picturesque continues to offer contemporary practitioners with many points of reference. Suzanne Mooney's

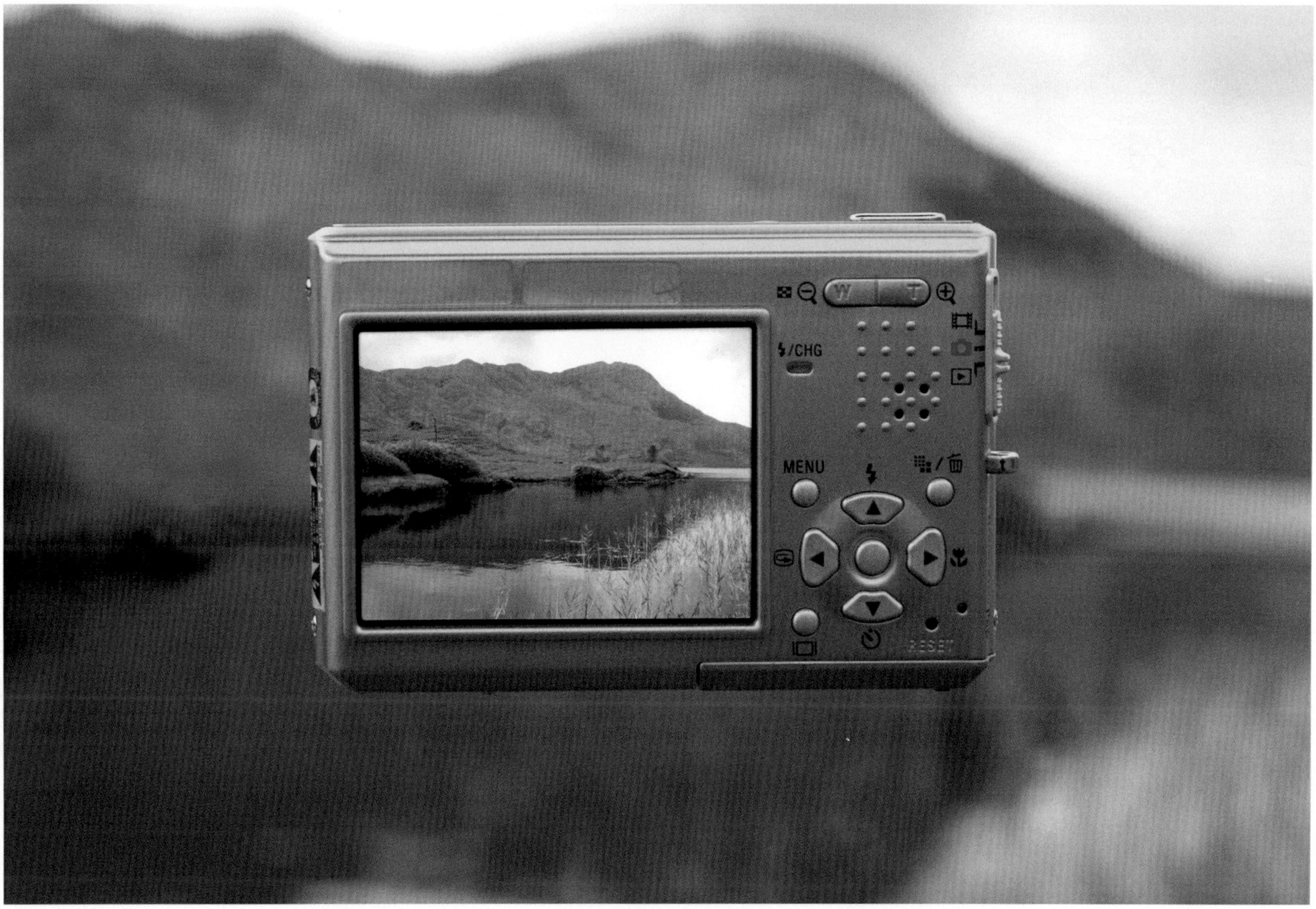

Fig. 2.8

Fig. 2.8
SUZANNE MOONEY
Lough Fee* from the series *Behind the Scene, 2006
In Suzanne Mooney's series, picturesque viewpoints are fused with the kind of image that might be found advertising a new camera. The pin-sharp image of the camera and the landscape it presents the viewer on the LCD screen clearly dominates the frame. What little that is around the camera is inaccessible. The camera that allows us to preserve a view simultaneously blocks it, perhaps alluding to how powerful such clichéd images are at imposing a definitive, enduring representation of a place.

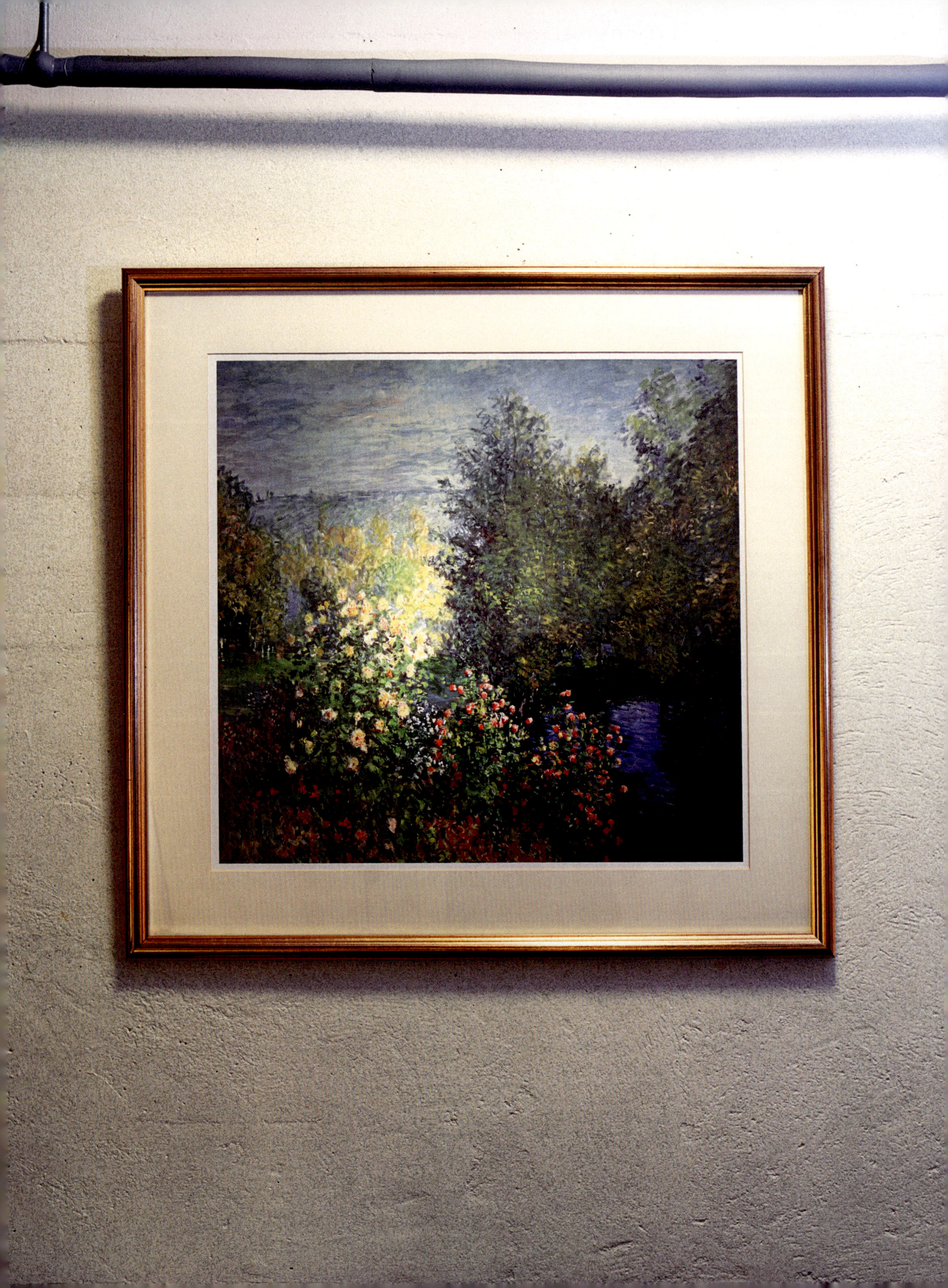

Discussion of the picturesque is mostly in negative terms, but this underestimates the extent to which it can be valued positively, as something that enlists you into a composure, but one which may nevertheless be complacent. DAVID BATE[16]

Fig. 2.9
DAVID MOORE
The Principal Office* from the series *The Last Things, 2008
Political apparatus and the power of state institutions are themes behind the work of David Moore. To make the project *The Last Things*, Moore negotiated access to the British government's "secure crisis management facility" beneath central London. The resulting series of photographs have an unembellished, perhaps even forensic aesthetic, which mirrors the functional nature of the space. In this series as well as in other bodies of work, Moore turns the camera on powerful institutions that exercise a degree of surveillance and control, making visible the spaces that are invisible to the rest of us. As well as picking out features and structures that are particular to an underground bunker, Moore's gaze settles on incongruous details like potted plants, ornaments, and framed post-impressionist prints, which have a surreal presence among such a sobering environment. It is these features that are perhaps the most revealing and chilling. These familiar, everyday things allow us to relate to such a secretive location, which makes the horrifying prospect of, for example, a major terrorist attack on the capital requiring the bunker to spring into action, seem so much more vivid.

series *Behind the Scenes* (Figs. 1.1 and 2.8) refers to the picturesque in various ways. The work was inspired by the artist's animosity toward the prolific postcard views of County Galway in Ireland, where she grew up. Mooney photographed some of these well-trodden viewpoints as well as more generic countryside scenes. These photographs were digitally superimposed with a floating digital compact camera on which we see the same scene, yet pin sharp as opposed to the out-of-focus background surrounding the camera. This device, along with the familiarity of these kinds of views, at first appears to relate to advertising or—perhaps in light of Mooney's ongoing project, *Make Love to the Camera*—might have another sort of instructive function. In a sense it does, so far as the camera acts as a device to tell the viewer that this work is about framing, excluding, looking, and consuming the view. The spectator of the photograph is simultaneously both viewer of the artwork and in the position of the photographer. The camera depicted in Mooney's photographs becomes a barrier between the viewer/photographer and the actual, out-of-focus landscape in the background. Twinned with the shift in focus between the two pictures, the places become inferior to their represented images—the camera is singled out as a mediating device for how we consume the land.

The myopic picturesque way of seeing has been criticized widely, primarily because picturesque imagery idealizes and romanticizes places, offering a limited or even superficial representation of the landscape. Today's picturesque artists and photographers might question where the harm lies in representing nature looking at her best, perhaps fostering a sense of nature's importance within those who might take their environment for granted. As William Gilpin proposed in his *Observations*, the picturesque might still reside in exotic territories and tourism, but today it occupies our routine existence. The proliferation of picturesque landscapes in myriad vernacular contexts (in our homes, on computer screen savers, within advertising, and displayed in public and corporate spaces) points to a compulsion toward escapist imagery. As David Bate suggests, picturesque imagery almost serves a social function, offering viewing pleasure and instilling calm: a soothing rural scene or a relaxing seascape to alleviate an anxious patient in a dentist's waiting room perhaps? The picturesque reminds us that in times of uncertainty, we turn to a certain image of nature. David Moore's photograph of a post-impressionist print in the British government's central London bunker (Fig. 2.9) presents a dark take on this: With the capital under attack and perhaps the rest of the world in the shadow of a mushroom cloud, how would our leaders cope without a pretty landscape scene to lighten the mood?

The passion caused by the great and sublime in *nature*, when those causes operate most powerfully, is Astonishment; and astonishment is that state of the soul in which all its motions are suspended with some degree of horror. In this case, the mind is so entirely filled with its object that it cannot entertain any other, nor by consequence reason on that object which employs it. EDMUND BURKE[17]

THE SUBLIME

The sublime is a key theme in landscape art and also important to other aspects of cultures past and present, as well as our more general understanding of the concept of nature. The sublime has been the subject of discourse over centuries, even millennia. One of the earliest thinkers on the topic was the Greek philosopher Longinus (c. 300 AD), whose treatise related to literature rather than to visual works. Various scholars, including Immanuel Kant, Georg Hegel, and Johann Schiller, wrote about beauty and the sublime, but no writing on this subject has been as influential or widely discussed as Edmund Burke's 1757 treatise, *A Philosophical Enquiry into the Origin of Our Ideas of the Sublime and Beautiful.* Burke was interested in how certain things impressed themselves upon people's senses and prompted a particular response, such as pleasurable feelings and terror. Burke articulated his understanding of the sublime and distinguished it as a category almost in binary opposition to beauty. Where beauty was the domain of contentment and harmony—a gentle and enjoyable experience of something—the sublime prompted unsettled feelings and emotional awakening; it was often the raw, heart-stopping power of Mother Nature.

Both beauty and the sublime are matters of the senses and aesthetics, but the sublime occupies the imagination to a greater extent. There are no such things as sublime *objects*, but when something triggers a feeling of fear, dread, or horror (for example, encountering a mountain, a great canyon, or something equally perilous), then you are in the *presence* of the sublime. The sublime is something that is triggered in people by certain things. Burke identified specific objects that he believed were "productive of the sublime,"[18] ranging from the general, such as vastness, suddenness, and darkness, to the very specific, "the angry tones of wild beasts."[19]

The sublime was a prominent theme within nineteenth-century landscape and history painting. Philip James de Loutherbourg's (1740–1812) depiction of an avalanche in the Alps (Fig. 2.11) is a classic example from this period. It is a scene of sheer chaos: the plummeting cloud of snow swirls around the canvas, almost obliterating the light from the sky. The cool tones of the snow, clouds, and mountain coalesce into almost abstraction. Three figures, perhaps making some sort of journey, are confronted with this perilous spectacle. The avalanche has smashed the wooden bridge to the right of the picture, which perhaps alludes to the fate of the travelers. The man on the far left flings both arms outward in despair while the man on the right presents clenched hands heavenward, with a gesture that is difficult to distinguish between a plea for mercy or a defiant outburst. The woman between the two men is the only person with the sense to flee away from the approaching snow, while the dog, with paws splayed and wide and terrified eyes, is catatonic with fear. The emotional states exhibited by these four characters make up a fairly complete—albeit caricatured—catalog of the range of responses to an encounter with the sublime.

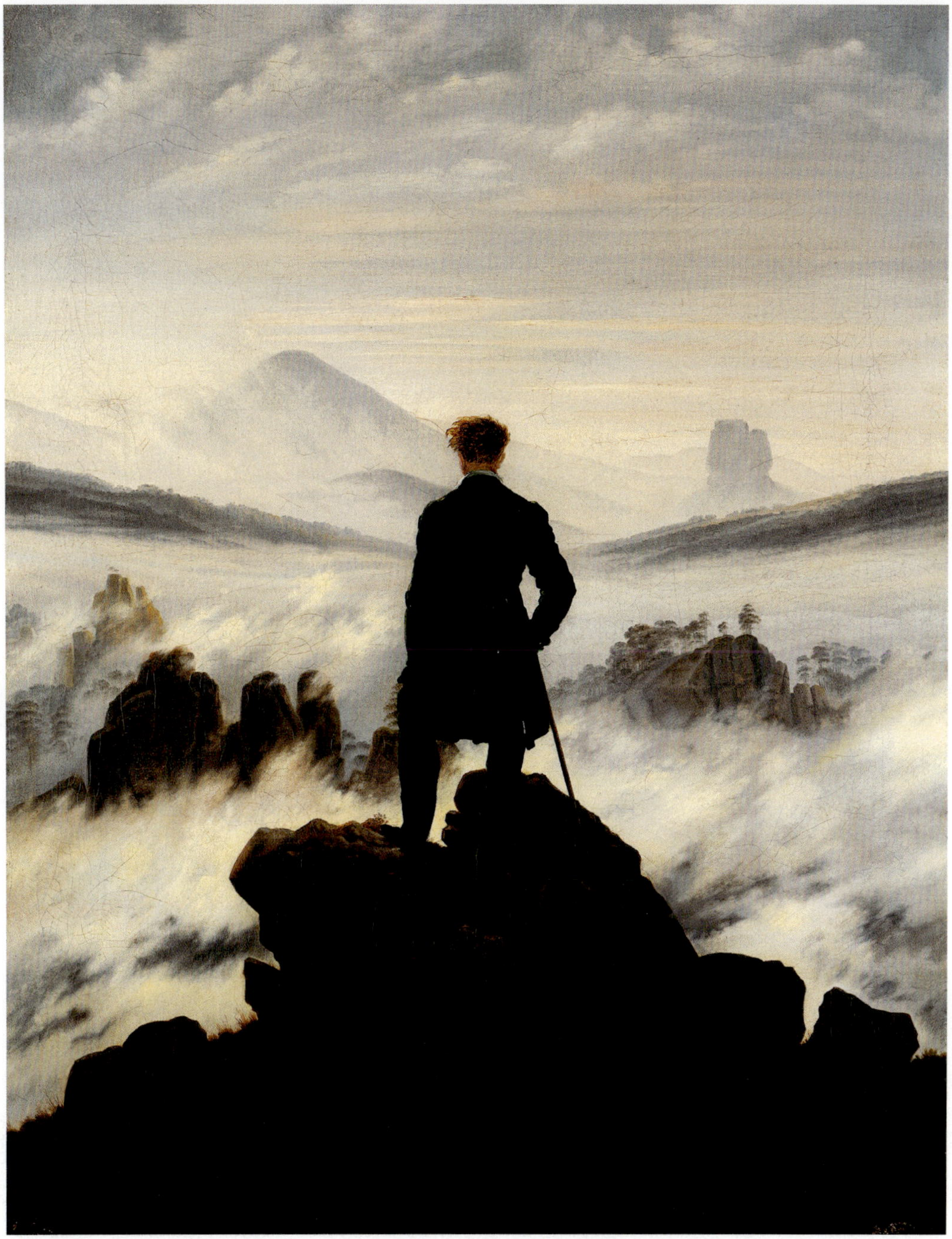

Fig. 2.10

Fig. 2.10
CASPER DAVID FRIEDRICH
Wanderer Above the Sea of Fog, 1818
Friedrich's painting of an anonymous figure stepping out into an expansive landscape provides a particular kind of illustration of the sublime. The anonymous man appears to be at a threshold with the wilderness, an expanse of unknown, craggy terrain partially obscured by mist or fog. The prominence of the single figure with his back to the viewer clearly distinguishes this work from a picturesque depiction, where figures are typically smaller and incidental to the scene. He is a protagonist engaging with the landscape, not merely performing a supporting role. This particular romantic motif, known as a *Rückenfigur* (which translates as "back figure"), was a common visual device employed by Friedrich, the contemplative state of the person depicted being an attempt to instill the same sense of reverence within the viewer of the painting.[20] The orientation of the picture is also worth noting—breaking from the traditional landscape orientation, the painting clearly attempts to establish a different approach to representing the landscape.

THE CULT OF THE SUBLIME

Natural disasters like the avalanche depicted by de Loutherbourg were not the only kinds of catastrophic events explored by painters inspired by the sublime. Apocalyptic scenes from religious narratives and folklore, as well as from antiquity, were popular subjects. The diversity of "disaster paintings" of this time connects the sublime potential of nature (tsunamis, plague, volcanic eruptions, etc.) to a mythological or spiritual sublime that can be transmitted only culturally. We can see this in the range of influences of the celebrated painter John Martin (1789–1854), whose practice included illustrating a work of fiction (*Sadak in Search of the Waters of Oblivion, 1812*) and scenes from antiquity (*The Destruction of Pompeii and Herculaneum, 1822*) and his epic *Judgment Series* triptych, depicting the Revelation narrative of the New Testament.

The popularity of art exploring sublime themes indicates the continued pleasure that is found in its consumption. This legacy can be seen in the abundance of both the historically based and futuristic narratives of the Hollywood disaster movie, as well as in other stories set in the present day that tap into the particular anxieties of paying audiences. Environmental apocalypses have been explored in movies such as *The Day After Tomorrow* (2004) and *The Road* (2009). In *Outbreak* (1995), a viral epidemic threatens to wipe out mankind, and in *The Birds* (1963) and *Arachnophobia* (1990), the collective forces of otherwise inferior creatures violently consume placid towns.

Perhaps most terrifying of all, screenwriters have prophesized extinction events caused by things from beyond our world in films such as *Independence Day* (1996) and *Deep Impact* (1998). While some might like to believe that such tales of impending doom are part of a wider conspiracy to lull the population into political subservience, it is more likely that audiences simply take great pleasure in being frightened.

In practice, beauty and the sublime are not necessarily mutually exclusive. The pleasure derived from an experience of the sublime may well be felt as something positive; the setting sun might well be considered sublime inducing, and perhaps the ever-increasing number of sunsets on Flickr, for instance, confirms this.[21] There appears to be, however, a clearer distinction between the sublime and the picturesque. The word "picturesque" literally means "like a picture," and by definition, a picture is contained by a viewfinder or picture frame. This implies an inherent formalism, that everything a viewer needs to understand the work lies within the confines of this picture, where its narrative begins and ends. With the sublime however, while it practically may be possible to convey or suggest the sublime, ultimately the real significance of the subject is ineffable. Herein lies the paradox of representations of the sublime. It could be argued that to attempt to contain the sublime within the frame is just as false as picturesque efforts to reproduce idealized depictions of serenity.

[I]f psychoanalytic theory is right in asserting that every affect arising from an emotional impulse—of whatever kind—is converted into fear by being repressed, it follows that among those things that are felt to be frightening there must be one group that has been repressed and now returns. This species of the frightening would then constitute the uncanny, and it would be immaterial whether it was itself originally frightening or arose from another affect. SIGMUND FREUD[22]

PSYCHOLOGY OF THE SUBLIME

In *A Philosophical Enquiry*, Burke refers to the "soul" and the "mind," which leaves a discussion of the sublime open to scrutiny from other discourses. In fact, part of the radicalism of Burke's ideas was that it described profound human experience in secular terms.[23] In 1919, Sigmund Freud developed ways of thinking about the sublime, relating it to the field of psychoanalysis, the invention of which is also attributed to Freud. A key principle of Freud's psychoanalysis was the idea of a human unconscious, the realm of the psyche that is not readily accessible. Freud did not invent this term, but he popularized it and expanded our understanding of it to a great extent. The unconscious could be accessed through Freud's techniques, which included free association, dialogue with patients suffering with mental disorders and abnormal behavior, and most famously, deciphering the symbolism of their dreams.

Fig. 2.11
PHILIP JAMES DE LOUTHERBOURG
***Avalanche in the Alps*, 1803**
De Loutherbourg's *Avalanche* is a typical example of sublime painting of the romantic period. It is worth noting that, like today, the Alps were a popular destination for wealthy travelers of the time and this kind of imagery helped mythologize the region in a particular way. The Alps are also vividly depicted in Mary Shelley's gothic literary masterpiece, *Frankenstein* (1818).

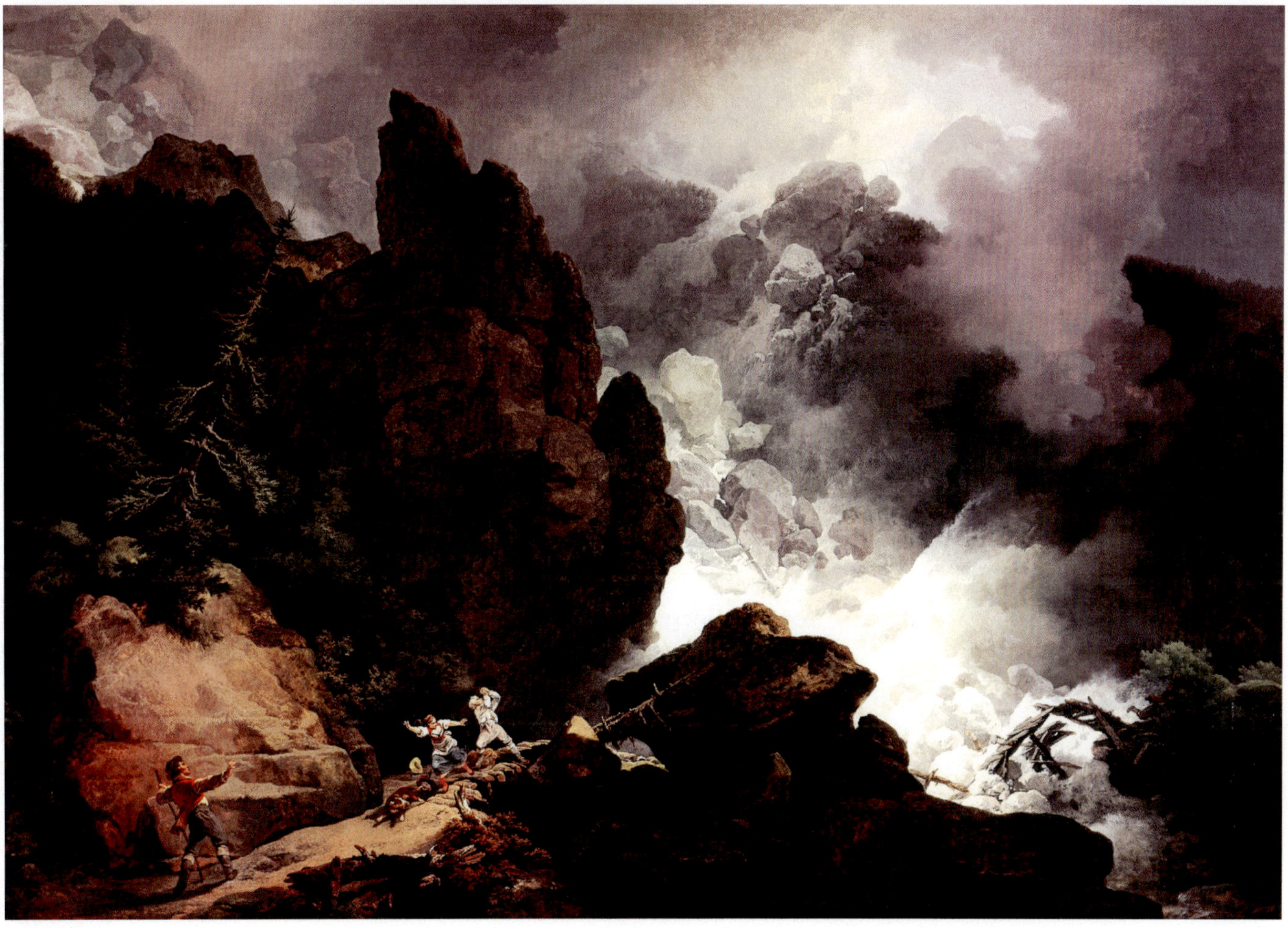

Fig. 2.11

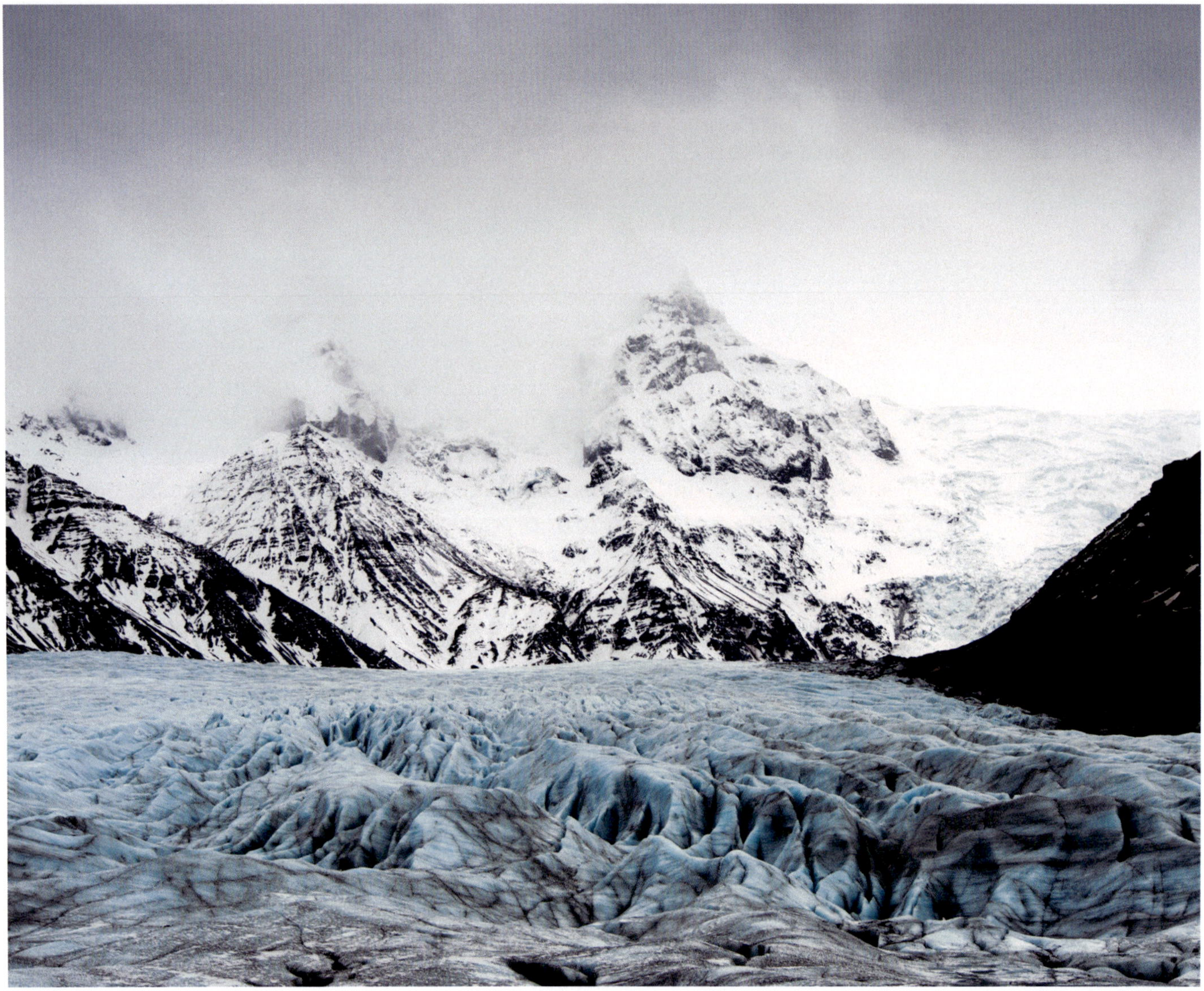

Fig. 2.12

Fig. 2.12
JOSÉ NAVARRO
Viderni, Iceland
Navarro's photograph displays classic sublime-inducing subjects, which are composed accordingly: the icy glacier in the foreground fills the bottom of the image like an impenetrable barrier to the landscape. It is rendered very differently to popular imagery of glaciers—often curving and winding up valleys toward mountains offering a route for the eye to travel through the picture and, conversely, suggesting a real possibility of entering the landscape. The gray sky along the top of the frame seeps down and shrouds the summit of the mountains, further underscoring the hostility of this environment.

In Freudian psychoanalysis, the key to understanding apparent mental problems—or "neuroses," as they were referred to—lay in the unconscious. Freud's work has also had a major influence on how we interpret both historical and contemporary art.

In Freud's essay, he expands his thoughts on the "uncanny," which "belongs to the realm of the frightening, or what evokes fear and dread."[24] He does not use the term "sublime," but he was discussing essentially the same ideas as were Burke and others. Freud elaborated the term "uncanny" with the German word, *unheimlich*, which more literally translates as "unhomely," unfamiliar, or out of place. Freud asserts that the sensation of being frightened is triggered by the recognition of something from the unconscious through what is actually being experienced. There is then a conflict between what is recognizable in the external environment and what rises uncontrollably from the unconscious. Freud's examples were typically a lot more nuanced than the works discussed here; however, the principle is the same: the uncanny and the sublime both relate to a feeling of being displaced by, or being at the mercy of, a force greater than ourselves.

Fig. 2.13
NADAV KANDER
Chongqing XI, Chongqing Municipality, 2007* from the series *Yangtze, The Long River

The Yangtze traverses over 4,000 miles through China, and more people live along the river than the entire population of the United States. To complete his project, Nadav Kander explored different parts of the river, from its mouth in Shanghai westward across the country to Quinghai Province. As geographic features, the sheer scale of the river and its surrounding topography certainly have sublime qualities. Kander's photographs effectively convey this vastness, and many readers might recognize a sense of the sublime in what they see. Indeed, the photographer identifies his own work with that of John Martin, J.M.W. Turner, and C.D. Friedrich. However, perhaps the truly frightening aspect of what Kander addresses in the project is not the scale of nature in this part of the world, but the magnitude of man's impact upon it. Throughout the series, we see a country in rapid, seemingly exponential growth, almost overcoming the magnitude of the landscape. The ever-present murky smog that diffuses Kander's images is a reminder of the ecological toll that this economic expansion is costing this environment. This photograph, taken in central China, captures these issues and conflicting interests. The half-constructed bridge acts as both literal illustration and metaphor for Chinese social and economic development. This structure might also be seen to be bridging political and social issues as well. The cluster of fishermen in the foreground draws attention to the river as an essential resource that has been integral to the lives of millions of people over thousands of years. Beyond the fishermen, the barges highlight the economic importance of the river as a means to transport goods and resources through the country. There are two conflicting kinds of sublime here: the vastness of nature and the unstoppable sublime force of a world superpower.

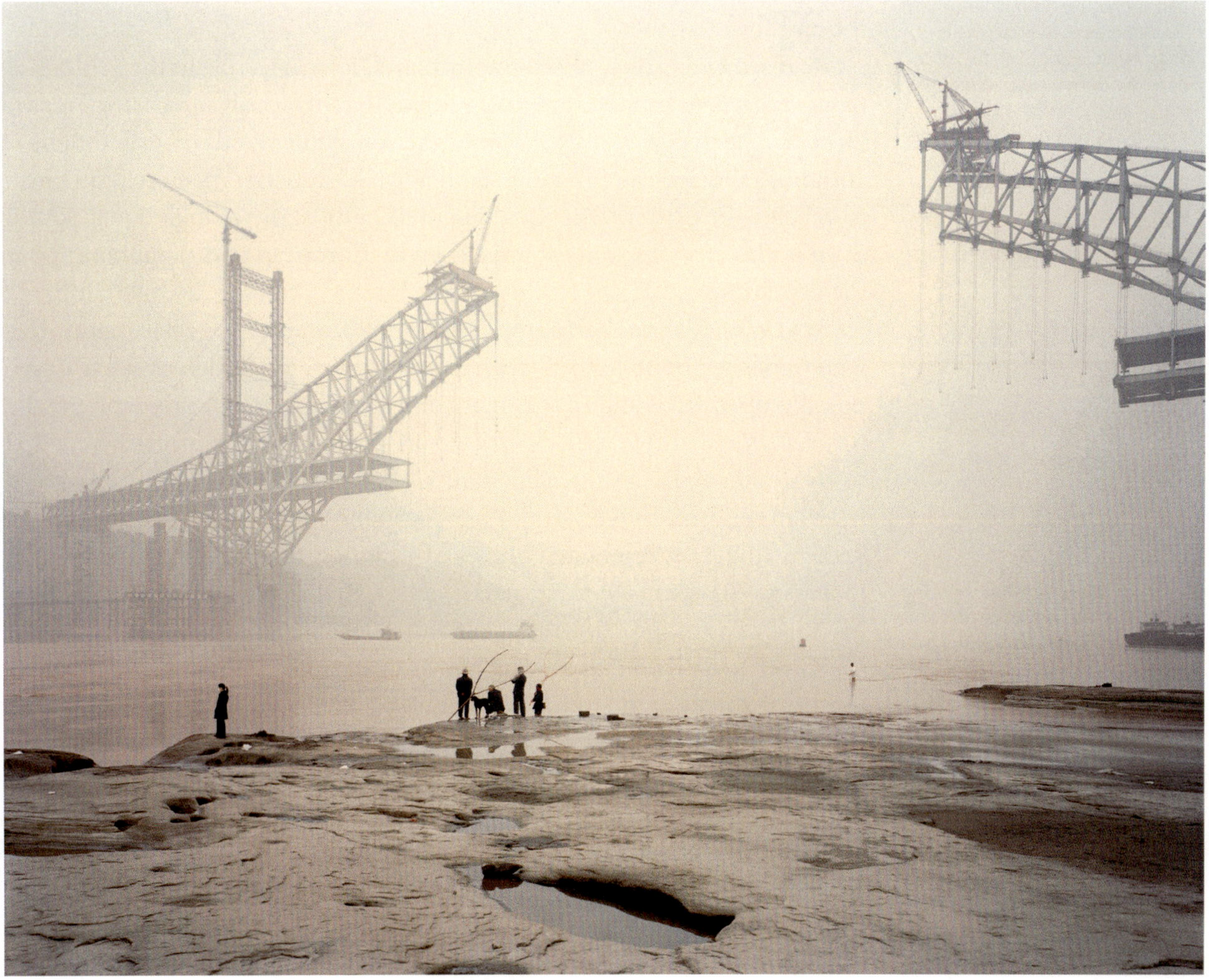

Fig. 2.13

Fig. 2.14
TIMOTHY O'SULLIVAN
Ancient Ruins in the Cañon de Chelle, New Mexico, 1873
Timothy O'Sullivan's photographs taken on geological surveys around the Great Basin region are remarkable in contrast to pictorial landscape photography of the period, particularly that made by European practitioners. This photograph is typical of O'Sullivan's work from these expeditions in that it communicates a sense of the drama and inhospitability of the landscape. The irony is that the area is actually one of the longest-inhabited parts of North America. There are no fore- or middle-ground objects to lead us to what remains of the "White House" on the other side of the canyon or the distinctive patterns on the towering cliffs above: the subject engulfs the frame and there is neither a "way in" nor any means of escape for the viewer.

EXPLORATION

Much landscape photography inevitably requires traveling to particular locations to make work. Sometimes, however, the journey itself is more important than the destination, and the means of locomotion (walking, driving, taking the train) is itself integral to the creative strategy of the project. As with the work of Susan Derges (Fig. 1.16) in Nadav Kander's project, the river itself is an analogy of renewal and change. In Kander's work, the river also acted like a transect through the country and plotted the route for the photographer to conduct his study. Alec Soth's project *Sleeping by the Mississippi* (2004) used the great river as a tributary through which to examine the diversity of the people who live along it. As with Gawain Barnard's work (Fig. 0.3), while only a handful of the photographs from this series might be considered as landscape pictures per se, in this project, the landscape plays an integral role in drawing the photographer to his subjects and linking the pictures and the narrative together.

As discussed earlier, photography played a famous role in the geological surveys that explored, examined, and mapped out the previously uncharted North American interior. The presence of a photographer on similar kinds of expeditions was common, and it is easy to understand why: What better medium than photography to validate the existence of these far-flung, almost mythological places? Some of the earliest photo books were albums taken by European photographers documenting the exotic corners of the world, such as Francis Frith (1822–1898), John Thompson (1837–1921), Maxime Du Camp (1822–1894), and Auguste Salzmann (1824–1872), who published photographs from their travels to the Middle and Far East. The possibility of travel still entices many toward practicing photography, and travel magazines and coffee-table books are, of course, familiar places where we continue to encounter landscape imagery at its glossiest.

As in the greatest works of other disciplines, such as literature and cinema, some of the most celebrated bodies of photographic work have centered around journeys—road trips in particular. Examples include *American Photographs* (1938) by Walker Evans, *The Americans* (1958) by Robert Frank, and Paul Graham's *A1—The Great North Road* (1983), which is a more specific study of one of the busiest motoring routes in the UK. There are great benefits to making photographic projects around specific places that are familiar and accessible or that have a particular historic or sociopolitical relevance into which you can conduct additional research. However, there are also great possibilities in *not knowing* exactly where a journey might take you, what subjects a particular strategy or route will lead you to, and what the outcomes might be in terms of your photographs.

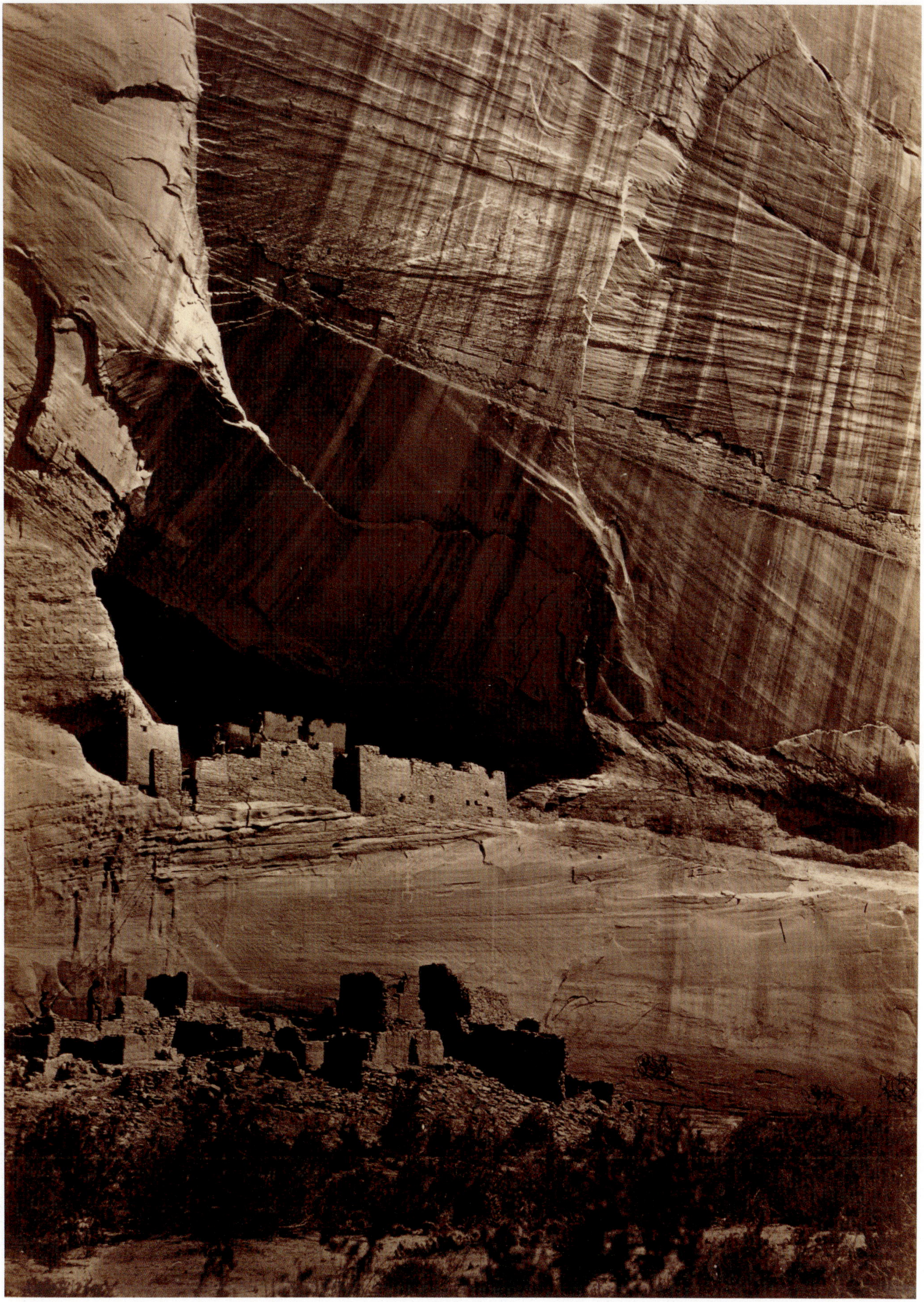

Fig. 2.14

Fig. 2.15
ALEC SOTH
USA, 2006* from the series *Broken Manual
Alec Soth's project explores the idea of escaping from modern life and documents people in America who have established homes for themselves in remote locations. This project expands a notion of wilderness not so much by displaying a particular kind of terrain but by hinting toward what some people are desperate for. Climate and topography are perhaps irrelevant here; an absence of others is perhaps the defining characteristic of being in the wild.

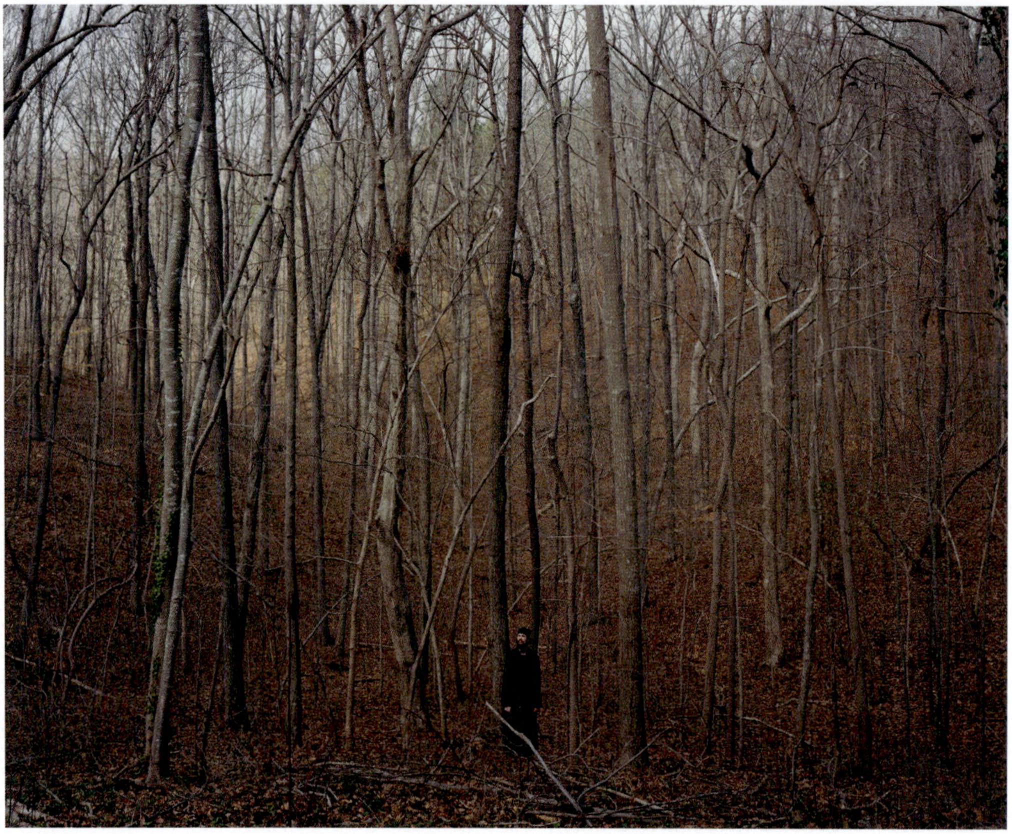

Fig. 2.15

Fig. 2.16
NASA
***Santa Anita Panorama, May 2004* (detail)**
This color "mosaic" was taken over several days by the panoramic camera on NASA's Mars exploration rover *Spirit*. It comprises a total of 384 images and is an approximate true-color rendering of this area, near the Bonneville Crater. Many of the photographs taken by *Spirit* are compelling, although the tire tracks in the Martian "earth" (or perhaps less problematically "dirt") are particularly striking, having a resonance with the famous image of astronaut Buzz Aldrin's crisp footprints on the moon, taken on the Apollo 11 mission in 1969.

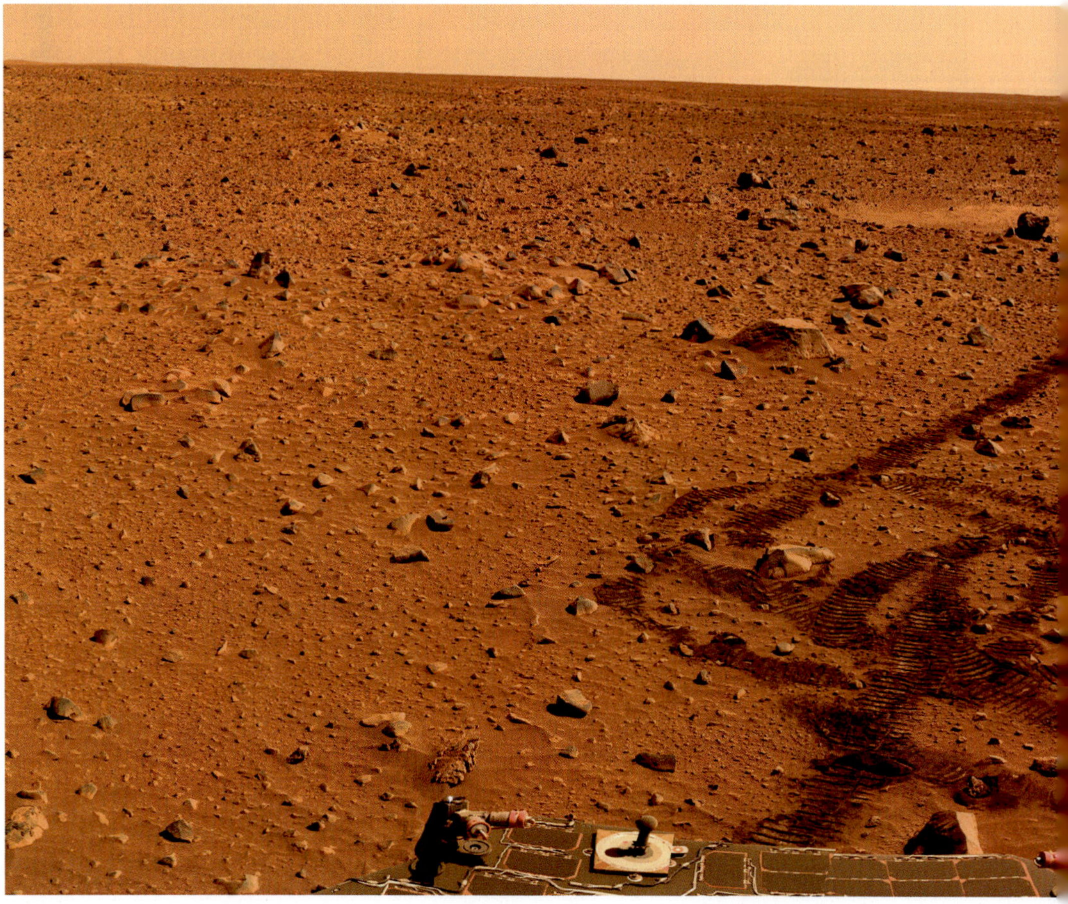

Fig. 2.16

THE WILDERNESS

Although it may sometimes feel like the world is increasingly diminishing in size, there are still plenty of wild places to explore. Nonetheless, "wild" is a permeable term and is subject to cultural interpretation. In an everyday context, the idea of the wild depends upon the perception of a lack of domestication. The nuances of a carefully managed landscape might go unnoticed to someone who is unfamiliar with a particular environment. There are certain places that surely can be considered a wilderness by anyone. Thomas Joshua Cooper's *Atlantic Basin Project*, for example, has taken him to the extremities of the five continents (see Fig. 1.3).

In *Broken Manual* (2006–2010), Alec Soth photographed people in a different kind of wilderness; people who have made a deliberate effort to extricate themselves from society and pursue a reclusive existence. For some this is a lifestyle choice, but others, for all sorts of reasons, need no excuse to get "off the grid." Soth began working on the project as the sun was setting on the George W. Bush administration,

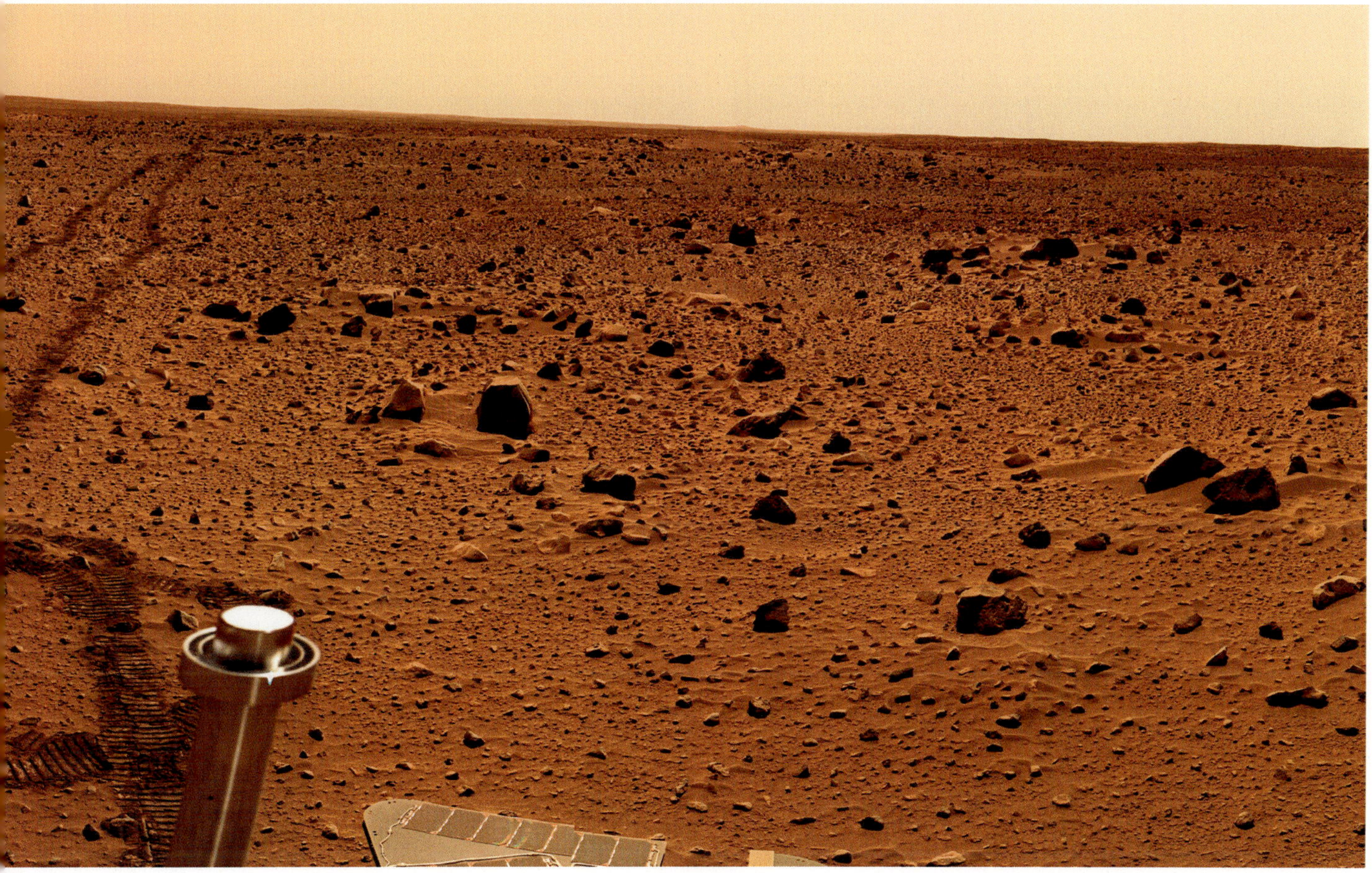

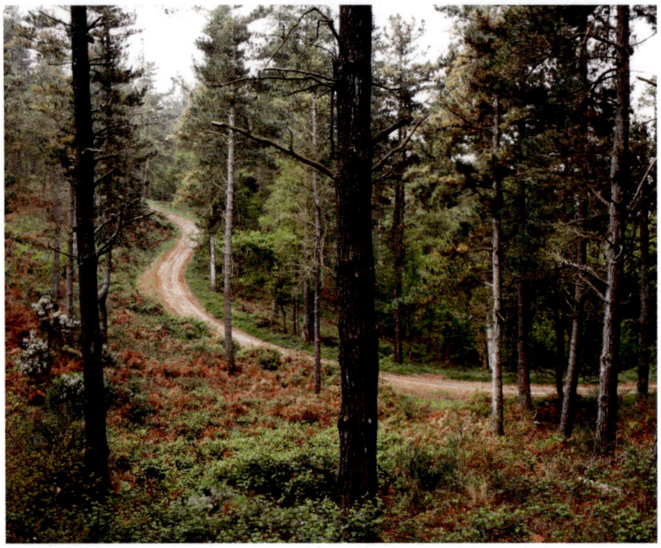

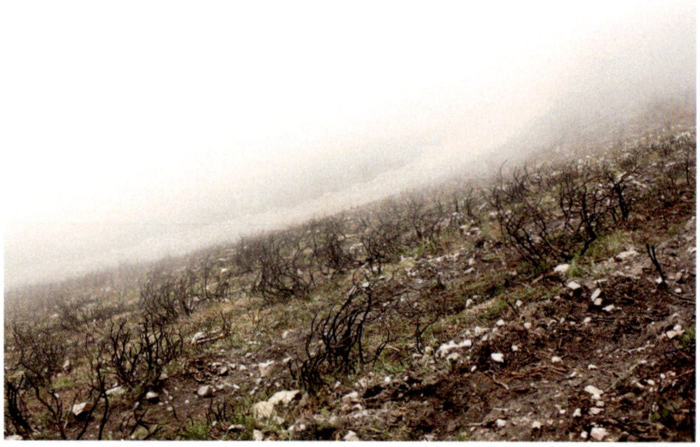

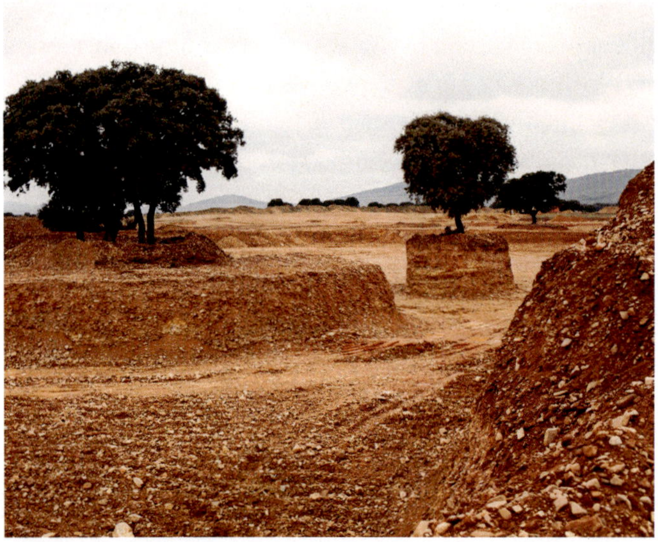

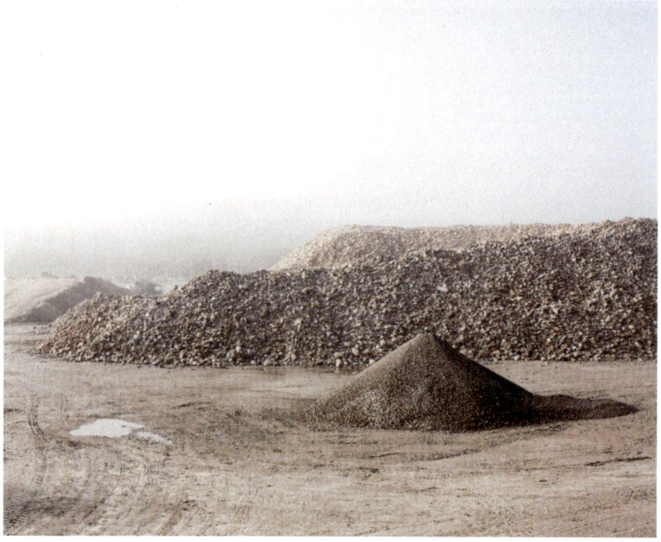

Fig. 2.17

Fig. 2.17.i–2.17.iv
PAUL GAFFNEY
From the series *We Make the Path by Walking, 2013*

Paul Gaffney completed his project over a period of two years and many different journeys traveled on foot. In total, the photographer walked nearly 3,000 km across various parts of Europe. While areas of the terrain may be recognizable to some, the actual locations are not Gaffney's particular concern, and he does not link individual images to any country or other particular category. There are no famous landmarks or designated viewpoints to be found in Gaffney's photographs. In contrast to the economy of the content of the work of Paul Seawright (Figs. 5.1 and 5.9), the modesty and sometimes mundane nature of Gaffney's views does not allude to anything malevolent but instead to something pensive. Central to Gaffney's practice is adopting an Eastern approach to landscape, whereby his process is more that of reflecting upon his experience within the landscape rather than utilizing a Western tradition of *framing* the landscape into a particular image. This philosophy is suggested in the title of the project, and the images and their sequencing leave space for the audience to make their own way through Gaffney's work.

which was partly characterized by extreme anxieties over national security and the erosion of civil liberties. Soth met many sorts of recluses, such as those who have withdrawn as part of their faith. But the image of the paranoid survivalist is perhaps the most potent in relation to the sociopolitical backdrop of the project.

Part of the impetus for the work was Soth's own fantasy of withdrawing from busy modern life to a more solitary existence, and as the title suggests, the photographer's monograph serves as a kind of guide to going under the radar. Many readers will not personally identify with Soth's fantasy of disappearing from society, which goes hand in hand with a physical escape to a remote location. In Jon Krakauer's book *Into the Wild* (1996) (and the feature film directed by Sean Penn in 2007) about the real-life mishaps and eventual tragedy of Christopher McCandless in Alaska, we see how this sort of adventure has the potential to end badly.

Perhaps some of the most extreme environments we are aware of are not on this planet at all. The extract of a panorama of a Martian landscape, made by the Mars expedition rover *Spirit* (Fig. 2.16), depicts a terrain that is quite literally out of this world and just about as remote as it is possible to imagine. It certainly remains unmolested by mankind, save for the remains of ill-fated exploration missions and, of course, the tracks left by the intrepid robots. The images from these devices remind us of the continued significance of the photographic image to how we relate to and mythologize faraway places. The novelty of the rovers' images can give insight into how, for instance, John Thompson's albums of China (c. 1874) must have appeared to a Victorian layman who, we might speculate, would never have imagined the opportunity to visit the place for himself.

STRATEGIES

Producing a series of photographs around certain parameters might seem like a restrictive way of working and contrary to the creative process. Professional practice invariably involves adhering to the particular needs of a client or the specific context in which your photographs must function. On the other hand, having too much creative freedom (too open-ended a brief) can be equally problematic, as when faced with too many options, it can be difficult to be confident with creative decisions. Incorporating a particular strategy into a project can, paradoxically, be an effective way of leading you to new creative possibilities while at the same time allowing you to stay on course and not deviate from your original idea. A strategy might be a very distinct set of parameters by which you will complete a project, or it could be something more ambiguous. In fact, whether we are aware of it or not, we are all working with a strategy when we are out taking pictures. Even to try to take a set of photographs without a particular direction or idea in mind could be considered a strategy, although not one that is likely to result in a remarkable set of pictures.

Fig. 2.18
CHRIS COEKIN
The Hitcher, 2007
Chris Coekin embraced hitchhiking to make this work, which removed the responsibility from the photographer to select whom he could photograph. This method of collecting portraits reflects the haphazard nature of this way of getting around, which relinquishes some control over route and sometimes even the destination.

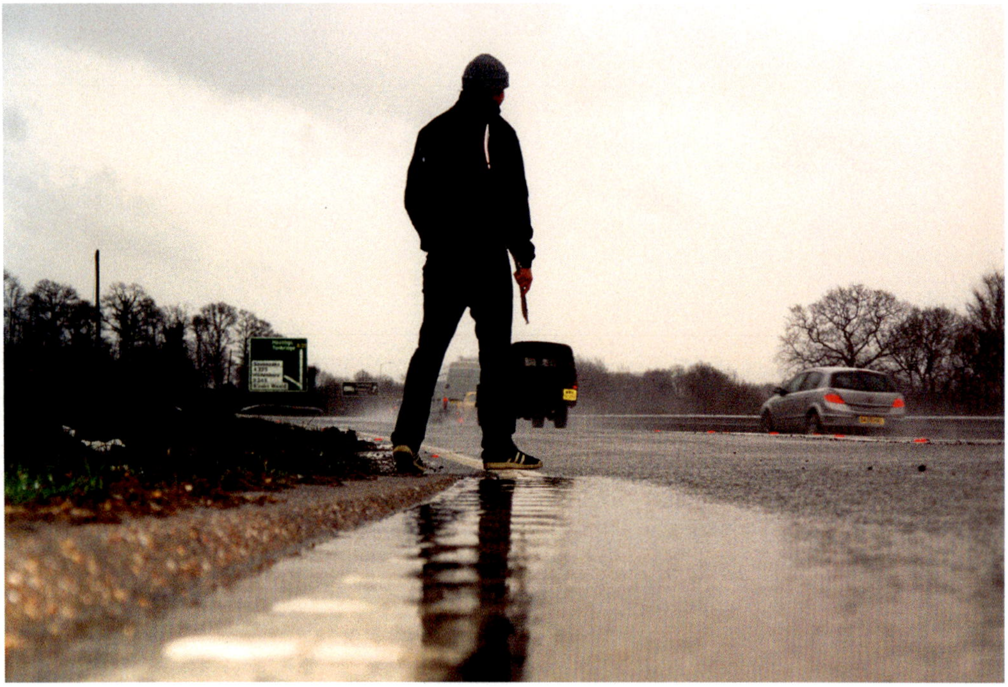

Fig. 2.18

A strategy for a project is more than simply a novel passing thought, although there is never any harm in pursuing an idea or an approach that still requires some development, to see what might emerge. Like the materials and technology a photographer chooses to employ, a strategy should complement the subject and the conceptual underpinning of the work. We can see these different concerns overlap (subject, strategy, technique, idea) in Chris Coekin's project *The Hitcher*. This work brings together several years' and many hundreds of miles' worth of hitchhiking around the UK. Hitchhiking, which has become less common in recent years, was an integral part of Coekin's strategy for the project.

The Hitcher comprises self-portraits of the photographer and incidental details that record his journey, mostly the diversity of rubbish and detritus that is discarded along Britain's roads. These were taken on a compact consumer camera, and the visual qualities reflect the impromptu nature of the project and also have an autobiographical aesthetic. Another key part of the work are the portraits of the drivers who chose to give the photographer a lift, which Coekin took on a medium-format camera. As well as providing better image quality for the portraits, the distinction between the different sets of pictures by the two camera formats elevates the men and women who gave Coekin a lift and could be seen as an acknowledgment of their kindness. In this body of work, an unusual means of traveling through the landscape combines with a strategy for collecting a unique set of portraits. Unlike with the majority of portrait photography, where the photographer makes a conscious decision as to whom he chooses to photograph, with Coekin's methodology, just the opposite is true: the drivers selected themselves to be photographed—albeit inadvertently—by deciding to offer Coekin a lift.

Matt White's project *This Is the Place* also deals with journeys but contrasts sharply against the meandering nature of Coekin's hitchhikes. White explores historic journeys and stories behind places, using photographs and video to engage with these past narratives. For this project, White looked at the history of Joseph Smith and the first Mormons, who were the first white settlers of Las Vegas before moving

Fig. 2.19
MATT WHITE
Rest* from *This Is the Place, 2008
Matt White's project takes as its starting point the history of the Mormon Church and its founders, which led him to a point in the desert between Las Vegas and Salt Lake City. It is important to consider the symbolism of the desert as a type of environment: in mythological narratives, it is associated with spiritual clarity and personal revelation—an archetypal wilderness—which makes it a suitable location for narratives around initiation and rites of passage. The type of terrain is a space for contemplation and contributes to the allegorical nature of the work. The project brings together photographs as well as several pieces of video work, including a sequence of the artist in a state of self-hypnosis, which posits White's physical voyage in relation to a very different kind of journey.

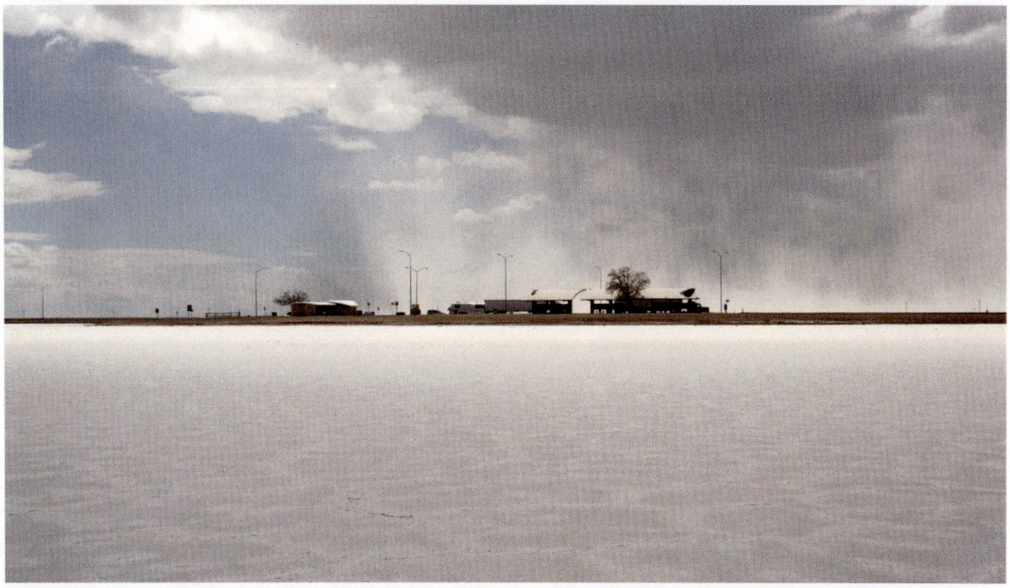

Fig. 2.19

to Salt Lake City. Both cities have a shared history but differ hugely in terms of the moral values associated with them. Salt Lake City remains closely aligned with the piety of the Church of Jesus Christ of Latter-Day Saints, whereas Las Vegas is the spiritual home of decadence, gambling, and other sins. White produced short video sequences from research undertaken in both cities and in addition to these, explored the territory between these two places using GPS to locate the precise midpoint between them. This took the artist into the depths of the Utah desert, where he made a series of photographs and video works. While this spot might be an unremarkable point on a map, it becomes—metaphorically—the midpoint between two strongly opposing ideologies: virtue on one hand, vice on the other. White's imagery depicts a kind of moral no-man's-land.

THE EDGELANDS

For many contemporary landscape photographers, the idea of exploration has less to do with traveling to far and exotic lands than it has to do with territories much closer to home. "Territory" is used quite deliberately here, because for the most part, types of land tend to fit into one of a few distinct categories: inner city, suburban, rural countryside (cultivated land, villages, and hamlets), and the more expansive open spaces like national parks. All of these zones are intriguing in their own ways and continue to be examined by photographers in innovative and exciting ways. The places *between* these kinds of landscape are also a source of fascination for artists and photographers. In *Edgelands: Journeys into England's True Wilderness* (2011), writers Paul Farley and Michael Symmons Roberts discuss the characteristics of these peripheral spaces that are, to some extent, defined by their failure to fit comfortably into one of the zones defined above. The lack of identity of the edgelands lies partly in their functional nature: industrial units, business parks, and conference centers; brownfields; household recycling plants; electricity substations, and so forth. Edgelands are not, however, exclusively utilitarian spaces and might be somewhere we go for leisure, such as an out-of-town shopping center (e.g., see Fig. 3.6) or a golf course.

Thanks to Marion Shoard, who articulated the term in 2002,[25] these spaces now have a name of their own. Farley and Symmons Roberts's book answers Shoard's call

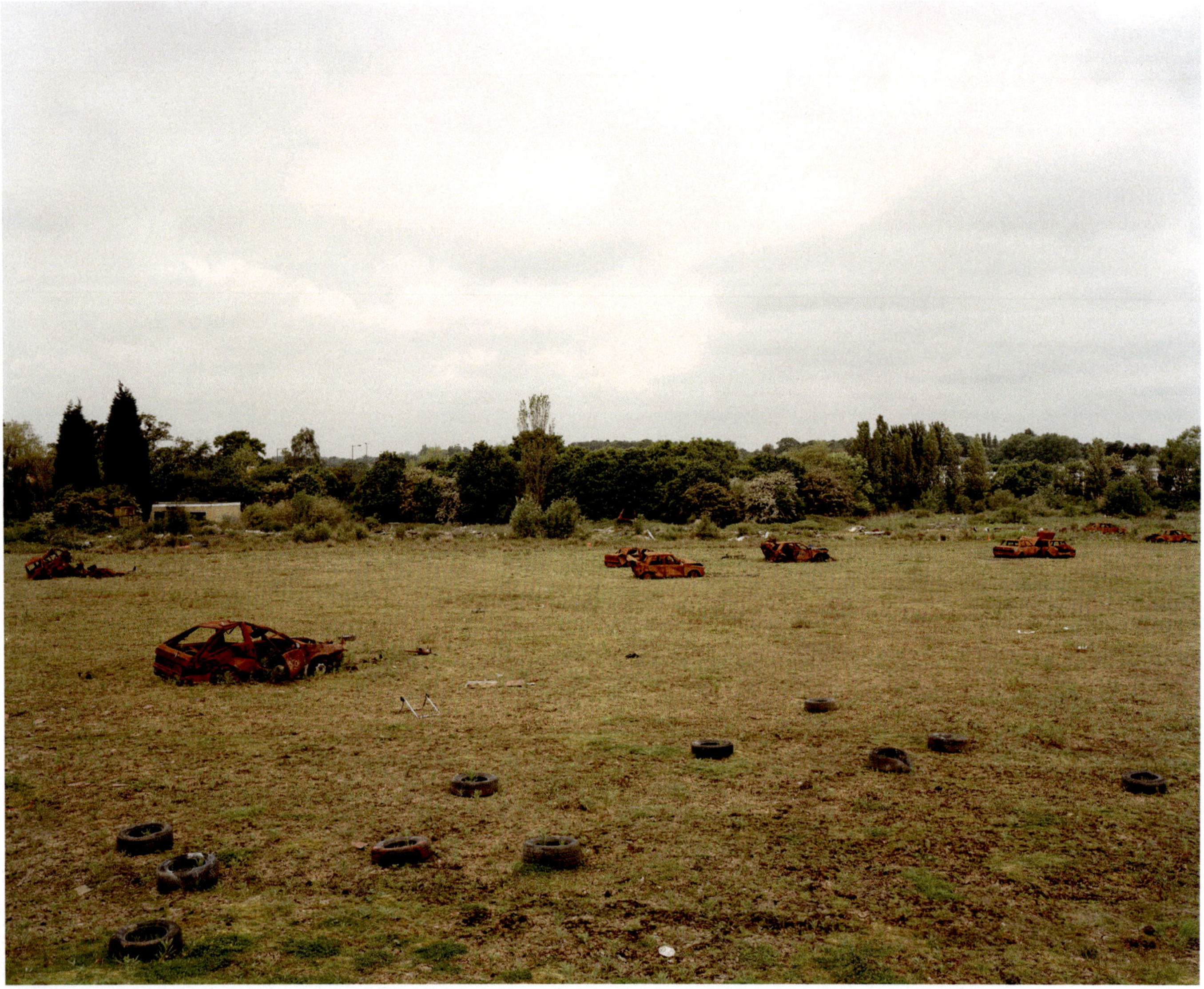

Fig. 2.20

Fig. 2.20
MARK POWER
K 13 North* from the series *26 Different Endings, 2003–2006

Mark Power's project, defined by the title of the touring exhibition of the work as *A System of Edges*, examines the spaces around the city's perimeter. Many of Power's photographs clearly depict suburbia, but others are—according to Farley and Symmons Roberts's definition—archetypical edgeland: industrial units, shipping containers, and scrapyards. In this photograph, we are in a distinct no-man's-land between the city and the rural countryside. A paddock that might have once been home to the odd pony or cow has apparently become a popular spot for joy riders to torch stolen cars that have screeched out of the city, through suburbia, to their final resting place.

for artists to consider the value of these spaces and the impact they have upon both their urban and rural neighbors. But judging by the breadth and quality of the works discussed in the book (many of them photographic projects), perhaps the edgelands are already more prominently represented in our culture than Shoard supposed. Mark Power's project *26 Different Endings* is typical of this kind of terrain, depicting precisely the types of infrastructure and characteristics discussed in *Edgelands*. Power responded to the once ubiquitous *A–Z London Street Atlas*, which, in the age of the smartphone and satnav, is perhaps becoming a thing of the past. With each updated edition of the atlas, it is somebody's responsibility to adjust the boundaries of the map. From year to year, a place may or may not find itself within the London area, as defined by the *A–Z*. In a series of excursions, Power traveled along the perimeter of the map, exploring the land along the edges of the fifty-six different pages, where the landscape dropped off the map.

The subtitle of *Edgelands—Journeys into England's Tue Wilderness*—might be a little ironic: What is so wild about some fairly grubby bits of postindustrial wasteland? The authors acknowledge the remarkably domesticated landscape of England: the less densely inhabited parts being never truly remote and not within very expansive areas relative to other parts of the world. Perhaps the enchantment of the edgelands is not so much because they are closer to an idea of wilderness or sense of isolation but rather because they make up the least well-documented and most ignored bits of the country.

1 Stephen Shore, *The Nature of Photographs* (London: Phaidon Press, 2007).

2 Feminist debates of the same period examined this discussion in relation to the gender construct of women (nature) and men (culture). See p. 136. See also M. MacCormack and C. Strathen, *Nature, Culture & Gender* (Cambridge: Cambridge University Press, 1980).

3 Numerous authors have used this phrase, such as Alexander Wilson for his book *The Culture of Nature: North American Landscape from Disney to Exxon Valdez* (Toronto: Between the Lines, 1991).

4 David Campany, ed., *Art and Photography* (London: Phaidon Press, 2003), 190.

5 Dave Beech, *Beauty* (London: Whitechapel Gallery, 2009), 12.

6 Edmund Burke, *A Philosophical Enquiry into the Origin of our Ideas of the Sublime and the Beautiful* (1729) (Oxford: Oxford University Press, 1990), 15.

7 This philosophy has resonance with postmodern debates about photographic history, such as the writing of John Tagg, who criticized modernist narratives of the medium's history as being too inward looking. Instead of thinking about photography in terms of a "canon" of great figures, allied to art and academic institutions, there were in fact many histories of photography's diverse and varied applications that contribute to a broader, more complex narrative of the medium. See John Tagg, *The Burden of Representation: Essays on Photographies and Histories* (London: Macmillan, 1988).

8 See Liz Wells's critique of the national park system: *Land Matters: Landscape Photography, Culture and Identity* (London: I.B. Tauris, 2011), 140.

9 Fay Godwin. *Southbank Show*. Produced and directed by Hilary Chadwick, London Weekend Television, 1986.

10 Malcolm Andrews, *Landscape and Western Art* (Oxford: Oxford University Press, 1999), 166.

11 William Gilpin, *Observations on the River Wye* (1782) (London: Pallas Athene, 2005), 17.

12 Ibid., 10.

13 See Andrews, *Landscape,* 116.

14 Susan Sontag described this as "aesthetic consumerism." See Sontag, *On Photography* (New York: Picador, 2001), 24.

15 In a letter from Archdeacon Fisher to John Constable, the benefactor wrote: "Let your Hay Cart go to Paris. . . . I am much too pulled down by agricultural distress to hope to possess it." Quoted in Andrews, *Landscape,* 175.

16 David Bate, "Notes on Beauty and Landscape," in *Art and Photography,* ed. David Campany (London: Phaidon Press, 2003), 287.

17 Burke, *A Philosophical Enquiry*, 53.

18 Ibid., 75.

19 Ibid., 77.

20 See also Friedrich's *Woman Before Setting Sun, 1818.*

21 The exponential, seemingly unstoppable rate at which digital images are accumulating might also be seen in relation to the sublime. Installations such as Erik Kessel's *24 Hours in Photos*, where the artist prints out and fills a room with all of the photographs uploaded to Flickr in a day, vividly express this sentiment.

22 Sigmund Freud, *The Uncanny* (1919) (London: Penguin Books, 2003), 147–48.

23 Adam Phillips in Burke, *A Philosophical Enquiry,* xi.

24 Freud. *The Uncanny*, 123.

It is worth noting that Freud's relatively brief discussion of the uncanny relates, as he makes clear in his introduction, to aesthetics, and he gives examples of the uncanny in literature rather than those in clinical observation, although he states that "whatever has an uncanny effect in real life has the same in literature" (157). This was partly because Freud believed that particular use of language (common phrases and expressions) revealed details of the unconscious.

25 Marion Shoard, "Edgelands," in *Remaking the Landscape*, ed. Jennifer Jenkins (London: Profile Books, 2002), 117–47.

ASSIGNMENT 2

A JOURNEY

PROJECT Make a series of between six and twenty-four photographs in response to a journey. This might be a journey that is very familiar to you. If this is the case, use it as an opportunity to look for new things along the route that you normally overlook or perhaps that have intrigued you but you've never explored further: this is an opportunity to indulge your curiosity.

Or, you might use this assignment to make a completely new journey into unknown territory and use the camera to record your findings. The journey might be very short, such as a walk around the block, or something much longer, incorporating other means of transport. Your journey might not be from A to B but could be a circular walk: perhaps try drawing around the rim of a glass on a map and follow this route.

Perhaps your journey might not actually involve *moving* anywhere. Could you use photography to record an imaginary journey?

When you have edited and sequenced your series write a short introduction to your project that includes:

- A title.
- Details of which photographers, writers, and other artists inspired you during this project.
- A brief rationale outlining why you adopted a particular shooting strategy or style and why you think it was appropriate for this project.
- A description of what you think the strengths and weaknesses of your work are. What would you do differently next time?
- Show your work to your peers or post it on your blog or Flickr account along with your written introduction, and invite comments.

RESEARCH AND DISCUSSION Consider the following questions and write down your thoughts in your reflective learning journal or on your blog. Then discuss with peers in a group or use the questions to start a thread on an online forum.

- What do you understand of the terms "nature" and "culture"? How do these terms contradict or complement each other?
- What is the distinction between the "picturesque" and the "sublime"? How do these two concepts overlap? Can you identify themes around the sublime in recent bodies of photographic work or elsewhere in popular culture?
- What does "wilderness" mean to you? Do you think the term still has relevance?
- How does travel influence your photography? Can an outsider offer a more useful insight to a place than someone native to or living there?

Chapter 3
SYNTHETIC VISIONS

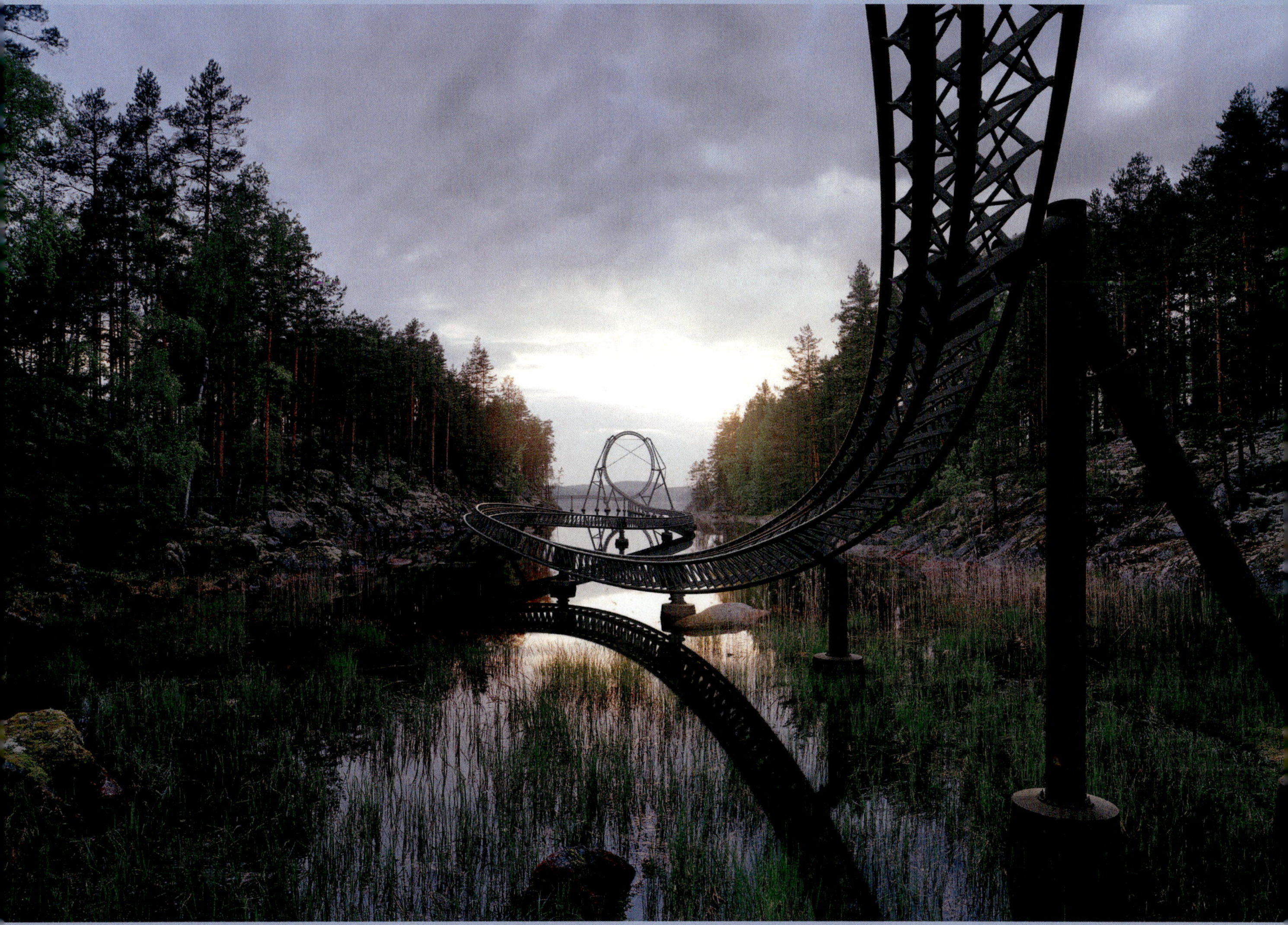

Fig. 3.1

Fig. 3.1
ILKKA HALSO
***Roller-Coaster, 2004* from the series**
The Museum of Nature, 2003–2008
In order to protect and restore nature we need stronger means. Ilkka Halso has continued his conquest in order to save the world. He presents plans for a brighter and more durable millennium.
Ilkka Halso[1]

Soon after photography was revealed to the world, artists and critics were quick to dismiss it as an expressive medium. This was in part because the process relied upon a methodical chemical procedure and also because photographic images were discussed and presented as uncorrupted analogous *facsimiles* of real life as opposed to expressive *interpretations* of it. William Henry Fox Talbot himself—who invented the positive/negative Calotype process—described photography as *The Pencil of Nature*.[2] Implicit within this subtitle for photography was, perhaps, an idea that the photographic process had the same kind of affinity with the purity and virtuousness that could be found only in the natural world: photography was itself a process of nature.

Now, photography is accepted as a means of artistic expression, but to most of us, notions of its objectivity are a thing of the past. Although photography is still a series of mechanical procedures, there are plenty of opportunities for the camera's operator to meddle—creatively or maliciously. Acceptability of the extent of such creative interventions is hotly contested. For some, extensive processing of the photograph is integral to the artistic process, while to others, such interference is a disservice to photography's unique characteristics and a distraction when it comes to using landscape photographs to communicate ideas. This chapter looks further into techniques that are commonly practiced in landscape photography and explores some of the different ways that contemporary practitioners have embraced alternative materials, processes, and technologies. What we are chiefly concerned with here is not so much *how* they have created a particular picture, but *why* they selected a particular process or strategy and how their decisions impress upon what their work communicates.

PLANES OF FOCUS

When starting out with photography, one of the first things we learn to manipulate is what part or proportion of the subject or view is in sharp focus. The visual contrast between sharply focused and out-of-focus areas of a photograph can provide an effective device for drawing the viewer to what is sometimes called the "point" of a picture, just as our own eyes adjust to movement and things of interest. Portraiture is a particular area of photography where using a shallower depth of field can allow the viewer to literally *focus* on the subject without the distraction of a background. Although focus is not an exclusively photographic characteristic, with the exception perhaps of photorealist painting, the visual effect of something being out of focus is a trait peculiar to the lens-based arts. Intriguingly, movie directors and computer-generated imagery (CGI) animators, who have complete control over the appearance of their sequences, choose to mimic the effect of shallow depth

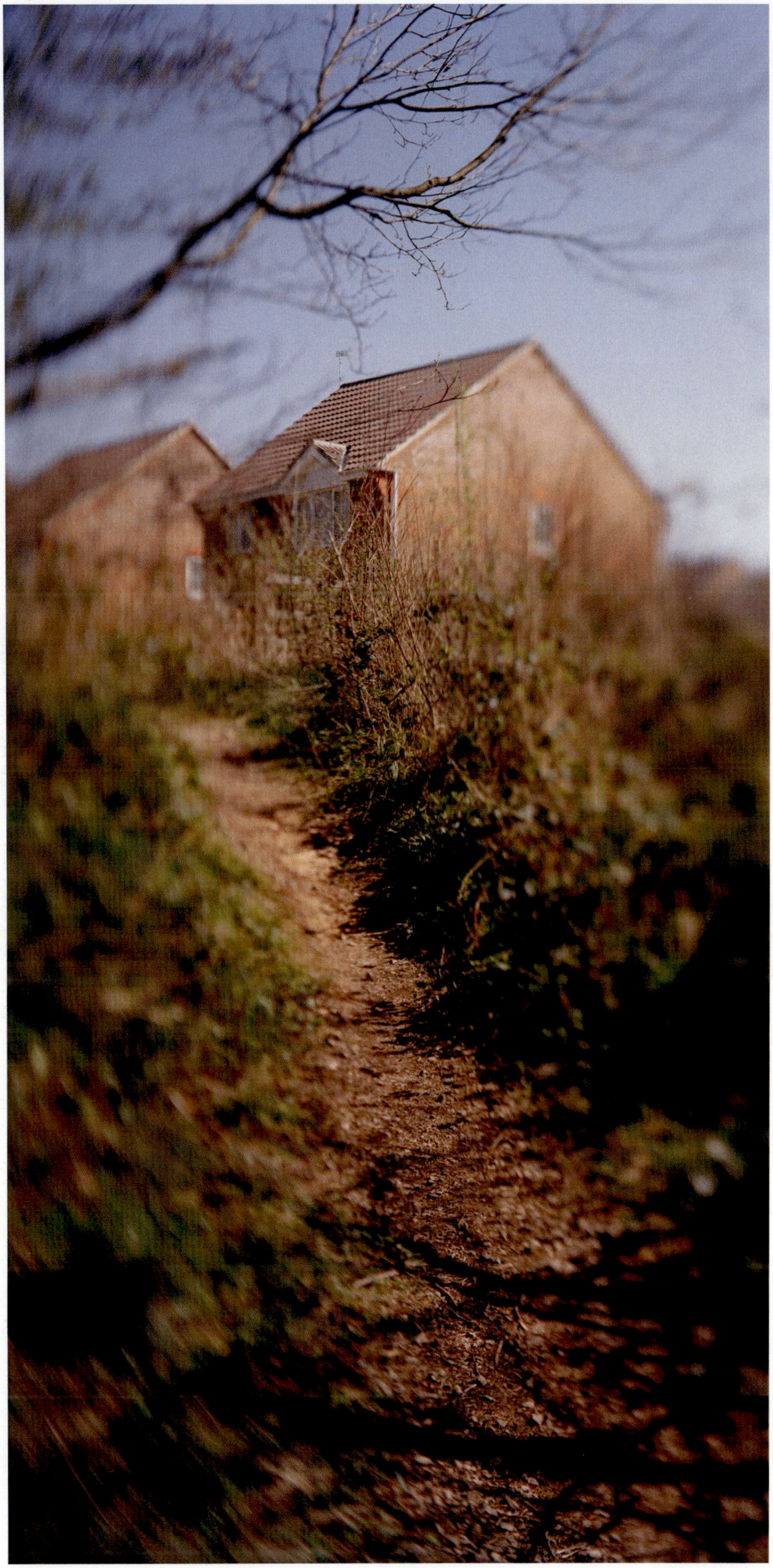

Fig. 3.2

Fig. 3.2
RICHARD PAGE
Suburban Exposure no. 2, 2003 **from the series** ***What We Already Know***

The world is simultaneously familiar and alien, banal and fascinating, revealed in a new light and obscured. Fantasy and reality converge in a way that suggests something that was previously repressed might be about to "come to light," but this resolution is perpetually withheld and each image denies any specific narrative, leading us back to search for answers in "what we already know" about these strangely familiar scenes and their mode of depiction.
Mark Bollan[3]

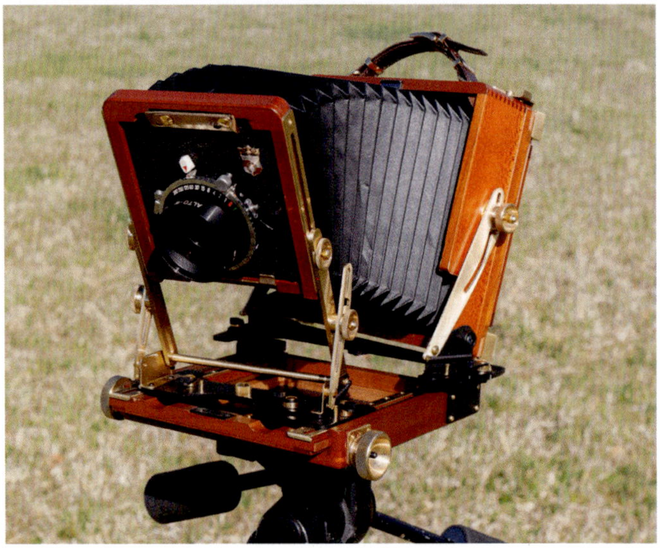

Fig. 3.3

Fig. 3.3
5" x 4" baseboard or field camera.
This photograph shows how the large-format field camera can be articulated. The large-format monorail camera, which is less portable and more likely to be found in the studio, offers an even greater range of camera movements. As well as giving a photographer the opportunity to have complete control over both the focal plane and perspective, the scale of large-format negatives offers exceptional image detail in enlarged prints (see p. 33). The movements of the front standard are especially helpful in interior and architectural applications, as these can alter the perspective of the image. For instance, by "shifting" the front standard upward, the tall vertical lines of buildings and structures are rendered in parallel with each other, thus avoiding the appearance of converging vertical lines that occur when a regular camera (i.e., one without tilt-shift capabilities) is pointed upward.

of field, to support the illusion that it was actually filmed by a movie camera as opposed to modeled in a computer.

In addition to the distance between subject and lens, and of course aperture size, depth of field is influenced by the focal length of a lens. It is particularly important to manage depth of field when using large-format cameras because of the longer focal lengths of standard lenses, which result in a shallower depth of field (see p. 34). Large-format camera lenses tend to have much smaller minimum apertures than 35-mm or medium-format cameras, which help extend the depth of field. Large-format cameras are designed to allow the photographer to align the camera so that it complements the plane of focus of the subject. Whereas most cameras have the lens and film or sensor in a fixed, parallel position, with large-format cameras the lens plane and the film plane (or the "front" and "rear standards" of the camera) can be articulated so that they can be aligned with a plane of focus that is not parallel to the lens and film plane. Being able to control the depth of field so meticulously offers advantages within the field of close-up product photography in particular, when the distance between camera and subject is particularly small.

The dramatic effects of deliberately *misusing* camera movements and manipulating the focal plane of an image can be seen in the work of Richard Page and Miklos Gaál. In Page's series *What We Already Know* (Fig. 3.2), made throughout the wake of 9/11 and the subsequent climate of anxiety, the obscured image around the skewed focal plane stands for misconstrued information. The shift in focus alters how we read Page's photographs of very ordinary places, turning the mundane into something potentially more malevolent. There is another side effect from this visual trick that can be seen in the work of Miklos Gaál. Typically made from a high vantage point looking down into a city or place of activity, the shift in focal plane alters the sense of the scale of the view and the subjects within it, as if you are pressed up against a miniature model. It is likely however, that these interpretations of these two bodies of work will be difficult to recognize, given that this technique has become so ubiquitous in recent years. It is used to stylistic effect in advertising imagery and across a variety of types of television programs and is even replicable as a smartphone postproduction filter and within the firmware of some consumer cameras.

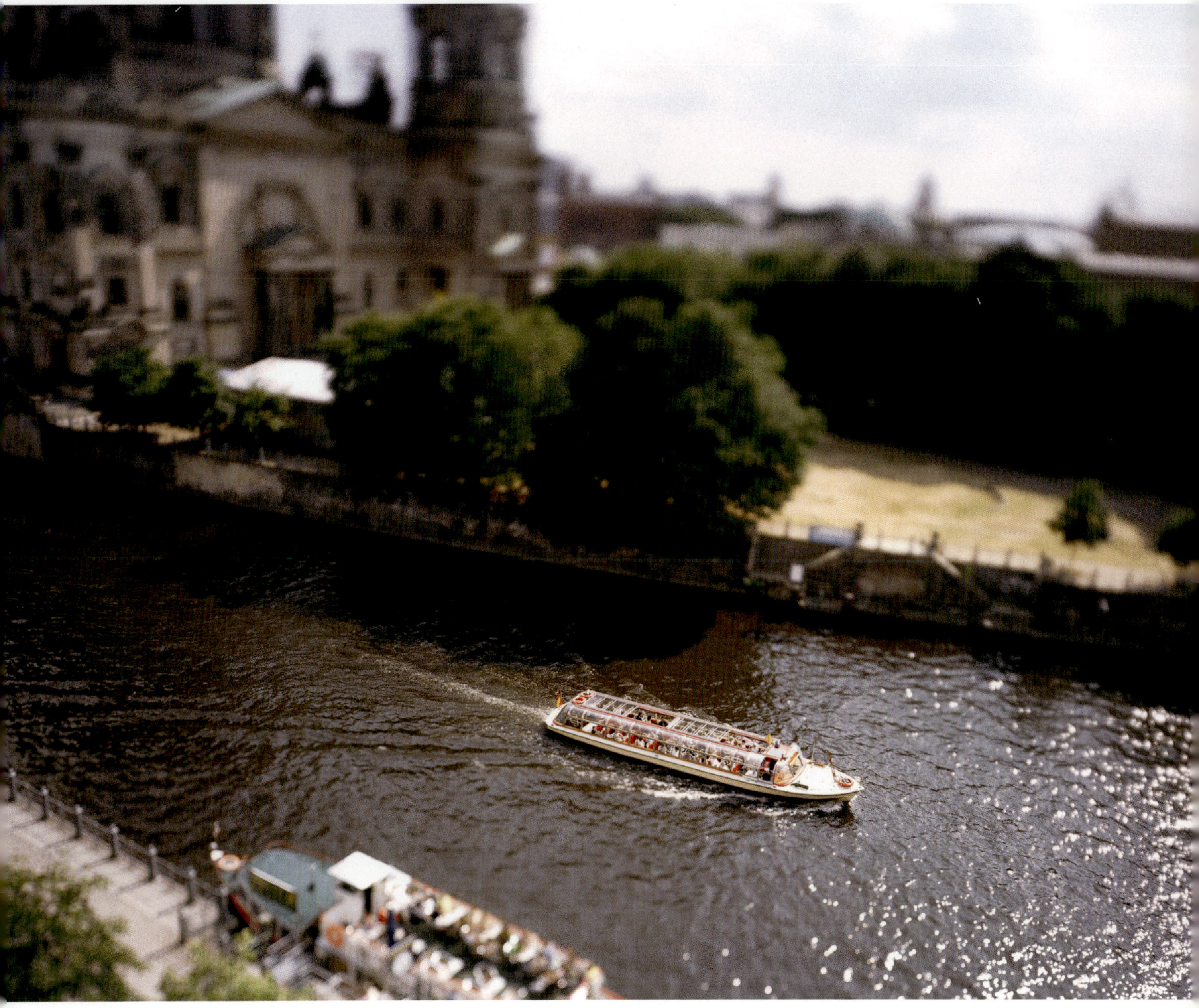

Fig. 3.4

Fig. 3.4
MIKLOS GAÁL
Sightseeing Tour 2, 2008

The tilt-shift is an optical-spatial event that adjusts the depth of field independently of parallel distance, manipulating the scope of view and making shifts to the sense of space. It focuses in a form of a sheet inside the perspective, resulting in a focused strip in the flat output image. Besides the focus, the detached viewpoint and the undisturbed view is a suggestive thing. The remote and elevated position of the viewer—of a seemingly uninvolved spectator—implies questions about objectiveness and the impossibility of it. For me it involves meditative, relieving, and sentimental connotations. Generally speaking, I am interested in how the viewing of familiar things as estranged can give rise to a kind of a contemplative, introverted process. A surprising point of view contrasts the preexisting ideas to the ones seen and poses questions about the spectator's own possibilities and responsibilities in constructing the reality.
Miklos Gaál

THE TEMPERATURE OF LIGHT

In color photography, the color temperature of a particular light source needs to be understood in order to take complete control over the appearance of a final image. Not all types of light sources emit the same colored light. Some sources, such as a naked flame, are red or warmer, while others, such as daylight and a camera's flash, are bluer or cooler. Our eyes generally do not make us aware of the color temperature of different light sources; however, with both digital and analog photography, it is necessary to be aware of how different light sources will influence the color balance of your pictures so you can select film and filters or process your image files accordingly. Failure to do so will potentially result in an image that has a color cast, which will distort the appearance of the photograph and produce an unrealistic rendering of the subject. While adjustments to the color temperature can be a matter of personal interpretation and an important stage in the creative process, in most circumstances—and in particular commercial applications, such as product photography—achieving a neutral white balance is the objective for most practitioners.

In digital photography, the white balance can be adjusted from frame to frame, and this is a simple matter of matching the white balance setting to whatever the shooting scenario is. In practice, leaving the white balance setting on automatic will generally suffice, and assuming you are shooting in RAW, there should be plenty of information to adjust the image in postproduction. But matching the white balance to the light source at the time of capture will result in a greater range of color information to work with. You may also find yourself in a particular scenario where the light sources are mixed and it is necessary to take greater control over the white balance.

Matters are actually simpler in analog photography than they are in digital photography, in so far as the photographer has a choice of whether to use tungsten-balanced (3,200 K) or daylight-balanced film stock (5,500 K). In practice, either one of these film stocks can be used all the time, with the use of either an orange or a

Fig. 3.5
Color temperature scale, measured in Kelvins. These numbers are approximate values. Precise temperature may vary.

1,900 K	2,200 K	2,700 K	3,400 K	3,800 K	4,100 K	5,400 K	5,500 K	6,500 K
wax candle	sunlight at sunset	domestic lightbulb	tungsten-halogen continuous lighting	white fluorescent studio lighting	moonlight	sunlight at noon	flash	cloudy

Fig. 3.5

Fig. 3.6
DAN HOLDSWORTH
A Machine for Living 01, 1999
Dan Holdsworth's suite of photographs that make up *A Machine for Living* ironically reference the modernist architect Le Corbusier, who asserted that "a house was a machine for living in." Much of Holdsworth's practice involves photographic interrogations of the landscape as it is transformed by the night. This shopping mall, completely absent of people or vehicles, is typical of the kind of generic space and architectural features that the photographer is drawn to. In this image, the effect of the artificial light swelling inside the view demonstrates the transformative potential of artificial light and the otherworldly visual effect that these conditions lend themselves to. By adjusting the color to provide a neutral color balance for the artificial lighting of the mall and the parking lot, the color of the sodium street lighting across the foreground and the light pollution from the city in the sky beyond the horizon is exaggerated dramatically. The deliberate use of color cast enhances the sense of discord in Holdsworth's landscape: a shimmering consumerist utopia contained within a fiery red, angry landscape (see p. 178).

blue filter. As with digital photography, prints from color negatives can be adjusted for color casts during the printing process. However, image quality and the accuracy of colors can deteriorate when color balance is altered by greater degrees. As with care regarding exposure when using both film and digital cameras, attention to white balance at the time of capture will result in better image quality and less time required in postproduction.

When using film and extended exposures (i.e., greater than 1 second), the reciprocity law in photography (Exposure = Light Intensity × Time) breaks down, which means that exposure times need to be extended further to make up for this reciprocity failure. As a result of reciprocity failure, the different layers of colored emulsions in the film can respond slightly unusually, which results in colors appearing untrue. Although this is usually to quite subtle degrees and can be adjusted in the darkroom or with software, it underscores the fact that judgment over color balance is subjective. As we can see in the example of Dan Holdsworth, nighttime long exposures often present the challenge of mixed light sources: working to the white balance of one can lead to the extreme appearance of another.

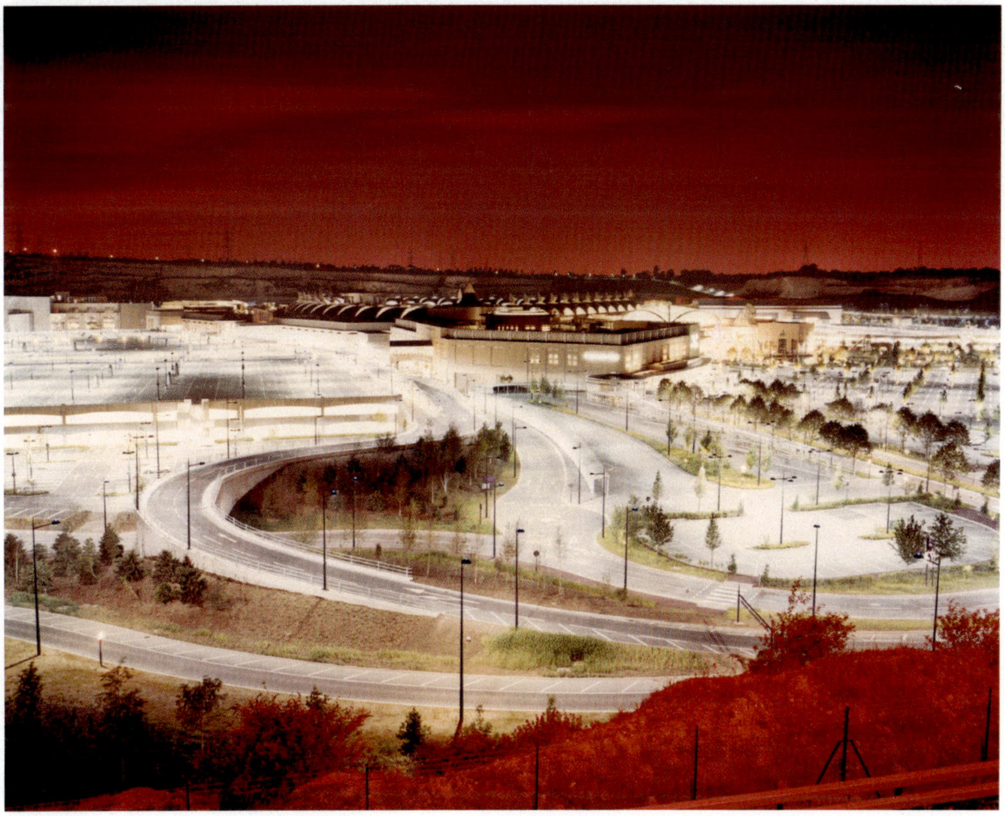

Fig. 3.6

Since the sky and the clouds are changeable and varied, COKIN Filters invite you to imitate them in your own interpretation of colors. These secondary characters will become essential actors in a dialogue with the countryside. COKIN PHOTO VIDEO ACCESSORIES SALES BROCHURE, C.1990

ANALOG AND DIGITAL FILTERS

Although filters are used for all kinds of professional scenarios, they have become synonymous with landscape practice. Whether or not, as the manufacturers would like you to believe, you feel they will be essential actors in your camera outfit or will have much to contribute to your imagery is a matter of your own judgment; however, it is useful to understand why they are used and how they can be employed in practice. In black-and-white analog photography, the use of colored filters allows the photographer to affect how certain tones will be rendered on the film *before* experimenting with tonal balance in the darkroom. Although monochrome film renders an image in shades of black and white, it is sensitive to all colors of visible light ("panchromatic"). Likewise, if you are shooting digitally with the camera set to black-and-white mode, the sensor is still forming an image from the colored light reflected from the subject or view. However, monochrome film is generally more sensitive to light toward the blue end of the visible light spectrum, and therefore, blue skies are rendered *lighter* than they appear to the naked eye.[4] To manage these deficiencies, colored filters are used to make certain subjects appear darker or brighter. They allow light waves of colors similar to those of the filter to pass through. Although colored filters are useful to all applications of black-and-white photography, there are typical scenarios in landscape practice that make the use of filters invaluable. For example, the problem of the density of blue skies can be rectified with the use of an orange filter, which will absorb much of the blue light, leading to greater tonal density in the final, reversed print. Skies can be made to appear even darker with a red filter. A subtler effect can be achieved with a yellow filter, which will also reduce the appearance of distant haze caused by ultraviolet light.

Polarizing filters are used with both digital and analog photography and also are particularly useful in landscape photography. They work by partially blocking

Fig. 3.7.i–3.7.iii
Paul Alexander Knox
Retraced: St. Cuthbert's Final Journey, 2013
While making *Retraced*, Paul Alexander Knox embraced the spontaneity and aesthetic that his smartphone and associated processing filters offered. The photographer found that the quality of the images, which was poorer than that offered by his "proper" camera, actually lent themselves well to the concept of a journey and complemented his other, more considered photographs.

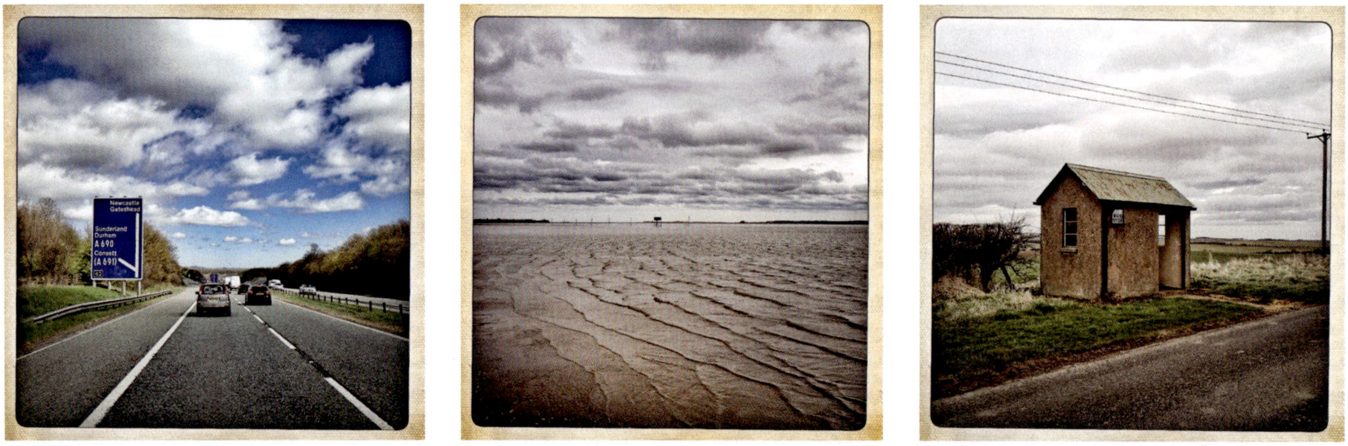

Fig. 3.7

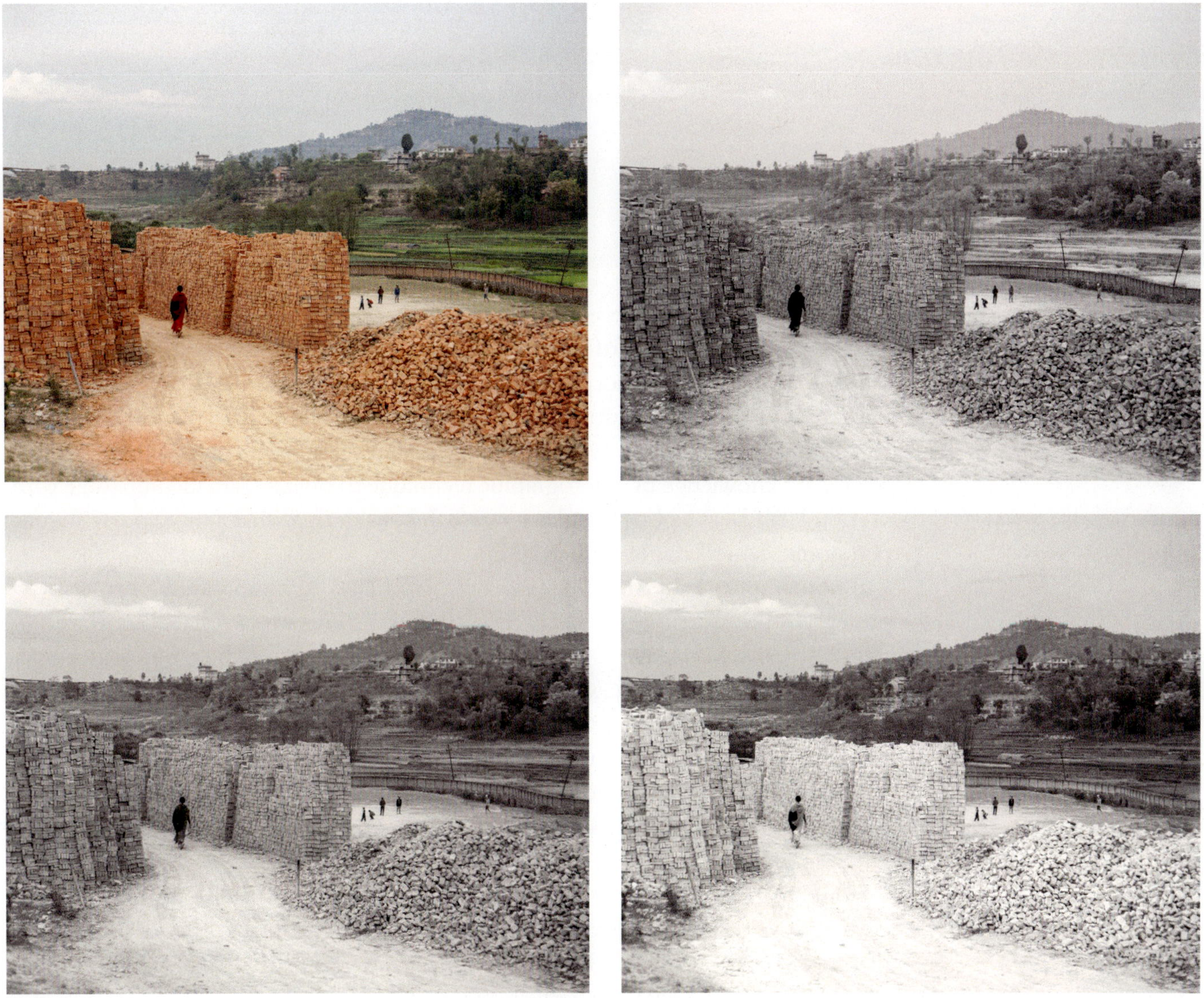

Fig. 3.8

Fig. 3.8
Selective channel mixing of a digital color file
Tonal adjustment in monochrome digital photography can be managed to an even finer degree with selective channel mixing. As demonstrated here, an image file captured with the full range of color information can be adjusted so that particular tones stand out more than others.[5] This file has been adjusted digitally to approximate the effects that red, green, and yellow filters would have if the photograph were taken with black-and-white film.

off the polarized light that reflects from shiny surfaces, therefore reducing the intensity of light in certain parts of a picture. For example, by blocking out some of the reflected light from a glass window, a polarizing filter can sometimes make the subject behind the glass visible. Also, by reducing the polarized light from clear blue skies they can have the effect of darkening the sky.

Within the digital context, software has brought us myriad options for refining and altering the appearance of our pictures. Moreover, digital filters have brought with them something of a level playing field: previously, filters tended to be available only to professional and semiprofessional camera systems, thus excluding the consumer and perhaps adding to the mystification of landscape photography in particular. Smartphones and consumer digital cameras allow special-effect filters, such as desaturation or a deliberate color cast, to provide a retro aesthetic. Rather than enhancing the optical quality and density of images (which is the purpose that analog filters have traditionally served), these filters are designed to "obscure our view,"[6] to simulate the look of poor-quality lenses and outdated point-and-shoot analog cameras and faded vintage prints. Stephen Bull asserts that rather than keeping popular analog photography alive, the nostalgia that accounts for the trend toward these kinds of retro filters actually underscores the datedness and contributes to the demise of popular analog photography.[7] We are increasingly seeing the devices that incorporate these filters within spheres of commercial photography and photojournalism,[8] demonstrating that the level playing field is in fact a game of two halves. While it may seem that these pieces of equipment, which require no knowledge of photographic technique to operate, are incompatible with "serious" landscape photography, it is worth considering what a more portable and ergonomic camera might have to offer.

Photographer Paul Alexander Knox incorporated "iPhonography" into his project *Retraced: St. Cuthbert's Final Journey* (Fig. 3.7). This was a collaboration with writer Richard W. Hardwick that followed in the footsteps of the ninth-century community of Lindisfarne, which fled from Viking invaders with the 200-year-old remains of St. Cuthbert.[9] Knox initially used his smartphone to make visual notes and to generate material to upload onto his blog that documented the project. The smartphone also offered a geotagging function that connects GPS data to images and provided useful information for piecing together his photographs. However, Knox soon found that the phone's camera offered creative as well as practical uses and provided a spontaneity and visual quality that resonated with the idea of voyaging. In the exhibition that was the outcome of the project, Knox's iPhone pictures were hung around the larger prints, taken on a professional camera, and provided a sense of rhythm to the installation.

Fig. 3.9
HELEN SEAR
Inside the View 14, 2004–2008
Helen Sear used neither digital nor analog filters per se to create the series of works that comprise *Inside the View*. However, her technique of digitally layering several images on top of one another makes an interesting point of reference for a discussion of what filters add, or perhaps detract, from a photograph. Several different pictures, with portions of the image removed from each, are overlapped, with striking visual effect. Close inspection reveals a lace-like patina across the surface of the final image, the result of the artist's painstaking process of cutting out individual segments of the top image, like kitting individual stitches or tying intricate knots. Each of the different perspectives that comprise *Inside the View* is an individual filter revealing a partial image that abstractly complements the others. This series has various contextual references, but the back of a woman's head that emerges through the fog of information alludes to Casper David Friedrich's *Wanderer Above the Sea of Fog* (Fig. 2.10). Unlike in Friedrich's painting, the figure depicted here overpowers the frame, restricting us (the viewer) from sharing what she is looking at. There is a dual sense of obscurity here: the view, blocked by the woman, and the woman, shrouded by a digitized veil. Consequentially, our gaze is forced inward and becomes self-reflective: we look *inside* the view.

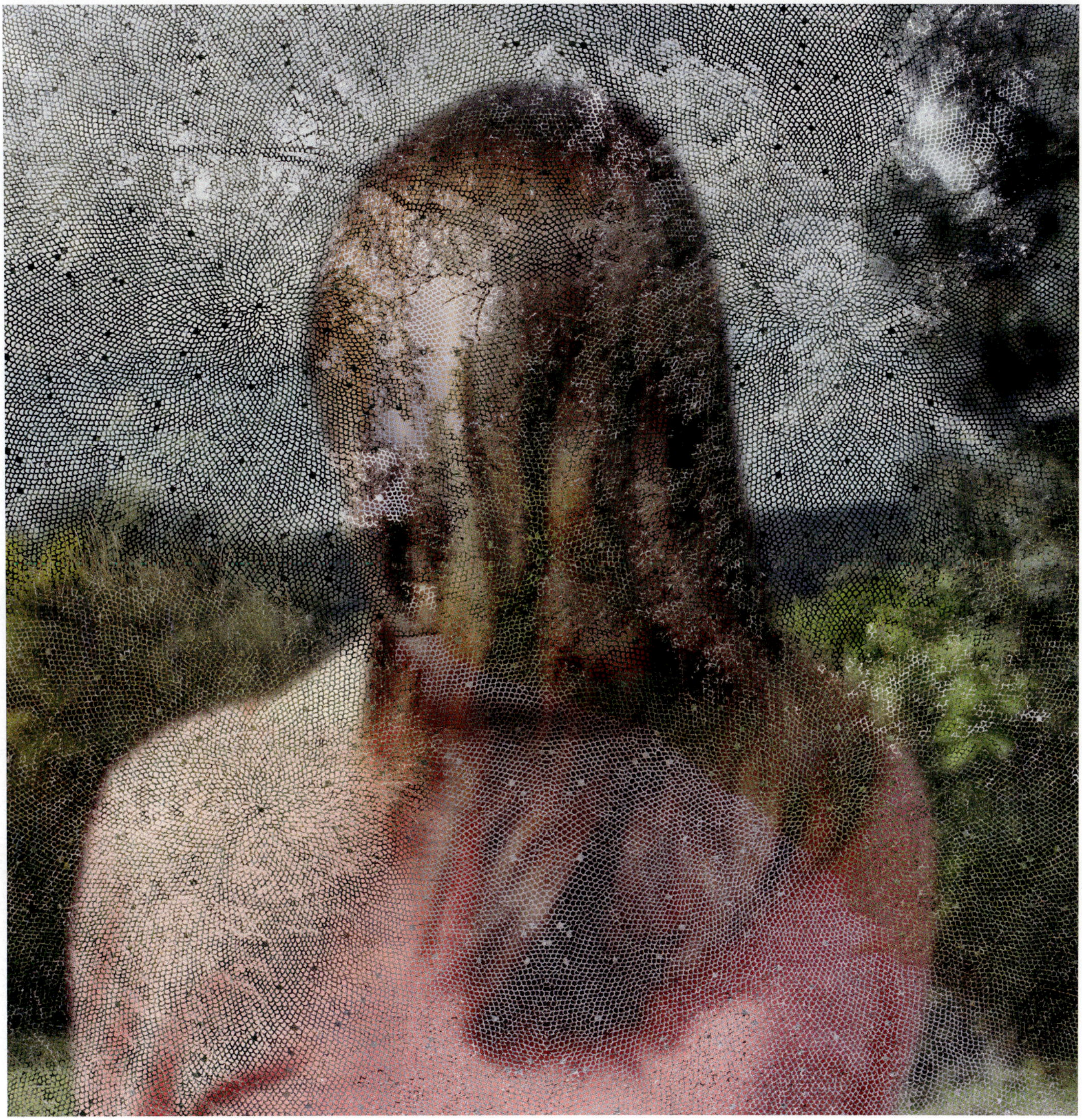

Fig. 3.9

MANAGING DYNAMIC RANGE

In Chapter 1 we looked at the limitations of photographic film and digital sensors in terms of their dynamic range (see p. 44). Assuming the aim is to capture an image that records as much detail and as wide a tonal range as possible, a typically challenging landscape scenario might be trying to expose for a bright sky and capture some tone and detail in the clouds and also manage to register detail in the foreground shadows. However, as Figure 3.10 illustrates, there is no reason such a view should be impossible to capture. In black-and-white analog photography, achieving prints with detail in the highlight areas as well as in the shadows is often achieved through dodging and burning techniques in the darkroom, giving a particular part of the print less or more exposure time than the rest of it. The same words are used to describe tools in digital image editing software that perform the same task. Dodging and burning is generally necessary, even with a "correctly" exposed negative, because the dynamic range of photographic paper is narrower than that of film. However, when dodging and burning is employed excessively, the print will appear grainy.

The extent to which an exposure can be compensated for in postproduction describes the latitude of the material. Monochrome film has a greater latitude than does color negative, which is much more versatile than slide film. Now, digital sensors have the greatest dynamic range, and exposures can be corrected to a relatively substantial degree (+/– one or two *f*-stops) with acceptable results. However, image quality (i.e., the visibility of grain or noise and the appearance of color casts in certain tonal ranges) depends upon the extent to which an image is enlarged. Also, what is deemed to be acceptable is subjective. It should be clarified that there isn't necessarily anything wrong with a photograph that lacks detail in the shadows or in the highlights: contrast in a print can enhance its visual presence. However, increasing the contrast—which is effectively narrowing the range of tones in an image or increasing the concentration of either the highlights or shadows (or both)—can be achieved easily postproduction in both the wet and digital darkroom, but it is advisable to capture as wide a tonal range as possible at the time of capture so that you have plenty of information to work with later.

BRACKETING AND BLENDING

A technique for making sure that you manage to capture an image that is as evenly exposed as possible is bracketing, in which one or two exposures are made under or over the light meter reading. Depending on the shooting situation or the material used (e.g., on digital or slide film), bracketing may be only one- or two-thirds of an *f*-stop to either side of a "correct" meter reading, or it may be several whole stops. When shooting on medium- and large-format cameras, bracketing is generally not

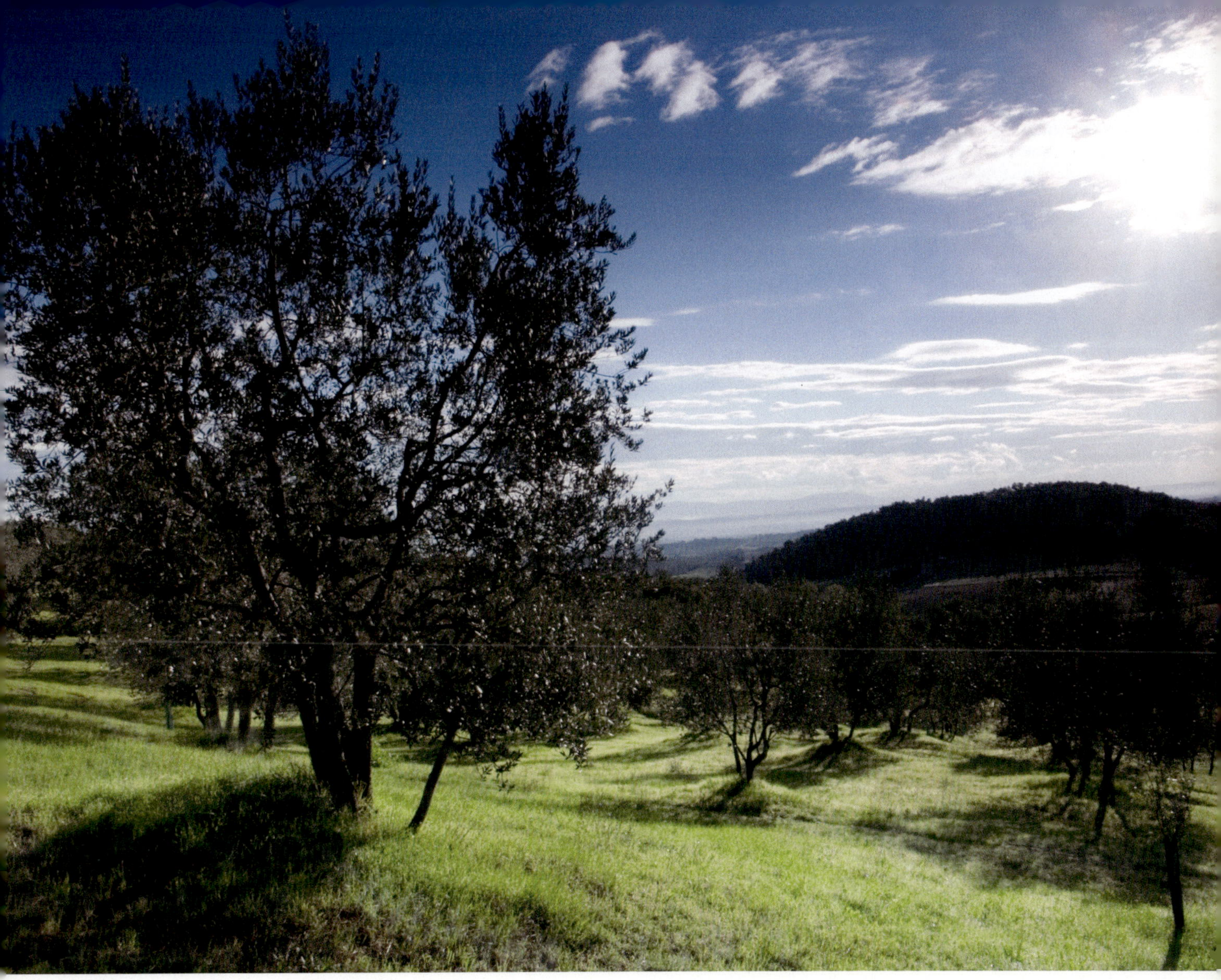

Fig. 3.10

Fig. 3.10
JESSE ALEXANDER
Olive Grove, Tuscany, Italy, 2005

Early morning and late evening, when the sun is low on the horizon and casts long shadows, offer some of the most challenging lighting situations in terms of exposure difference between the land and the sky. Graduated neutral density (ND) filters are particularly useful in landscape practice. These filters are clear on the bottom and *graduated* to a darker gray at the top and can be either held in front of the lens or slotted into a specially designed holder and adjusted accordingly. Depending upon the particular type, the denser gray portion of the filter will block off up to three *f*-stops of light. This allows tone and detail from the sky to fit within the dynamic range of the digital camera or film. It is necessary to expose for the foreground *before* the filter goes in front of the lens; otherwise you may well end up with an underexposed foreground. Even when rendering detail in the foreground would not lead to an overexposed sky, a graduated ND filter might be used to make the sky appear darker or exaggerate the color. A plethora of tinted graduated filters are on the market that can make an overcast day appear to be bright blue or allow the sun to appear to set at noon.

Fig. 3.11
EADWEARD MUYBRIDGE
Unidentified Estate, California. Possibly the Stanford residence, c. 1872–1880
Because early photographic emulsions were much less sensitive to blue light than they are today, it was often not possible to achieve detail in the sky as well as in the foreground within a single exposure. To overcome this, photographers such as Muybridge created a collection of sky and cloud photographs and combined these negatives with landscapes as required. As well as drawing a parallel with today's techniques for extending the dynamic range of photographic materials, this approach can be seen alongside the work of other nineteenth-century photographers who used combination printing techniques to produce montages from multiple negatives to create the illusion of a single moment, such as Henry Peach Robinson (1830–1901) and Oscar Rejlander (1818–1875) (see p. 112).

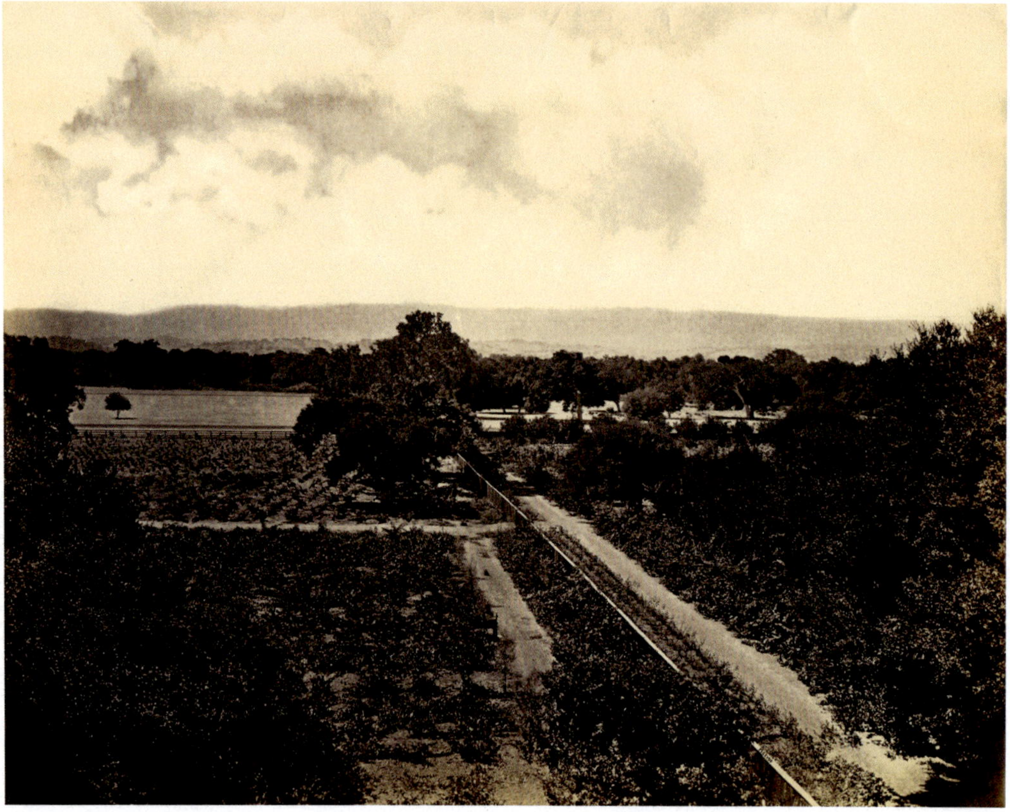

Fig. 3.11

economically viable, although if you are working with 35-mm film or digitally it is often a sensible approach. Bracketing may seem like an idle or amateurish method of achieving an optimum exposure, but in some circumstances it is necessary, such as when you are working with infrared film or when failure to achieve a well-exposed image is not an option.[10]

As well as the possibility of having a negative that has a better average exposure than the setting indicated by the light meter, having these additional versions means that you have much more material at your disposal in postproduction. Whether you are working with digital, analog, or a hybrid of these processes, separate images can be combined, resulting in a photograph with an extended dynamic range, achieving detail throughout the image from the shadows to the highlights. This technique, known as high dynamic range (HDR) merging, has its roots in nineteenth-century photography and has become particularly popular in recent years among amateur landscape photography with the increased accessibility to image editing software. Many digital cameras and smartphones now are capable of creating merged HDR images in camera. The amount of information that can be contained within a RAW file means that it is also possible to process a single file to approximate different exposures that can be combined in the same way. While HDR montage is a technique worth familiarizing yourself with, the common mistake is to use it unnecessarily and without subtlety. The results of the technique can be conspicuous, such as the appearance of halos around foreground objects where a brighter background has been darkened. When applied excessively, imagery can look unrealistic—or rather "nonphotorealistic," or painterly—which for some is the attraction of the technique.

Fig. 3.12
Digital composite of three files at one *f*-stop increments
HDR merging can be performed automatically by computer applications or by assembling the different layers manually. HDR merging can be useful when trying to capture particularly contrasting lighting conditions that are too challenging for a single exposure. It is important to take the sequence as quickly as possible so that the subject is as similar as possible in each frame, and of course the use of a tripod is always necessary to achieve consistency of framing.

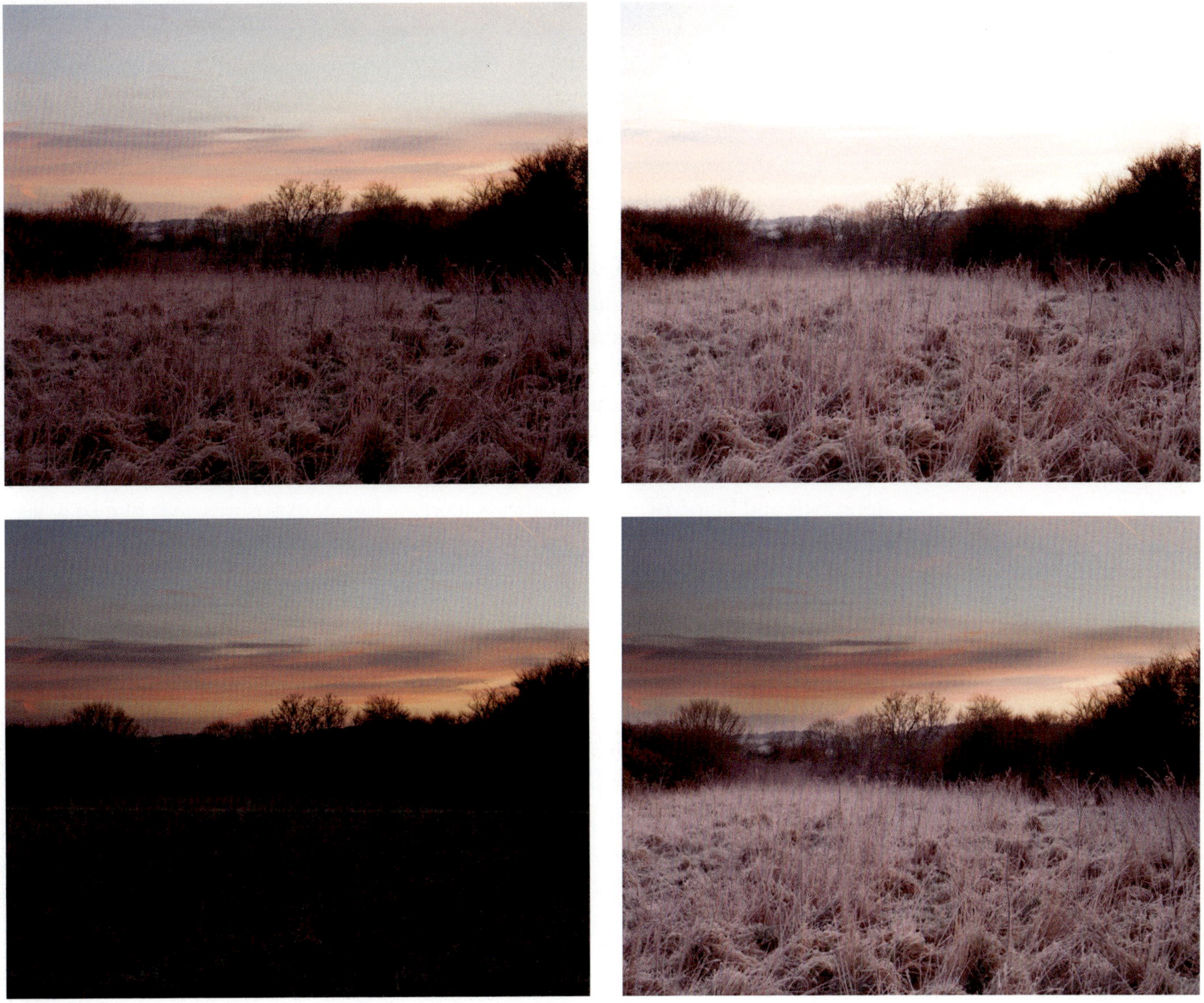

Fig. 3.12

LIGHTING THE LAND

The night can offer exciting opportunities for landscape imagery. Working in the dark does not come without its challenges, but it can be enjoyable and visually rewarding. The dark can transform a space, both in terms of how it appears to the camera and the atmosphere of the picture. Depending on exactly where you are shooting and whether you are working alone or have assistance, you may consider the thought of working at night uninviting. On the other hand, you might find the solitude and the experience of consuming a place that you have all to yourself a kind of indulgence. We often associate "good" photographs with an appreciation for the nuances of lighting conditions, so there is perhaps something that perverts traditional landscape values by shooting when there is very little natural ambient light.

Photographing at night inevitably requires extended exposure times. Depending upon the exact lighting conditions (i.e., how bright the sky is, whether there is moonlight, the presence of street lighting, etc.), it may be a fairly straightforward matter of taking a light meter reading and making a long exposure. If you wish to capture as fine a detailed image as possible, it is necessary to keep the ISO low (particularly if you are shooting digitally), as longer exposures can make images look very "noisy." It is also sensible to shoot with a smaller aperture to increase depth of field and help guarantee a sharp image, as focusing accurately in low light is difficult.[11] When using film and exposures of longer than one second, the reciprocity law fails. Therefore additional exposure time needs to be added to achieve an image that is as equally dense as an equivalent exposure value with a faster shutter speed. The actual length of time by which you will need to increase your exposure will vary depending upon type and brand of film, but always increase longer exposures with film by at least one stop, or ideally, try several different exposures.

LANDSCAPE AS STUDIO

Although these calculations may sound complicated, not all situations actually will be as straightforward as this. Just as it can be difficult to expose detail in backlit subjects in bright sunlight, balancing the exposure of different elements within the viewfinder at night can be challenging. However, one of the benefits of longer exposure times is that they provide an opportunity to introduce supplementary lighting, such as a handheld flash unit or a torch. Of course, if you have access to them, more powerful battery-operated flash units or continuous lighting might be used. However, similar effects can be achieved by repeatedly firing a small flash unit throughout the duration of an extended exposure. The size of a flash unit also means that light can be used with precision, to illuminate particular parts of a scene or introduce light from a certain direction.

Fig. 3.13
RAFAELLA MARINIELLO
Porto di Napoli [The Port of Naples], 2001
One thing stands out immediately . . . the fact that they were taken at what is often the crucial moment in many fantasy stories; dusk. For many—even in these times of technological and rationalist certainties—this is still an anxious time (as light disappears and the immensity of night falls, from the innermost depths even of modern man emerges a—conscious or unconscious—fear that the sun may never return). This is Raffaela Mariniello's favourite hour.
Diego Mormorio[12]

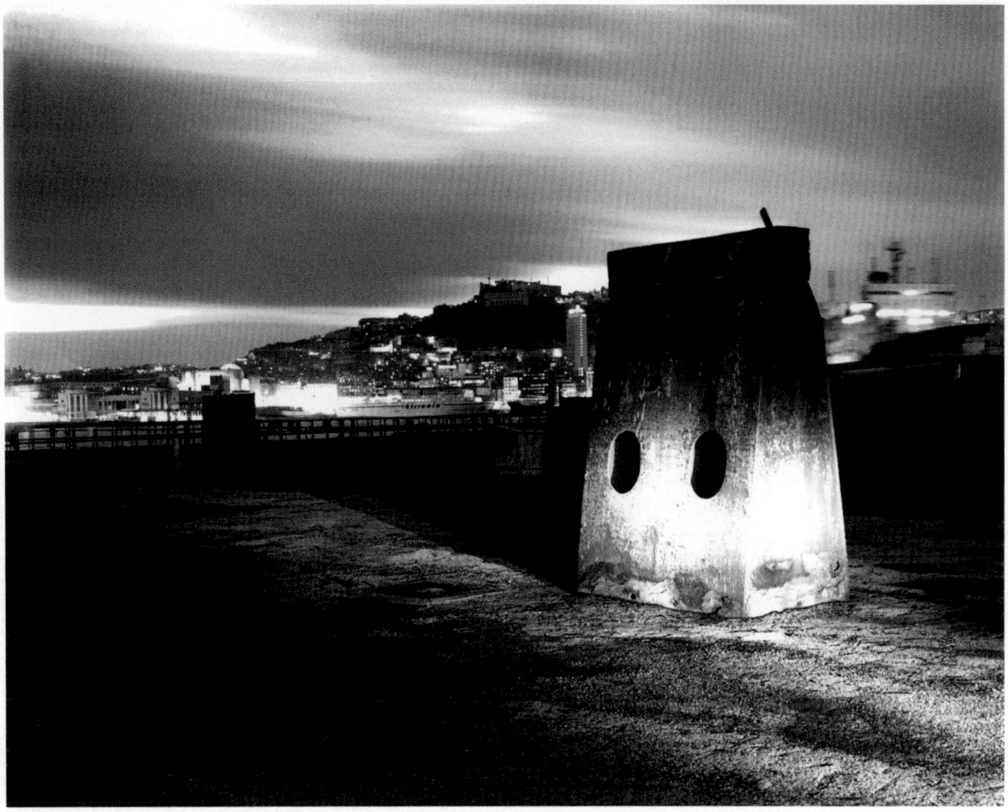

Fig. 3.13

Rafaella Mariniello is one photographer who exploits the drama of twilight within her practice. The locations she gravitates toward to make her long exposures are often the kinds of places one might prefer to avoid after dark, especially with a conspicuous large-format camera, such as dockyards, building sites, and other edgelands (see p. 83). Mariniello works at twilight with exposure times of up to twenty minutes, which allows her to incorporate a little light from the sky with industrial and street lighting as well as her handheld flash. Her use of black-and-white film means that an array of light sources with different color temperatures—which could result in a kaleidoscope of saturated colors—are rendered in neutral monotone. This denial of visual information also adds to the strangeness of Mariniello's photographs. The technique allows the photographer to use flash to both highlight some objects and conceal others: overexposing some objects washes them out of the picture, while keeping the flash away from others keeps them in the gloomy darkness.[13]

In many respects, working with artificial light in the landscape at night is a contrasting approach to working with daylight. Whereas in the daylight the photographer can affect how a subject will appear to only limited effect, during the nighttime, the photographer starts with a *black* canvas and to some extent chooses what to illuminate and what to hide in a composition. Edgar Martins incorporates long exposures with multiple bursts of flash in many of his projects—even with interiors that appear to be brightly lit. The nuances of photographic technique and how this disrupts the way we process imagery is an important aspect of Martins's practice, such as the subtle manipulation of perspective or an incongruously placed object that might be lit differently from the rest of the scene, leaving the viewer to wonder whether perhaps it has been photoshopped in. Several of Martins's projects examine the landscape at night, and he exposes foreground elements with artificial lights, leaving the background cloaked in darkness. Lighting the subject frontally from a range of angles reveals the subject with a distinctly shadowless, tonally flat appearance. Within his contextualization of Martins's project *The Time Machine, 2011,* Geoff Dyer creates a vivid image of the photographer at work:

> *Many of the apparently bright places photographed by Martins are, in reality, quite dark. During the necessarily long exposures required remedying this, he darts around with a flash filling in bits that would otherwise be consigned to shadow. So somewhere in these pictures the photographer lurks invisibly. They are self-portraits in which the author-subject has been irradiated, vaporized or somehow absorbed. The effect is to make it seem as if the equipment on display has somehow photographed itself, recording what it has observed during the lengthy exposure time of its functioning.*
> Geoff Dyer[14]

Tim Simmons also explores the notion of the landscape as a studio. His photographs are produced with elaborate lighting assemblies to meticulously

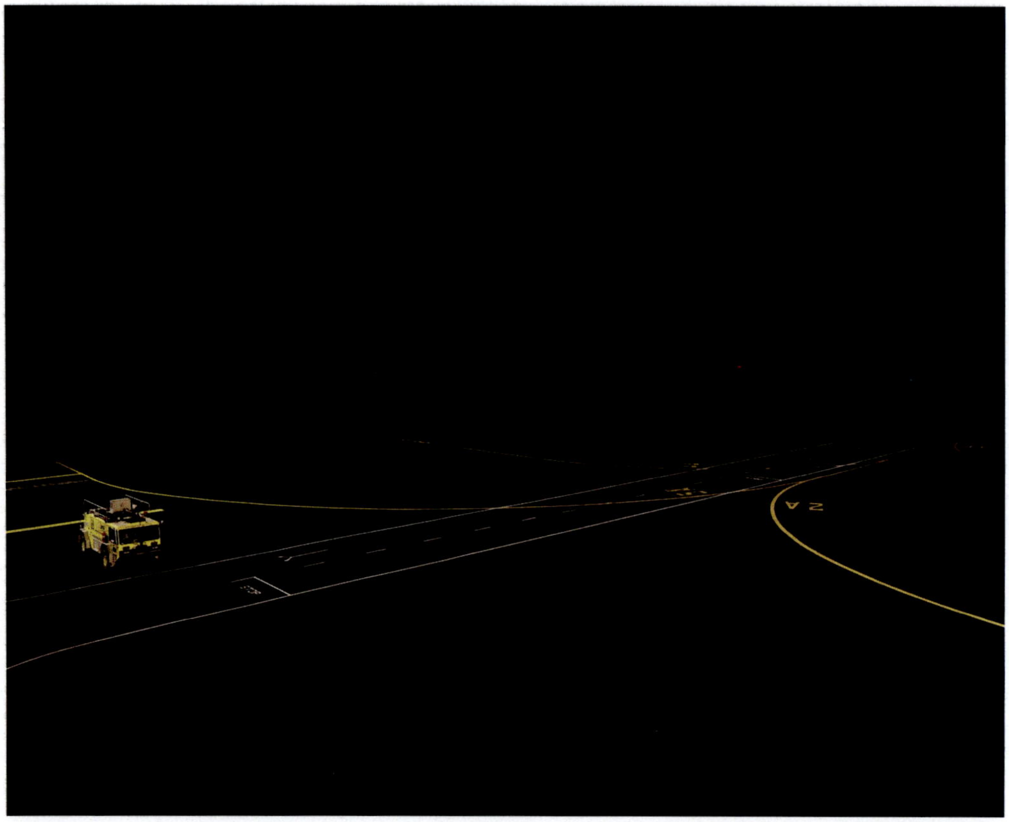

Fig. 3.14

Fig. 3.14
EDGAR MARTINS
Untitled (Santa Maria—55 minute exp.)* from the series *When Light Casts No Shadows, 2008
The black of the runway tarmac in Edgar Martins's series contrasts vividly with the bright markings that delineate these sites as airports. Martins's photographic technique—incorporating long exposures with carefully controlled flash and other artificial lighting—leads to disorienting imagery whereby the details seem to emerge from a blank page like a brass rubbing. Although the architecture and runways are generic, some of these airports have relevance to the history of trans-Atlantic aviation as stop-off points for passengers and refueling. This reminds us that airports function as points for people in transit and, like Dan Holdsworth's shopping mall, are somewhere we might describe as "non-places" (see p. 175).

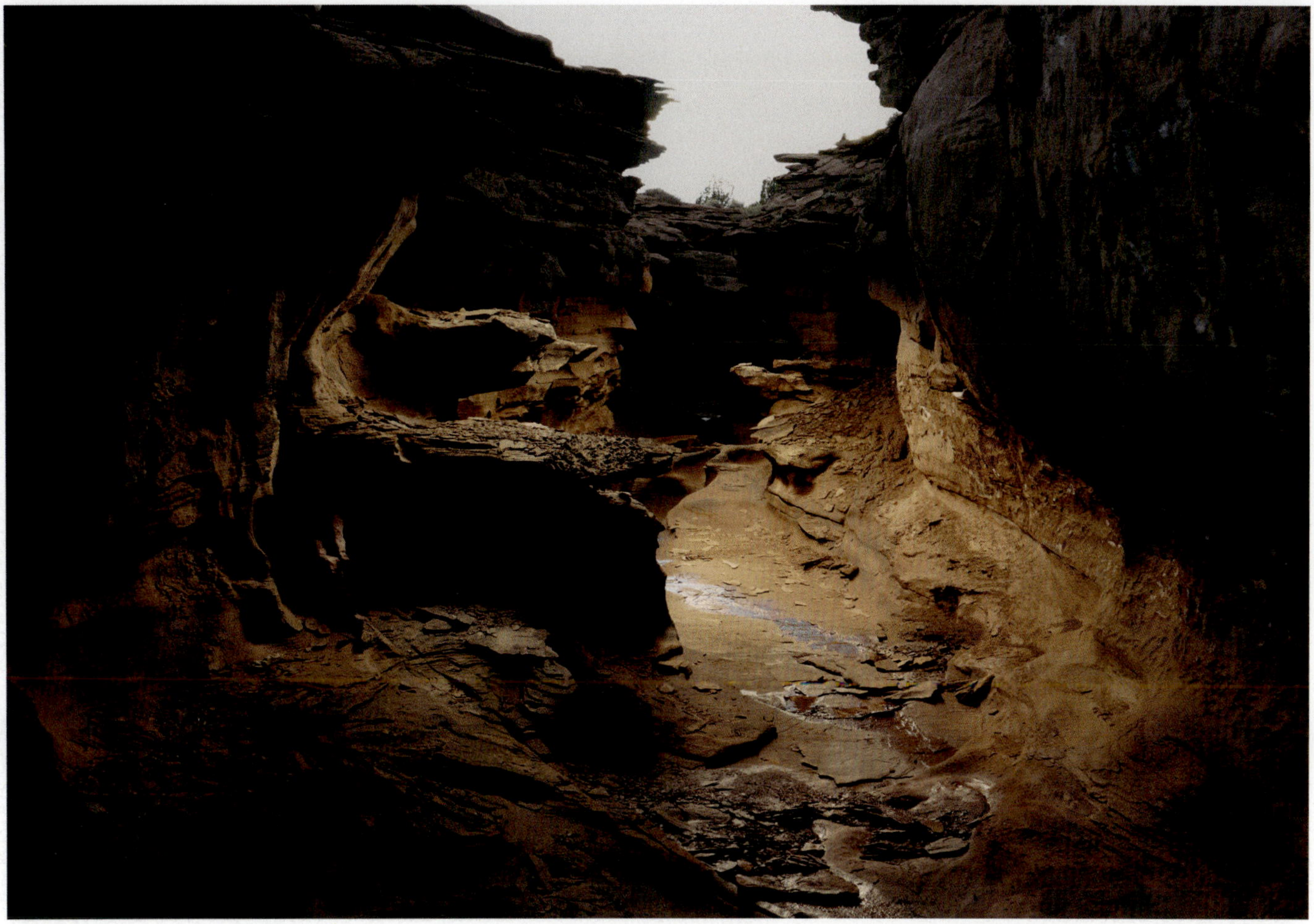

Fig. 3.15

Fig. 3.15
TIM SIMMONS
Capitol Reef #2, 2010
Tim Simmons uses extensive artificial lighting to striking effect in the landscape at night. His photographs have a distinctly nonphotographic look, recalling aesthetics of popular culture, specifically computer-generated cinematic imagery and video games.

manage the appearance of close-up and wider views of a variety of terrains. As a result of these extensive production values, his photographs have a distinctive and peculiar aesthetic. By using artificial light to mimic the effects of moonlight, or perhaps how our eyes might attempt to render the view when accustomed to the dark, Simmons's pictures lose their photographic quality. They assume the appearance of something else, perhaps a still from a video game—ironically, a medium that tends to strive toward creating photorealistic imagery. This deliberate disorientation, and the *otherworldly* qualities that Simmons's landscapes assume, prompts the viewer to question the veracity of the representation: Where are the lights coming from? Is it an image formed by a camera or something computer generated? This strategy proposes further-reaching questions around what constitutes a *real* image of *nature* and the complexities of these two concepts.

Fig. 3.16
Michael Wolf
Interface 9* from *Paris Street View
Michael Wolf's collections, which are take from Google Streetview, comment on this now ubiquitous digital platform as a kind of universal interface between users and their environment. The appropriation of Google Streetview images by practitioners has been seen as an alternative response to traditional street photography. Recent legislative changes in particular countries, as well as a heightened suspicion of the camera in certain public spaces more generally, have brought challenges to those wishing to photograph within the metropolis. The hijacking of Streetview's surveying, all-pervading eye highlights the absurdity of the notion of the documentary street photographer as a legitimate source of suspicion.

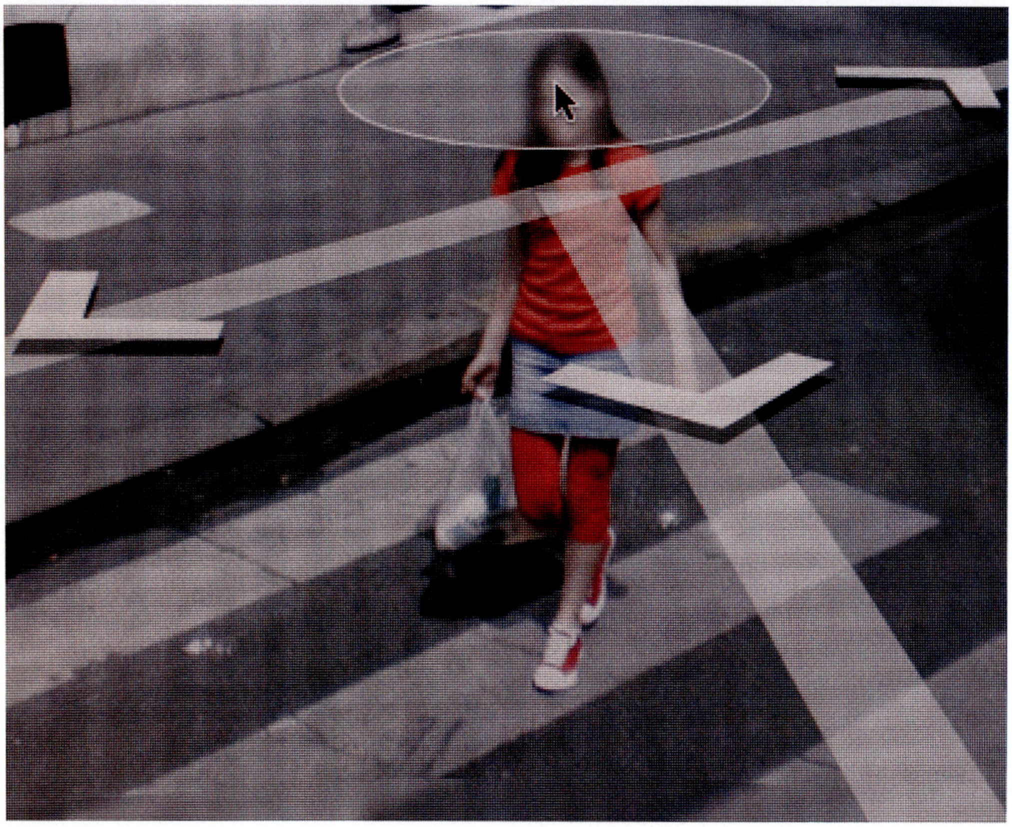

Fig. 3.16

ART BY ALGORITHM

Advances in technology continue to provide us with new and exciting ways to visualize our immediate surroundings as well as more distant places. Numerous institutions, including those attached to all areas of science, engineering, the movie industry, and the military, are at the forefront of digital imaging. However, many of these advances eventually filter through to our everyday lives. Technology is important to how we think about landscape because it alters our perception of our environment. Google Earth (2005) and Streetview (2007) have adjusted our sense of the scale of the world because we have images of *everywhere* at our fingertips. Google has faced criticism for what has been felt by some as the invasiveness of their epic Streetview project. Several practitioners, including Mishka Henna, Jon Rafeman, and Michael Wolf, have engaged with the platform and the vast quantities of imagery as the raw material of their work. At first glance, the images from Henna's *No Man's Land* (2011), which are free of the decoration associated with the software (i.e., navigation tools, labels, and watermarking), look like fairly straightforward documentary photographs. By comparison, Michael Wolf's images reveal their origins much more conspicuously and perhaps less self-consciously. His pictures are clearly photographs of his computer monitor and confirm an idea of the photographer painstakingly trawling through digital mile after digital mile, capturing views for his various collections.

Since the 1990s, Joan Fontcuberta has been keen to experiment with the creative possibilities of Adobe Photoshop as well as other new technologies as they have emerged. Before that, however, Fontcuberta's practice also was preoccupied with fabricating organic objects within photographic images. The photograph and its relation to reality continue to be a point of fascination for the artist, as well as

Fig. 3.17
DAN HOLDSWORTH
Yosemite, Plan View, 2012* from the series *Transmission: New Remote Earth Views

Although sparse of pictorial information, Dan Holdsworth's images are recognizable as aerial views. The chiaroscuro defining the contours and topographic features resembles the relief of some distant territory: the monotonous grays of the surface of our moon or perhaps an image captured from a satellite exploring deep in the solar system. They depict, however, rather more familiar places—at least in relation to photographic history. Holdsworth's photographs reveal an alternative perspective of the well-photographed American West as first visualized by the photographers of the U.S. Geological Surveys (see p. 21). Aligning himself to the collaborative spirit of those expeditions, to complete this series, Holdsworth worked with geomorphologists, who make use of satellite imagery to measure land and climate change.[15] In these minimal canvases, made possible by radar scanning technology, we see a terrain completely devoid of traces of mankind. Although different in visual appearance, we are confronted with the kind of untouched, primordial landscape akin to the representations of those early expeditionaries.

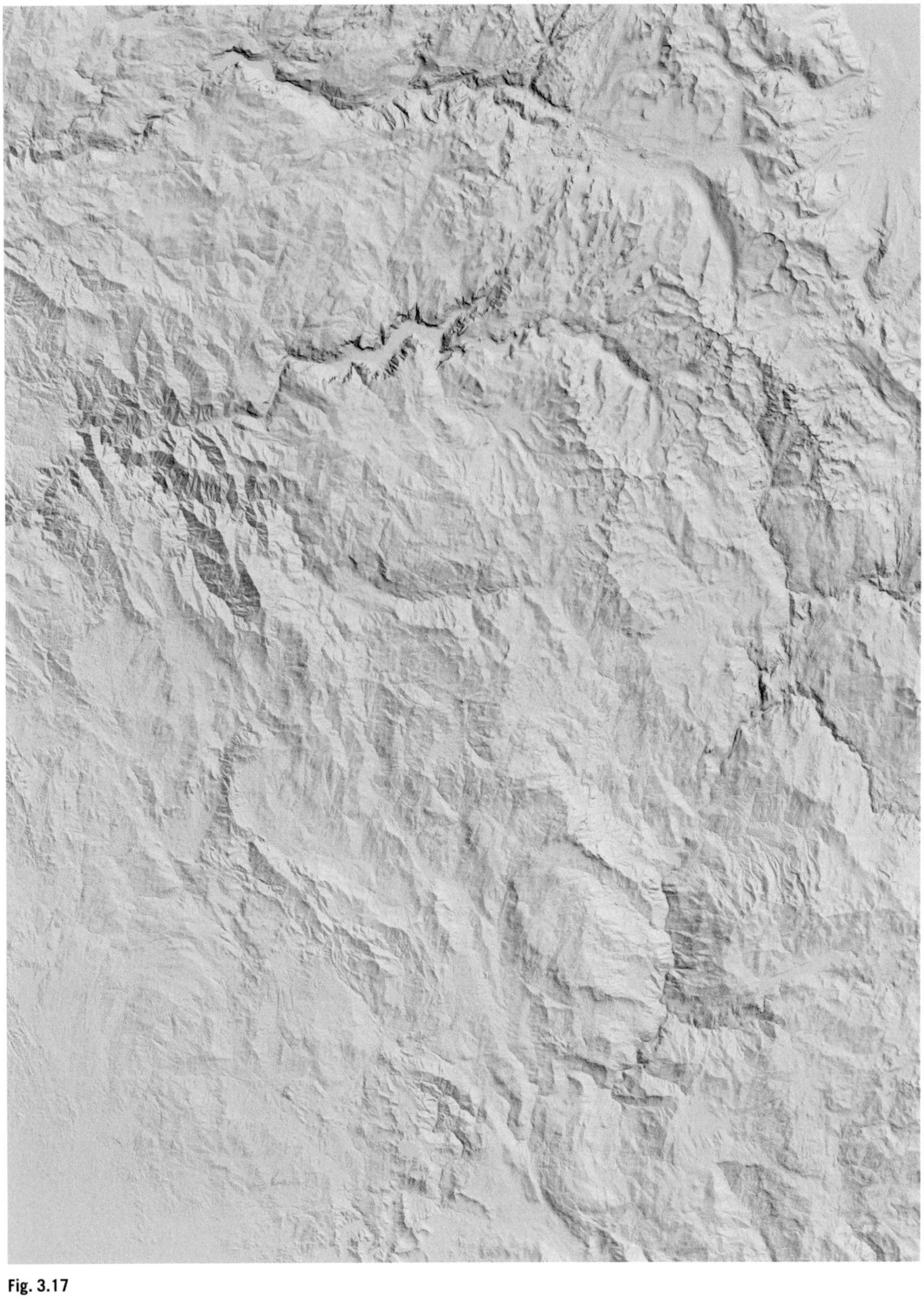

Fig. 3.17

tinkering with the possibilities of new pieces of software and processes. His series *Orogenesis* was made with three-dimensional landscape-simulation software, which interprets maps and topographical data into photorealistic images. As well as having practical applications in industry, programs like Terragen have a strong following of enthusiasts who share their compositions on forums in the same way that amateur photographers use more developed platforms like Flickr. Many users of these forums are of course digital technicians who use the software professionally, such as in film and television. However, a comparison can be made here to other popular virtual platforms, such as Second Life (2003), that allow users to create their own digital avatar and engineer environments to play in.

Terragen allows the finer topographical details of compositions, including things like the simulation of the weather and atmospheric effects, to be adjusted manually—although these digital, three-dimensional worlds generally begin from some sort of cartographic binary data. For his series, Fontcuberta fed the software misinformation in the form of digitized versions of some of the most famous examples from the history of landscape painting. Typical of the artist's irreverence, he also used photographs of parts of his own body as the source code for his pictures, so that rather than forming an image from a different format of information, the software was forced to *reinterpret* another image. The artist has compared this strategy to the intertextuality of postmodernism, whereby rather than creative works from the past being eschewed, they are re-examined and interrogated.[16] Unlike the majority of the best-known landscape paintings, however, Fontcuberta's landscapes are devoid of other people. We are presented with truly untouched locations that are as infinite as the virtual world in which they were

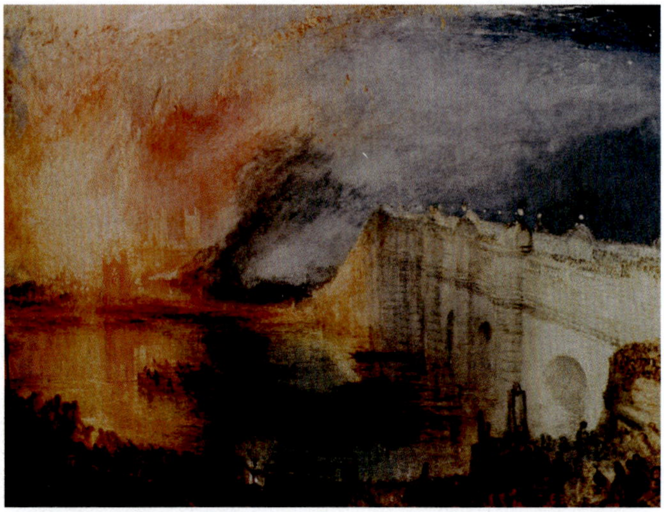

Orogenesis: Turner 2003
Joseph Mallord William Turner
***The Burning of the Houses of Lords and Commons, 16th October 1834*, 1835**
Oil on Canvas
Philadelphia Museum of Art

Fig. 3.18.i

Fig. 3.18.i–3.18.ii
JOAN FONTCUBERTA
Turner, 2003* from the series *Orogenesis
Fontcuberta's imaginary landscapes are a computer's interpretations of celebrated masterpieces of landscape painting. Fontcuberta often incorporates software and applications into his practice, irreverently perverting their intended function.

cast. There are, of course, comparisons here to Burke's assertions about vastness and the sublime (see p. 70). Ilkka Halso also works with three-dimensional design software to produce his unlikely imagery. Halso combines straight photographs with structures and textures rendered with computer-aided design applications to produce his futuristic, dystopian visions. Far from Fontcuberta's primordial, untouched landscapes, Halso's visions simultaneously describe the landscape both as something under the threat of extinction and a sort of kitsch theme park. The "photographs" in Halso's *Museum of Nature* (Fig. 3.1) are entirely fabricated—the artist's pastiche of the efforts of a heroic conservationist.

Fig. 3.18.ii

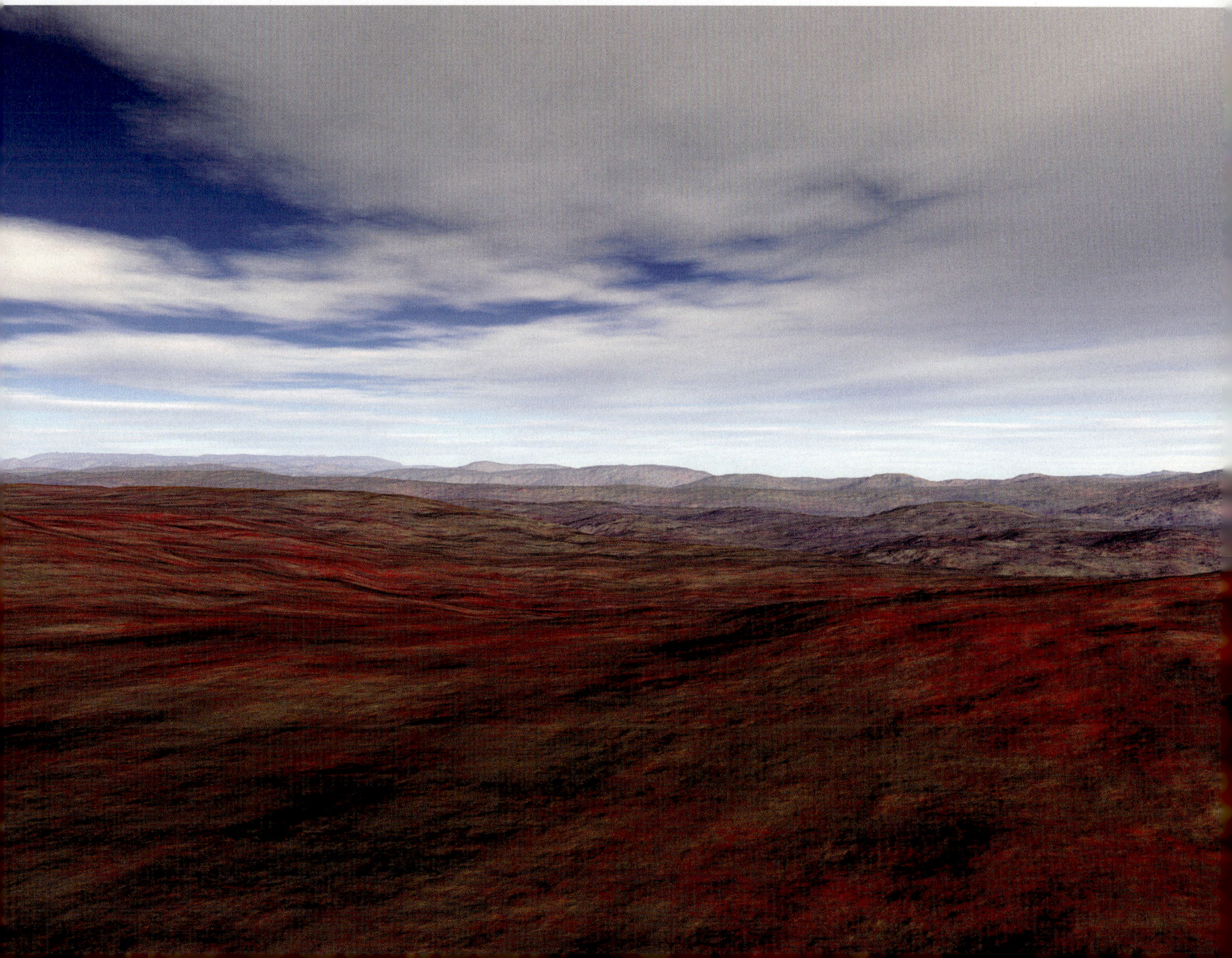

"Pictorialism" is only an exaggeration of what the Photograph thinks of itself. ROLAND BARTHES[17]

PICTORIALISM VERSUS "STRAIGHT" PHOTOGRAPHY

The extent to which a negative or a digital file should be adjusted has always been contentious. At what point does aesthetic fine-tuning of a photograph—such as control over exposure, cropping, dodging, and burning—become a *manipulation* of the image? Some of the earliest experimental photographers were practicing painters who wanted to explore the creative and artistic possibilities of the photographic process. Oscar Rejlander, for instance, was inspired by allegorical and history painting of the period and completed his epic photomontage *The Two Ways of Life* (1857) from thirty separate negatives in his studio over the course of several weeks.

What made Rejlander's approach stand out was that he had aligned his photography with allegorical painting. At the time, in an attempt to elevate photography to the status of the "high arts" of painting and sculpture, photographers were more likely to be found simulating *the look* of paint on canvas and related media. To achieve these effects, photographers would employ soft focus and use poor-quality optics. Instead of spreading photosensitive emulsions across papers and negatives as clinically as possible, these photographers would use brushes, deliberately leaving imperfections across the surface of the final image. These measures were a concerted effort to obfuscate the realism of the photograph and disguise the method of production. The conspicuous brushstrokes were a very blunt declaration that the picture was not the sole product of a mechanical process but instead, a *handmade*, individual expression. The extent to which the image was manipulated was seen to be central to a picture's artistic credentials.

This approach was known as "pictorialism" and was one of the greatest follies in the history of photography. In the 1930s, Ansel Adams described pictorialism as "superficial" and "shallow" in its attempt to mimic the appearance of other art forms.[18] However, pictorialism was remarkably popular and was the dominant style among photographic salons across the world. Attitudes began to change, however, and in 1912 an exhibition in New York at the 291 gallery, which was curated by Alfred Stieglitz (1864–1946), marked a dramatic rethinking of the aesthetics of "art" photography. Stieglitz and his contemporaries, including Edward Steichen (1879–1973) and Clarence White (1871–1925), believed that rather than masking the photographic qualities behind darkroom effects or attempt to emulate the look of other art forms, practitioners should embrace the intrinsic qualities of photography that delineated it from other expressive media. Instead of dainty, fuzzy pictures, they advocated sharply focused images and printed negatives to render as much detail and tonal clarity as possible. Stieglitz's *The Steerage* (Fig. 3.20) typifies this approach, which was defined as "straight" photography. It is necessary to clarify that these kinds of unembellished photographs were, of course, circulating

Fig. 3.19
ALFRED MASKELL
Landscape, 1898
Maskell's *Landscape* is a typical example of late-nineteenth-century pictorialist photography. In an effort to have their pictures accepted as artistic works, pictorialists deliberately degraded the optical quality of their photographs to make them look less like photographs and more like drawings and paintings. Alternative processes (i.e., those that were not practiced commercially) were also employed to further distance creative photography from other applications and to demonstrate the importance of darkroom skills within the artistry of the process.

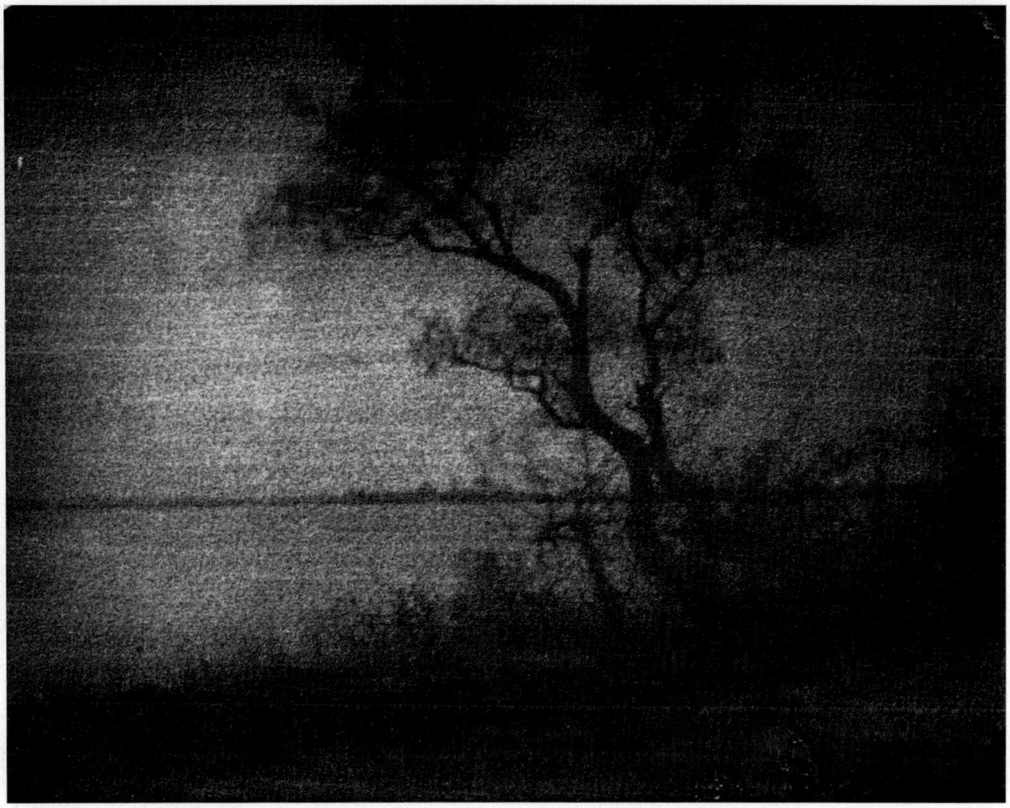

Fig. 3.19

in abundance during the early twentieth century; however, they were not to be found in serious art institutions. In addition to new photography, at the 291 Stieglitz also exhibited work by modern artists, including Rodin, Matisse, Cézanne, and Picasso, which provides a sense of the progressive company in which this kind of photography was placed.

The rejection of pictorialism by Stieglitz and his peers has endured, cemented by the contribution of Group *f*/64 on the opposite coast, which included Imogen Cunningham (1883–1976), Edward Weston (1886–1958), and Ansel Adams. As the name implies, sharply focused subjects throughout the image was an aesthetic priority for the group. A celebration of form, both natural and man-made, was common to their interests in terms of subject matter. Adams's dramatic views of Yosemite, as well as the other national parks that he photographed in the 1930s and 1940s, overshadow Group *f*/64. These majestic scenes continue to sell calendars and coffee-table books, ensuring that the image of an American West sublime endures.

The idea of previsualization of the final print at the time of capture was also a central component to Adams's creative philosophy (see p. 44). Working on the final print in the darkroom was important to Adams's artistic process, although meticulous attention to framing, exposure, and filtration at the moment of capture was arguably a greater priority. Adams's commitment to the education of landscape photography is admirable, and his eagerness to share his technical expertise can be seen in his numerous publications.[19] Perhaps though, in the drive to promote the craft of landscape photography that this formalist approach to photographic practice typifies, there is a danger of overlooking the importance of a more personal, individual connection to place, even if this comes at the cost of technical refinement.

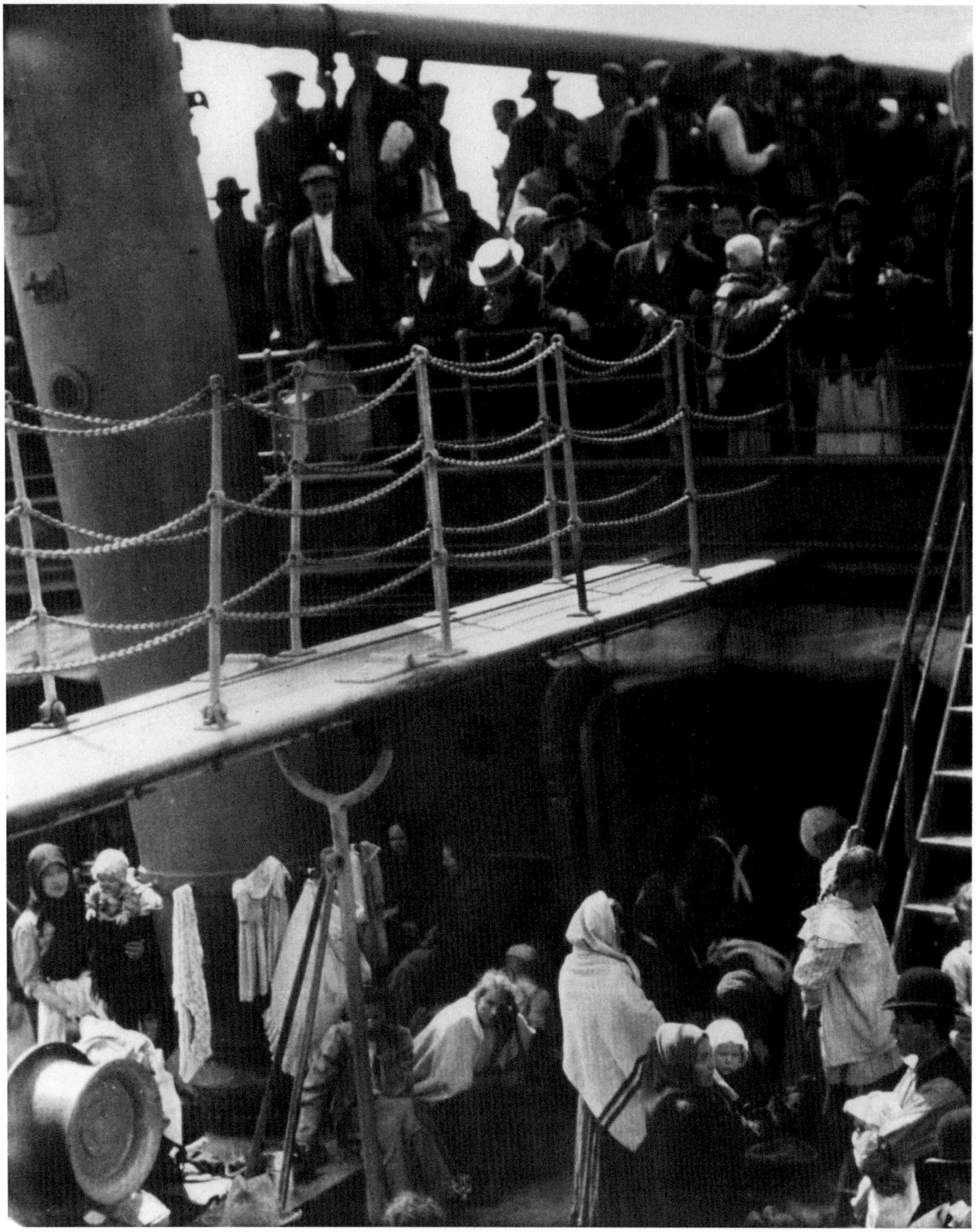

Fig. 3.20

Fig. 3.20
ALFRED STIEGLITZ
The Steerage, 1907

"A round straw hat, the funnel leaning left, the stairway leaning right, the white drawbridge with its railings made by circular chains, white suspenders crossing the back of a man in the steerage below, round shapes of iron machinery, a mast cutting into the sky, making a triangular shape. . . . I saw a picture of shapes, and underlying that the feeling I had about life." [20] Alfred Stieglitz describes his motivation for capturing a photograph that marked a turning point in the aesthetics of early-twentieth-century art photography. The scene depicted was taken aboard the *Kaiser Wilhelm II*, from the first-class deck, looking down onto the passengers traveling on the steerage deck, which offered appalling traveling conditions. The steerage passengers are believed to have been refused entry to the United States and are on their way back to Europe.

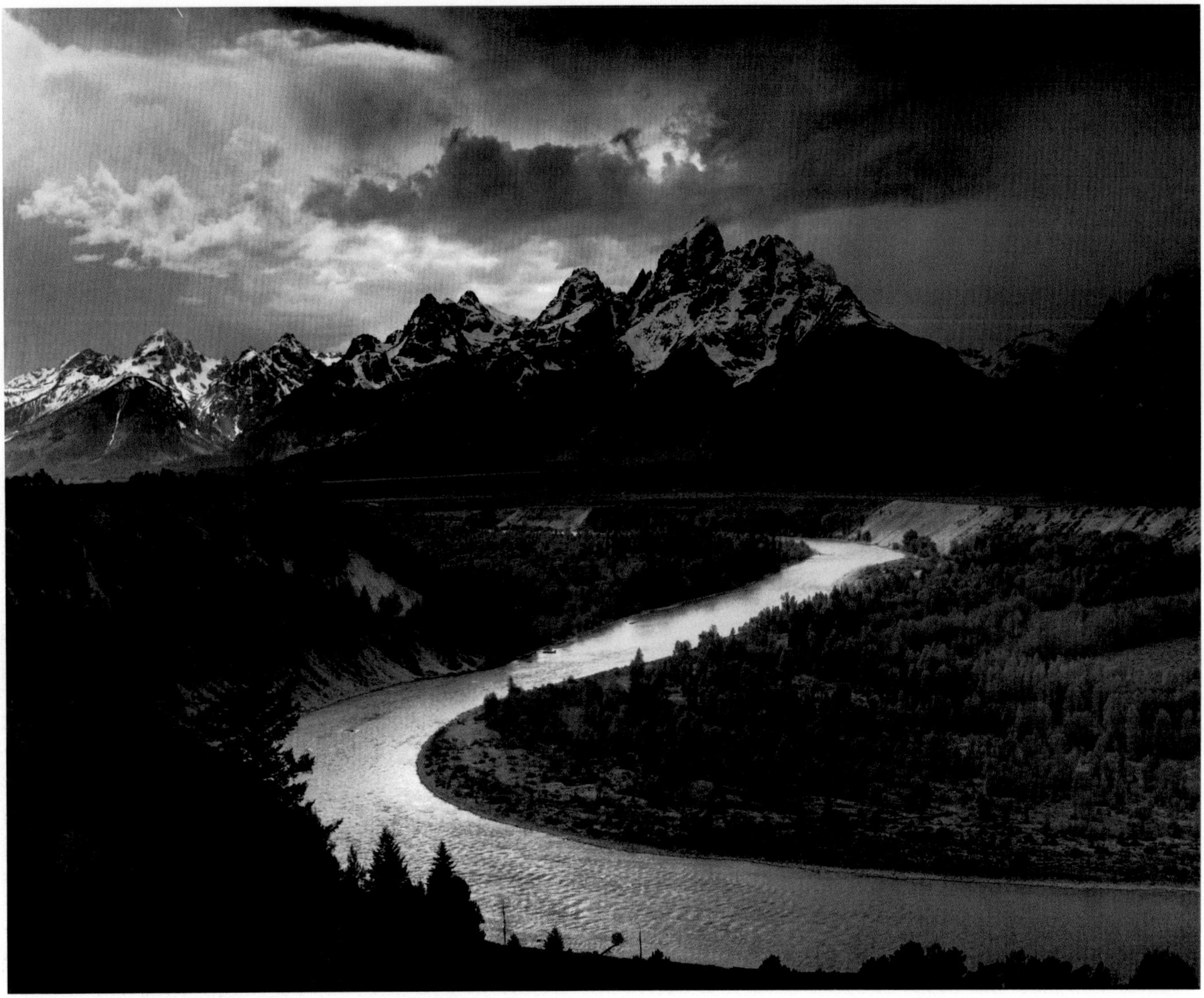

Fig. 3.21

Fig. 3.21
ANSEL ADAMS
The Tetons and the Snake River, Grand Teton National Park, Wyoming, 1942
Ansel Adams's views of U.S. National Parks are some of the most celebrated imagery in the history of landscape photography. *The Tetons and the Snake River* is typical of Adams's ostentatious imagery, combining epic topography with evocative lighting and weather conditions, reminiscent of romantic painting from the previous century. Adams was a staunch environmental activist, particularly around Yosemite, and his efforts have been associated with the expansion of the U.S. National Park system.

1 Artist's statement, http://ilkka.halso.net.

2 This was the title of Fox Talbot's book of photogenic drawings, the first volume of which was published in 1844.

3 Mark Bollan, "The Decoy," in Richard Page, *What We Already Know* (Cardiff: ffotogallery, 2007), 10.

4 Because of the reversal process in black-and-white analog printing, overexposure—or increased density—of an area of a negative will result in underexposure—or less density—in the final print.

5 Pieter Hugo's project *There's a Place in Hell for Me and My Friends* (2012) demonstrates a particularly thought-provoking use of selective color mixing. In these portraits, the photographer reduces particular color levels, showing faces that are rough and uneven in tone: the antithesis of digital retouching. The portraits can also be taken as a comment on racial issues in South Africa, illustrating that none of us are simply black or white, but we are all *colored*.

6 Stephen Bull, "Digital Photography Has Never Looked So Analogue: Retro Camera Apps, Nostalgia, and the Hauntological Photograph," in *Photoworks*, Spring/Summer 2012: 24–25.

7 Ibid.

8 Benjamin Lowey, Damon Winter, and Tim Hetherington are professional photographers who put down their digital SLRs and reached for their iPhones in conflict zones for the intimate images that could be captured as well as the practical benefits of disseminating image files in the field.

9 See http://stcuthbertsfinaljourney.com.

10 One of the most influential images of the twentieth century, *Earthrise* (Fig. 4.10), which was taken aboard *Apollo 8* by William Anders, was taken in a sequence of bracketed exposures.

11 This might mean that the exposure time needs to be considerably longer than the slowest shutter speed of your camera. In this instance, you will need to set the shutter speed to "bulb" and control the length of exposure manually using a shutter release cable and a stopwatch. To calculate a correct exposure time, first increase the ISO and set the aperture to its widest setting. When you have taken a satisfactory image, decrease the ISO and stop down the lens, extending the exposure time by the total number of stops.

12 Diego Mormorio, "Photographs of the Nightfall," in Rafaella Mariniello, *Napoli veduta immaginaria* (Milan: Motto edizioni, 2001).

13 Mormorio, "Photographs."

14 Geoff Dyer, "Edgar I Nothing Am," in Edgar Martins, *The Time Machine* (Bedford: The Moth House, 2011).

15 Emma Lewis, "Dan Holdsworth's *Transmission: New Remote Earth Views*." See http://www.danholdsworth.com/information/45/.

16 Interview with Marc Feustel (02/12/10). See www.eyecurious.com/interview-joan-fontcuberta-landscapes-without-memory/.

17 Roland Barthes, *Camera Lucida* (London: Jonathan Cape, 1982), 31.

18 Ansel Adams, "The New Photography," in *Modern Photography, 1934–35,* ed. Geoffrey J. Holme (New York: The Studio, 1935), 13.

19 See for instance: Ansel Adams, *Examples: The Making of 40 Photographs* (Boston: Little, Brown & Co., 1983).

20 Alfred Stieglitz in Clarke, *The Photograph* (Oxford: Oxford University Press, 1997), 169.

ASSIGNMENT 3
ALTERNATIVE PERSPECTIVES

PROJECT Choose a location or a view that interests you. Don't worry if you can't explain *why* you are drawn to it at this point. Hopefully this exercise will help you to understand why it intrigues you.

Photograph the location or view using as many of the techniques as you can that have been discussed so far. Experiment with exposure, white balance, and artificial lighting. Try working at different times of the day and in different weather conditions. In postproduction, try out different filters, effects, and processing methods. Save at least six different images, which might be a combination of different pictures and images processed in different ways. They may be subtly or more dramatically different.

Then write a brief evaluation of each picture, explaining how that particular one differs in appearance—and mood—to the others. Does one of these images begin to answer the question of why you chose to photograph this location? If you had a clear idea of why the location interested you, identify which photographs or technique you think most effectively communicates your personal point of view.

Show your work to your peers or post it on your blog or Flickr account, along with your written introduction, and invite comments.

RESEARCH AND DISCUSSION Consider the following questions and write down your thoughts in your reflective learning journal or on your blog. Then discuss with peers in a group or use the questions to start a thread on an online forum.

- Do you think the stylistic enhancement of an image gets in the way of communicating the photographer's message?
- What technical adjustments (either digitally or working with analog) can be applied to a photograph before it could be described as manipulated?
- What do you think are the unique characteristics that set photography apart from other media? Is it important for these qualities to be identifiable in your photographs?

Chapter 4
LANDSCAPE AND POWER

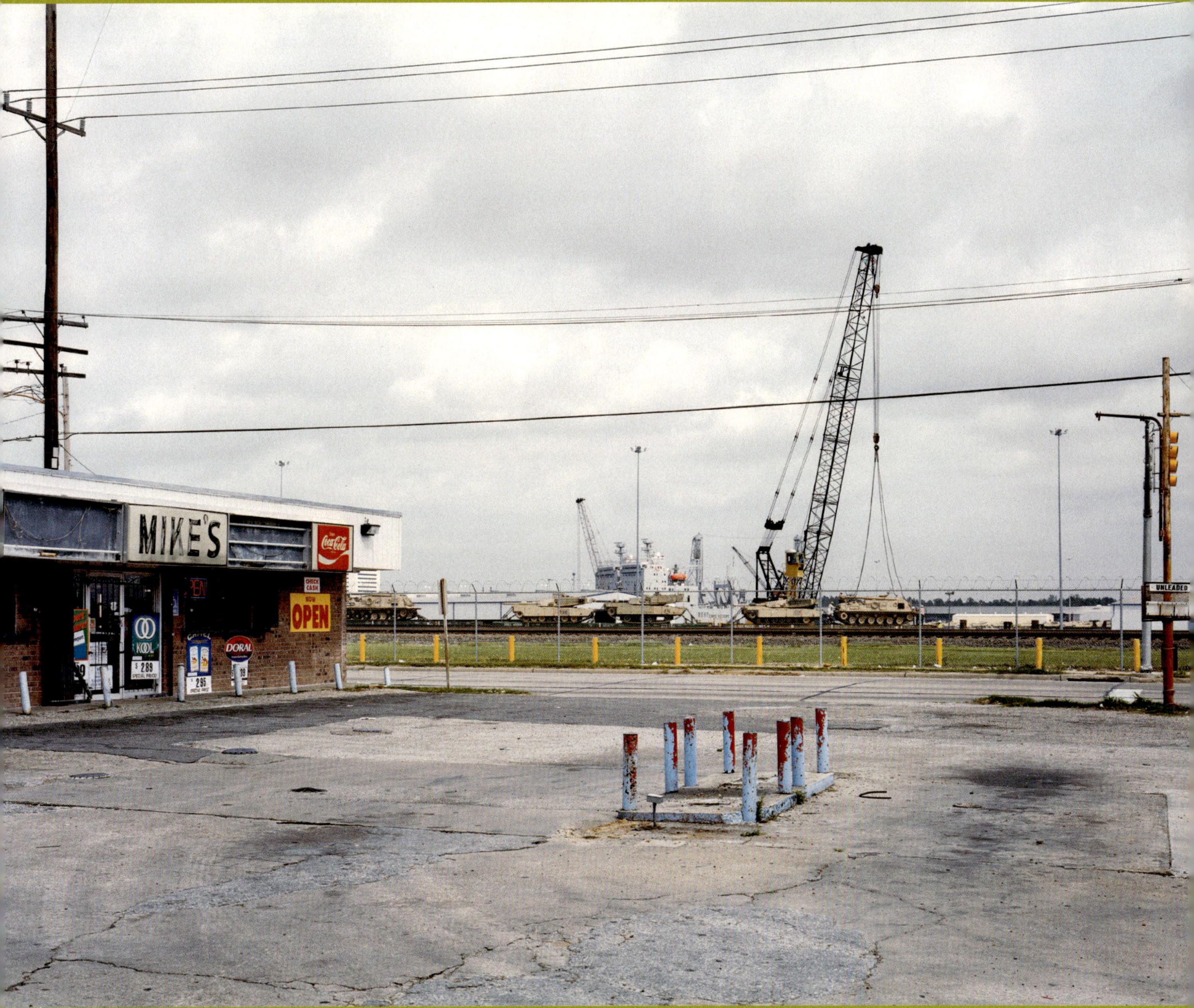

Fig. 4.1

Fig. 4.1
MITCH EPSTEIN
***Port of Beaumont, Texas*, 2006**
from *American Power*

Since land is invariably somebody's possession, landscape is inextricable from notions of ownership. For instance, many early landscape paintings were commissioned by wealthy merchants and aristocrats to show off their country estates as well as properties overseas. Thomas Gainsborough (1727–1788) was famous for painting his wealthy sitters *outside* of their plush country houses, using their estates as backdrops to reference their wealth and elite social status. The photographic collections from the U.S. Geological Surveys might be seen as a way of taking ownership of the image of the country—a symbolic means of extricating the land from Native American communities. The creation of national parks has been seen as a democratic gesture, placing ownership and stewardship of the exceptional parts of the country with *the people* and their successors. However, some have been critical of the true accessibility of such places to marginalized groups and individuals, suggesting that, far from the charitable spirit in which the parks were imagined, imagery of them widens the gulf between those who can afford to visit them and those who cannot.[1] This chapter explores power as the subject matter of landscape pictures and the politics that lie behind the making and the consumption of landscape views. We shall explore how landscape pictures have been employed in the pursuit of national unity and how such imagery can be equally divisive. During this discussion, we will look at certain historical and social narratives that are important, to shed light on the ideas and meaning of the works mentioned. This discussion should serve as a reminder of the importance of learning about your subject matter, not just focusing on innovative ways of photographing it.

Fig. 4.2
PHILIP JAMES DE LOUTHERBOURG
Coalbrookdale by Night, 1801
On casual inspection, de Loutherbourg's striking depiction of ironworks in Shropshire could be mistaken as a scene of devastation from the Napoleonic Wars, the horse-drawn carts taking refugees with whatever possessions they can carry and fleeing from the inferno, which makes the outline of the cottages to the center left of the canvas shimmer from its scorching heat. The painting has become a symbol of the industrial revolution and alludes to how it dramatically affected the British countryside around the turn of the nineteenth century. Industrialization prompted concerns over its negative impact upon the landscape, and this contributed to the popularity of the romantic movement, to which the picturesque belongs. Although the subject matter is very different from his other landscapes, the painting is typical of de Loutherbourg's preoccupation with the sublime.

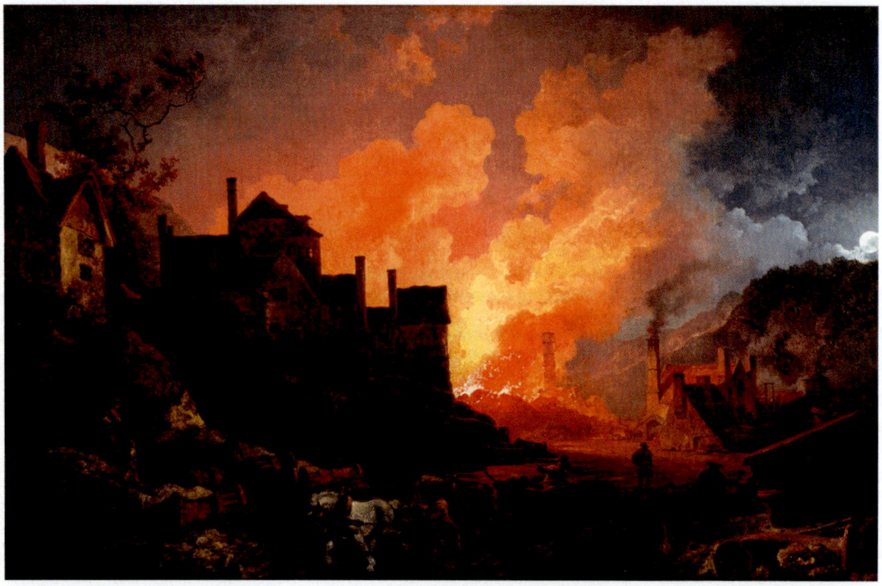

Fig. 4.2

THE INDUSTRIAL SUBLIME

In recent years, the calls to re-evaluate our energy needs and the impact of energy production upon our ecosystems have become familiar subjects within landscape photography. On initial inspection, Mitch Epstein's project *American Power* (2003–2009) is typical of this. Throughout the series, Epstein captures the epic infrastructure of coal-fueled power plants, oil fields and refineries, hydroelectric facilities, nuclear power stations, and other means of energy generation. The project takes this a step further and rather than simply being a survey of energy production, explores power in a more abstract sense. His photographs depict infrastructure in the context of both the immediate domestic landscape—how people cohabit alongside these new kinds of man-made topography—and the political implications. *American Power* makes an implicit connection between U.S. energy security and the perception of security more generally, as well as tacit connections to recent foreign policy. In *Port of Beaumont, Texas* (Fig. 4.1), desert-camouflaged tanks are off-loaded from flat trucks bound for—or perhaps returning from—deployment in the Persian Gulf. In the foreground of the photograph, the forecourt of Mike's Gas Station looks distinctly empty, implying a connection between U.S. foreign policy and the country's reliance upon oil.

American Power demonstrates one approach to how landscape can be used as a vehicle to assert a political or ideological voice. The work also shows how it is possible to turn the camera on subjects close to home yet reference narratives taking place many miles away. The work also fits into a tradition of industrial landscape, which can be traced back to the industrial revolution itself.

Coalbrookdale, which lies next to the River Severn in England, was a popular point on the picturesque circuit in the late seventeenth century (see p. 64). The melodrama of Philip James de Loutherbourg's painting of the ironworks in Shropshire might go some way toward suggesting what an arresting—perhaps even sublime—sight this must have offered travelers in search of more pleasant and genteel views of the countryside. De Loutherbourg's image evokes the same kind of terror and awe as does his *Avalanche* painting (Fig. 2.11), but instead of plumes of white snow, it is fire and smoke that fill the canvas—the products of the open coke hearths at the Bedlam Furnaces, which cast many components of the industrial revolution. Exactly as a truly sublime representation should, the painting is a cautionary message about the uncontrollable force within the frame while at the same time inducing a kind of reckless, hedonistic euphoria. It has become an iconic expression of the sudden impact of industrialization on the English countryside. It is also one of the earliest examples of what could be described as an "industrial landscape." Although many continue to insist upon a plethora of prefixes to pin on various types of landscapes, this kind of separation is essentially unhelpful.[2]

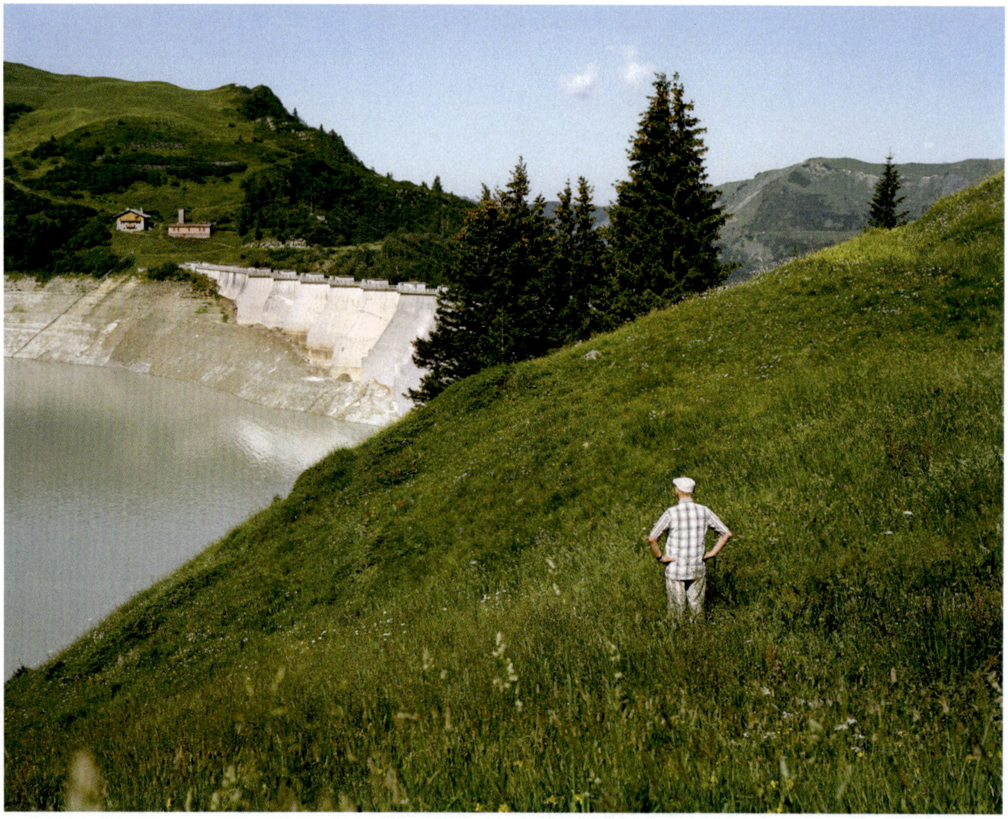

Fig. 4.3

Fig. 4.3
CÉLINE CLANET
Nino Manfiotto, workman at La Girotte dam from 1942 to 1949* from the series *Des Barrages et des homes en Savoie
Clanet's series surveys hydroelectric infrastructure around the French Alps, which exploits the natural topography and resources to generate energy. Her pictures show the vastness of the structures, which at times seem to be squeezed awkwardly between valleys, while at others they sit alongside the land more comfortably. Clanet photographed several people who had a working relationship with the structures, either as formal portraits or almost anecdotally within the composition. The figures appear contemplative, as if recalling their past, rather than heroic *Rückenfiguren* (see Fig. 2.10). They also serve an almost symbolic function, suggesting a more intimate, individual perspective on these mighty structures that disarms their prowess.

De Loutherbourg's two canvases propose that representations of man-altered spaces do not belong within a discourse separate from images of the untouched or unspoiled environment, since although they are vastly different in terms of subject matter, the nature of the emotional response they elicit and their visual similarities are synonymous.

It is perhaps within the recent and numerous depictions of the interaction between industry and the environment in contemporary photography that we can most vividly trace the legacy of the sublime. Mountains are replaced by cooling towers; vast open spaces by dams and bridges; tributaries of water with highways and intersections; and brooding storm clouds with plumes of acrid smoke. The remarkable imagery of Edward Burtynsky, whose 2012 exhibition was titled *The Industrial Sublime*, exemplifies this trend.[3] Where more conventional depictions of the landscape within a sublime tradition might elicit a reflection of the viewer's inconsequentiality in relation to the awesome power of nature, the industrial sublime prompts a realization of the collective force of man and the significance of his unrelenting impact upon nature. The methods of production and presentation

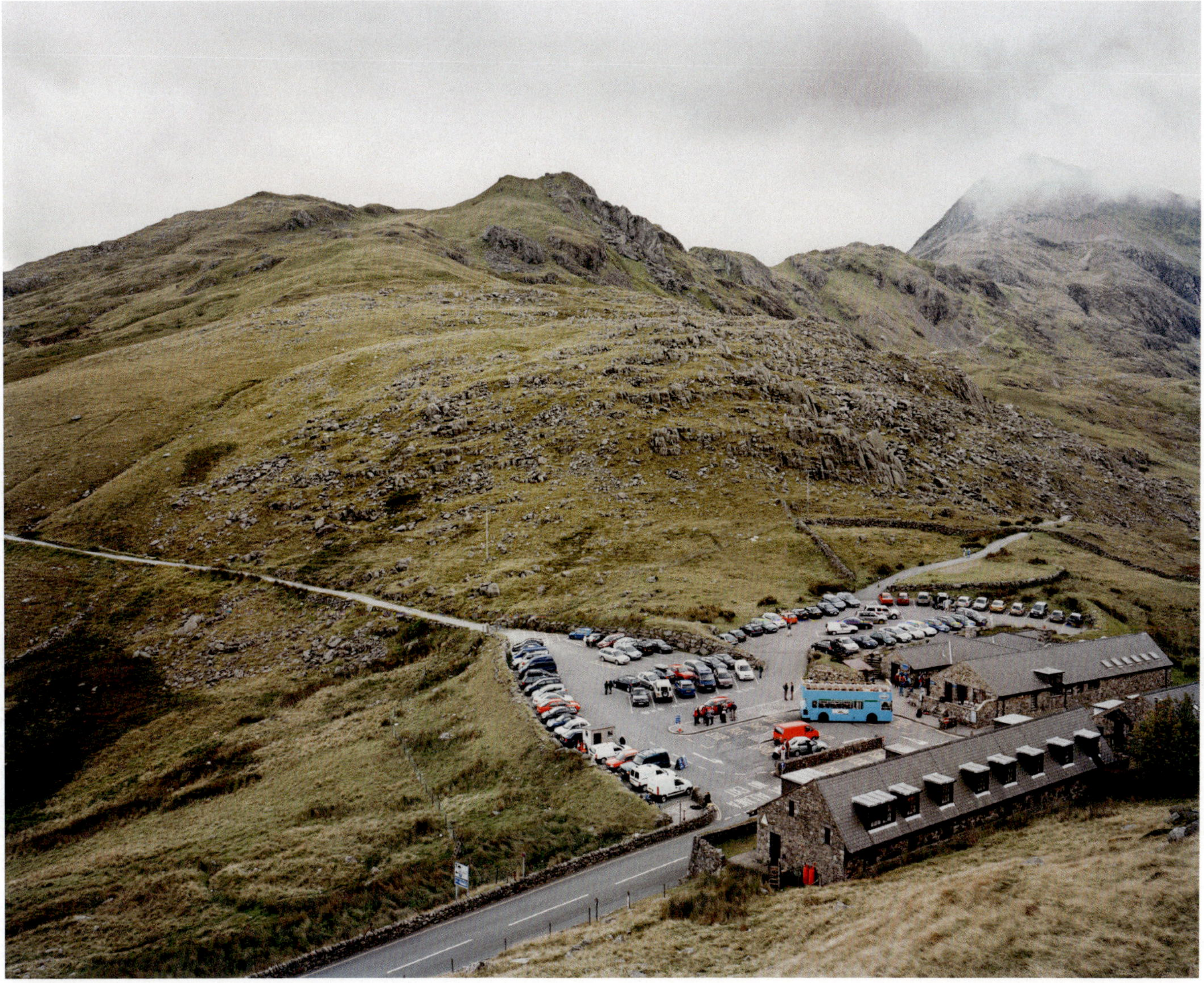

Fig. 4.4

Fig. 4.4
JAMES MORRIS
Llanberis Pass, Snowdonia, Gwynedd
from the series *A Landscape of Wales, 2010*
While the phrase "industrial landscape" might bring to mind images of factories and power stations, it is important to bear in mind that the rural landscape is a significant aspect of a country's economy. Agriculture is the dominant industry throughout the countryside, although tourism plays a hugely significant part in most rural economies. James Morris's photograph taken at Snowdonia National Park in north Wales shows some of the infrastructure associated with outdoor leisure activities (e.g., parking lot, visitors' center, and youth hostel), suggesting an exploitation of the land that may be different from extraction industries but, nevertheless, a viable form of industry.

of Burtynsky's work—as well as that of Mitch Epstein and many others—complement the scale of the subject matter. Often with the assistance of a small team, Burtynsky uses a 10" × 8" camera, which allows for negatives to be enlarged to at least a meter in width without the loss of any detail in the print. As well as elevated shooting positions, Burtynsky has taken aerial views from helicopters to capture the epic proportions of his subjects.

Larger print proportions of exhibition prints are a relatively recent development within the presentation of John Davies's work (see Fig. 1.24), who is celebrated for his documentation of the industrial heritage of the British landscape. It has been suggested that the larger sizes of Davies's prints run the risk of the aesthetic qualities of his photographs overshadowing their documentary value.[4] Some have similarly criticized the likes of Burtynsky for representing pressing environmental concerns within the aesthetic dialect of the sublime, eroding its sociopolitical imperative by reducing the subject to visual spectacle. For instance Joshua Schuster notes that "the sublime is breathtaking at a distance that stays distant and thus involves an uneasy relationship with forms of hands-on environmentalist activism."[5]

It is when there is some kind of human interaction with landscape, when the landscape, having been manufactured or altered, is in the process of being reclaimed by nature . . . that its "inward meaning" is most powerfully felt. GEOFF DYER[6]

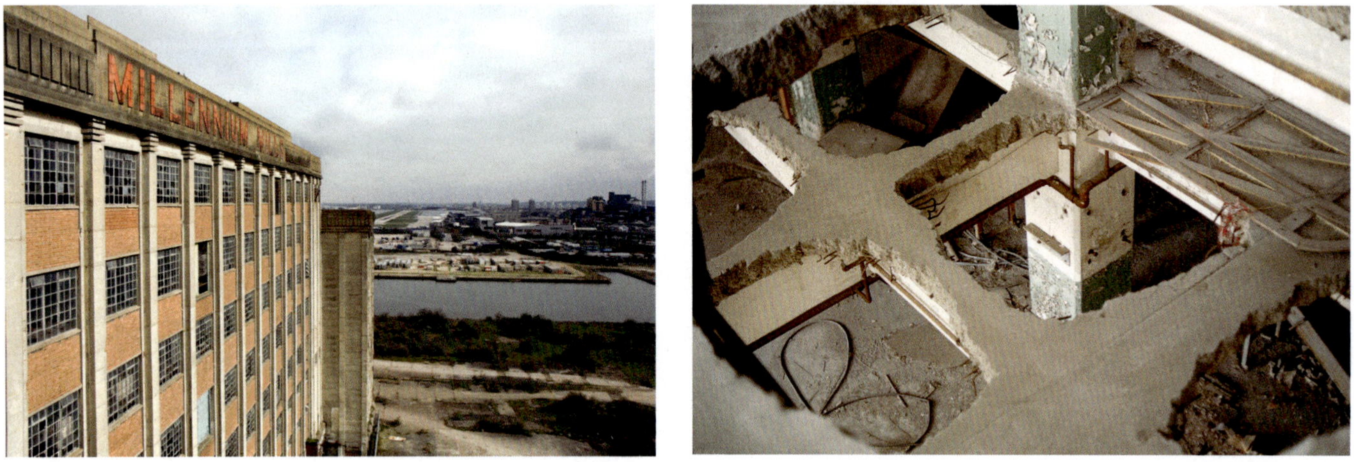

Fig. 4.5

THE PLEASANT STATE OF DECAY[7]

The industrial heritage of Wales comprises a substantial part of James Morris's study titled *A Landscape of Wales*. The legacies of stone quarrying and coal mining are conspicuous across the country, which has undergone substantial economic change in recent decades (see the work of Gawain Barnard, p. 12). The startling visual impact of these heavy extraction industries is articulated with a complementary melodramatic dialect of expansive views, usually taken under somewhat sodden conditions. Despite their bleakness, Morris's vistas are compelling, even when the subject matter is more mundane. The decaying and the dilapidated, and what to the naked eye might be deemed unsightly, seem to have a particular affinity with photography. In the same way that castles ravaged by the English Civil War were pleasing to those in search of picturesque aesthetics a century later, crumbling architecture, infrastructure, and wreckage more generally seem to have a magnetic attraction to both accomplished photographers and those at much earlier points in their practice. It is often precisely the ability to translate an unappealing subject into a satisfying visual expression that is the most alluring aspect of the photographic process.

Photographing spaces, buildings, and infrastructure that have been abandoned or are otherwise off limits has become an increasingly popular pursuit in recent years, so much so that it has its own term, "urban exploration," or the vernacular "urbex." Shooting in these kinds of locations presents technical difficulties that

Fig. 4.5.i–4.5.iv
SUZANNA DAVISON
Millennium Mills
It could be said that urban exploration is a way of escaping the banal. For me, this is true: as you hop over the fence you break the daily routine set out by rules and regulations—it is true playtime. *When exploring the famous Spiller's Millennium Mills it was necessary to duck and dive through a field to avoid the security van, but on various occasions we got caught, at which point the security guard would say, "Next time I catch you I'll call the police." Little did he know that the use of the words "next time" instead of "if" was received as an invitation to play a game—the trespassing game. When you enter these often decrepit buildings, or even when infiltrating sites that are still in use, not only are you filled with adrenalin but you are met by intimate history. Urbex shows me a physical insight into the past of these places like no book could ever provide. Be it the workings of a flour mill or the layout of an old manor house, I become almost like an archaeologist or historian in that I see, feel, and document the past first hand and then share these experiences within the Urbex subculture, giving these lost buildings a life again.*
Suzanna Davison

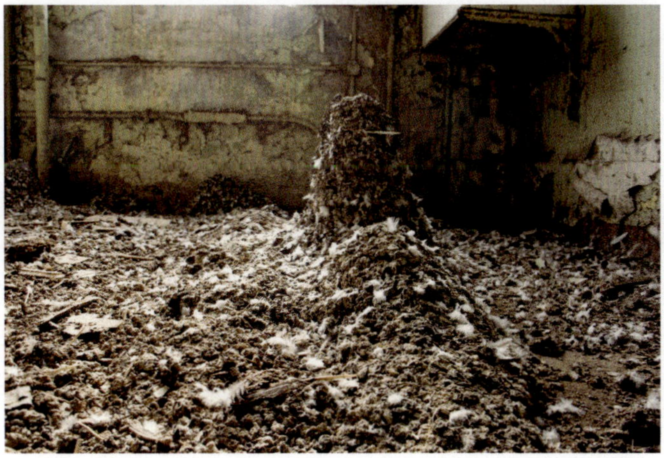

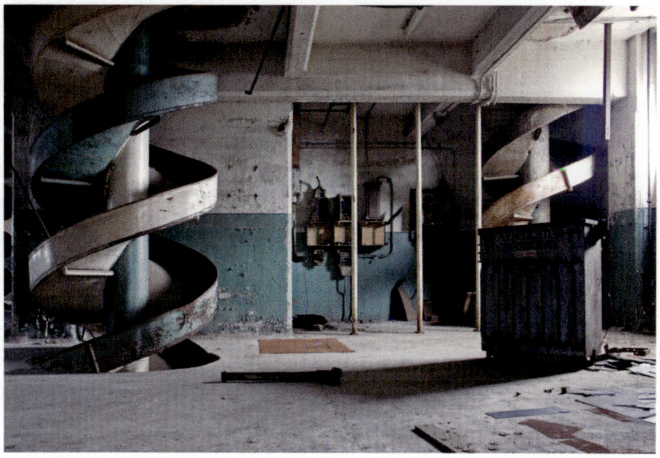

might be as challenging to overcome as infiltrating the spaces without being caught. Storm drains and sewers, factories and depositories, decommissioned railway tunnels and quarries, asylums and old office blocks are the kinds of spaces that excite these recreational trespassers.

While it might be easy to dismiss these furtive activities as juvenile thrill seeking, for many it is the expression of a sincere desire to engage with history firsthand and to make a connection with the past that is not mediated by any institution or organization. Urbex also has been suggested as a politically motivated response to increased surveillance and restriction of access to public spaces more generally.[8] For those who choose to visit subterranean spaces, the opportunity to experience a place that is unknown to the majority of the inhabitants above ground level is a motivating factor. The Internet provides a host of websites and forums for users, logging in under pseudonyms, to share their knowledge and experiences.

Photography plays two key roles in urban exploration: for some, taking photographs is the purpose of excursions, while for others it appears to be part of the affirmation of the experience. In the same way that countless holidaymakers repeat the same pose in front of monuments and landmarks, photographs across urbex websites and blogs often repeat the Friedrich-esque *Rückenfiguren*, looking out across a metropolis from some precarious vantage point, or, in a silhouetted deadpan stance, looking straight at the camera, their anonymity preserved by the blinding light of their head torches in the stygian gloom.

NEW TOPOGRAPHIC OUTLOOKS

Few events in the history of contemporary photography are as widely accepted as truly being pivotal in terms of the development of the medium as the 1975 exhibition *New Topographics: Photographs of a Man-Altered Landscape*. The show comprised the work of Robert Adams (Fig. 4.6), Lewis Baltz (Fig. 4.7), Bernd and Hilla Becher (Fig. 4.8), Joe Deal, Frank Gohlke, Nicholas Nixon, John Schott, and Stephen Shore and was held at the International Museum of Photography at the George Eastman House in New York. The show was curated by William Jenkins, who cited the pop artist Edward Ruscha as being an inspiration for the curatorial direction of the exhibition. Ruscha, who works with photography as well as other media, published *Twenty-Six Gasoline Stations* in 1963, which as the title suggests, was a typology of the gas stations on the artist's journey home on Route 66 from Los Angeles to Oklahoma City.[9] In 1966, Ruscha published the even less ambiguously titled *Every Building on the Sunset Strip*. The simplicity of Ruscha's strategy and the straightforwardness of his pictures, which according to Jenkins had the effect of "eschewing entirely the aspects of beauty, emotion and opinion,"[10] exemplify the methodologies of the practitioners included in *New Topographics*, which has persisted in the deadpan approach of many current practitioners.

As the title of the show implies, the exhibition confronted the discourse of landscape representation and, specifically, the *new* topography of twentieth-century North America, including its sprawling suburbs, parking lots, and other burgeoning industrial and domestic infrastructure. This kind of realism challenged the trend for celebratory, conservationist representations of the country, which advocated a vision of unspoiled wilderness. While the show has served to unite the interests of the participating photographers to some extent, it is easy to mistake them as any kind of activist collective. Although it is true that most of the contributors knew one another, it is more accurate to consider the impact of the exhibition in terms of defining a "new topographic outlook,"[11] which was developing in art photography, rather than *the New Topographic photographers* as an artistic movement. The sociopolitical posture of the show also can be seen in the context of heightened political awareness in America and beyond, which was facilitated by the civil rights movement, dissent against the war in Vietnam, environmental politics, and the women's movement.[12] The very generalized title of the show, as well as the apparent lack of an artistic style, made a link between contemporary landscape practice and the efforts of the nineteenth-century geologic survey photographs. Jenkins's show was a different kind of survey of the American landscape, not describing the *potential* of the landscape for development, but rather the various ways that the land had been exploited. Each contributor focused on a particular area or region, and the geometric layout of the framed prints on the walls enforced a cartographic reading of the exhibition. This underscored a pseudomechanical approach to the making of the work and curation of the exhibition.[13]

DEADPAN AESTHETICS

What the *New Topographics* exhibition articulated about the possibility of landscape photography was as radical as what it said about the medium more generally. The aesthetic qualities of the works included were, of course, fundamental to the conceptualization of the show. Just as the subject matter in the photographs was commonly considered mundane or bland, the visual qualities of the photographs were simple and unembellished and were met by traditionalists with skepticism and perplexity. The environmental conditions under which they were taken contributed to their plainness, where overcast and the solid tones above the horizon reigned over the angry skies or fluffy clouds commonly associated with landscape imagery. Jenkins wanted to represent photographers whose work was not overtly expressive: that appeared to be free from the self-conscious anxieties about "artistic" credentials that so preoccupied both the early pictorialists and their modernist successors (see p. 112). The new topographic outlook took on board the technical rigor of straight photography but took it further, or rather took a radical step *backward*. Instead of espousing the importance of master craftsmanship as

Fig. 4.6
ROBERT ADAMS
Lakewood, Colorado, 1974* from the series *What We Bought: The New World, 1970–1974
Robert Adams's major project *What We Bought* illustrated the dramatically altered urban and suburban landscape around Denver, Colorado. Using a 6 × 7 cm camera, Adams photographed commercial spaces as well as acres of sprawling housing creeping out into the desert (see also Fig. 5.12 by Hala Elkoussey), including factories, offices, and supermarkets. As the title suggests, Adams draws a parallel to the early European colonization of North America and is critical of the commercially driven overdevelopment of the landscape.

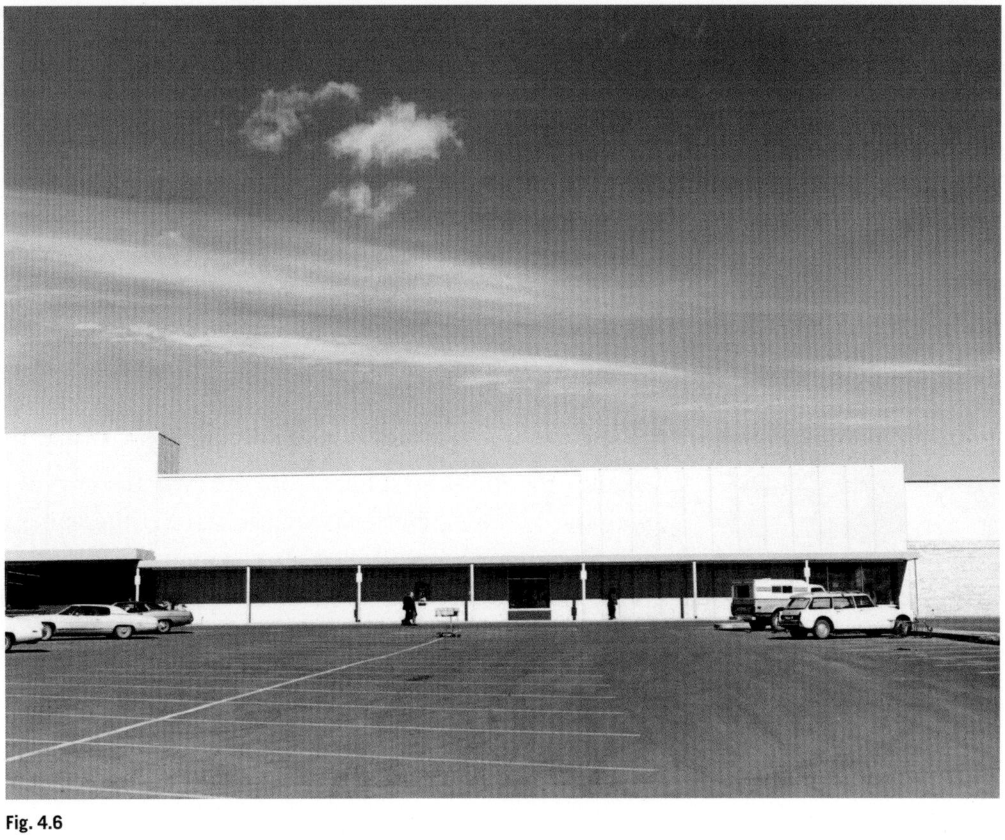

Fig. 4.6

Fig. 4.7
LEWIS BALTZ
Tract House no. 22, 1971* from *The Tract Houses
The *New Topographics* exhibition placed our relationship with architecture, something that previously had been confined to representations of the city, firmly within the discourse of landscape photography. Like Adams, Baltz was compelled to photograph commercial buildings and the economical, mass-produced tract housing. Baltz's photographs are perhaps more visually stylistic than the other contributors', whereby his frame often cuts into the scene and architecture to render at times abstract pictures. Nevertheless, compositionally these are strictly rectilinear and rigorously framed, never suggesting any sense of organic form within the subject or any kind of harmony with its environment.

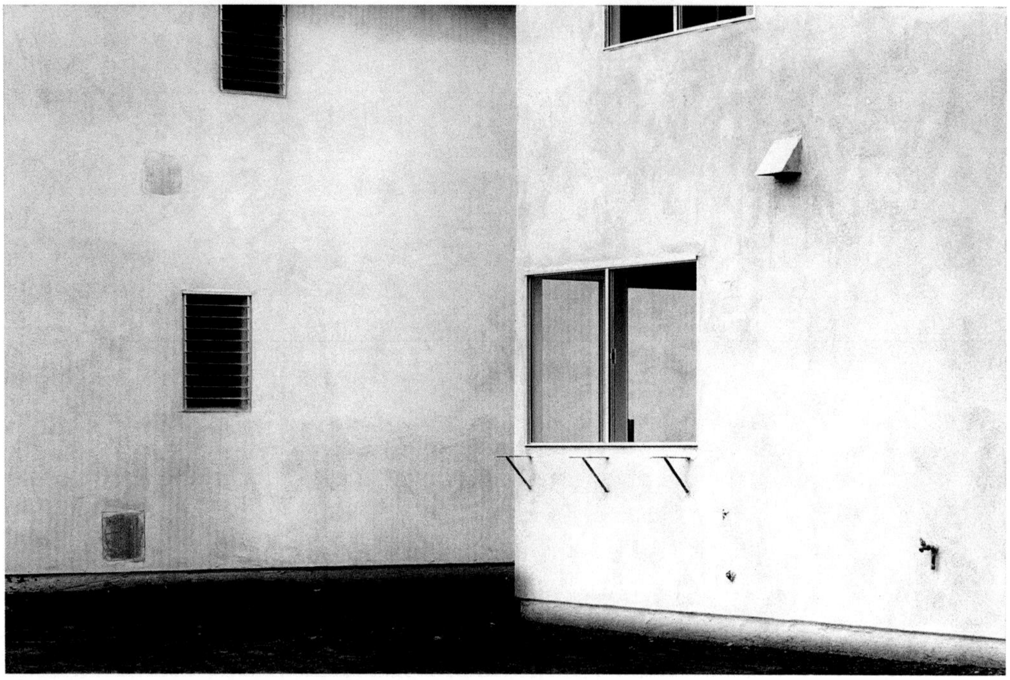

Fig. 4.7

fundamental to artistic expression, Jenkins wanted to celebrate the mechanical—literally "documentary"—qualities of the medium. As he explains, "Rather than the picture having been created by the frame, there is a sense of the frame having been laid on the existing scene without interpreting it very much."[14] Technical rigor (for example, precision of exposure and framing) remained a facet of this deadpan aesthetic, but artiness (darkroom effects, layered composition, and visual lyricism) was expunged. This approach was precisely the opposite of what the early photographer artists wanted to emancipate themselves from—the perception of photography as simply a copying device.

However, through the concerted rejection of style, a very distinct aesthetic emerged. While the *New Topographics* exhibition placed the swiftly changing terrains of America on the map in terms of landscape subjects, the aesthetic of its practitioners has been equally influential. This, as has been seen through the contribution of the only non-American practitioners in the show, Bernd and Hilla Becher, who are best known for their typological strategies. As exemplified in their *Coal Bunkers* grid, the concept behind typology is that by arranging a group of similar types of objects, the differences between them, and sometimes their evolution, can be traced.[15] The Bechers's technical rigor is also exemplary, the strength of their work owing in part to their consistency of framing and evenness of the light on their subjects. The simplicity of their practical approach—and that of the other photographers from the *New Topographics* exhibition—has endured within landscape practice as well as within other spheres of contemporary photography. The exhibition also brought a greater awareness of the suburbs as being fertile territory for artistic investigation, a previously uncharted no-man's-land that often sits awkwardly between the urban and the rural.[16]

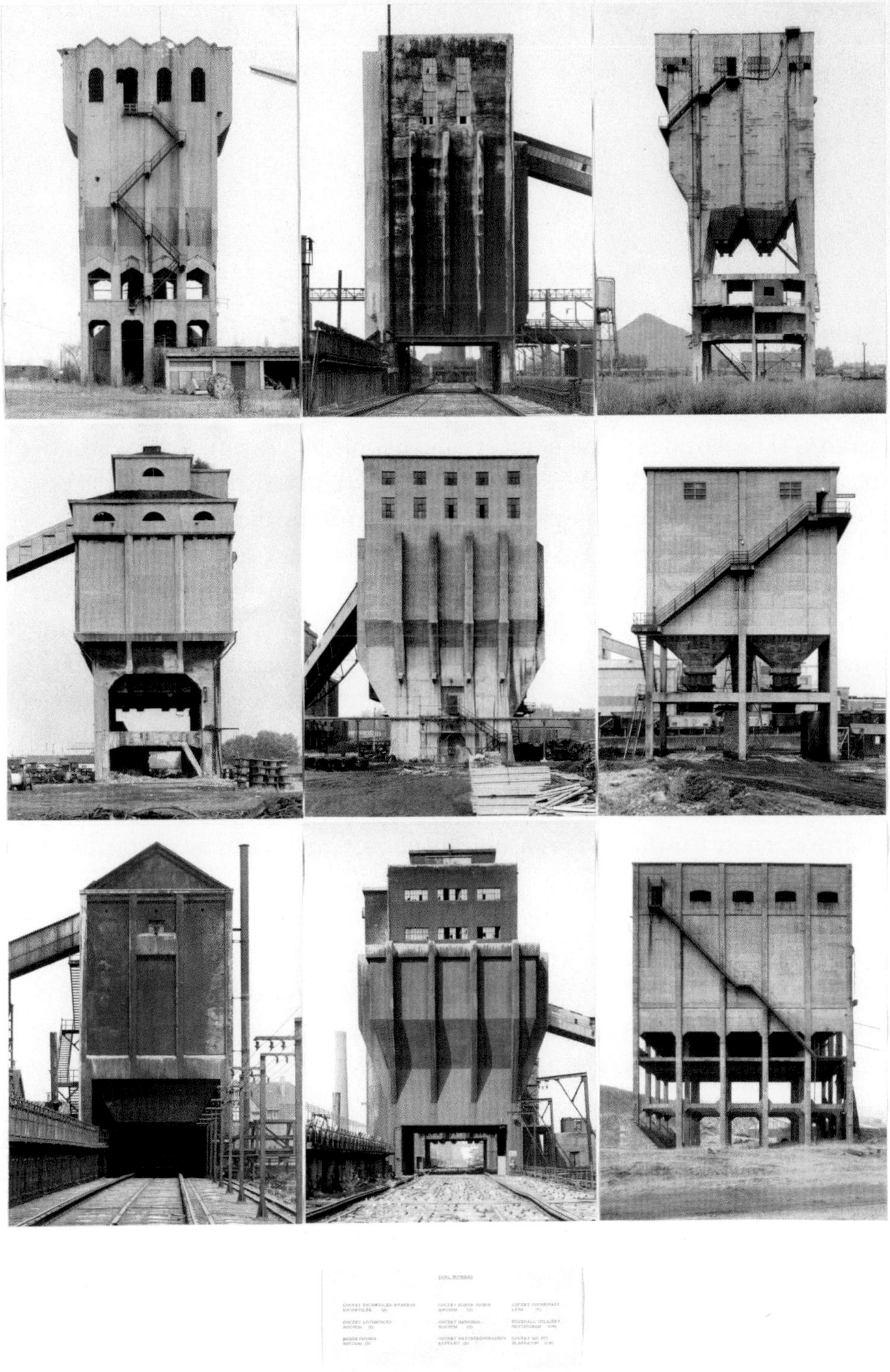

Fig. 4.8

Fig. 4.8
BERND AND HILLA BECHER
Coal Bunkers, 1974

Typological approaches are deceptive in that what at first seems to be a statement about commonality or homogeneity actually reveals nuances of formal individuality. In the case of the Bechers, mundane structures (water towers, coal bunkers, pitheads, and so on) take on almost alternative identities. As described in *Edgelands*: "*A single cooling tower may look beautiful, but nine cooling towers on one sheet looks like a series of ancient monoliths, or temples, or plinths for statues of long forgotten gods.*"[17] The legacy of the participants of the *New Topographics* is enduring, although the Bechers's influence can be seen most acutely within the commonalities among their students from the Kunstakademie Düsseldorf, who include Andreas Gursky, Thomas Struth, and Thomas Ruff.

The heightened consciousness in the western world about the environment in the late twentieth century makes us increasingly aware of what, in different ways, has always pertained: landscape is a political text. MALCOLM ANDREWS[18]

ENVIRONMENTAL POLITICS

In the 1930s—which saw the Great Depression and the rise of fascism in Europe—Henri Cartier-Bresson was severely critical of certain approaches to photography, declaring, "The world is going to pieces and people like Adams and Weston are photographing rocks!" Ansel Adams responded to this attack with, "I still believe there is a real social significance in a rock—a more important significance therein than a line of unemployed."[19] Although the moral superiority of either party is debatable, the heated exchange is a reminder that despite their pictorial appearance, there was an ideological motivation behind Adams's photographs and the simple message—*this* must be conserved at all costs.[20] Adams's approach of highly celebratory imagery may be very different to more didactic photographs depicting the overexploitation of our natural resources. However, historical examples have shown that more positive imagery can be equally powerful.

NASA's Apollo 8 space mission took a manned spacecraft beyond the safety of Earth's gravity for the first time, but the photograph taken by astronaut William Anders from the window of the lunar module while orbiting the moon on Christmas Eve 1968 (Fig. 4.10) has arguably become the most historically significant aspect of that mission. It is often said that the *Earthrise* image was pivotal in the narrative of the environmental movement, although the precise extent of the photograph's impact is difficult to qualify.[21] Compositionally, the *Earthrise* photograph is very familiar: it is a kind of inverted sunrise, with a black sky instead of a bright one, and instead of an Earth foreground to offer scale, the lower frame is contained with lunar topography. But the picture offered a radically different view that no one had seen previously. The blue marble of Earth occupies a relatively small portion of the frame and is isolated roughly within its center. In spite of the moon in the foreground, this formal organization suggests a sense of the fragility of the planet and the remoteness of the people of Earth. Yet the photograph simultaneously implies the inhabitants are inextricably linked—bound to one another in spite of differences of race, creed, or political ideology. The image illustrated the concept behind environmental economist Barbara Ward's book, *Spaceship Earth* (1965), which promoted environmental sustainability, likening the people of Earth to the crew of a space shuttle hurtling through space with finite resources at their disposal. On Christmas Day, American poet Archibald MacLeish wrote in *The New York Times*:

> *To see the Earth as it truly is, small and blue and beautiful in that eternal silence where it floats, is to see ourselves as riders on the Earth together, brothers on that bright loveliness in the eternal cold—brothers who know now they are truly brothers.*

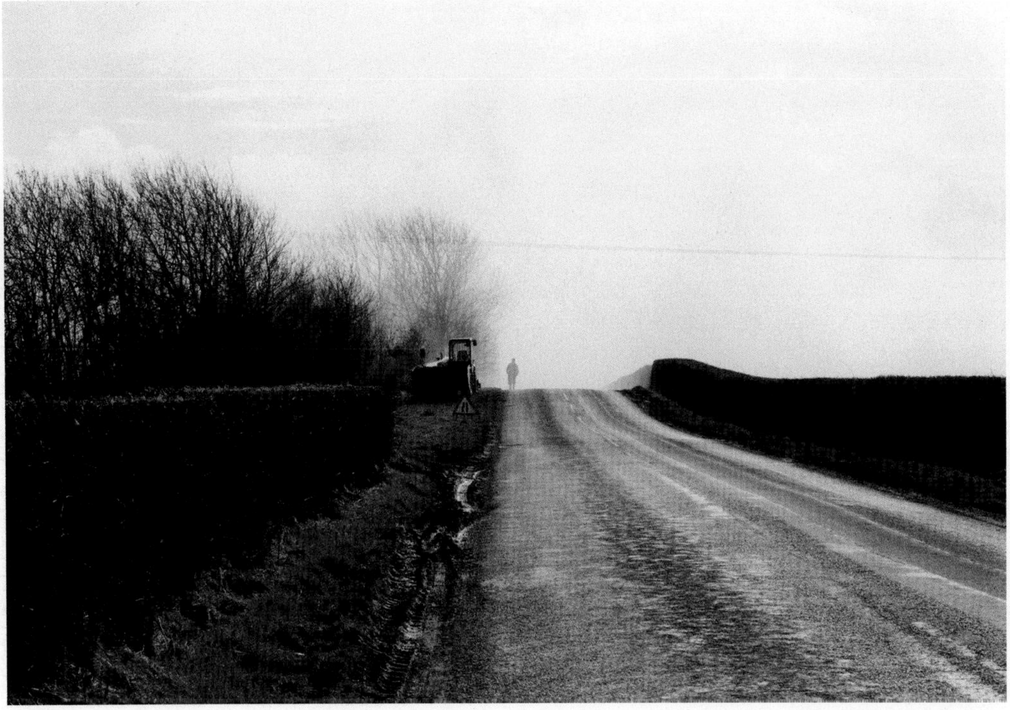

Fig. 4.9

Fig. 4.9
JOHN DARWELL
Entrance to Welton Pyre* from the series *Dark Days, 2001–2002
In 2001, John Darwell began documenting the visible signs and effects of the British foot-and-mouth outbreak. His photographs reveal macabre piles of carcasses and the efforts to contain the spread of the disease. He visited several farms across Cumbria, and his pictures describe the realities of the disposal and decontamination operations. Many of his photographs provide a sense of the impact of the outbreak from the perspective of someone who used the countryside at the time: access to open country and use of footpaths was curtailed or forbidden, and the rural countryside resembled the scene of a crime. This image, shot from the confines of a main road and revealing relatively little, gives an impression of the restriction under which the countryside was placed.

It should also be noted that a clear color photograph of Earth was captured by a NASA applications technology satellite (ATS) the year before. Also, a similar *Earthrise* image had been captured in 1966 by the remote spacecraft *Lunar Orbiter 1*. This black-and-white image is almost the mirror image of Anders's photograph and is distorted with vertical banding. However, it would be simplistic to suppose that the superior technical quality of Anders's photograph, taken on color slide film with a medium-format camera, completely accounts for its elevated historical significance. On Christmas Eve 1968, the day the *Earthrise* photograph was taken, the largest television audience of its time tuned in to listen to the three astronauts relay their experiences back to Earth live, as well as their reciting verses from the Book of Genesis. Although the mission was concerned with learning more about the moon, the symbolism of sending a manned craft beyond Earth's orbit was of greater significance, and its legacy was a rethinking of our relationship to our home planet.

THE ENVIRONMENTAL CONTEXT

The rhetoric of the broadcasts of the crew of Apollo 8 and those of subsequent astronauts serves as a reminder of the political significance of the space race within the broader historical context. The terrifying scale of man's potential for devastation was seen through the destruction of Hiroshima and Nagasaki with atomic bombs at the end of the Second World War. The continued threat of nuclear conflict during the Cold War following World War II was instrumental in sustaining a level of concern over the environmental future of the planet.[22] The Second World War also prompted a deep concern for food security, particularly in the UK, which was almost forced into capitulation by Nazi U-boat blockades of food imports on which Britain depended. Anxiety over livestock and arable crop yields contributed to the acceptance of intensive farming methods and use of fertilizers and pesticides like DDT. In her book *Silent Spring* (1962), biologist and writer Rachel Carson was highly critical of the indiscriminate use of DDT, as well as other chemicals,

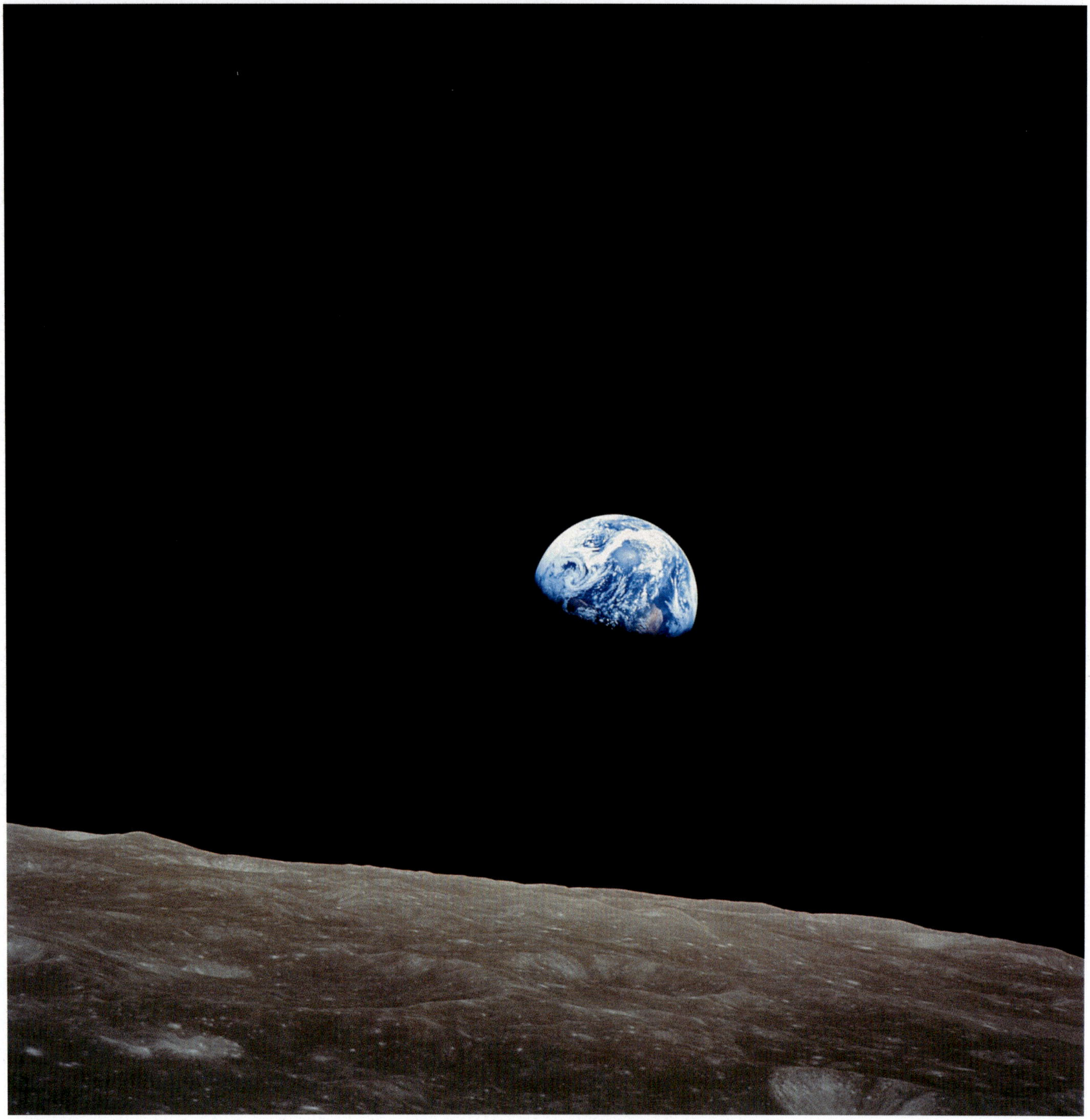

Fig. 4.10

Fig. 4.10
WILLIAM ANDERS
AS8-14-2383 Earthrise, December 24, 1968

The social importance of *Earthrise* was foreseen by astronomer Fred Hoyle two decades before it was taken: *Once a photograph of the Earth, taken from outside, is available, we shall, in an emotional sense, acquire an additional dimension. . . . Once let the sheer isolation of the Earth become plain to every man, whatever his nationality or creed, and a new idea as powerful as any in history will be let loose.* [23]

Fig. 4.11
DANIEL BELTRÁ
from the series *Spill, May 27, 2010*

Daniel Beltrá's image depicts crews cleaning the marshes, which are swamped with crude oil when the Deepwater Horizon oil rig exploded on April 20, 2010. On the one hand, Beltrá's aerial photographs reduce the environmental disaster to a pleasant abstraction of lines, colors, and textures, and stylistically they echo Yann Arthus Bertrand's popular project *Earth From the Air*. On the other hand, however, the distanced point of view provides a kind of narrative summary of the event and is an alarming reminder of the scale of the disaster and the cost to the environment when our harvesting of oil goes badly wrong.

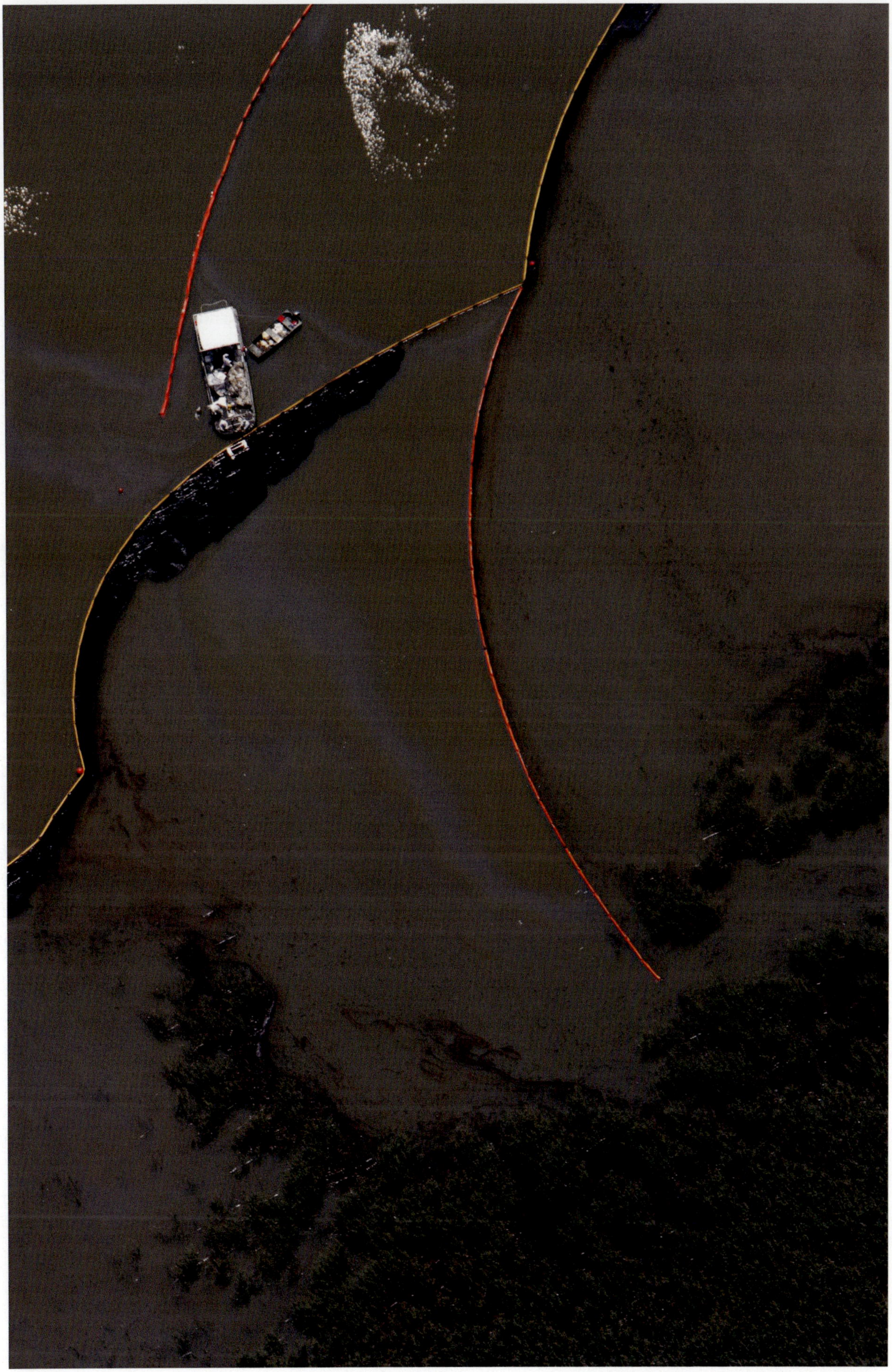

Fig. 4.11

linking its application to leukemia and other serious health risks. *Silent Spring*, which circulated among a nonspecialist readership, discussed the use of such chemicals within the broader ecological context and the corruption of specific ecosystems.

Like the *Earthrise* photograph, many cite Carson's book as marking a crucial turning point in mainstream environmentalism. Carson begins her discussion with a bleak, almost postapocalyptic fictional description of a town in the heart of America, where the population gets sick, the birds disappear, and the livestock becomes infertile. She concludes her prologue with

> *I know of no community that has experienced all of these misfortunes I describe. Yet every one of these disasters has actually happened somewhere. . . . A grim spectre has crept upon us unnoticed, and this imagined tragedy may easily become a stark reality we all shall know.*[24]

Similar arguments have raged since the 1990s in relation to whether the genetic modification of crops is a legitimate means to feed the world while reducing the need for pesticides or these Frankenstein foods are, in fact, a dangerous experiment that risks contaminating the gene pool and ties farmers to multinational biotech corporations like Monsanto.

In the UK, the gradual move away from intensively farmed produce to locally sourced and sustainably produced food has been fueled by a string of food scares, particularly around animal welfare and the safety of meat. The BSE/vCJD outbreak in the 1990s, which was the result of feeding cattle on recycled meat, and the spread of the foot-and-mouth disease outbreak in 2001 led to the destruction of millions of sheep, cattle, and other livestock.

While the BSE epidemic had a more profound impact in terms of changing consumer choices, the foot-and-mouth outbreak, which was exacerbated by the transportation of livestock, had a more visible effect upon the rural countryside. Fires were used to dispose of the carcasses of—in many instances healthy—livestock, which were slaughtered on an industrial scale to curb the spread of the disease. The restrictions that were placed upon public access to the countryside to further prevent transmission were felt by almost anyone who visited the countryside for business or recreation. Projects made at the time by Clive Landen[25] and John Darwell (Fig. 4.9) provide a record of this particularly bleak chapter in the British countryside's not-too-distant history.

Today, climate change, carbon emissions, and sustainability of energy consumption are at the forefront of the political agenda. Increased general awareness of environmental issues has, perhaps inevitably, led more photographers to engage with such topics within their practices, but it also has made the consumption of

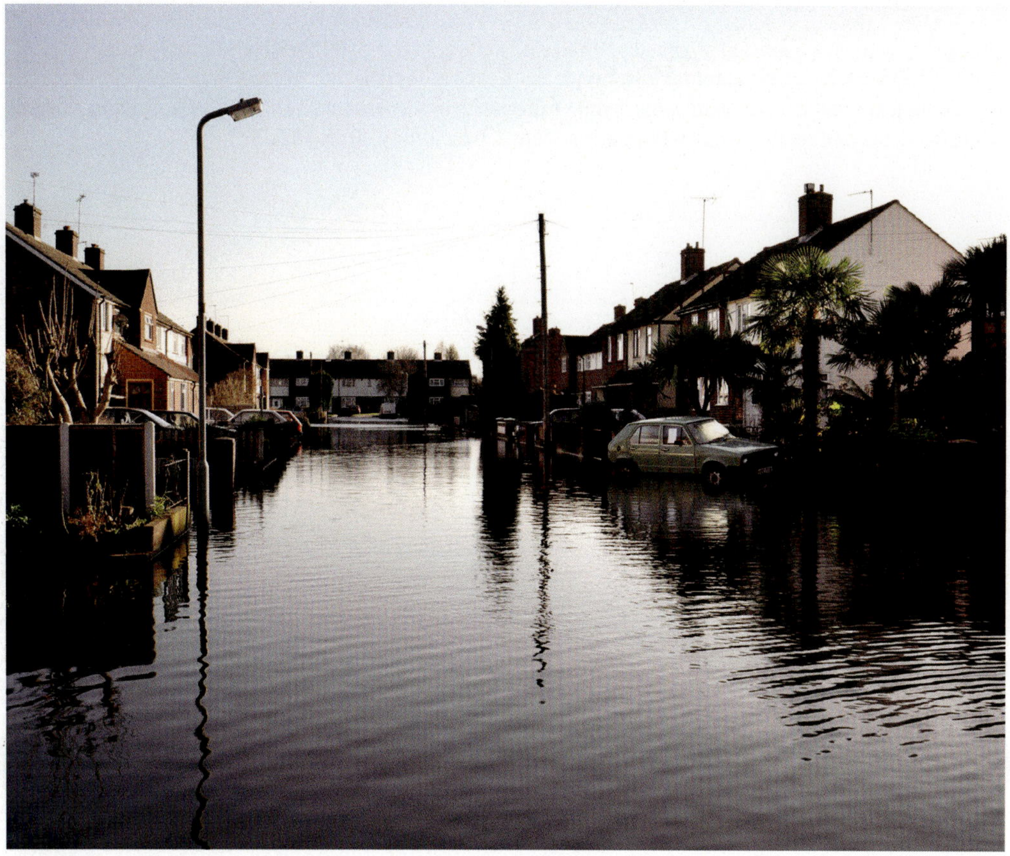

Fig. 4.12

Fig. 4.12
JONATHAN OLLEY
Flood, New Jubillee River Flood Relief Scheme. Churtsey, Greater London, Surrey, England, UK* from the series *The Sea Wall, 2002–
As an island nation, the UK is particularly interesting with respect to coastal erosion. In *The Sea Wall*, Jonathan Olley—who is better known for examining the marks of conflict left across the landscape—depicts England's east coast, which is susceptible to the encroaching seawaters, and the failure of infrastructure to cope with unexpected storm water. Like Olley's other projects, including *Castles of Ulster* (2000) and *Land Between Two Rivers* (2004), *The Sea Wall* reveals a kind of battlefield, one that perhaps isn't quite as lethal as unexploded bombs and land mines but is perhaps, in fact, a much mightier adversary. Olley's photographs often are taken under melodramatic conditions, which hint toward the peril of the elements. However, the compositional simplicity also adds to a sense of unease and uncertainty. We see what has historically been Britain's greatest defensive asset almost turning upon itself (see also Fig. 0.4).

work of a critical nature more palatable to public audiences. Ilkka Halso's digital montages depicting the imminent extinction of habitats and organisms (see Fig. 3.1) blend photographic realism with a futuristic, dystopian vision. The series *Naturale* builds upon his *Museum of Nature* series, revealing a glimpse behind the scenes of the museum's diorama or perhaps the exhibits that the museum does not have the space to show. Great warehouses have microclimates on palettes ready to go—even an authentic house complete with a garden. Halso's series recalls mythological flood narratives and the desperate collection and classification of species to avert extinction, his warehouse playing the role of Noah's ark.

Many photographers, including Jonathan Olley (Figs. 0.4 and 4.12), Dana Lixenberg, and Neil A. White, have explored the very real effects of rising sea levels, the result of melting Arctic sea ice due to global warming. In these projects, which have studied coastal erosion and the impact upon nearby communities, we can actually see the land crumbling and vanishing. They have a certain resonance in relation to notions of the altered landscape, whereby it is the environment that is doing the landscaping. The rapidly changing physical landscape will, of course, continue to fascinate contemporary practitioners, and the urgency of our environmental crisis is likely to remain at the forefront of landscape photography. Hopefully photography will continue to play a part in building awareness of these issues and strengthening a common conviction to bring about meaningful change. Without questioning the significance or urgency of climate change, we should be wary of environmental photography overwhelming the discourse of landscape practice, as the aestheticization of these issues might easily supersede the ecological imperative that is presented.

Though women have been and remain identified with nature, in the mythic text nature remains an enclosed space which men enter for leisure, pleasure, and to test themselves and their authority. Nature is what men are not. In other words, the mythic experience of nature is not primarily addressed to women, but establishes and reinforces a patriarchal version of masculinity. JOHN TAYLOR[26]

ENGENDERING THE LANDSCAPE

Landscape photography is often perceived as a gallant pursuit: the intrepid photographer battling against the elements in remote locations, forced to exercise technical expertise under pressure and fatigue from the burden of all *his* equipment. The images of the imperialist explorer (Roger Fenton, Francis Frith, John Thomson) or the commercial explorer (Carleton Watkins, William Henry Jackson, Timothy O'Sullivan) are enduring, masculine archetypes that typify the historical patriarchal relationship between man and the land. Much like elsewhere in the photography industry, an imbalance remains in terms of the ratios of female practitioners to their male counterparts. Analysis of the numbers of female-to-male practitioners in contemporary group exhibitions of landscape photography reveals that men consistently outnumber their female counterparts.[27]

The reasons women have participated to a lesser extent in landscape photography historically are practical as well as social: nineteenth-century equipment was cumbersome, and even in Britain, the countryside was genuinely hazardous. The restrictive clothing of the time was also something of a challenge to female photographers, which mirrors the social restrictions under which middle- to upper-class women (who would have been the only sort of women who could afford to practice photography) were placed.[28]

While a canon of great *female* photographers from the medium's birth do exist, their studies tended to focus on the domestic or more geographically confined areas. The nineteenth-century pioneer Evelyn Cameron stands out as amassing an exceptional collection of photographs that, confined by her homestead commitments, provides a detailed visual study of her Montana community.[29] Historically, women have been credited for an aptitude for detailed studies of things *within* the landscape (flowers, cottages, and so on), but *taking command* of an entire view was considered to be feasible only by a man.[30] Such a notion is, of course, incompatible with today's more enlightened attitudes, and if women had the same liberties as men had to consume the landscape, it is likely that such myths would have failed to take hold. Increased equality between the sexes facilitated greater access to the landscape for women. However, it is important to consider that until the twentieth century and legislation to give women the same rights as men to inherit property, landscape imagery depicted the exclusive belongings of men.

MOTHER NATURE

The question of to whom the view belongs relates to broader issues around nature and culture. Since the land is part of nature, which is symbolically associated with the feminine, man's presence within the land thus becomes a symbolic penetration of nature. Reducing nature to a formal representation is therefore a means of

Fig. 4.13
TOM STODDARD
Impotent Cowboy, Los Angeles, 2002
The stereotype of the heroic male protagonist within the remote landscape frequently appears in advertising imagery, no more vividly perhaps than in Philip Morris International's Marlboro Man. When Marlboro decided to market their new filtered cigarettes to men instead of to women in 1954, they experimented with various professions before settling on the role of cowboy or rancher in the 1960s. He would be seen working hard or relaxing—often enjoying the scenery—on a well-deserved cigarette break somewhere in the Rockies. Gradually, the imagery became less preoccupied with the Marlboro Man and his buddies and more concerned with the Rocky Mountain and Western landscape, in some cases even to the exclusion of figures altogether. "This Is Marlboro Country" and "Come to Where the Flavor Is" remain the brand's iconic straplines. Whether the Marlboro Man's whips, spurs, and chaps were actually manly or the image, in fact, tapped into something more homoerotic has been debated, and the cowboy has receded into retirement. The simplicity and recognizability of the campaign has made it an easy target for parody by antismoking groups, particularly in a social climate that is highly critical of smoking and its associated health risks.

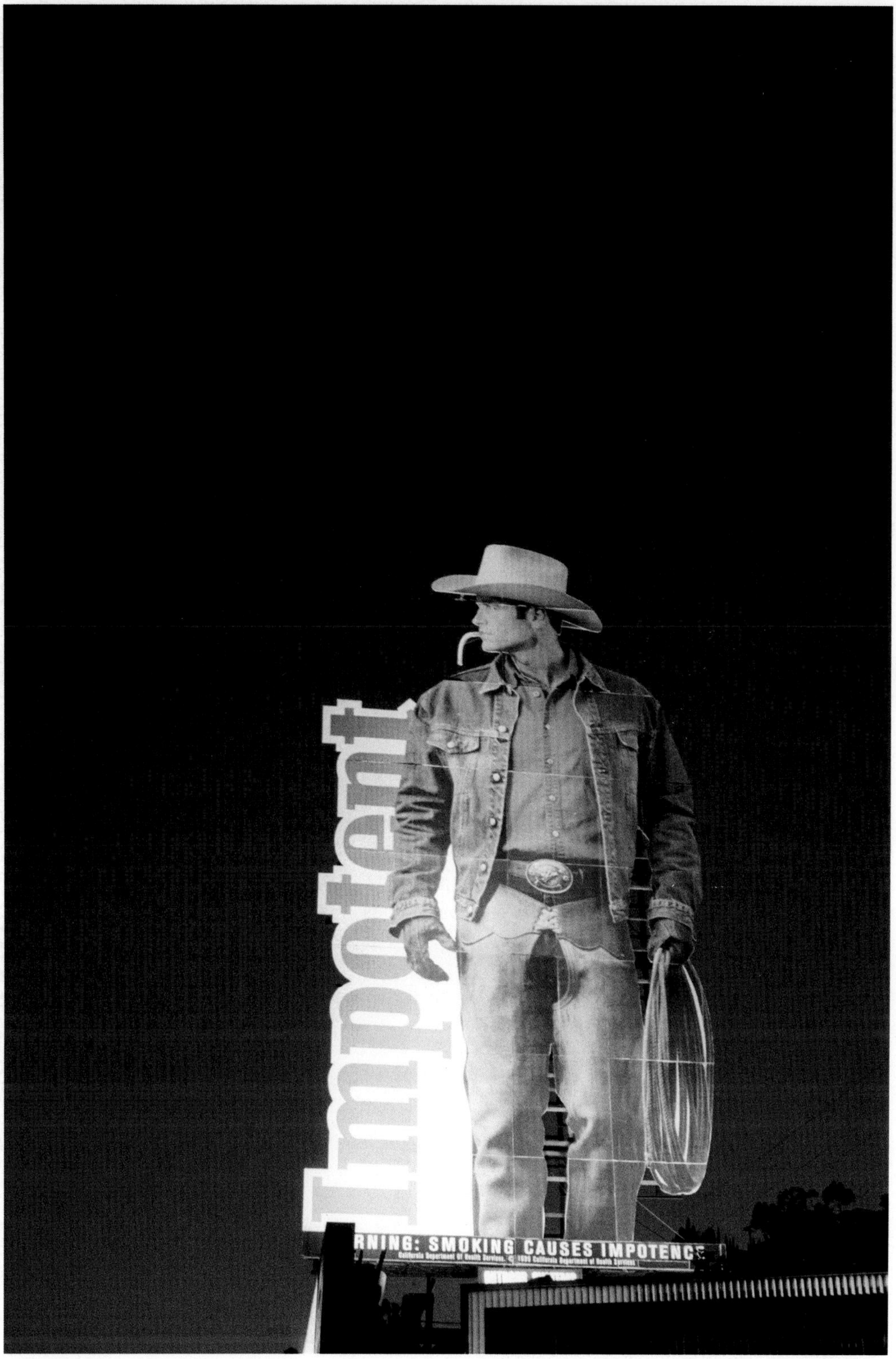

Fig. 4.13

overcoming the untamed *otherness* of nature. Penny Watson's series *Her Eyes On* (Fig. 4.14) is uncannily illustrative of how we innately perceive the land in terms of a feminine object. In an attempt to explore alternative practical approaches to photographing the celebrated English Lake District that transcended traditional clichéd views, Watson tried rotating her pictures through 90 degrees. To her astonishment, the abstraction of the images resembled the torsos of figures.[31] Watson's pictures of placid, lake-mirrored landscapes function a little like the psychoanalyst's Rorschach inkblot test. The identification of female figures in

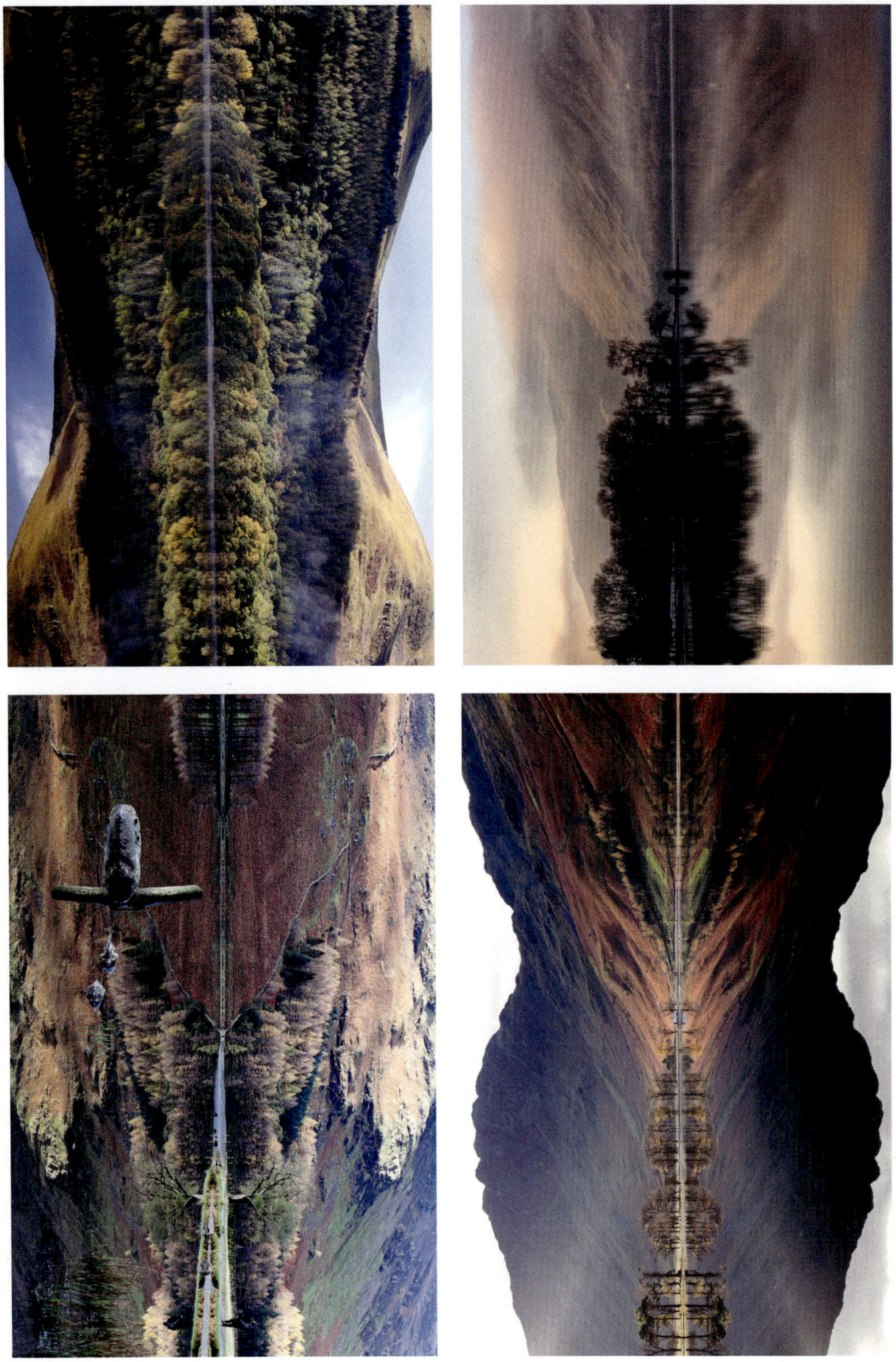

Fig. 4.14

Fig. 4.14
PENNY WATSON
Her Eyes On, 2013

The genre of landscape photography is historically the playground of the male photographer, both as maker and viewer. While not a conscious expression of feminism, I became interested in exploring the gendered gaze. Residing in the heart of the Lake District, I was provided with a "sublime" canvas, and suppressing the urge to be lured by its beauty was a key priority. In Her Eyes On, *by shifting the orientation 90 degrees, an entirely fresh syntax was created. No longer restricted by the conventional discourse of the landscape genre, an entirely new perspective of the landscape presented itself. The picturesque had been transformed into depictions of the female form, consequently challenging my own views on feminism, what the female gaze could be, and how this related to the landscape. The work aims to interrupt the conventional discourse of landscape photography by—literally—shifting orientation. It looks beyond the picturesque interpretation of the Lake District, pioneered by the romantics, and diligently observed by visitors ever since. Alternative references are invited on gender, the sublime, and feminism using the Lakeland landscape as the canvas.*
Penny Watson

Watson's photographs perhaps confirms that subconsciously we do indeed gender the landscape. A female identity of the unspoiled landscape also can be found in vernacular language. The word "rape" for instance, is used rhetorically to describe anything from pollution, the extraction of minerals, or the unsympathetic *erection* of renewable energy infrastructure.[32]

An underlying male perspective of the land and control over its representation becomes tantamount to an intrinsically "male gaze" in landscape photography.[33] This issue surfaced within feminist interrogations of visual culture during the 1970s and 1980s, and inquiries into gendering the landscape and its consumption continue to provide rich seams of investigation for contemporary practitioners.

Fig. 4.15
ALEKSANDRA MIR
Installation shot, *First Woman on the Moon, 1999*
Aleksandra Mir's monumental project *First Woman on the Moon* involved creating a giant beach sculpture that recreated a lunar landscape on a beach in the Netherlands. To complement the installation, the artist made accompanying documents, such as publicity material about the all-female team of astronauts. The structure, in contrast to other earthworks projects by the likes of Robert Smithson (1938–1970), Michael Heizer, and Christo and Jeanne-Claude, was an ephemeral construction and razed to the ground by a massive party on the same day that the diggers moved in. This poked fun at the grandiose nature of many earthwork or earth art projects. With this delightfully excessive and irreverent gesture, Mir makes the ironic, self-deprecating statement that for a *woman* to have any chance of standing on the moon she will have to first build it for herself. The further implication is that *man's* power over the landscape might as well be considered to extend beyond his own planet.

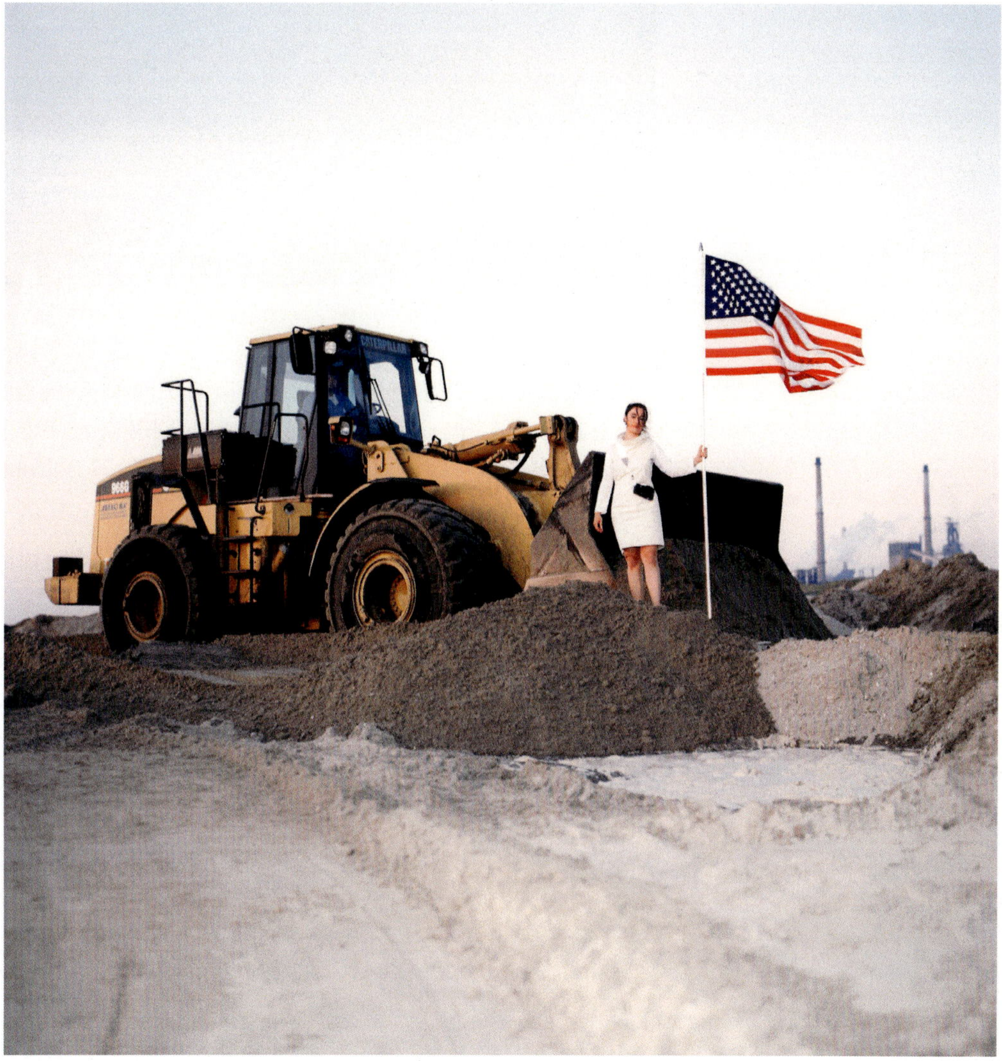

Fig. 4.15

Fig. 4.16
JO SPENCE AND TERRY DENNETT
Victimization* from the series *Remodelling Photo History, 1982
In Jo Spence and Terry Dennett's performative work, the pair candidly interrogate the patriarchal dominance of the landscape in both a physical sense and in terms of the male gaze. *Victimization* also touches upon issues around access to open land that were prominent political issues and explored in greater depth by practitioners including Fay Godwin (Fig. 1.10).

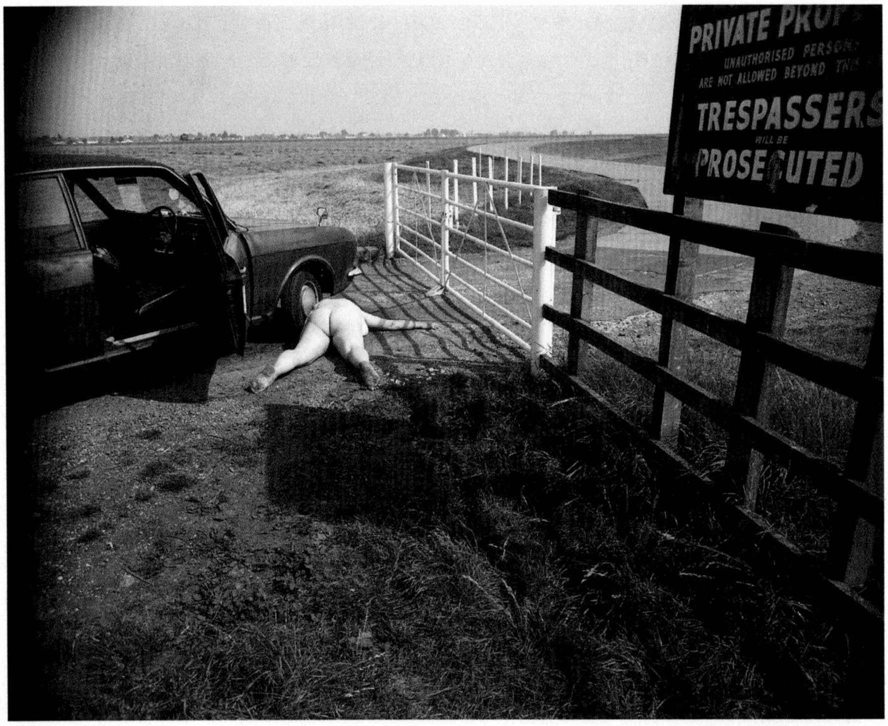

Fig. 4.16

In Helen Sear's *Inside the View* (Fig. 3.9), a female figure occupies at least half of the frame and interrupts the default male perspective. In presenting her back to the camera, the subject also denies the viewer the possibility of letting her own image suffer the same fate as nature's, becoming yet another object of the male gaze. Placing oneself and others in the landscape foreground has been a familiar strategy for many female practitioners and has been put into practice for various strategic and conceptual reasons.[34]

In some instances, we can see this as a sardonic response to the painter's tradition of the nude in the landscape. Within the history of painting, these typically depicted allegorical and mythological narratives (such as Claude's *Landscape with Narcissus and Echo,* 1644), although more recent photographic incarnations seem to have had more formal preoccupations: Edward Weston's beach nudes in New Mexico in the 1930s and Bill Brand's extreme wide-angle nudes from the 1950s, where female forms blend seamlessly into the landscape, are the most apparent historical examples. In several pictures from Jo Spence (1934–1992) and Terry Dennett's collaborative series *Remodelling Photo History*, which caricatures the medium's inherently patriarchal perspective, Spence places her naked body in the foreground. In *Industrialization,* the gesture of Spence's form stretched out on

Fig. 4.17
HELEN CHADWICK
Viral Landscape No. 3, 1988–1989
The five works that comprise *Viral Landscapes* were made with a combination of cellular body samples and photographs. Although the images have a strong formal presence—the abstract cellular formations are similar to Jackson Pollock's abstract paintings—they suggest a discordant, *parasitic* relationship between nature and both man *and* woman.

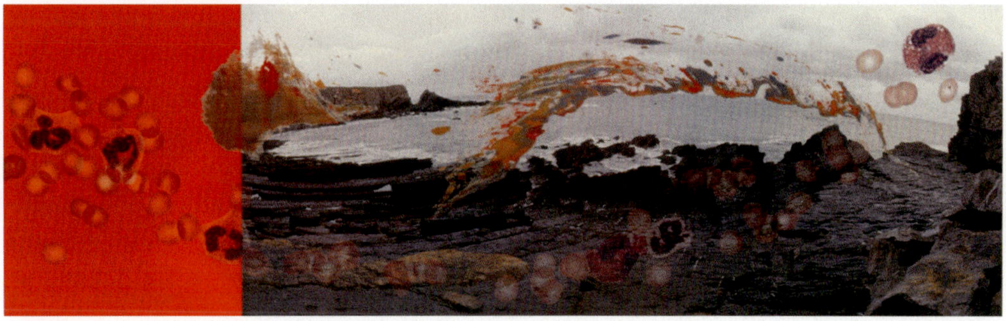

Fig. 4.17

the grass in the shadow of a tree subtly references a typical nineteenth-century pictorialist figure study in a landscape. In *Victimization*, however, Spence's pose is somewhat less elegant. She presents herself at the threshold of a place that declares in no uncertain terms that it is off limits. Spence, with face flat in the dirt, and as the title of the work suggests, expresses a state of utter defeat. The car door left open also adds a sense of haste and desperation. She ironically offers unconditional surrender to the landowner in relation to her right to access his land and through her nakedness, relents to the male gaze.

In *Viral Landscapes*, conceptual artist Helen Chadwick (1953–1996) similarly lays all bare. However, contrary to many of her previous works, instead of images of her external body she digitally combined cellular samples taken from her cervix, vagina, mouth, and ear with photographs of the rugged coastline of Pembrokeshire in west Wales. In one sense, this is a very literal amalgamation of nature and the female body, and formally, the expressive cell marks complement the shapes and textures in the landscape pictures in a similar manner to Brandt's *bodyscapes*. Chadwick expressed self-criticism that some of her earlier works were too self-centered and therefore overconcerned with gender, which was one of the reasons for seeking *internal* representations of the body for *Viral Landscapes*.[35] Bearing in mind the social context of the work (made in the wake of the emergence of HIV/AIDS as well as the political prominence of the environmental movement), the series addresses the notion of mankind (as a species rather than man as a gender) and its relation to the planet in the same terms as a parasite and its host.[36]

PASTORAL REALITIES

Since we depend on the land for nourishment, it follows that evidence of the cultivation of food and rearing of livestock is likely to creep into depictions of it. "Pastoral" is a term that often emerges in discussions of landscape, and its implications merit a closer inspection. Traditionally, pastoralism is associated with nomadic agricultural strategies whereby livestock are continually moved to find water and fresh pastures. More generally, pastoralism relates to a mixed economy of what is harvested, which can improve food security if one crop or herd fails.

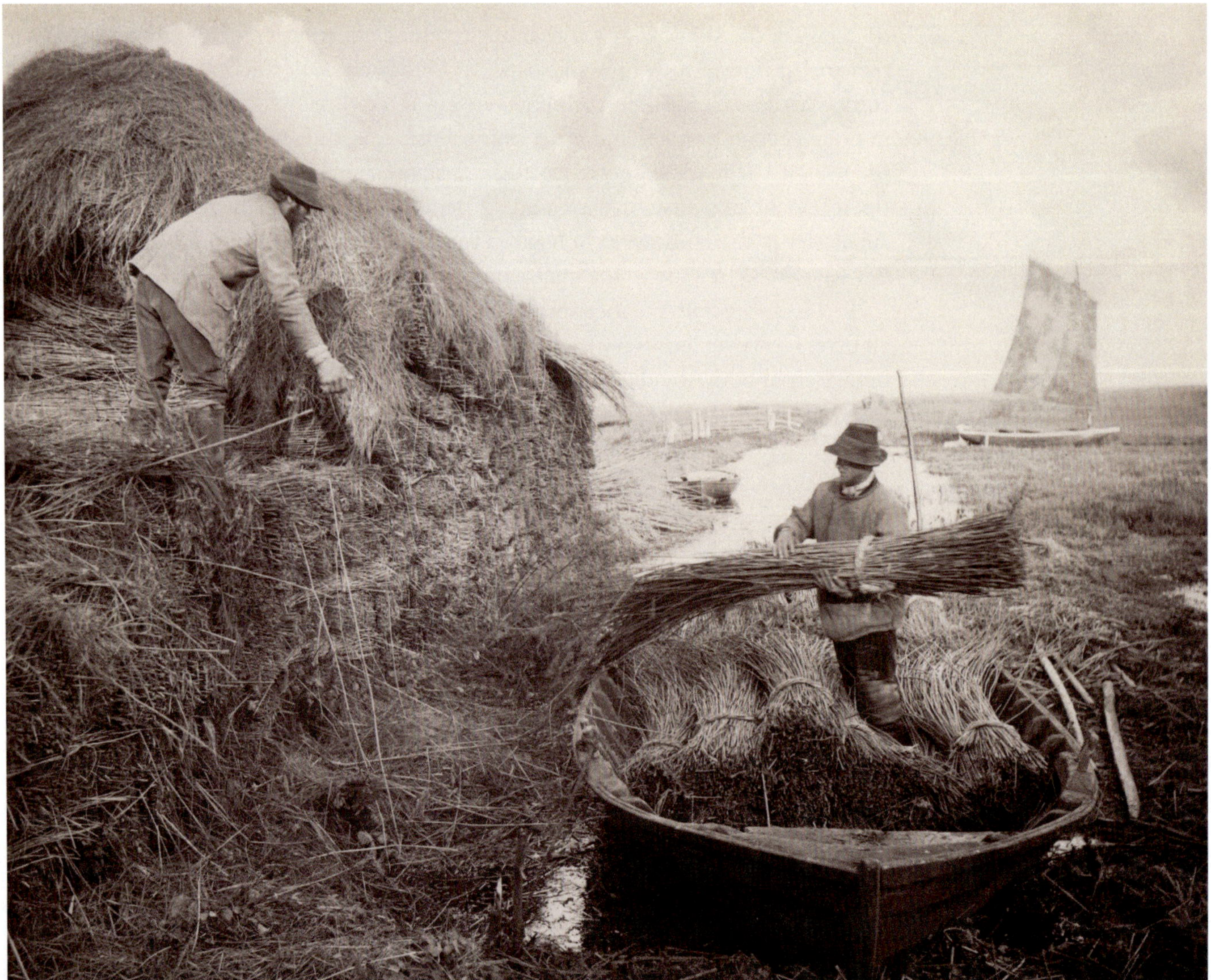

Fig. 4.18

Fig. 4.19
JACK DELANO
Chopping cotton on rented land near White Plains, Greene County, GA, 1941
Following the social upheaval of the Wall Street crash and hardships of the early 1930s, the U.S. government established the Farm Security Administration (FSA) to initiate various programs to improve the lives of farmers, particularly those effected by soil erosion in the Dust Bowl era, which was caused by the long-term effects of intensive agricultural methods. Perhaps the most celebrated legacy of the FSA was the substantial body of photographic work that was commissioned on an unprecedented scale. The FSA archive served to record the efforts of the government and to induce unifying support for state programs and initiatives. It was also profoundly important in establishing the genre of documentary photography.

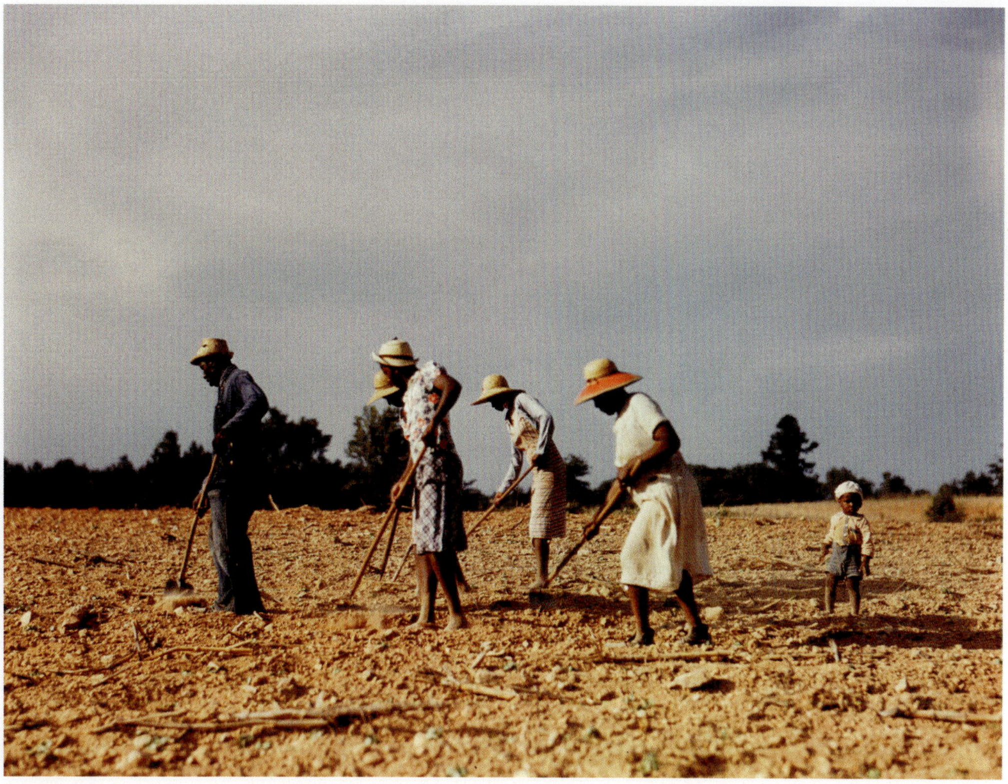

Fig. 4.19

Fig. 4.18
P.H. EMERSON
"Ricking the Reed"* from *Life and Landscape on the Norfolk Broads, 1886
Although Emerson's sepia photographs have a quaint appearance today, he was an advocate for straightforward, unembellished photography. Compared to his contemporaries, Emerson's photographs offered exceptional clarity in terms of depth of field, affording viewers the unusual privilege of purveying the image from foreground to background on their own terms. Unlike picturesque representations, Emerson's subjects were typically placed in the foreground, occupying a substantial proportion of the frame. His pictures of the Norfolk Broads, which constitute one of the most detailed accounts of a rural community to date, concentrated on the workers and their activity: they are not merely decorations to the landscape picture but shown as central to it.

In visual culture, the term "pastoral" is used in relation to works that incorporate agricultural details as either ancillary details or entire subjects within a narrative. A typically pastoral motif might be a shepherd or smallholder with a couple of sheep, goats, or cows or an exchange between a small group of rustic-looking people (see Figs. 2.6 and 4.22). Such details also animate otherwise relatively static imagery, providing a scene with dynamism in much the same way that actors animate a theater set. Similarly, pastoral imagery is essentially a performance of "the countryside," a generally idealized representation of uncomplicated rural life. These quickly identifiable motifs, the shepherd boy for instance, were incorporated into more complex allegorical works as a means of exploring multifaceted narratives: pastoral motifs are shorthand for "simple."[37]

Before the seventeenth century and the emergence of distinctly pastoral elements within landscape painting by artists such as Claude Lorrain (1604–1682), the pastoral was more formally acknowledged in classical literature, poetry, and music. Pastoral imagery, irrespective of medium, has always spawned from fictional narratives. As with other works of the picturesque, which tend to be rife with pastoral motifs, we well may be cynical of such idealized representations. However, it would be unjust to berate Lorrain for exercising "artistic license" within his narrative landscape paintings without criticizing the tomes of other artists and authors who have also set imaginary accounts and narratives within the open spaces beyond our cities. A problem has arisen whereby collectively we have lost consciousness of the artifice of pastoral representation, amounting to a myth of a countryside idyll that overshadows the actual complexities of rural life. As Fay Godwin asserted, this kind of misrepresentation can lead to a polarization between

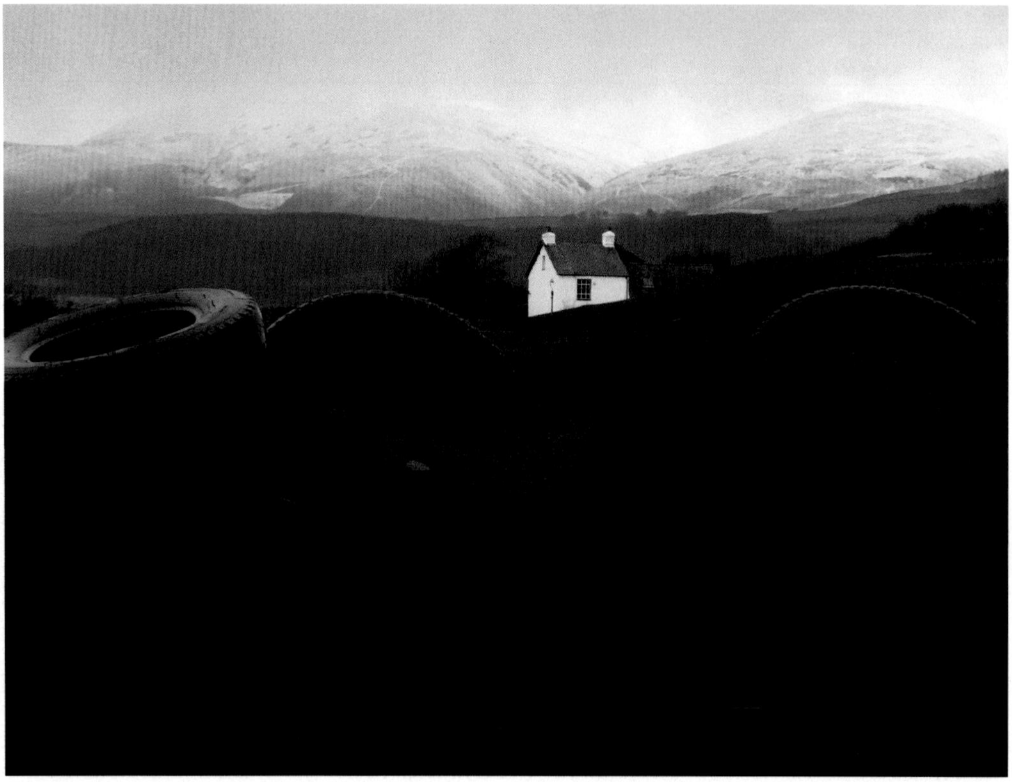

Fig. 4.20

urban and rural populations, citing the continued development of designated places in the British landscape as tourist destinations:

> *People are let out into the country . . . there are nice benches and lavatories, but they don't really experience the country and they don't understand the problems of the countryside. And so there is more and more polarization between people who live in big cities and people who live in the country. Some city dwellers . . . like to know that these spaces are still here, but one can become very unrealistic by saying that an area shouldn't be spoilt by a fish factory or various other things that the local population need in order to survive. If there is nothing at all for people to do, the only work for people in this sort of area will be services for hotels, and that is totally unreal.*[38]

The urban/rural divide that Godwin identifies is a politically poignant topic, particularly in the UK. In 2002, the prospect of a ban on hunting with hounds was a particularly emotive issue and triggered a demonstration of around 400,000 people to march on London demanding "liberty and livelihood." It is worth noting that what might seem like a fairly trivial issue received 700 hours in parliamentary debate compared to just seven on whether the UK should invade Iraq.[39] Although the march prominently articulated support for fox hunting, its principal message was a concern that the government was out of touch with the needs of rural communities and did not appreciate the importance of field sports to their economies. As well as more fundamental issues around employment and rural poverty, today prominent rural issues in the UK center on infrastructure, such as the increased cost of energy in remote parts of the country and the inaccessibility of high-speed Internet connections and mobile telephone networks.

As well as distorted and idealized impressions of the countryside and its inhabitants, an urban/rural binary remains entrenched within visual culture. In the

Fig. 4.20
KATE KIRKWOOD
Towards Blackcombe, Cumbria, 2007
Kate Kirkwood's photography of her Lakeland surroundings is illustrative of alternative possibilities of depicting the rural. In this image, a dramatic view is spliced with an oily black foreground of discarded tires holding down polyethylene over silage—an unlikely pastoral motif. Although Kirkwood's images have formal appeal, they reject clichéd or romanticized representation. Like Penny Watson (Fig. 4.14), Kirkwood sought to distance the Cumbrian landscape from its associations with nineteenth-century romanticism. Working more in the vein of a street photographer, Kirkwood's pictures are spontaneous, appearing to have been made *on the go* (even through the car windscreen) responding to immediate observations as opposed to a painstaking study of specific views or places. Nevertheless, Kirkwood's work amounts to a poetic document of her rural environs.

UK, this narrative is vividly satirized in Bruce Robinson's black comedy *Withnail & I* (1987). It is a tale of two unemployed and disillusioned actors who attempt to find rejuvenation in the Cumbrian Lake District. The ill-prepared friends soon regret leaving the city, begging the neighboring farmers to sell them some food—unconvincingly trying to assure them that they are "not from London." The hostility of the suspicious locals toward the pair, who are portrayed in similar caricature and completely overwhelmed by their circumstances, epitomizes the stereotype of two incompatible cultures.

Despite its hilarity, *Withnail & I*, set in 1969, is infused with pathos throughout and is a transparent lament for the death of the "swinging sixties." This melancholy, and the conspicuous use of rural motifs—particularly since they are subdued rather than glorified—echoes the subgenre of pastoral elegy in poetry, whereby the author writes about the death of a friend, traditionally from the imaginary perspective of a shepherd. Indeed, the film concludes with an explicit elegiac gesture: when the two characters part company, Withnail recites Shakespeare's monologue *What a piece of work is a man,* in which Hamlet expresses his grief upon the death of his father. And within the pastoral tradition, the simple matter of two friends parting is a simile for something more significant—the conclusion of a historic era.

Fig. 4.21
MURRAY CLOSE
Production still from *Withnail & I, 1986*
Murray Close's production still from Bruce Robinson's cult film depicts a scene where the main characters Marwood (played by Paul McGann) and Withnail (Richard E. Grant) argue over who will dispatch the chicken, reluctantly sold to them by a neighboring farmer. The film is a satirical illustration of a perceived urban/rural cultural incompatibility.

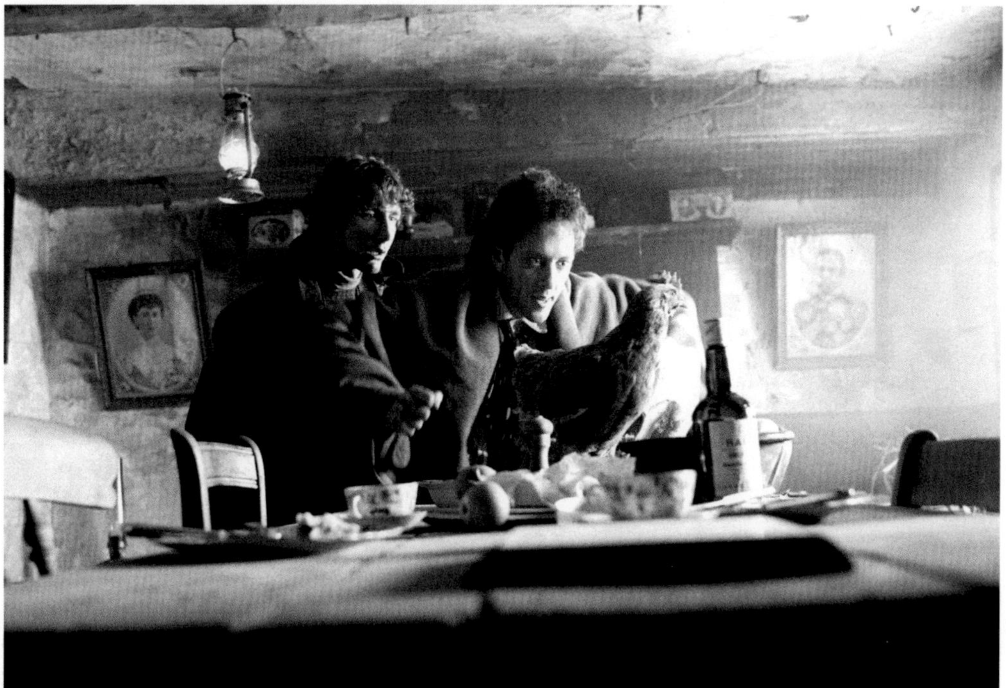

Fig. 4.21

INSPIRING NATIONHOOD

People continue to be actively encouraged to enjoy views of their own country and the views of those that they visit. From the picturesque tourist's Claude glass (see p. 65) to the modern-day viewpoint denoted on maps and road signs, we are guided toward what are considered to be the most splendid aspects that a country has to offer. Whether to be photographed to add to one's holiday snaps or to admire and contemplate the scenery only temporarily, the consumption of landscape is a popular activity. In the same manner as the family album with its repeated pictures of birthday parties, holidays, and other rituals, we share similar landscape views within our personal photographs.

In this sense, this branch of landscape photography can, like the family album, be described as "vernacular": landscapes not taken for art's sake but as personal records of one's experience.

On a daily basis we also encounter idealized imagery of what one's country is *supposed* to look like. In advertising tableaux, television programs and movies, postcards, posters, and decorative wall art, depictions of *our* land contribute to a sense of our national identity. Other public institutions, such as galleries and museums, decide which pictures are considered important enough to be acquired and added to a country's art collection. Over time and with repeated appearance, these pictures contribute to a country's sense of its unique identity.

Fig. 4.22
FRANK NEWBOULD
The South Downs* from the series *Your Britain. Fight for it now, 1942
Frank Newbould's series of four posters depicted a variety of idyllic rural views of the south of England. The style of the series does not deviate from Newbould's posters commissioned by railway companies from throughout the 1930s, advertising various parts of the UK as tourist destinations. The campaign coincided with a strategic shift by the Luftwaffe, bombing regional towns with little strategic importance. The Baedeker Blitz in 1942 was in retaliation to the Allied attacks on Lübeck, Cologne, and Rostock. Bath, Canterbury, Exeter, Norwich, and York, which were celebrated in the German *Baedeker* tourist guide to Great Britain for their picturesque beauty, were targeted. It was a strike not against the Allied war effort per se, but an attack on *Englishness* and British morale.[40]

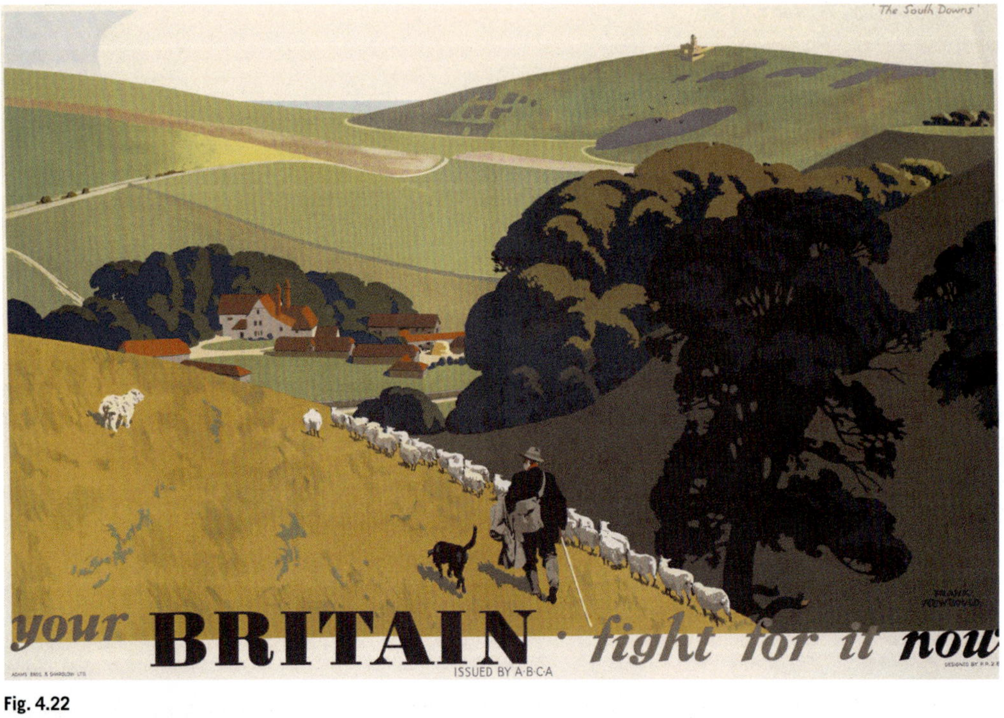

Fig. 4.22

Fig. 4.23
SIMON ROBERTS
Stanage Edge, Hathersage, Derbyshire, August 3, 2008* from the series *We English*, *2009
In the foreground, a Muslim couple wearing distinct gray robes walk on a footpath through the landscape. Our tendency to read this view in terms of traditional English activities is hard to resist, and the couple therefore seem to be out of place. On speaking to them, I learned that they were from Leicester on a week's walking holiday, staying at a B&B in the nearby village of Hathersage. They spoke of feeling completely at ease in the area and described how they often spent their holidays exploring the English countryside.
Simon Roberts[41]

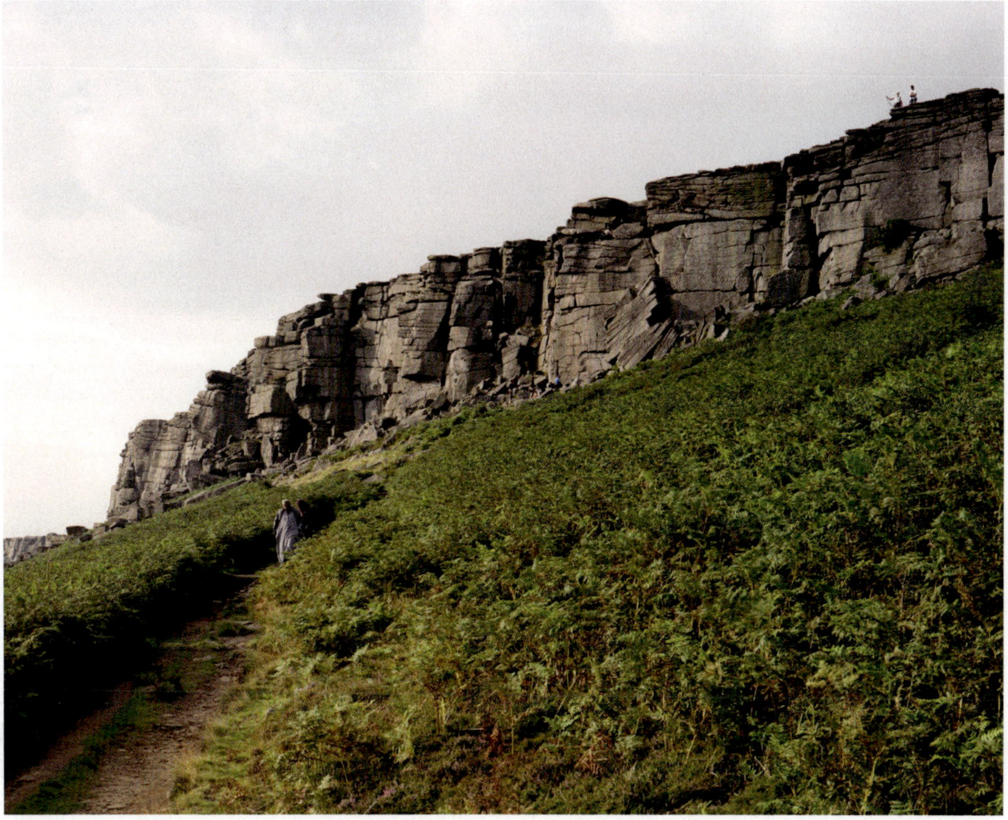

Fig. 4.23

The effectiveness of subverting one such national treasure can be seen in Peter Kennard's *Haywain with Cruise Missiles* (Fig. 2.7). The art historian Kenneth Clark (1903–1983) wrote the following about John Constable's original painting: "Its leading motives have been the inspiration of a hundred thousand calendars, but personally I find that it has survived this destructive popularity and remains an eternally moving expression of serenity and optimism."[42] Accordingly, *The Hay Wain* has contributed to the mythologizing of the southern English landscape as among other adjectives, "serene." Often, landscape pictures have a unifying effect upon the viewer; however, this can come at the expense of the exclusion of others who, for various reasons, do not identify the image perceived by the majority.

NATIONAL IDENTITIES

In periods of social unrest and war, depictions of the landscape have historically been used to inspire national unity. During the Second World War, all sides used imagery of their landscape to make the public aware of the importance of the land in terms of simultaneously fueling the war effort and reminding the public what they were fighting for. Frank Newbould's famous series of posters, which were commissioned during the Second World War, is a vivid example (Fig. 4.22). Rather than using macabre or frightening imagery typical of First World War propaganda, Newbould, who was an established advertising artist and famous for his railway company posters, painted tranquil scenes from the south of England. These were juxtaposed with the rousing strapline, "Your Britain. Fight for it now." His depiction of the South Downs features the archetypal pastoral motif of a farmer and his dog with a flock of sheep and a farm in the center of the composition, which appears to be nestled within the protective countryside around it. In the background, a tiny slither of the English Channel is visible, perhaps a subtle suggestion of where the enemy might arrive. This faint detail is a reminder of Britain's relationship to the coast as a natural defensive asset, which is also at the root of an "islander" mentality that continues to be a stereotype of the British perceived by others.

The Second World War also prompted a major initiative to document the British landscape and its architecture, which aimed at making artistic records of the country facing rapid and unprecedented change as well as sustaining a sense of the preciousness and precariousness of the countryside. The scheme, called "Recording Britain," was an extension of the War Artist's Advisory Committee (WAAC), which coordinated the commissioning of artists, such as Henry Moore, Stanley Spencer, and Paul Nash, to interpret the war effort both along the home front and throughout overseas theaters. The establishment of the WAAC and the Recording Britain scheme was in no small part owed to Kenneth Clark, then director of the National Gallery. As well as propaganda and posterity, Clark had more realistic motivations—to keep artists employed and away from the front lines. While the scheme and the resulting archive have their merits, the overwhelming majority of the collection—which almost exclusively comprises watercolors and pencil drawings—are benign rural studies and scenes of market towns, amounting to a charming yet myopic depiction of Britain: Scotland was surveyed in a separate scheme altogether, and Clark's project omitted paintings of Northern Ireland and contained a relatively small number from Wales, with the majority of the collection comprising views of the south of England.

MINORITY PERSPECTIVES

Occasionally there are moments when an image will strike a chord that transcends political or national boundaries, such as the *Earthrise* photograph (Fig. 4.10), and themes within landscape, such as the sublime, exert themselves on a psychological level. However, much landscape imagery is coded with cultural motifs that are lost on viewers who are unfamiliar with certain references. Although landscape is essentially a shared activity, the messages are not always received entirely as they were meant to be read.

Simon Roberts's major project *We English* is a survey of the contemporary English landscape and picks out peculiarities and eccentricities, as well as more commonplace activities of its inhabitants. While the project is likely to be immediately accessible to British audiences, there is a danger this kind of project might leave foreign audiences at a loss as to how to interpret the subject matter or even how to confine a nation to conformed stereotypes.

Roberts's work has been compared to Martin Parr's *Think of England* (2001), which isolates English stereotypes more explicitly. Roberts's photographs are,

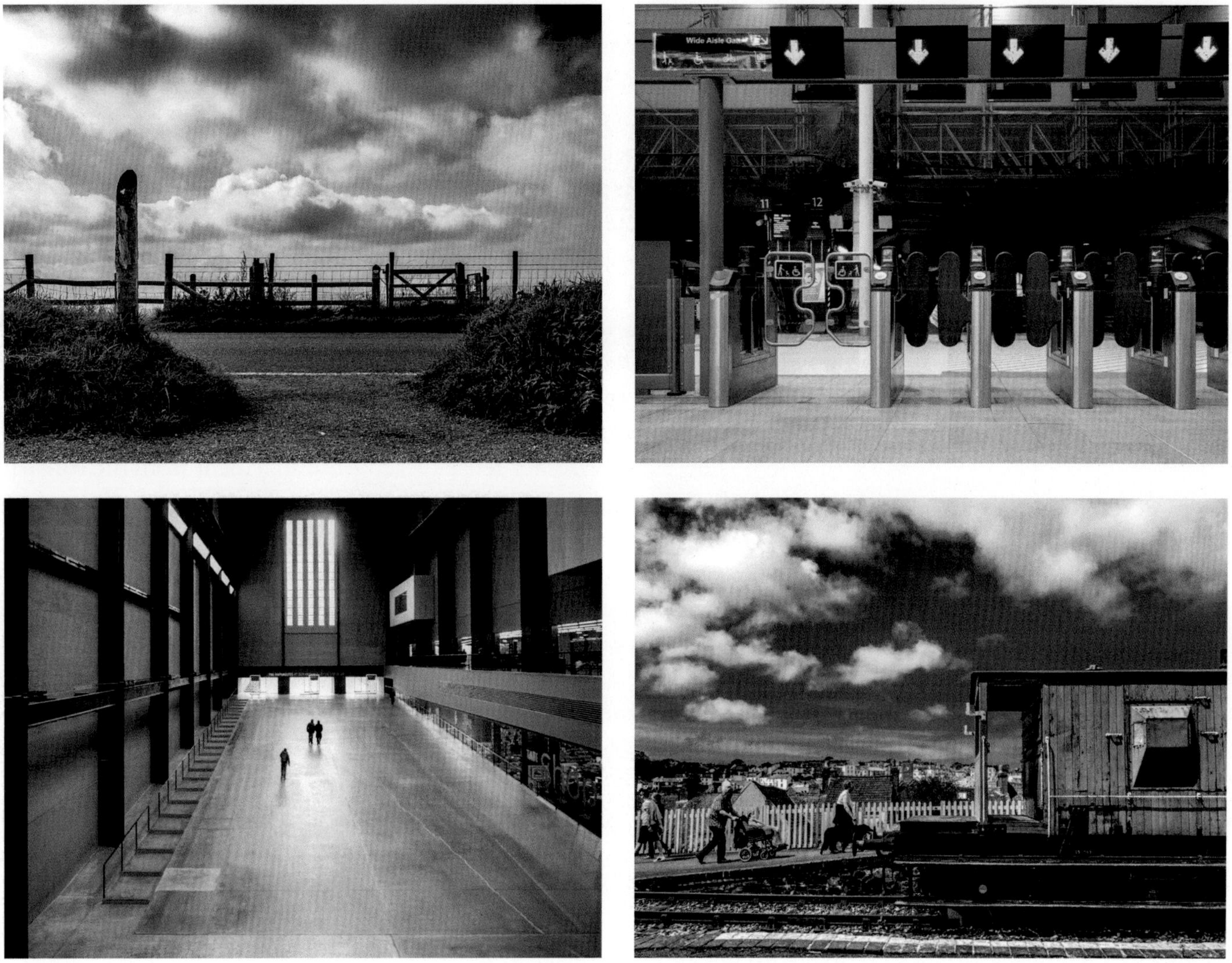

Fig. 4.24

Fig. 4.24.i–4.24.iv
PETER MANSELL
Landscape of Disability, 2013
Peter Mansell offers a personal insight into what it is like to navigate public spaces from the perspective of a wheelchair user. He identifies particular structures and design features that turn out to be poorly thought through or easily undone: an accessible station but an inaccessible train, or instead of making all the ticketing gates wide enough for wheelchair access, installing a single designated extra-wide gate. Mansell questions the wisdom of special provisions for people with special needs, suggesting that design with both able-bodied and disabled people in mind will ultimately better serve everyone and also dismantle societal barriers between able-bodied people and those with disabilities.

of course, created and read in a landscape paradigm. The photographer looks specifically at the diversity of English leisure activities in relation to the landscape, ranging from the bizarre—the annual Mad Maldon Mud Race in Essex—to the intimate—Roberts's photograph of the South Downs in Sussex shows what we assume is a young couple relaxing in a field, a curious echo of the pastoral motif of young villagers courting. As well as the presentation of clichés, such as the couple picnicking barely a few meters away from their car in the Yorkshire Dales, Roberts challenges stereotypes about the English landscape.

Within his commentary on the project, published on the blog that accompanied the project, Roberts wrote of his satisfaction at being able to question a widely held perception that the English countryside is dominated by the white middle classes.[43] These comments stand in stark contrast to the celebrated series *Pastoral Interlude* (1987) and *Miss Pollard's Party* (1993) by Ingrid Pollard, who was born in Guyana and asserts in no uncertain terms her sense of acute estrangement from the English rural identity. In *Pastoral Interlude*, Pollard appears as a slightly awkward-looking rambler. The photographs are hand-tinted monochrome prints, which is a reference to the quaint heritage of the landscape that she temporarily occupies, adding to a sense of incongruity. The depth of her discomfort is articulated vociferously in the accompanying captions, for example:

> *It's as if the Black experience is only lived within an urban environment. I thought I liked the Lake District, where I wandered lonely as a Black face in a sea of white. A visit to the countryside is always accompanied by a feeling of unease, dread.*[44]

The sense of isolation and of failing to recognize a common image of the landscape that Pollard voices in her early works is explored in the work of Peter Mansell. Because of a spinal cord injury, Mansell relies on a wheelchair to engage with his environment both in his daily life and in his photographic practice. His series *Landscape of Disability* (Fig. 4.24) is shot from the slightly lower than usual perspective of a wheelchair user and identifies design nuances (and nuisances) of public spaces that are intended to aid accessibility. Often, however, such measures are dysfunctional, which has the effect of underscoring difference rather than promoting equality of locomotion through the urban environment. The series offers an insight to approaching landscape from the point of view of an outsider, not in terms of cultural identity but in terms of how one might physically interact with public spaces.

1 E. Jussim and E. Lindquist-Cock, *Landscape as Photograph* (New Haven: Yale University Press, 1985), 140.

2 These prefixes include *sea*scapes, *town*scapes, *urban,* and *industrial* landscapes, which uphold an implication of a rural bias in unprefixed, *regular* "landscapes."

3 Burtynsky comments, "I was born a hundred years too late to be searching for the sublime in nature. To me, pursuing this would have just been an expression of nostalgia." From *Manufactured Landscapes: The Photographs of Edward Burtynsky* (Ottawa: National Gallery of Canada, 2003), 47.

4 Liz Wells, *Land Matters: Landscape Photography, Culture and Identity* (London: I.B. Tauris, 2011), 170–71.

5 Joshua Schuster, "Between Manufacturing and Landscapes: Edward Burtynsky and the Photography of Ecology," *Photography & Culture*, 6(ii) (2013): 194.

6 Geoff Dyer, *Zona* (Edinburgh: Canongate Books, 2012), 116.

7 Phrase expressed by Richard West and John Duncan in *Source* 52 (Autumn 2007), 32.

8 See B.L. Garrett, "Undertaking Recreational Trespass: Urban Exploration and Infiltration," in *Transactions of the British Institute of Geographers*, 2013 doi: 10.1111/tran.12001. Also see Garrett's blog, http://www.placehacking.co.uk.

9 For a detailed discussion, see Ian Walker's essay in Patrizia Di Bello (ed.). *The Photobook: From Talbot to Ruscha and Beyond* (London: I.B. Taurus, 2012).

10 William Jenkins, *New Topographics: Photographs of the Man-Altered Landscape* (New York: International Center of Photography at George Eastman House, 1975), 5.

11 Greg Foster-Rice and John Rohrbach, *Reframing the New Topographics* (Chicago: The Center for American Places at Colombia College Chicago, 2013), xiv.

12 Ibid.

13 Ibid., 90.

14 Jenkins, *New Topographics.*

15 This technique has a sinister heritage in photography, particularly in Sir Francis Galton's investigations into eugenics and Alphonse Bertillon's studies of criminal types.

16 Gregory Crewdson is one practitioner who effectively explores the strangeness of the American suburbs through elaborate narrative tableaux.

17 Paul Farley and Michael Symmons Roberts, *Edgelands: Journeys into England's True Wilderness* (London: Jonathan Cape, 2011), 194.

18 Malcolm Andrews, *Landscape and Western Art* (Oxford: Oxford University Press, 1999), 175.

19 Jussim and Lindquist-Cock, *Landscape,* 140.

20 Adams was an active member of the Sierra Club, which was founded in California at the end of the nineteenth century and continues to lobby for environmental and conservation issues across the world.

21 See Robert Pool, *Earthrise: How Man First Saw the Earth* (London: Yale Books, 2010).

22 See the photomontages of Peter Kennard, who collaborated with the Campaign for Nuclear Disarmament (CND).

23 From Vicky Goldberg, *The Power of Photography: How Photographs Changed Our Lives* (New York: Abbeville Publishing Group, 1991), 52.

24 Rachel Carson, *Silent Spring* (London: Penguin Books, 1991), 22.

25 Landen's project *The Abyss* was published in *Source* 51, Summer 2007.

26 John A. Taylor, *A Dream of England: Landscape, Photography and the Tourist's Imagination* (Manchester & New York: University of Manchester Press, 1994), 273–74.

27 In the following sample of seminal landscape exhibitions, the ratio of male to female practitioners was as follows:
New Topographics (New York, 1975) 9:1
Perspectives on Landscape (London: 1978) 10:1
Landscape Without Horizon (Nuremberg, 2010) 13:2
Sense of Place: European Landscape Photography (Brussels: 2012) 30:10
Landmark: A Stroll Through the Fields of Photography (London: 2013) 68:12

28 Liz Wells, Land Matters: *Landscape Photography, Culture, and Identity* (London: I.B. Tauris, 2011), 188. See also Liz Wells, *Viewfindings: Women Photographers, Landscape and Environment* (Tiverton: Available Light, 1994).

29 Wells, *Land Matters,* 116.

30 See Andrews, *Landscape,* 157.

31 This anthropomorphism recalls the fruit and vegetable "faces" of sixteenth-century painter Giuseppe Arcimboldo.

32 See Taylor, *A Dream,* 272–73.

33 The concept of the male gaze is perhaps most clearly articulated in Laura Mulvey's essential essay "Visual Pleasure and Narrative Cinema," in *Screen* 16(iii), 1975.

34 See for instance Susan Trangmar (*Untitled Landscapes, 1986*), Elina Brotherus (*Large de vue, Hommage à Erik Satie, 2006*), and Karen Knorr (*The Virtues and the Delights, 1992–1994*).

35 Mary Horlock, "Between a Rock and a Soft Place," in Mark Sladen (ed.) *Helen Chadwick* (Ostfildern-Ruit: Hatje Cantz, 2004), 21.

36 Ibid., 39.

37 In precisely the same way that picturesque composition was ordered according to visual harmony, the use of pastoral motifs were used to imply social harmony. See David Bate, "Notes on Beauty and Landscape," in Campany, 2003, 287.

38 Fay Godwin, *Southbank Show,* produced and directed by Hilary Chadwick, London Weekend Television, 1986.

39 Geoffrey Wheatcroft, "Jaw-Jaw on Hunting is SOP to MPs for War-War in Iraq," *Guardian,* February 14, 2005. Accessed December 21, 2013. http://www.theguardian.com/politics/2005/feb/14/labour.hunting.

40 Christine Riding, "The Home Front: War and Peace," in Dimbleby, *A Picture of Britain,* 80.

41 "Contested Countryside," *We English,* January 16, 2009. Accessed December 27, 2013. http://we-english.co.uk/blog/?p=930.

42 Kenneth Clark, *Landscape into Art,* (2nd ed.) (London: John Murray, 1976), 151.

43 "*We English* Commentary," *We English,* September 7, 2009. Accessed December 27, 2013. http://we-english.co.uk/blog/?p=1864.

44 *Pastoral Interlude* reproduced in Wells, *Viewfindings.*

ASSIGNMENT 4

YOUR POINT OF VIEW

PROJECT This chapter has touched upon several topics that are either of social and political significance today or that were pertinent to the historical context in which they were made. With some of these issues in mind, compile a list of social and political topics that you find interesting. You may feel these are specific to your immediate location or circumstances or they may be more universal themes or topics. Whatever they are, make sure that these are things that genuinely interest you. Try to expand your list, prioritizing the topics that you feel are most relevant, and begin thinking about how you might use photography to investigate them. You may find that some of the issues on your list are interconnected: Is there a way of linking several themes together or making other connections?

Start thinking about how you will treat one of these topics, and begin working on your project with some test shoots. Try to incorporate techniques and materials sympathetically, to complement your subject matter. How you do this will depend entirely upon your chosen theme or topic. Once you have made some preliminary progress, discuss your ideas for subject matter and strategies with your peer group.

When you have developed your project, post your work on your blog or show it to your peers along with a brief evaluation of your project. Refer to specific images and explain your working process. Consider your audience and their prior knowledge of the subject your work addresses. You may need to supply an additional narrative about the subject; however, this information should complement, not override, your photographs. Discuss the strengths and weaknesses of your project and how successfully you believe it addresses the themes that you set out to explore.

RESEARCH AND DISCUSSION Consider the following questions and write down your thoughts in your reflective learning journal or on your blog. You may find these questions helpful to develop your ideas for your project.

- Are images of the negative impact of man on the landscape or pictures of an environmentally sensitive nature made within a sublime tradition helpful in raising awareness of certain issues? Or do such depictions simply turn the issues into spectacle, overshadowing the ecological urgency of the subject matter?
- Do you think that men and women relate to the landscape in different ways? Do you think that your gender determines how you look at a landscape?
- How have your personal circumstances shaped your perception of rural and urban lifestyles? What potential conflicts can you see between those living in towns and cities and those in rural communities?
- How do you think outsiders stereotype the people and the place where you live, either locally or nationally? Is there any truth in these perceptions or are they misconceptions? How do you think such impressions are formed?

Chapter 5
LAND MARKS

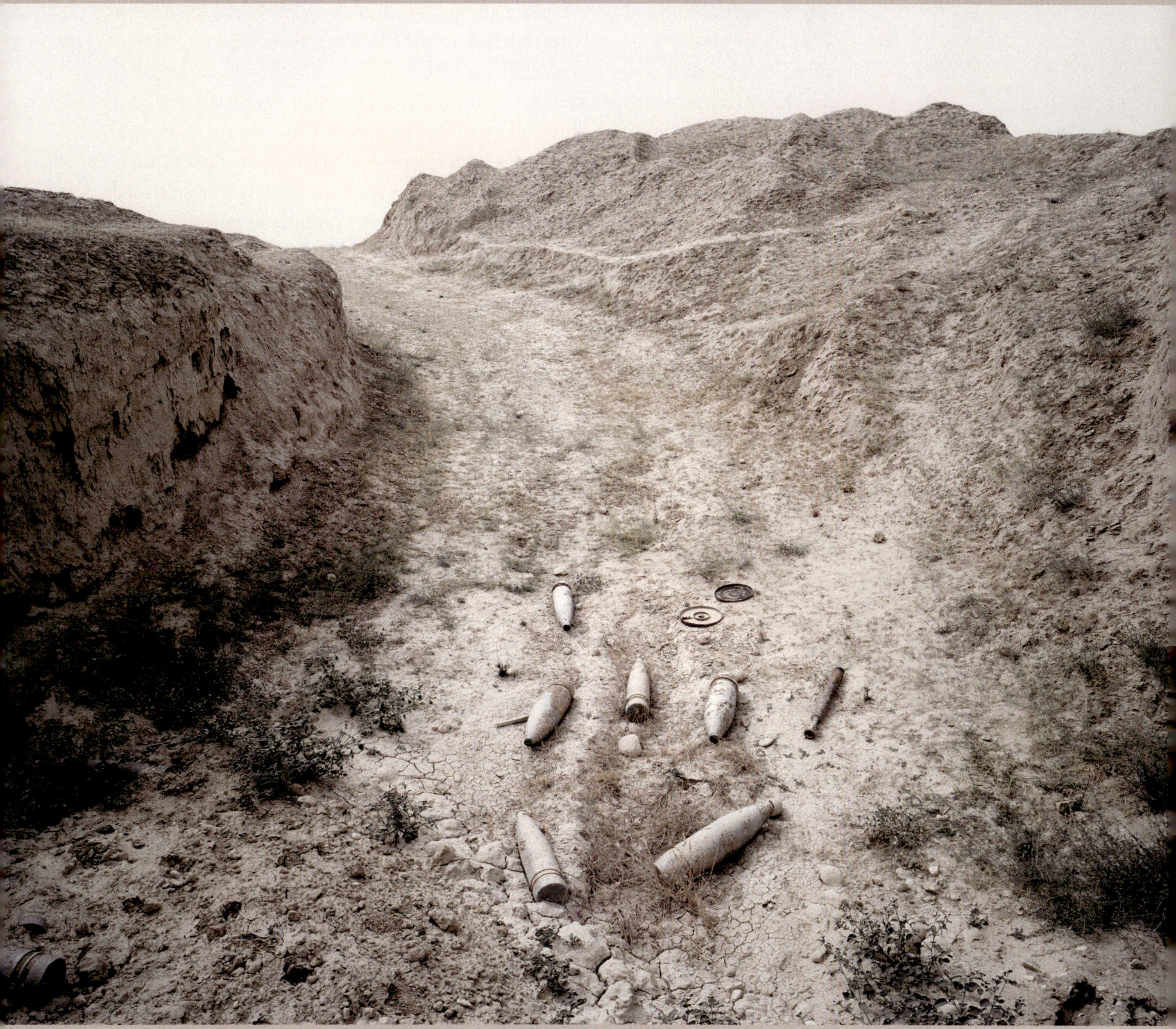

Fig. 5.1

Fig. 5.1
PAUL SEAWRIGHT
Valley, 2002 from the series
Hidden, 2003

Although we have already looked at many bodies of work where the artistic intention wasn't necessarily immediately identifiable from the single photograph alone, this chapter deals more explicitly with meaning that lies much deeper than the thin surface of the photographic image. The historical narratives and recent events that are bound to a particular part of the land are not always apparent or immediately visible. The effects of a violent episode in a nation's history or a terrible catastrophe may ripple for many years to follow, although its signs will often be nuanced and familiar only to someone very familiar with the area. In some areas of photography we see the medium at the forefront of history, recording momentous events as they unfold. In landscape photography, however, the nature of the relationship to history is often not so much as witness but as a more pensive and retrospective inquiry.

Often, the tension created within the frame is not caused by what can be seen but by what is absent. The forensic nature of the photograph is well suited to these subtle and sensitive approaches. We shall also consider the distinction between a space and a place and reflect on the many ways that one particular location assumes greater cultural significance over another. We shall begin with a discussion of a mythical place, Arcadia, which is not only a recurring motif in landscape art but perhaps lies at the root of all idealized fantasies of nature that so many makers and consumers of landscape pictures continue to believe in.

LANDSCAPE AND MYTH

The Renaissance period, which brought about the genre of landscape painting, saw the reinvigoration within the arts of mythical narratives from antiquity about a prehistoric "golden age." In their epic poems, the Greek poets Virgil and Ovid describe this period as an idyllic time of ease and plenty, when man existed in an unspoiled condition and lived according to his uncorrupted conscience. The Golden Age was defined as the first of the Five Ages of Man in Hesiod's *Works and Days,* which dates from around 700 BC. Hesiod outlined the decline of man's virtuosity and moral purity, denoted by decreasing mineral quality from silver to iron, the age in which Hesiod finds himself. Arcadia was the name given to the site of the Golden Age and the place where there was no sickness or death, food was plentiful, animals did not harm one another, and people lived without the need of governance or authority. This kind of uncomplicated Edenic idyll as a kind of birthplace of mankind can be seen across creation narratives in all cultures.[1]

Anthropological evaluations of the universality of images of this kind of prehistoric paradise conclude that they are rooted in the very real narrative of humankind.[2] Contrary to popular perception, the hunter-gatherers of the Mesolithic Age (before c. 10,000 BC) actually had greater access to food and leisure time than did many of their Neolithic successors, who with greater population densities, adopted sedentism, which was associated with agricultural systems and more complex social hierarchies.[3] It is believed that Hesiod's lament for the lost Golden Age mirrors a longing for a way of life that our ancestors were forced to give up. This kind of nostalgia for bygone eras can be seen in cultures at all points in their history. When we seek comfort, we often find reassurance in memories and images of the past. This translates into our taste for the types of landscape imagery that we surround ourselves with—images of the unspoiled, pristine landscape commonly decorate our domestic and public spaces. The popularity of these kinds of views indicates a collective aspiration for rural experiences and a desire to escape to less-densely populated spaces.

The myth of Arcadia has been extensively re-evaluated throughout the history of art and continues to be an object of fascination for contemporary practitioners. Christopher Down has used this image to explore issues around present-day conflicts. In *Visions from Arcadia* (Fig. 5.3), Down places soldiers within his interpretation of a tranquil Arcadian garden. Down's vision is a fairly modest impression of Arcadia, perhaps unpacking the myth or suggesting it as being a state of mind rather than a physical place. Unlike the early Renaissance paintings

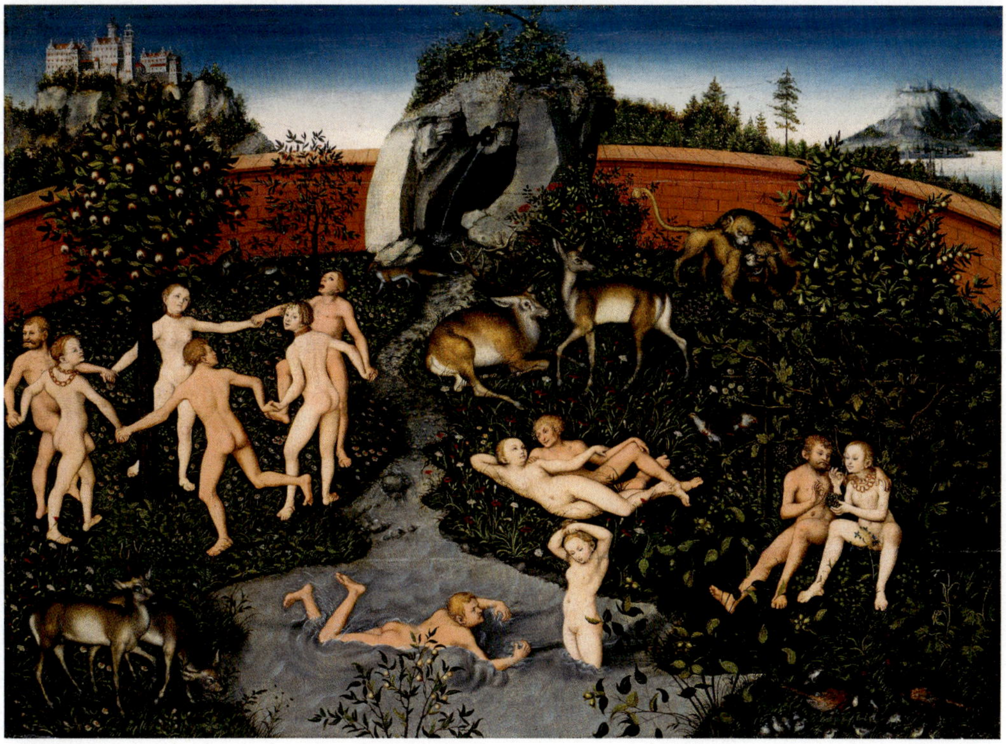

Fig. 5.2

Fig. 5.2
LUCAS CRANACH THE ELDER (1472–1553)
The Golden Age, c.1530
Cranach's depiction of Arcadia, the site of Hesiod's "golden age," summarizes the utopian aspirations of generations of scholars and artists who have continued to explore the possibilities of a "perfect" environment and lifestyle—the abundance of food, harmony between all animals, sexual freedom, and autonomy from governance being the key recurring themes. According to Hesiod, the god Zeus concluded the Golden Age with the Age of Silver, bringing with it the four seasons and making it necessary for man to build shelters as well as plant his own crops. Tales and mythology from antiquity such as Hesiod's were popular subjects during the Renaissance.

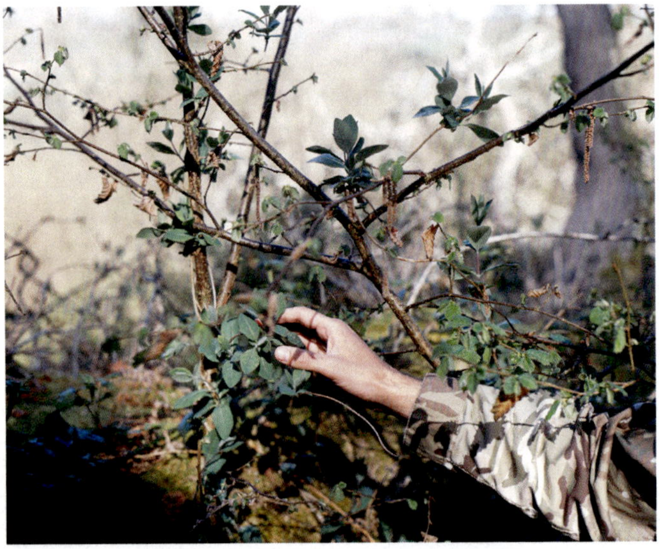

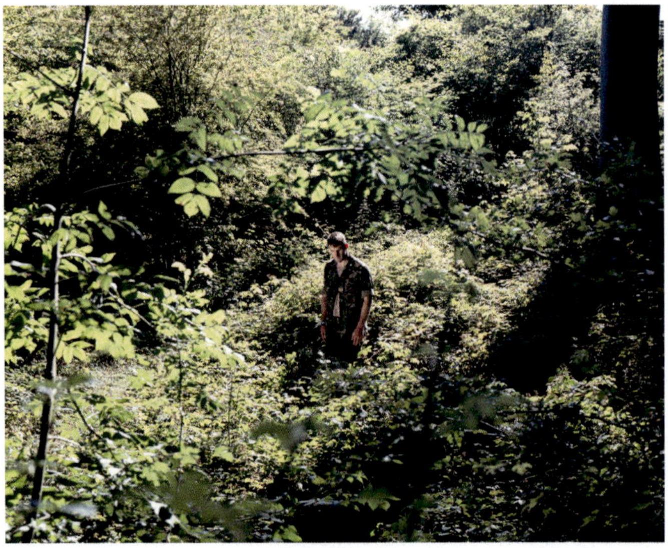

Fig. 5.3

Fig. 5.3.i–5.3.iv (left to right)
CHRISTOPHER DOWN
Man is a part of nature, Leipzig Wood, Before the clearing,* and *Orchard (part two)* from the series *Visions from Arcadia, 2012
Chris Down's collaborations with servicemen engage with themes surrounding the myth of Arcadia. The somewhat bemused expressions of the soldiers as they appear to be re-engaging with territory at peace—recently withdrawn we may presume from a theater of war—contribute to a more general sense of discord throughout the series. In Hesiod's *Works and Days*, narratives of fighting and conflict underpin the transitions from one age to the next, and the soldiers dressed in modern fatigues remind us of the state of war and conflict in which we seem to be perpetually engaged. The military uniforms are a more explicit reference to the mythologization of land in relation to war, for instance, the "green and pleasant" English landscape being worthy of a soldier's making the ultimate sacrifice for, as well as being a place of sanctuary in which to disengage from combat duties.

of Lucas Cranach the Elder (Fig. 5.2) or the early-twentieth-century interpretations of Cézanne and Matisse, there is no frolicking or jollity, only quiet reflection, contemplation, and personal exploration of this unassuming landscape, which appears to offer a sanctuary and temporary respite from the realities of the soldiers' duties. The linear nature of Down's series, which follows the four seasons (which were forced upon the people of Arcadia as punishment) becomes both pastoral motif and a further acknowledgment of the unrelenting cycle of war.

POLITICS OF ARCADIA

More general themes of utopia within philosophy, literature, and art owe much to the Golden Age narrative. In *The Republic* (c. 360 BC), Plato outlined his vision of the ideal society, detailing precisely the structure and laws that would make this prosperous civilization function. This is regarded as the earliest example of a utopia within literature. The bureaucratic and political nature of *The Republic* typifies what utopia has become, a description of a political system that defines a place rather than the physical appearance of the place itself. As Plato's utopia appears to contemporary readers, often—if not always—utopias have a tendency to descend into their counterpoints, dystopian nightmares. Indeed, post–Second World War evaluations of *The Republic* criticize Plato's work for its totalitarian message.[4]

Shimon Attie's project *The Writing on the Wall* (Fig. 5.4) confronts the crimes carried out by one particular political regime and atrocities committed in the fanatic pursuit of an ideologically perverted society. In *The Writing on the Wall*, Attie juxtaposed photographs of Scheunenviertel, Berlin's former Jewish quarter, taken

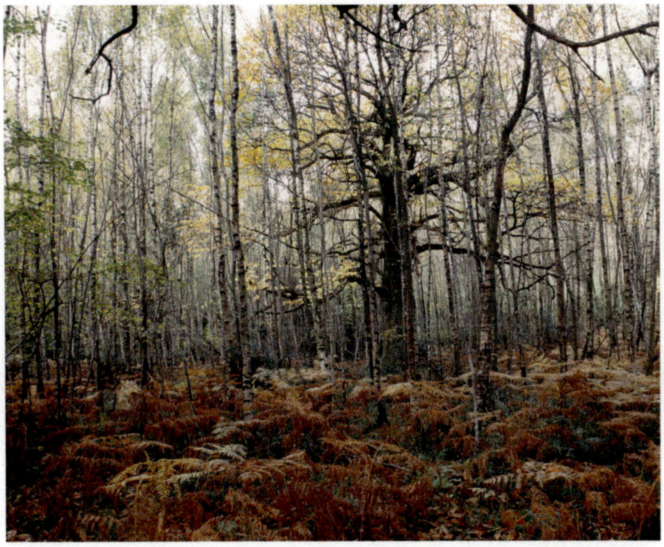

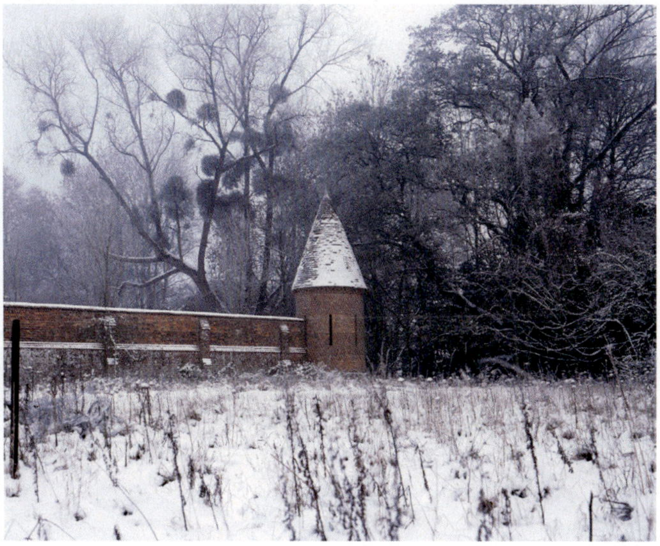

in the 1930s with the present-day architecture of this now-fashionable part of the city. Attie made use of what few photographs remain of the community and the buildings and projected these at life-size proportions back onto what period architecture remains in the Scheunenviertel. In Attie's temporary installations, archival photographs and the people who lived within them were reanimated by the space, sixty years after they were taken. The Jewish residents of Scheunenviertel—all of whom would have either emigrated or been murdered by the Nazis—are momentarily returned and defy the regime that so fanatically attempted to obliterate all traces of their existence. Jorma Puranen employed a similar strategy with his work *Imaginary Homecomings* (1991–1997), placing large prints of ethnographic portraits of native Scandinavian Sámi people taken during expeditions in the 1880s within the landscapes of Norway and Sweden.[5] The very symbolic *re-placing* of displaced communities, which the projects of both Attie and Puranen achieve, is a clear assertion that landscapes and the memories inscribed within them are intimately bound to the people who inhabited them.

Michal Iwanowski's series *Clear of People* (Figs. 1.23 and 5.5) addresses related themes of memory and identity. For the project, the photographer retraced the journey from Russia to Poland made by his grandfather and his grandfather's brother as fugitive prisoners of war at the end of World War II. These territories are rich in historical narratives and riddled with traces of past conflicts, such as concentration camps and mass graves. Central to Iwanowski's strategy was avoiding contact with people, mirroring the experience of his grandfather and great uncle as fugitives in a hostile environment. As a result, other figures seldom appear throughout the series,

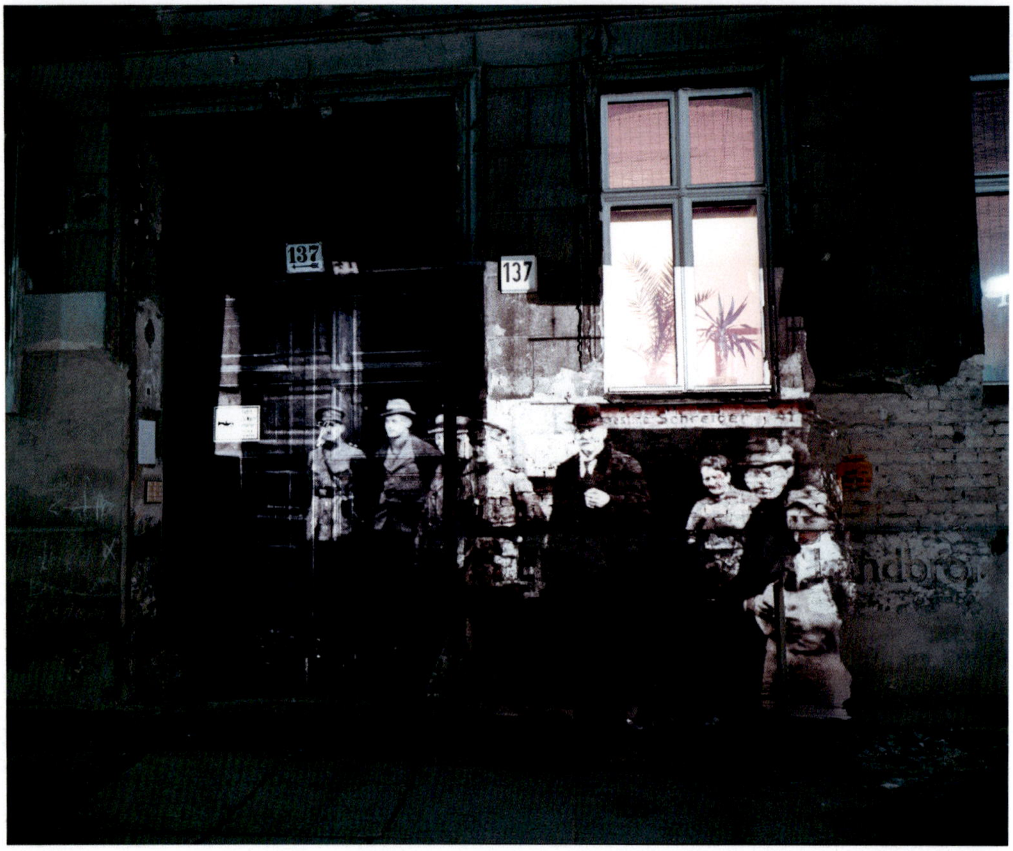

Fig. 5.4

Fig. 5.4
SHIMON ATTIE
Slide Projection of Police Raid on Former Jewish Residents.* Installation view from the project *The Writing on the Wall, 1992–1994
Shimon Attie's practice explores themes around migration and often involves working with communities that have experienced trauma or tragedy. In this installation he used archival images of residents taken in Berlin's historic Jewish quarter and projected these back on to the architecture of the contemporary site. This process reanimated these ghosts from the past into life-sized effigies. Many of the projections achieved practically perfect alignment of the architectural structures and details inside the photographs with the present-day buildings. As well as having a disturbing presence, the installation performs a curious kind of reversal of the photographic process, whereby the subject once captured through lens and film reappears within the space from which it was taken some sixty years ago.

and when they do, it is with an evident sense of detachment, often achieved from a high vantage point, such as illustrated in Fig. 1.23. This approach forced Iwanowski to traverse the peripheries of towns and villages and into the security of the more rural parts of the countries, much of which have remained relatively unchanged over the decades. The series is steeped in pathos and introspection, the visibly austere Eastern European climate contributing to a sense of isolation. This atmosphere, and the understated visual qualities of Iwanowski's photographs, underscores the distance between where they are on their journey and *home*.

While memories and narratives of the past are frequently reinterrogated by present-day practitioners, with the exception of certain practitioners who create conspicuously fictional landscapes, producing imagery of places and events that have yet to happen is, of course, not so straightforward for photographers as it is for those practicing in other media. Futuristic dystopias continue to captivate consumers of popular culture, from the regimented societies imagined by H.G. Wells and Aldous Huxley to complete societal disarray following environmental catastrophe in novels such as Cormac McCarthy's *The Road* (2006). In his documentary film *Into Eternity* (2009), Michael Madsen outlines the very real hazard posed to the environment by radioactive waste material. The didactic narrative is set against the construction of a vast subterranean storage facility in Finland called "Onkalo," which when completed around 2020, will store about a century's worth of spent nuclear fuel before it has been sealed, hopefully never to be opened again. The time scale of this project is staggering: scientists estimate that it will take up to 100,000 years for the radioactive material to become safe. The challenge that presents itself—assuming that there is anything left of mankind that far into the future—is how we set about dissuading forthcoming generations from tampering

Fig. 5.5
MICHAL IWANOWSKI
Pylon, Varliskes, Lithuania, 2012* from the series *Clear of People, 2013
I arrived in Lithuania for the first time in November 2012. I instinctively started walking, almost as if triggered by a memory gene that responded to the land under my feet. It had been nearly 70 years since my grandparents left their homes and their youth amidst the terrors of WWII. And equally as long since my grandfather escaped from imprisonment in Russia and crossed over 2000 km in search of his family. For many years, I thought that period of their lives was merely a funny anecdote or a nursery rhyme in a slightly strange language from some sort of a prehistory. Yet in a bizarre way, as I kept on walking through the forests and fields, from Kaunas to Vilnius, I could not help but feel, rather boldly, that I was coming home. And that inexplicable sensation of recognizing a landscape I had not seen before stayed with me throughout the journey. At the same time, due to the hypnotic nature of walking, and due to the relatively wild terrain I was moving across, time became irrelevant. It was both 1945 and 2013, the land had no boundaries, and it belonged to no country—only to the men and women who stood on it and recognized it as theirs.
Michal Iwanowski

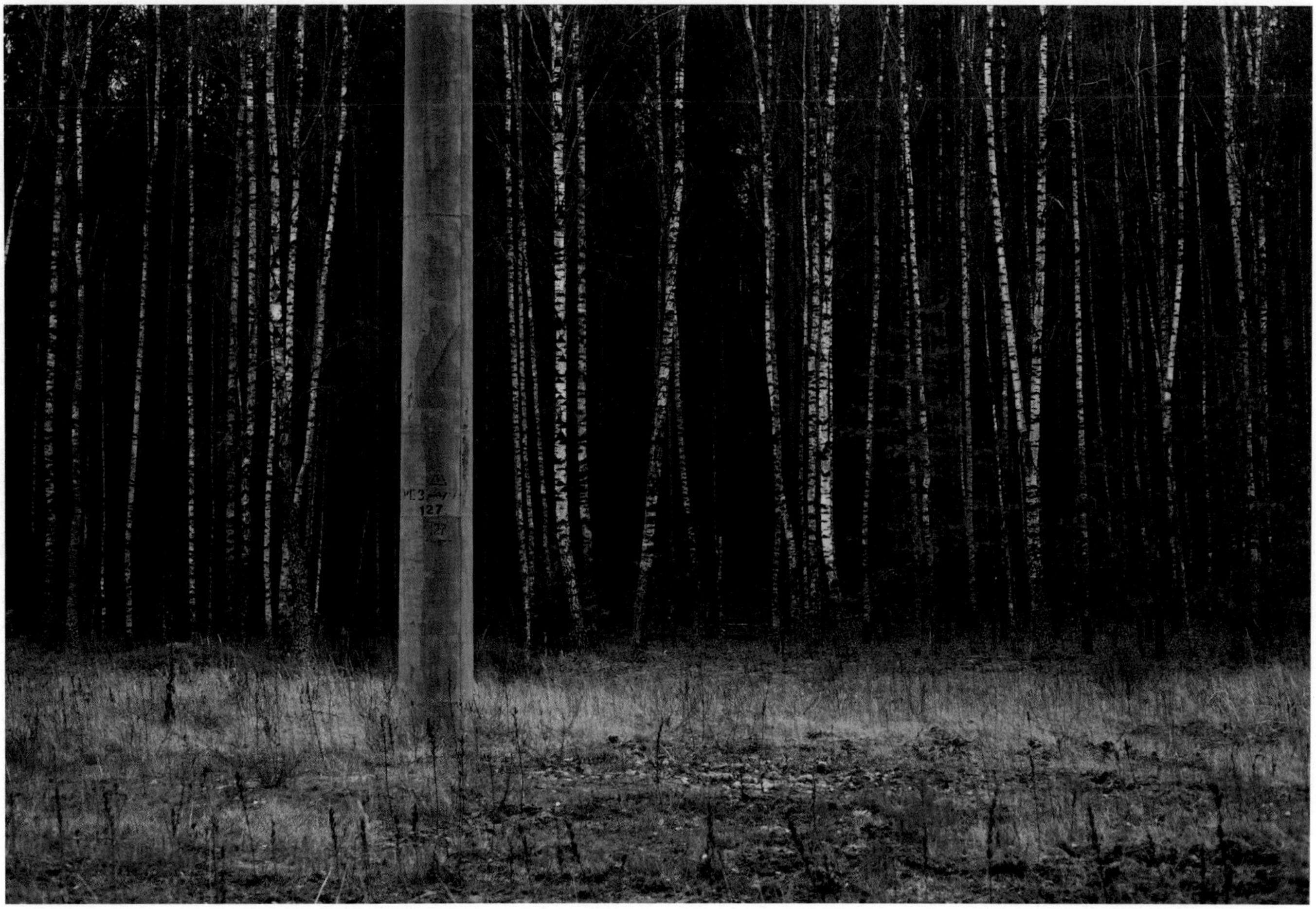

Fig. 5.5

with Onkalo. Aren't tales of a lethal material—a substance which has no visibly harmful properties—bound to become distorted over millennia, mythologized into stories about a mystical source of energy, power, or even knowledge? The practicalities of this task force us to consider how the mythology around a place might be *projected*—the reversal of an anthropological assessment of how past narratives inform current cultural perspectives of a landscape.

CONTESTED TERRITORIES

Since land tends to be the possession of someone, or indeed a nation, it is more than likely that from time to time disputes will arise over whom the land belongs to. Images of war and conflict pervade the history of all spheres of photography, and landscape is no exception. Some of the earliest photographs of conflict are widely considered to be more important in the broader narrative of photography than are landscape photographs taken at the time with more ostentatious claims to be taken seriously as art.

The Crimean War (1853–1856) provided the first opportunity to test the response of the photographer and the medium in a war zone and was the first time that any individual came close to what we would loosely identify today as a war correspondent. It is difficult to fathom the contrasting technical challenges that faced protowar photographers like Roger Fenton (1819–1869), James Robertson (1813–1888), and Felice Beato (1832–1909), who witnessed the Crimean conflict in Europe, and Alexander Gardner (1821–1882) and his contemporaries, who photographed the American Civil War during the following decade. The photographs of these conflicts established the "battlefield" within the discourse of landscape photography, which continues to motivate practitioners today of both fine art and documentary persuasions.[6]

These early conflicts tested certain ideas about the medium of photography, and they also set in motion ethical questions around the representation of conflict that are perhaps even more pressing in today's cultural climate, which is increasingly dominated by the photographic image. Fenton's presence during the Crimean campaign was owed to the requirement for some kind of evidence to put a positive spin on the British war effort, or in other words, generate some propaganda.[7] This endeavor is believed to have come at the behest of Prince Albert, who understood the need to counteract the negative accounts of the Crimean campaign in the press. Needless to say, photography, still in an age when it was very much believed to be a reliable witness, seemed like the perfect antidote to damning *written* accounts, particularly the dispatches of William Howard Russell.[8]

The cumbersome photographic equipment of the time and the slow emulsions of the wet-plate negatives, which had to be processed as soon as they were exposed, severely restricted the capabilities of nineteenth-century photographers working with all subjects. However, the chaotic and perilous nature of warfare exacerbated the situation for those working in the battlefield. Like his counterparts who covered the American Civil War, Fenton was therefore resigned to photograph depictions of the people, infrastructure, and landscape well behind the front lines or views taken after the fighting. The kinds of pictures that received widest publication were Fenton's individual and group portraits of commanders, officers, and soldiers; some

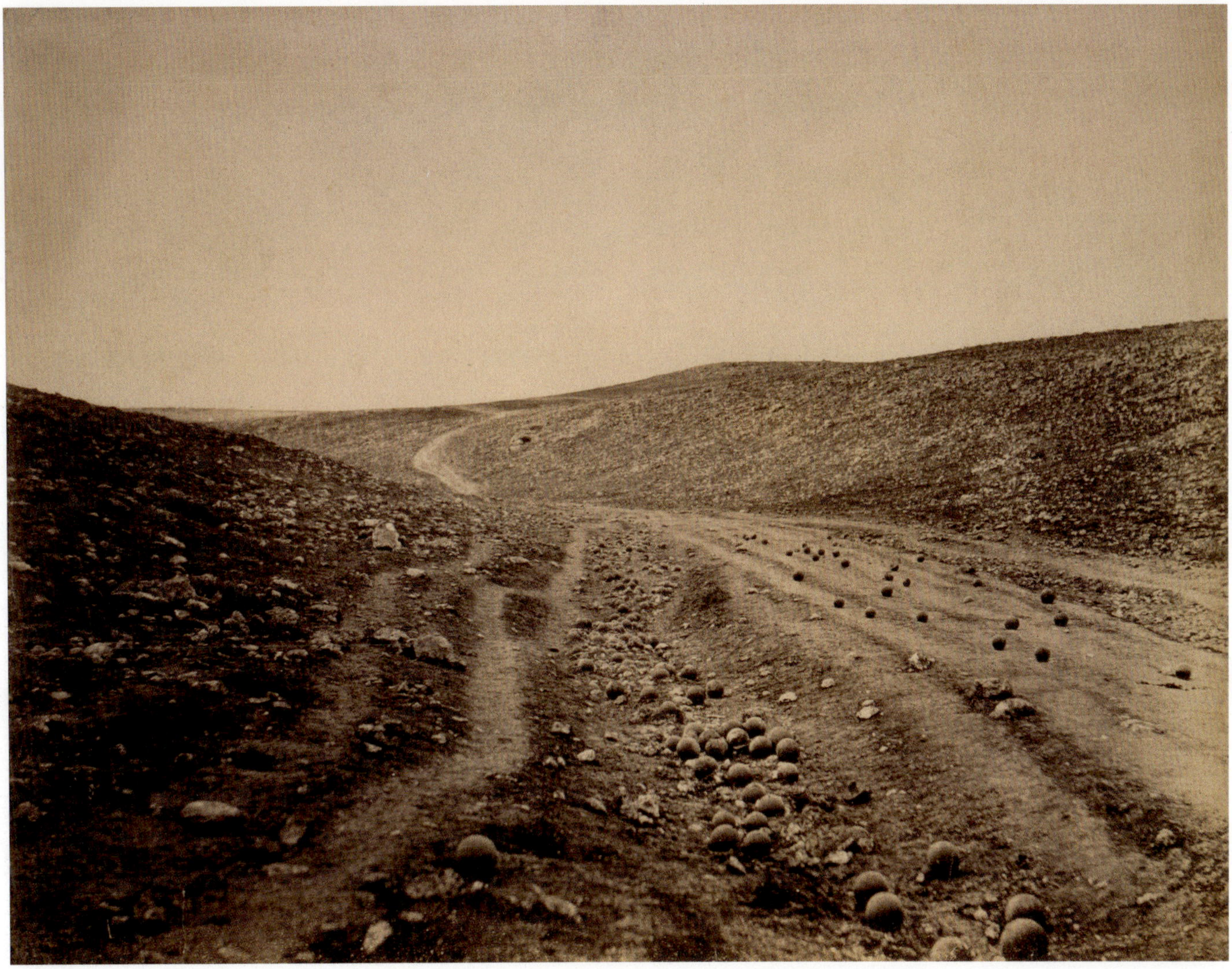

Fig. 5.6

Fig. 5.6
ROGER FENTON
The Valley of the Shadow of Death, Sevastopol, 1855
The one photograph Fenton took in the Crimea that reaches beyond benign documentation is "The Valley of the Shadow of Death." . . . Fenton's memorial photograph is a portrait of absence, of death without the dead. It is the only photograph he took that would not have needed to be staged, for all it shows is a wide rutted road studded with rocks and cannonballs that curves onward across a barren rolling plain to the distant void.
Susan Sontag[10]

offering heroic, militaristic gestures, others showing the wounded, weary yet stoic in the face of their Russian adversaries.

One of Fenton's photographs stands out conspicuously from the rest of his Crimean portfolio. His photograph *The Valley of the Shadow of Death* contains no figures, and casual inspection might even overlook the cannonballs that are spread across the track. It quietly alludes to the aftermath of battle, without any overt reference to the macabre realities of combat. Fenton's title references Alfred, Lord Tennyson's poem *The Charge of the Light Brigade* (1854), which helped immortalize the Battle of Balaklava, near Sevastopol, in British military history. The actual location of Fenton's photograph is not, in fact, the same site as where the infamous advance took place.[9] In addition, there are two contrasting versions of *The Valley*: one with cannonballs in the ditch to the side of the track and the other (*the* photograph) with the same cannonballs strewn across it. These two pictures have led to controversy over the image, raising questions about whether the apparent intervention of the photographer was unethical within the context of journalism or whether it exemplifies Fenton's artistic credentials, showing perhaps his aesthetic discernment and a methodology more in line with his celebrated still-life photographs rather than any of his other Crimean reportage work.

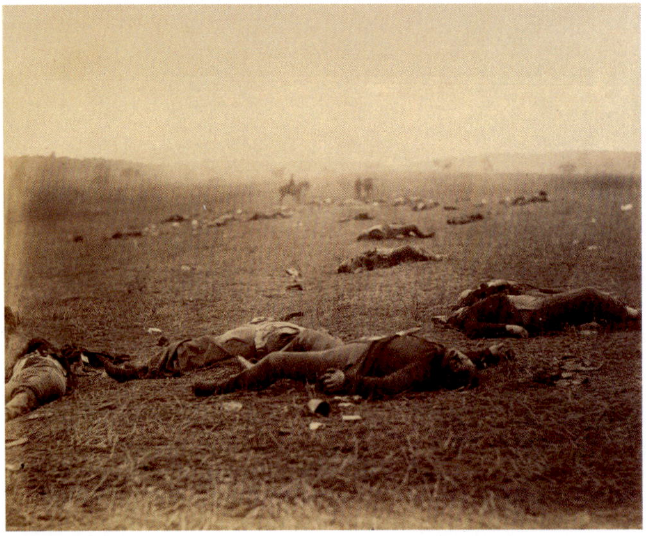

Fig. 5.7.i

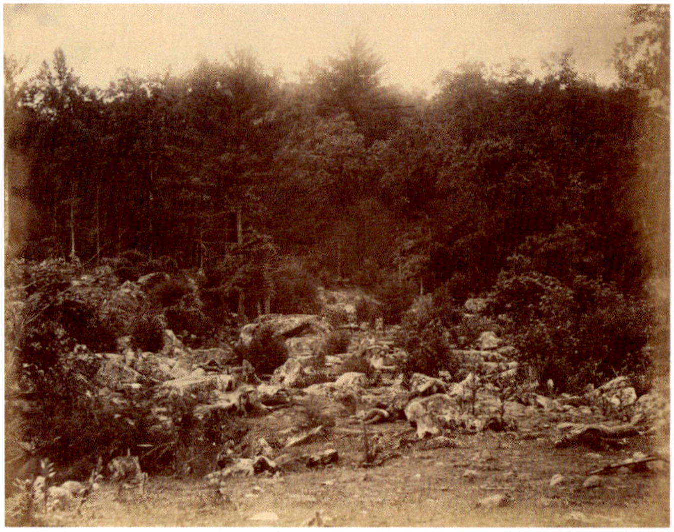

Fig. 5.7.ii

Fig. 5.7.i
TIMOTHY O'SULLIVAN
A Harvest of Death, Gettysburg, Pennsylvania
Fig. 5.7.ii
Slaughter Pen, Foot of Round Top, Gettysburg
from *Gardner's Photographic Sketchbook of the War, 1866*

Alexander Gardner traveled to America from Scotland in 1856 and began working for Matthew Brady, under whose direction he photographed the early stages of the American Civil War. Because of disputes over the attribution of authorship, Gardner parted company with Brady and photographed the rest of the war with new collaborators. Gardner published two *Sketchbooks* of the American Civil War, which included his own photographs as well as those of his associates, including Timothy O'Sullivan. Much of the content of the albums comprised portraits of soldiers and commanders and pictures of headquarters and barracks. The battlefield landscapes of the Civil War were among the first truly macabre sights to which the medium of photography bore witness, and they are a point of departure for photography's complex preoccupation with recording violence and conflict.

MEMORIALIZATION

Whether we consider Roger Fenton's approach as an artful, poetic response to a tragic event or instead as a sanitized representation of war epitomizing the political bias of his expedition, *The Valley of the Shadow of Death* has been sustained as an important image in the history of both landscape and war photography and is a reminder of the lyrical potential of both genres. Fenton's photograph, which references a specific event within the Crimean War, also has a relationship to the genre of history painting. More recently, the approaches of photographers such as Jeff Wall, who creates tableaux with high production values, such as the macabre *Dead Troops Talk* (1992), have been compared to history painting, whereby momentous events and scenes from history are expressed within a single impression.

Luc Delahaye's panoramic photographs also have been discussed in relation to history painting. Delahaye works alongside photojournalists covering political stories both at home and in war zones. Delahaye often captures the same moments as the other photographers; however, working with a large-format camera instead of the latest digital equipment, he photographs at a distance from the "action" that the reporters pursue—sometimes revealing the role of the journalists within the preceding. Printed around 2.5 meters wide and under the collective title *History*,

Delahaye's ongoing series conspicuously references the way that historically significant events are immortalized.

As a form of historical representation, Delahaye's and Fenton's photographs are pitifully modest in contrast to the diorama Franz Raubaud (1856–1928) created in 1905 to memorialize the siege of Sevastopol upon its bicentenary. *The Defence of Sevastopol* features a 115-meter, 360-degree painted panorama that, like a museum exhibit or zoo enclosure, is combined with a model of the "real" command post and paraphernalia of battle, including cannon, debris, and bunkers. This exhibition recreated the experience of surveying the city from its summit, looking out across the battlefield to the Black Sea. This kind of panoramic diorama features in Jeff Wall's photograph *Restoration* (1993). Wall's photograph unpacks the mechanism of the diorama's illusion, perhaps hinting at the role of the art institution in managing the spectacle and shaping our understanding of historical narratives.[11]

Paul Seawright's photograph *Valley* (Fig. 5.1), from the series *Hidden*, was made possible through the assistance of another institution, the Imperial War Museum. As part of its commitment to send artists into the theaters of war in which British forces are engaged (see p. 148), Seawright traveled to Afghanistan following the

Fig. 5.8
PAUL GRAHAM
Union Jack Flag in Tree, County Tyrone, 1985* from the series *Troubled Land, 1984–1986
Paul Graham's photographs of Northern Ireland are deceptive in several ways. Upon a casual glance we see fairly benign landscape views; however, closer inspection reveals the nuances of this troubled land: the Irish tricolor and the Union flag compete on pavement curbstones; a railing that at first seems to irritatingly disrupt the composition has actually been tagged with "IRA." In other photographs, the territorial markings are less discrete, such as the bright orange graffiti warning unwelcome visitors to a housing estate to "BEWARE." The deliberately wide-angle view of Graham's photographs requires viewers to commit their attention to the photograph, to scrutinize the scene for evidence of conflict within the immediately unremarkable pictures. What at first appear to be the blissfully ignorant observations of an outsider turn out to show an acute awareness of the politics of this landscape.

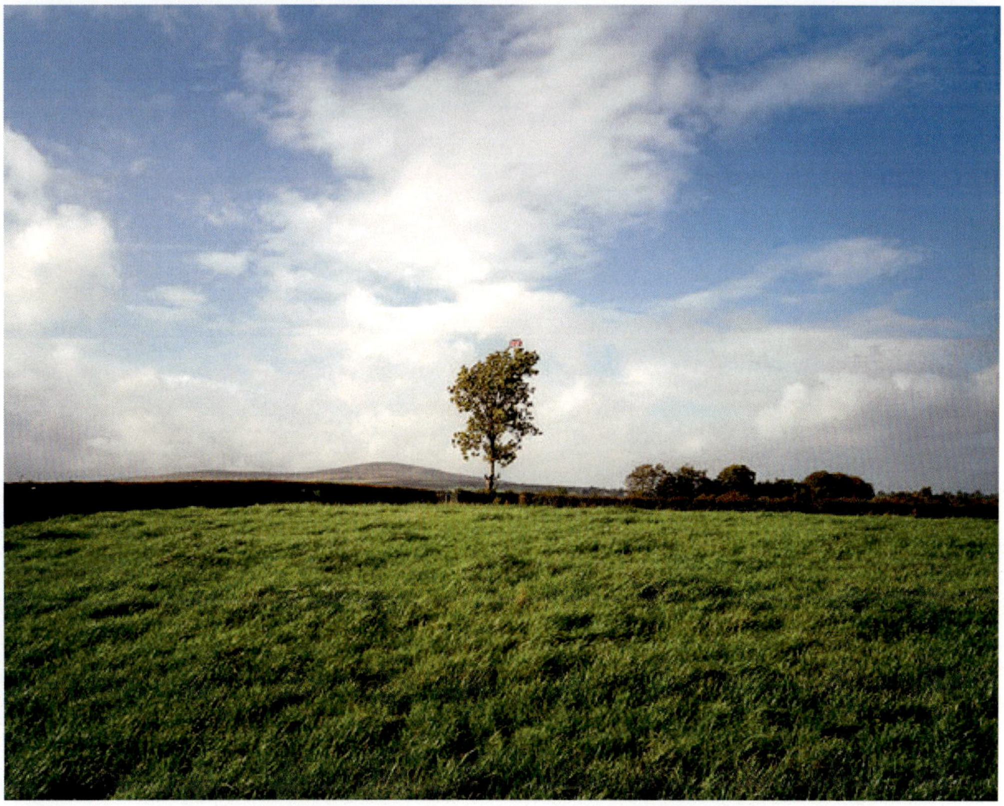

Fig. 5.8

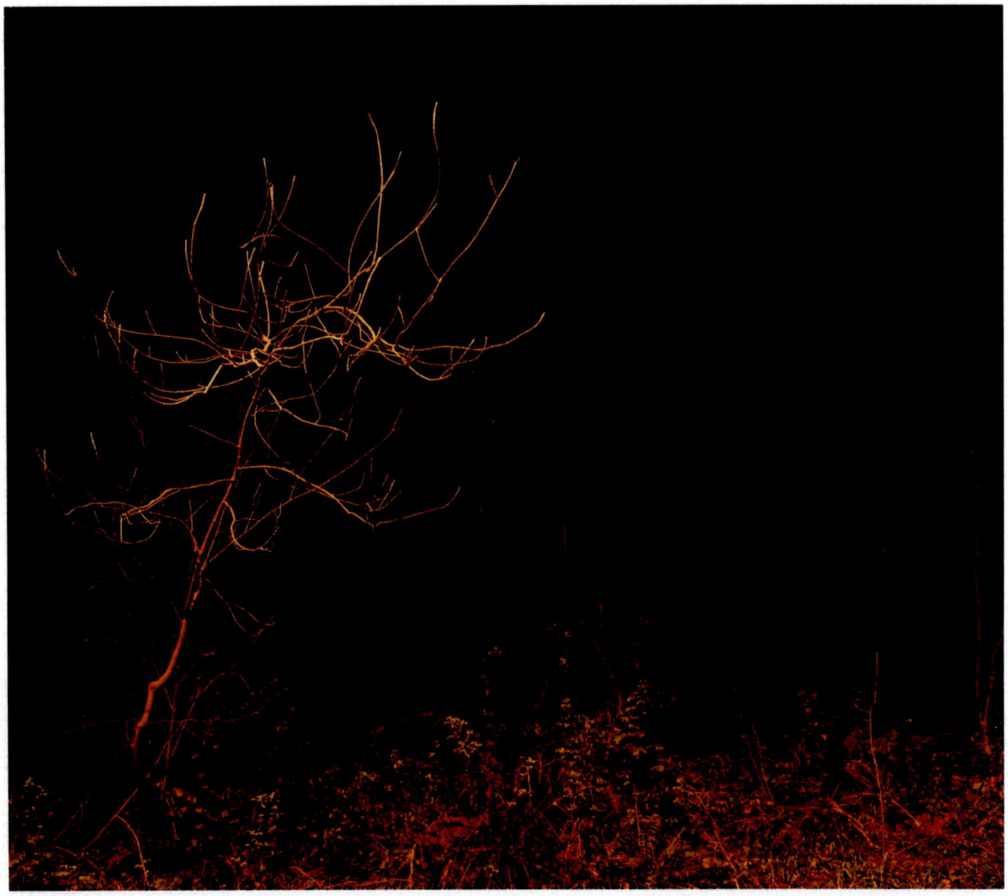

Fig. 5.9

Fig. 5.9
PAUL SEAWRIGHT
From the series *The Forest, 2001*
The orange street lighting lends the photographs from *Forest* a vivid and furious atmosphere. The spaces chosen by Seawright were dictated by where the street lighting ceased, which delineated where the city effectively reached its limits. Similar to the work of Martina Lindqvist (Fig. 1.17), the unfamiliar color asks us whether we dare venture any deeper into this potentially hostile territory. The sense of malevolence that can exude from this type of "in-between," *liminal* space is a recurring motif in Seawright's practice.

allied invasion in 2001. While the cannonballs may have been upgraded to even more destructive ballistics, the similarities between Seawright's *Valley* and Fenton's *Valley of Death* are uncanny. Even the muted tones of Seawright's photograph have more in common with the appearance of Fenton's sepia picture than does today's imagery of the country and the conflict.[12]

To an audience that witnessed the unfolding of the war on terror and its subsequent campaigns on live television, the quiet emptiness of *Hidden* is unsettling. *Hidden* contains no figures at all (save for the handful of camels that negotiate a minefield in one picture), yet it would appear that there was no shortage of traces of the many conflicts and armies that have ventured onto Afghan soil. The dramatic topography of Afghanistan, which features heavily in Donovan Wylie's *Outposts* (2011) (a project also facilitated by the Imperial War Museum), is only hinted at, looming behind haze in one or two photographs. For the majority of pictures, the camera looks out onto empty horizons, where identifying an enemy *should* be effortless. While in certain pictures hazardous objects are visible (i.e., landmines and other suspicious-looking objects), danger is mostly implied through absence. Whereas in Fenton's *Valley of Death* absence stands as a memorial for the fallen soldiers, in Seawright's series, emptiness implies uncertainty, alluding to the obfuscation of the true reasons for invading Afghanistan and the threat to the West that it was alleged to harbor.

The traces of conflict rather than scenes of violence themselves have dominated Seawright's practice. Like many of his contemporaries, including Willie Doherty, Jonathan Olley, John Duncan, Anthony Haughey, and David Farrell, the conflict in Northern Ireland, euphemistically referred to as "The Troubles," and its visibility across the landscape have had a profound impression on their practice.[13] Like many political and ethnic disputes over territories the violence in Northern Ireland has centered around particular parts of Belfast and its environs, where the delineation between a Protestant and a Catholic zone might be invisible to an outsider. The territorial aspect of the conflict in Northern Ireland is explored in Paul Graham's series *Troubled Land* (Fig. 5.8). Graham subverts the dialect of pictorial landscape imagery, tricking viewers into thinking they are looking at something little more than simply a visually pleasing picture; however, details within the frame (a British Union flag incongruously flying in a tree for instance) subtly and sinisterly allude to the conflict.

In one of Seawright's earliest works, *Sectarian Murder* (1988), he juxtaposed text from newspaper reports of killings from the 1970s—deliberately removing any reference to the religious or political affiliation of the victim—with his own contemporaneous photographs of the crime scenes. This strategy took Seawright to places around the city that he might otherwise not have visited. The roads leading out of Belfast became of interest for Seawright, not least because victims of sectarian killings had been dumped just off the road or in lay-bys. *The Forest* records these kinds of spaces as well as similar sites across Europe. Darkness plays an important role in the work, the photographs being lit by only the orange street lighting from the main road. Seawright's choice of location was effectively prescribed by where the local authority deemed it necessary to cease urban street lighting. The locations in Seawright's series and the spill of the street lighting therefore specify the threshold where the urban ceases and the rural begins. The genesis for this work stemmed largely from the photographer's memories and impressions of growing up in the height of The Troubles, of the places and kinds of spaces to avoid at all costs. As well as touching upon other matters around depictions of forests in folklore and mythology, *The Forest* points toward the legacy that violence inflicts, scoring lingering anxieties upon the people around it.

One might easily surmise that photography has of late inherited a major role as undertaker, summariser or accountant. It turns up late, wanders through the places where things have happened totting up the effects of the world's activity. This is a kind of photograph that forgoes the representation of events in progress and so cedes them to other media. As a result it is quite different from the spontaneous snapshot and has a different relation to memory and to history. DAVID CAMPANY[14]

"LATE" PHOTOGRAPHY

The traces of natural and man-made disasters that are left on the land inevitably crop up within both historic and contemporary landscape practice. In some of the photographs that we have discussed so far, these traces vary from conspicuous evidence of the aftermath of an event to subtler, sometimes even merely implied, references to a past narrative. In his influential essay "Safety in Numbness," published in 2003, theorist David Campany ascribed the term "late photography" to still photography of the aftermath of recently past events of historic proportions.[15] Campany uses the work made by Joel Meyerowitz of Ground Zero in the wake of 9/11 to exemplify the approach of one such practitioner. In the essay, as well as in his writing elsewhere, Campany refers to the work of Sophie Ristelhueber, Richard Misrach, Paul Seawright, Willie Doherty, Simon Norfolk, and Robert Polidori, whose works also typify the "late" approach within contemporary documentary practice.[16]

As well as arriving in the field after events have unfolded, these practitioners have similar working methodologies. They tend to work with large-format cameras and adopt a very "straight" compositional approach, echoing William Jenkins's celebration of the mechanical qualities of photography (see p. 126). The choice of technology further underscores the definition of "late photography": it is belated in relation to the television news crews and video cameras—as well as citizen journalists recording unfolding events with their smartphones—both of whom are more or less able to deliver the news in *real* time. In contrast to the priorities of television crews and photojournalists, to late photographers, time is almost inconsequential: they are in no hurry to arrive on the scene ahead of the competition, and when they finally get there, people and traces of movement tend to be absent from the frame. They are more like forensic crime scene photographers recording evidence rather than making any attempt to record pivotal moments or sequences of events.

Understanding the quality of *stillness*, which is peculiar to the medium of photography, is important to Campany's discussion. Popularly, we tend to think of photographs in terms of isolated moments—frozen slices of time within the continuum of time. As Campany points out, it was not until the development of smaller film and camera formats that such "decisive" imagery was made possible and, with it, the emergence of stillness as a defining characteristic of photography. The advent of the moving image technologies has also contributed to the motionless qualities of the still picture. The implications of the relationship between the still and the moving image are multifaceted, and with the expansion of digital platforms they become ever more complex. However, one enduring implication of the still image in relation to the moving image is how it hints

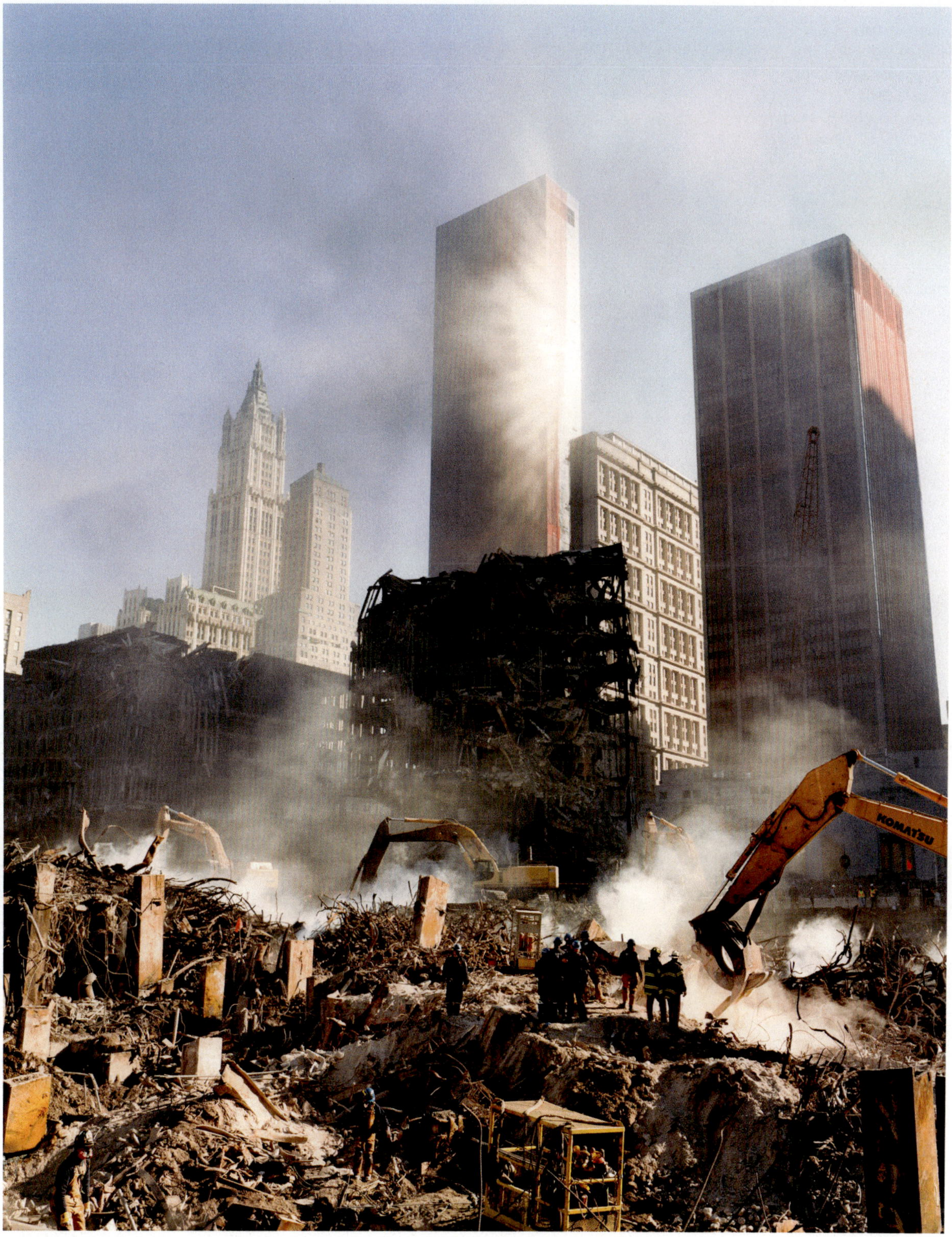

Fig. 5.10

Fig. 5.10
JOEL MEYEROWITZ
***Smoke Rising in Sunlight, November 11, 2001*, from the book *Aftermath: World Trade Center Archive*, 2006**
What began for Meyerowitz as an infiltration of the Ground Zero site to document the devastation and cleanup operation became a major collaboration with the authorities to create a memorial of the attack on the World Trade Center. For David Campany, the role of the still photographic image as the definitive mode of memorialization exemplifies the medium as secondary or subordinate to the moving video image that "breaks" the news.

Fig. 5.11
ADAM BROOMBERG AND OLIVER CHANARIN
Chicago #2* from the series *Chicago, 2006

Broomberg and Chanarin's series depicts a fabricated Arab town, nicknamed "Chicago," built by the Israeli military, which has hosted dry runs of many operations and campaigns over the past few decades. As well as addressing conflict and other political issues, the photographs in *Chicago* touch upon the superficiality of the photographic gaze and its inability to penetrate beneath surface appearances. Also, the artifice involved with these kinds of sites relates to Freud's notion of the uncanny (see p. 74): they seem recognizable at first glance, but upon closer inspection, their fabrication reveals itself, gradually dissipating what you thought you knew about the image before you.

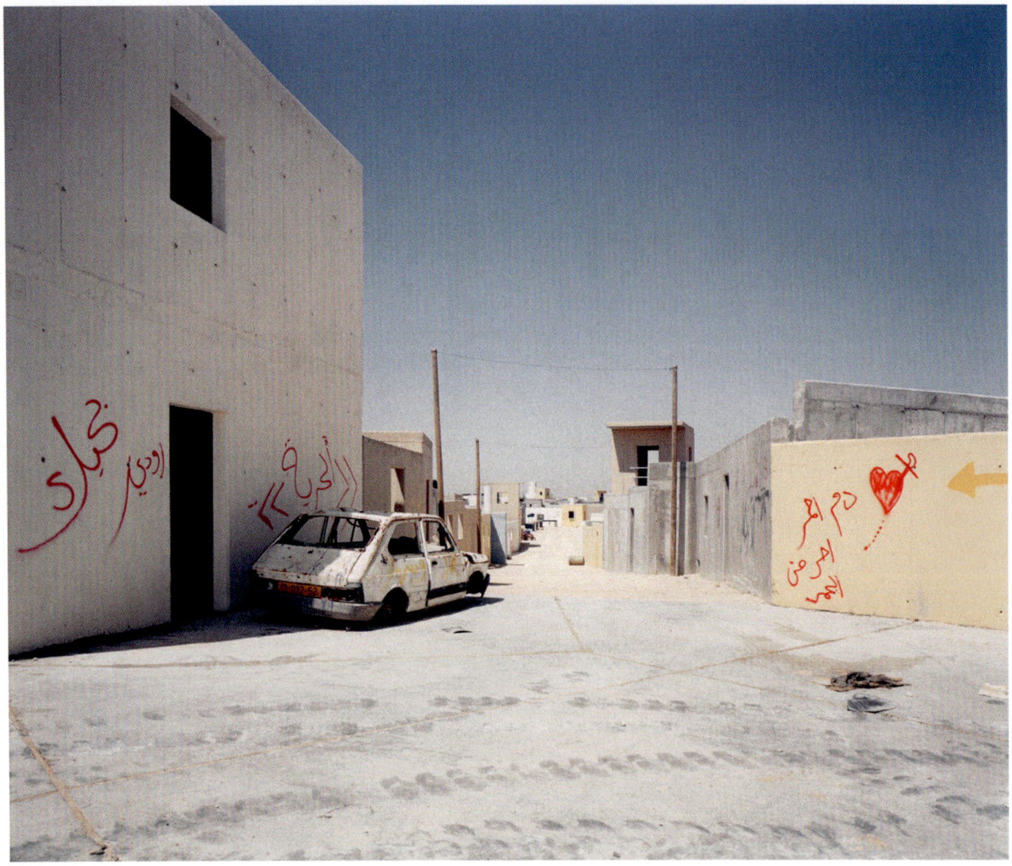

Fig. 5.11

toward past moments and events. As Campany asserts, "There is nothing like the 'presentness' of the moving image to emphasize the 'pastness' of the photograph."[17] The way that freeze-frames are used in movies and still photographs are incorporated into documentaries and news reports exemplifies the relationship that photography has to past moments, events that cannot be changed or repeated. To be more explicit, the still photograph has a relationship to death.[18]

The uneasy silence of the stillness of late photography is, for Campany, one of its problems. Although he singles out Joel Meyerowitz's Ground Zero photographs (published in a large, almost imposing monograph titled *Aftermath: World Trade Center Archive* in 2006), they are perhaps not the most indicative examples of late photography. While there is image after image of wreckage and devastation, the book includes many images of the dynamic, sometimes even frenzied, activity of the arduous cleanup operation as well as portraits of the excavation team. However, it was the formal commissioning of the stills photographer to create these *memorial* pictures, almost on behalf of the city of New York, that makes Meyerowitz's work such an interesting example in terms of the contemporary role of the photographer as history's "undertaker."

The quietness within the photographs of Norfolk, Misrach, and Polidori contrasts with the uneasy silence embodied in Meyerowitz's pictures. Campany suggests that in late photography there is a problematic disconnection between photography's fundamental mechanics, a mode where "the photographic image becomes less about the 'hot' decisiveness of the shutter and more about the 'cold' stoicism of the lens."[19] For Campany, particularly when the subject matter is of current sociopolitical significance and, like Meyerowitz's study, is in the service of commemoration, this slow stare might amount to a numbness or an ideological paralysis of viewers, forcing them to overlook the narrative of the events *before* the aftermath and confining them to the aesthetic experience of the "late" photographs.[20]

According to Campany, late photography signifies the still image coming to terms with being resigned to the "aftermath of culture,"[21] that is, no longer the mode of choice for communicating the latest news stories from around the world.[22] Since the late 1980s, documentary photographs have advanced aggressively into commercial galleries and become an increasingly credible part of the fine art economy. Perhaps this is of greater concern than the so-called "problem" of late photography. While there is abstract beauty in the shell holes and trenches as rendered by Sophie Ristelhueber's aerial photographs of the deserts of Kuwait, and there is also something strangely poetic in the more forensic treatment of Paul Seawright's unspecific vignettes of Afghanistan, the presence of Robert Polidiori's photographs of New Orleans following the devastation of Hurricane Katrina in the commercial gallery should be considered more critically. Unlike the anonymity of the subjects of the other bodies of work mentioned, many of Polidori's photographs reduce the private interiors of bedrooms and other living spaces to similarly generic tropes. As images of the personal and material cost of this environmental disaster, they are powerful and effective, and Polidori's invasiveness is arguably justified. But their social imperative is compromised perhaps by their impressive price tags and situation in the commercial gallery space.

In other writing, Campany relates late photography to another recent phenomenon within contemporary photography—bodies of work depicting places designed for training the emergency services and armed forces, such as An-My Lê's *29 Palms* (2012), which he describes as "not the 'theatre' of war but its rehearsal studio."[23] Similar bodies of work include Sarah Pickering's *Public Order* (2005) and *Incident* (2008), Paul Shambroom's *Security* (2007), and Adam Broomberg and Oliver Chanarin's *Chicago*. To greater and lesser extents, all of these works can be seen as alternative responses to the war on terror and domestic climates of anxiety following 9/11. While this kind of "pre-emptive" photography acts as a complementary foil to "late" approaches, these bodies of work, within all of which lie themes of performance, simulation, and artifice and in which the camera is complicit in the theater of the spaces depicted, sit more easily in the contemporary gallery context.

THRESHOLDS

As Paul Seawright's project *The Forest* (Fig. 5.9) demonstrates, spaces that are not obviously part of one particular type of space or another can have an evocative potential. We seem to be at our most unsettled when we struggle to identify and classify a space as belonging to a particular category, such as town, suburb, country, or the wilderness. In recent years, "in-between" spaces have featured heavily not just in contemporary photography but also across a range of media. Another way of describing these spaces is "liminal," meaning at the limit of one zone and on the threshold of another. While much of the following discussion relates to the earlier discussion of edgelands (see pp. 76–85), it should be remembered that Farley and Simmons Roberts's ideas relate to a specifically *English* context. The edgelands and their contents are, of course, international, and it is important to consider the ubiquity of liminal spaces within contemporary landscape practice.

The outskirts of Cairo are a feature of the work of Hala Elkoussy's body of work, *Peripheral.* This work comprises photographs as well as a series of fictional videos recreating stories of people who live on the edges of Egypt's capital city. Like most cities, as Cairo's population has burgeoned in recent decades, the conurbation has encroached ever deeper into the desert, planting into it increasingly Western architectural tropes. Elkoussy's landscape photographs literally document the *periphery* of Cairo, and this is done with a fairly restrained approach, often shooting from a high vantage point or looking across an open space. Although there is nothing blocking these views, equally there is little in the foreground to lead you into them either.

Elkoussy's photographs are tonally dense—even slightly underexposed perhaps—which renders slightly richer color tones and almost lends a sense of pathos to the landscape. This is extended by the way that tower blocks recede into the desert haze like a mirage in reverse. Although Elkoussy's landscapes have a heavily geographic dimension to them, her intention is to use these literal peripheries metaphorically, as a simile for the marginalization of individuals and communities that feel outside of a contemporary Cairene culture and identity. Elkoussy's choice of using aspiring actors in her short films to recreate rather than document the lives and stories of ordinary people is a strategy to further connect the work to the onslaught of popular culture and aspirations toward celebrity status.

Regeneration of the landscape is also seen in Paul Alexander Knox's series *The Space Between* (Fig. 5.13). His photographs of partly derelict and vacated houses in the North East of England illustrate the impact of the 2008 financial crisis on architecture across certain suburban landscapes. Because of the property crash, as with many similar places across the UK, redevelopment of these sites has been placed on hold, leaving these empty homes in an awkward state of limbo—on a kind of real

Fig. 5.12
HALA ELKOUSSY
Peripheral Landscape #3, Mokattam, 2004* from the series *Peripheral, 2005
Hala Elkoussy's photographs document the outskirts of Cairo, which encroach ever deeper into the Egyptian desert. Behind the apparently geographic preoccupation of the work are themes relating to social interpretations of "periphery" and marginalization. Her choice to install the photographs as inkjet vinyl banners—materials related to advertising and commercialization—references the plasticity of popular culture.

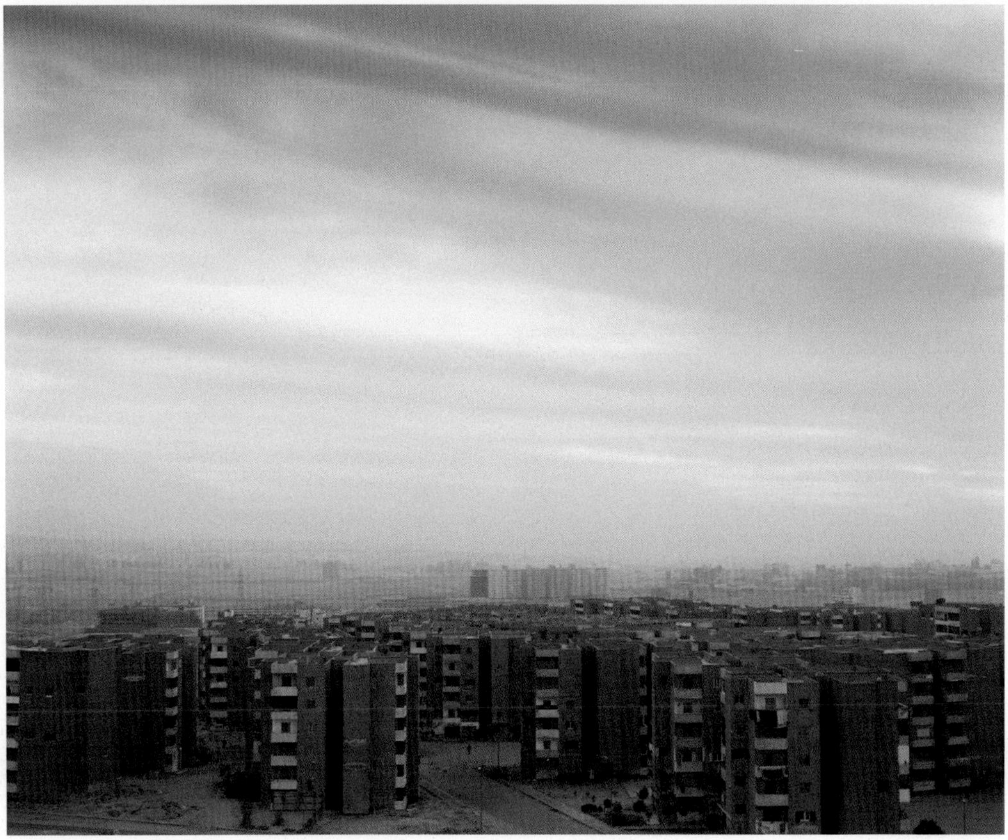

Fig. 5.12

estate death row—which is particularly exasperating at a time of property shortages. Knox's bleak treatment of this subject aptly mirrors the callousness of the situation: bare foregrounds; cold, stormy skies; and paths and roads leading to nowhere.[24]

UNCERTAIN PLACES

A photographic interest in these awkward urban/suburban spaces was identified as early as the 1930s. Waldemar George referred to the extremely influential photographer Eugène Atget as a photographer of "Paris *terre en friches* [waste ground], no man's land."[25] Atget was a prolific photographer and amassed a vast collection of photographs of the streets and architecture of Paris from the 1890s to the 1920s. Outside Paris from the mid-nineteenth century, a particularly defined territory between the city defenses and the *banlieue* [suburbs] existed and was referred to as the "Zone," which was identified with gypsies and travelers known as "zoniers."

As well as Atget, Robert Doisneau photographed the Zone throughout the 1940s. Surrealist photographer Man Ray was particularly taken by the work of Atget, finding something compelling in his modest views of street corners, shop windows, and the Zone, which were overlooked by the many who bought his prints, primarily for more prosaic purposes as architectural records.[26] Man Ray produced his own responses to Atget's photographs, titling one ambiguous image of a tree, grass bank, and steps, taken in 1932, as *Terrain Vague.*[27] This is most likely the earliest reference to this term within the discourse of visual culture and roughly translates as "uncertain place," which eloquently encompasses the diversities of many of the subjects discussed within this final chapter.

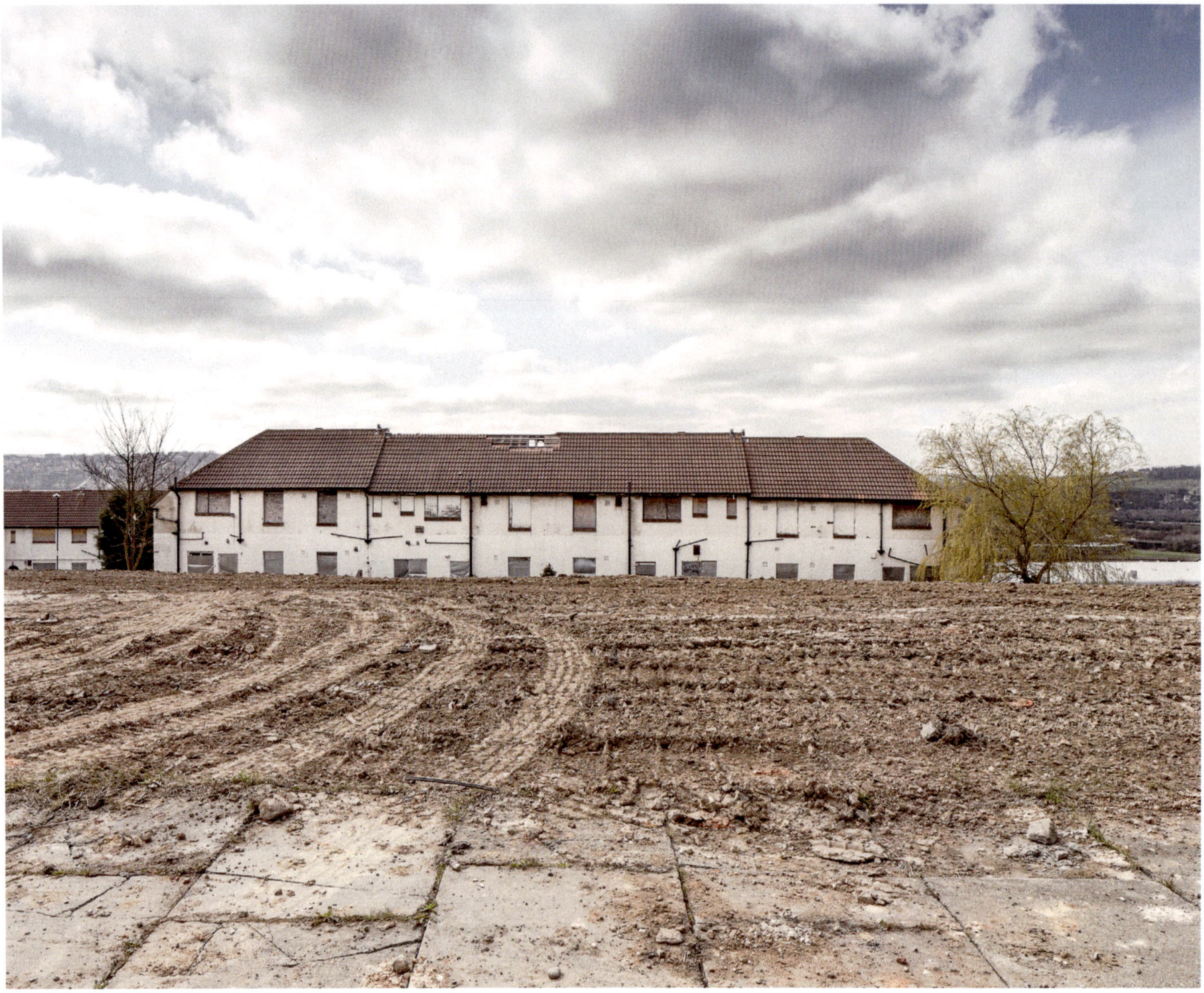

Fig. 5.13

The melodramatic connotations of the word "zone" are more fully realized in Andrei Tarkovsky's film *Stalker* (1979). This most undramatic yet highly revered film[28] follows the journey of two men who are guided by the "stalker" around an enigmatic abandoned landscape referred to as "the zone." Commentators of the film broadly agree that the zone, which is guarded by the authorities, is the crash site of a UFO, although this is not made explicit in the movie itself. Deep within this almost postapocalyptic landscape lies a fabled room in which everything that one desires can come true. The scenery of Tarkovsy's film is arguably its most alluring aspect, an eerie prophecy of what would be the long-term result of the nuclear meltdown at Chernobyl in 1986, which led to the abandonment of the nearby town of Pripyat (the aftermath of which has been documented by many, including John Darwell and Robert Polidori). In 2011, the Ukrainian authorities lifted the ban on entering the Pripyat exclusion zone, but the place has always remained an object of fascination, and not just for urban explorers, many of whom appear to regard the city as a kind of hallowed ground. It has seeped into popular culture elsewhere: locations within Hollywood movies as well as in video games such as *Call of Duty: Modern Warfare* (2007). As well as the allure of the aesthetics of decay, the historical value of Pripyat as a giant relic of the Soviet Union is understandable.

Fig. 5.13
PAUL ALEXANDER KNOX
Untitled*, from *The Space Between, 2011
Now condemned for demolition and redevelopment are estates such as those depicted by Knox. The tenants of the properties still owned by the local authorities would have been relocated, while those who bought their homes under the Right to Buy scheme in the 1980s would have been issued with compulsory purchase orders and forced to sell, perhaps below market value. Geographically, these kinds of estates are typically on the fringes of towns and cities and inhabited by economically marginalized groups, but the uncertainty of the fate of these properties and their communities places them in another kind of "liminal" space.

In certain respects Pripyat is not a peripheral space but rather an emphatically defined one, the health risks of entering demarcated in no uncertain terms. However, these symbolic barriers are not lined with lead, which is the only thing that will prevent radiation from spreading further.[29] There is no such boundary between the safe Ukrainian landscape and the evacuated exclusion zone, which many Ukrainians have had little choice but to cultivate as best they can. Pripyat is by no means the only worldwide conurbation to have been abandoned, but it is one that never will be fully inhabited again and will only decay further, its mythological status accruing. Or perhaps as the vegetation consumes what remains of the city, it will ultimately fade from our collective memory altogether.

TRANSIENT SPACES

In Anthony Hernandez's *Landscapes for the Homeless* (Fig. 5.14) and Henk Wildschut's *Shelter* (Fig. 5.15), we see spaces that are defined not simply by their physical location on the peripheries of towns but rather as sites that offer temporary sanctuary for mobile communities. Both bodies of work have a "lateness" to them, a forensic, scene-of-the-crime aesthetic whereby the viewer is left to scrutinize the picture for clues about the space's most recent inhabitant. In Hernandez's work, anonymous vignettes of landscape are claimed by those who have nowhere else to call home. The delicacy of Hernandez's compositions and their richness of color (which is amplified by their presentation as fine Cibachrome prints) extend a dignity, so often denied by other parts of society, to the temporary inhabitants of these spaces. This same sensitivity is exhibited in Henk Wildschut's photographs of makeshift shelters made across Europe by illegal migrants and would-be asylum seekers. The domesticity and composure of the interiors of shelters made in the woods near the port of Calais—for many, the last hurdle of their long journeys—is poignant. These shelters are not intended for long-term use by an individual but only for temporary use and are to be passed on to the next traveler in the same state in which they were found. In Fig. 5.15, as well as elsewhere in the series, the incorporation of packaging, advertisements, and other branded materials has a particularly striking effect. These materials offer a glimpse of the promise of Western luxury and culture that is mythologized, particularly by human traffickers who profit from the desperation of others. They also offer a kind of common currency linking a relatively affluent Western audience to an unknown, illegal alien "other" (or so certain spheres of the media attempt to lead us to believe). The spaces examined by Hernandez and Wildschut relate to other evaluations of spaces that are inhabited temporarily. Sociologist Marc

5.14
ANTHONY HERNANDEZ
Landscape for the Homeless #18* from the series *Landscapes for the Homeless, 1989–1995
Anthony Henandez has frequently photographed spaces people pass through or occupy temporarily. Using the scant possessions of the homeless people who make these spaces as comfortable as they can, Hernandez hints at their presence: to borrow Sontag's phrase, "a portrait of absence" (p. 163).

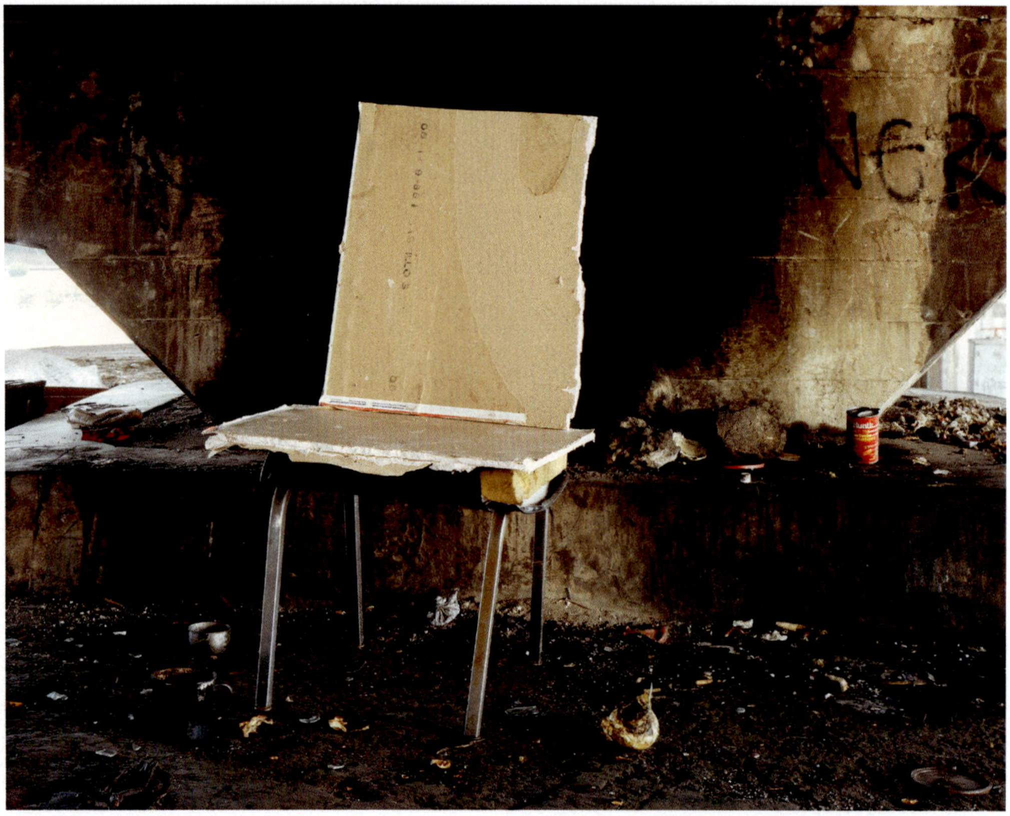

Fig. 5.14

Augé famously asserted the theory of "non-place" in relation to the condition of "supermodernity," which can be summarized as follows:

> *A world where people are born in the clinic and die in hospital, where transit points and temporary abodes are proliferating under luxurious or inhumane conditions (hotel chains and squats, holiday camps and refugee camps, shantytowns threatened with demolition or doomed to festering longevity) . . . a world thus surrendered to solitary individuality, to the fleeting, the temporary, and ephemeral.*[30]

Airports, out-of-town shopping malls, motorways, and gas stations are enmeshed with consumer lifestyles and characterized by Augé as non-places. It should not be forgotten that his description also includes those spaces utilized by the world's poorest. They are, of course, all different types of *spaces*, but they are neither destinations nor locations.

There is no escaping the fact, however, that non-places appear to be photogenic. It is not just their ubiquity but rather something else that makes them irresistible subjects

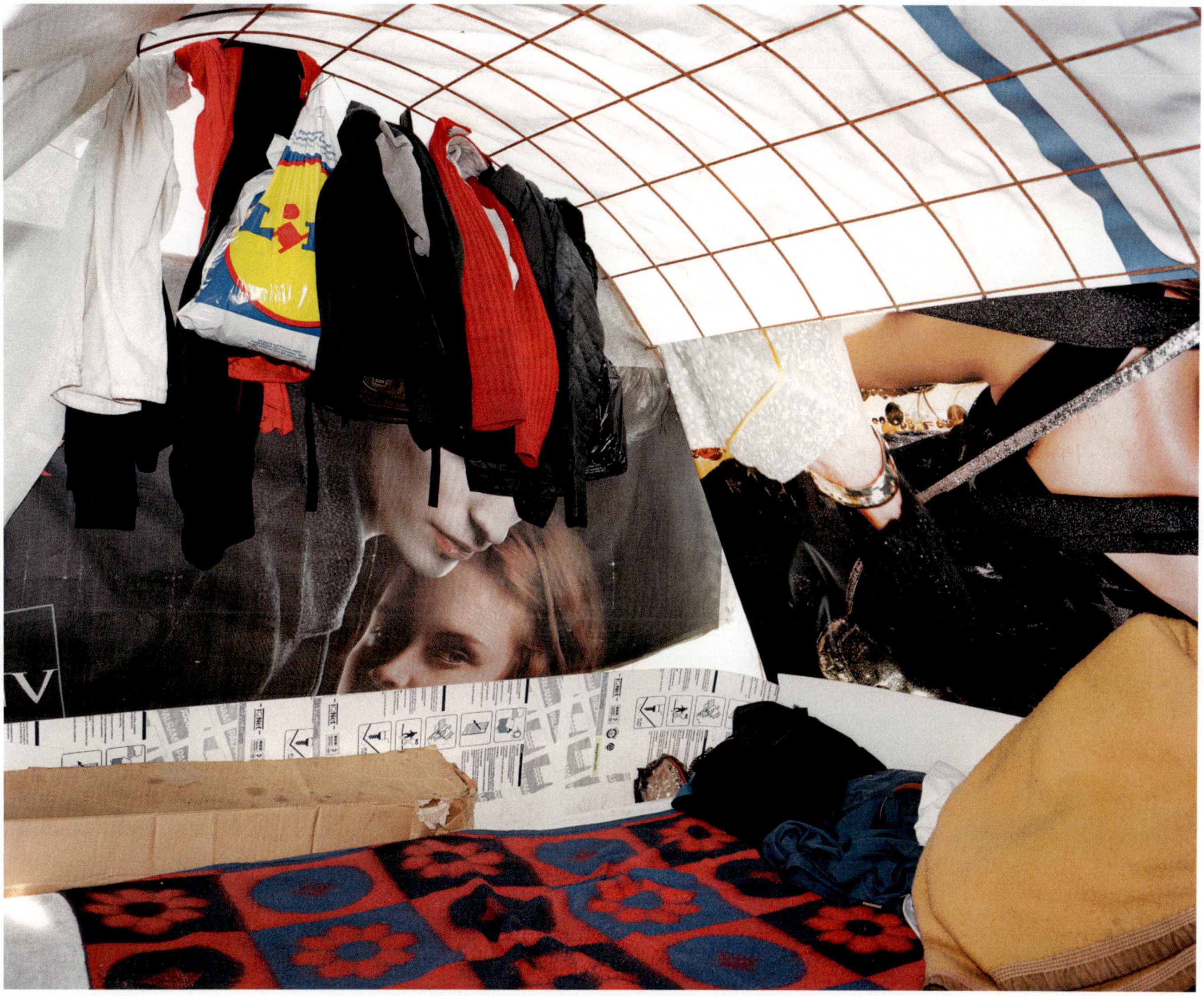

Fig. 5.15

5.15
HENK WILDSCHUT
Calais, France, 2009* from *Shelter, 2011
An analysis of this image resonates with Graham Clarke's description of a different photograph called *A Sharecropper's Home*, taken in 1937 by Margaret Bourke-White around the same time the FSA photographers were documenting the effects of the depression on American farming communities.

for so many contemporary landscape practitioners, their geometric blandness perhaps begging to be transcribed into two-dimensional photographic form (see Figs. 4.6 and 4.7). Since non-places so frequently occupy the peripheries of towns and cities, they have something that complements photography itself, which sits on the peripheries of other disciplines and media and serves a multitude of functions.

Although there are no figures in Wildschut's photograph, the themes of social polarization and aspiration echo a portrait taken some seven decades earlier by Margaret Bourke-White to such an extent that Graham Clarke's interpretation of Bourke-White's image can be overlaid onto Wildschut's photograph:

> *Surrounding the boy is a host of visual texts, newspapers from the time which advertise the essential elements of white consumer America. This is the good life, the "American Dream" from which the black child is excluded. Sharecroppers used newspaper on walls for insulation, but photographers use them endlessly as part of a political register. Here they create a direct contrast, a visual statement which asks political, social, and cultural questions. This is a photograph not just about poverty, but also about injustice and the inequalities of a political system.*
> Graham Clarke[31]

Photographs slice space into place; land is framed as landscape. Representation envelops reality; it becomes an act of colonisation. Photography contributes to characterising sites as particular types of places within the order of things. LIZ WELLS[32]

FROM SPACES TO PLACES

The words "place" and "space" are used in various ways, and what at first might seem like a simple distinction is actually more complex. Generally, "space" is used to define something that is open and expansive. We have given the word "outer space" to the infinity of the universe beyond our home planet. Contrary to astronomy, in architectural terminology "space" is the sum of the precise dimensions, features, and design of an interior, and architects remark on the psychological effects these things have upon whoever uses it. "Place" and "space" are used even more abstractly: in the vernacular they are used to describe someone's temperament or emotional state, to be "in a good place" or, alternatively, "in a dark place." In visual culture, "place" can have implications upon the reading of a work, for instance, "placing" a photograph in a public gallery will lend it certain values that the same image might fail to accumulate in an advertising context. To "place *something* upon *another*" implies a certain responsibility or even a burden. We can see this in the creation of premium open spaces like national parks, which commit future generations to its management. Objectively speaking, however, a place *is* just another sort of space. This proposition is essentially the argument that Marc Augé so provocatively suggests, that the buildings and infrastructure that define our modern existence are indistinguishable from each other and ultimately amount to, as Dan Holdsworth's title suggests, *A Machine for Living* (Fig. 3.6). Their lack of identity, individuality, and ubiquity limits their status to "spaces" or the even bleaker sounding "non-places." However, in practice we recognize and distinguish places from whatever surrounds them, whether in terms of topography, history, spirituality, or practically anything else.

THE TOURIST'S PERSPECTIVE

Although we tend to think of tourism as commencing from the nineteenth century, its routes are far more ancient. Even the eighteenth-century excursions of the upper classes along picturesque trails and their "Grand Tours" of Europe are relatively recent compared to the religious pilgrimages of our ancestors. Indeed, one of the first examples of literature written in English, Geoffrey Chaucer's *Canterbury Tales* (c. 1370) describes one such pilgrimage together with a few of the motifs of tourism that persist today, such as the sale of dubious religious "relics"—what today we might call souvenirs.

From the 1870s, photographic prints and postcards were readily available in local shops.[33] In an era in which mobility was relatively restricted and traveling abroad for most people usually meant resettling, it is easy to see how the realism of the photographic image was enthralling and photographs of distant places and exotic things were popular commodities. Stereocards—photographs made by a camera with two lenses—rendered a three-dimensional image when viewed in a cheaply produced stereoscope and were widely available and popular. Particularly in America, which had relatively few pictures of the country at the end of the nineteenth century, these mass-produced images contributed to the cataloging of particular topographical features and landmarks and the creation of *places* within such a vast country.

There are hints of Chaucer's satire in the photographs by Paul Reas and Martin Parr (Fig. 5.17). Reas's photograph *Constable Country* describes a contemporary feature of the tourist machine. The tourists depicted here are not on a religious pilgrimage but rather on a cultural one. The meaning of Reas's photograph is transparent: with one hand, the smartly dressed tour guide holds up a copy of one of John Constable's paintings made around Flatford Mill in Suffolk and with the other, points to *the place* from which Constable produced the sketch that would become his painting. Reas's image describes a multilayered dialogue between image and place. Like the effect Wordsworth's poetry had on the Lake District, Constable's paintings are credited for popularizing Suffolk as a tourist destination, so much

Fig. 5.16
PAUL REAS
Constable Country* from the series *Flogging a Dead Horse, 1993
Constable Country vividly illustrates how the perceptions of a southern English countryside have been formed through the paintings of romantic artists. The photograph also alludes to the significance of *destination* within the concept of place, of *going to* somewhere within a wider territory. In the case of Reas's *Constable Country*, the mode of travel for these tourists is the paintings of John Constable, which take them to certain well-trodden locations across the landscape. There is something endearing about the fact that these tourists have ventured beyond the capital in sensible shoes and intrepidly placed themselves within what appears to be—from Reas's perspective at least—a fairly unremarkable part of the English countryside.

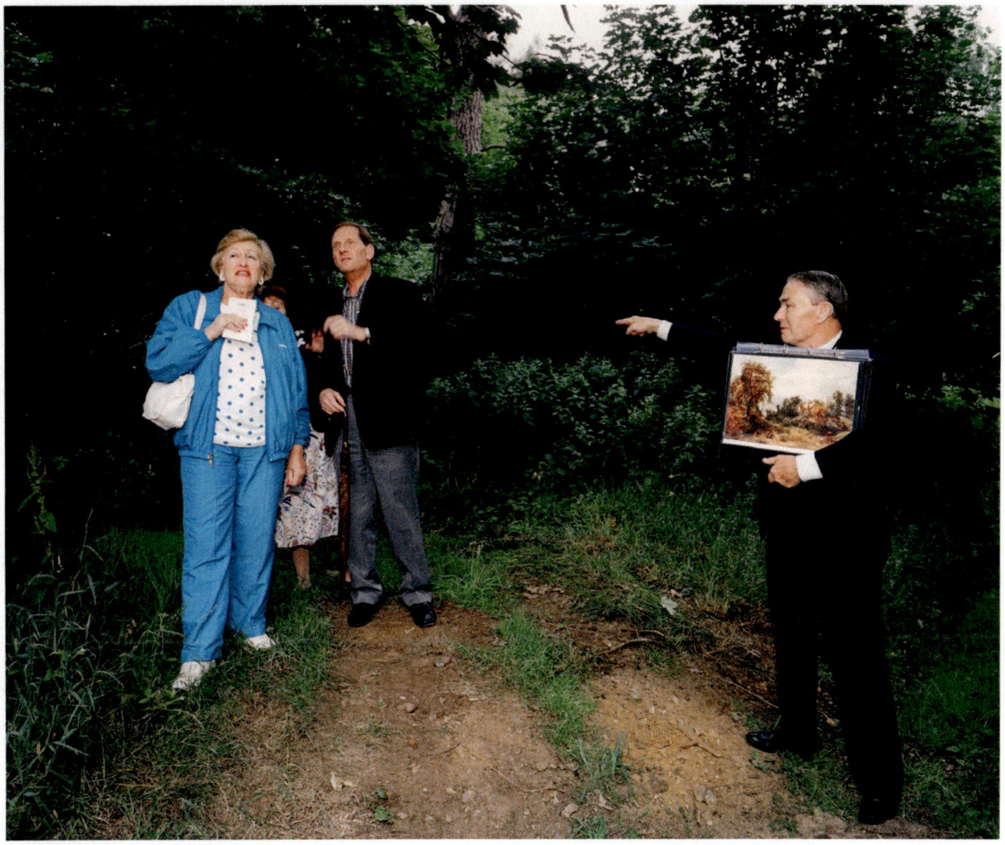

Fig. 5.16

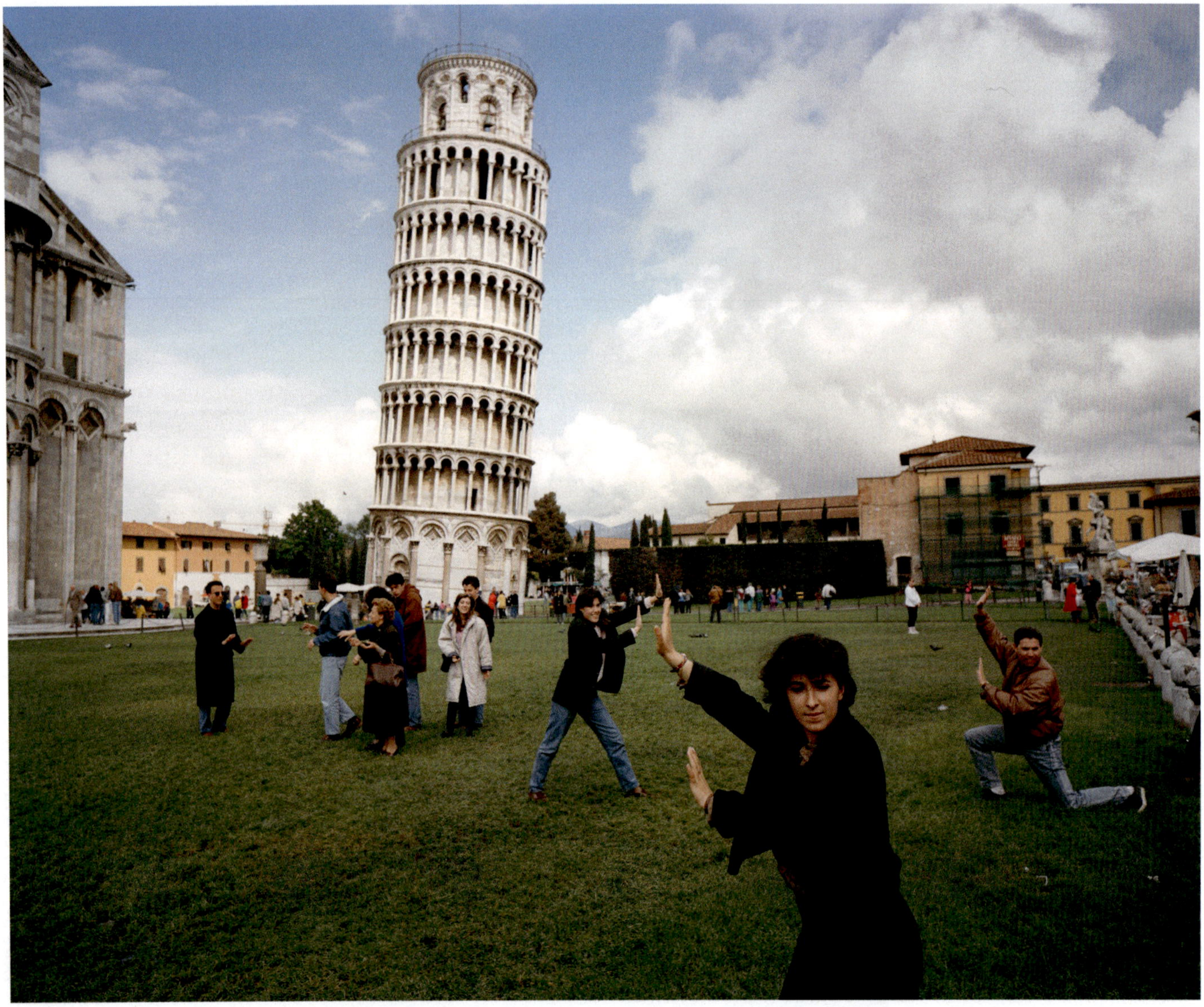

Fig. 5.17

so that the title of the photograph refers to how the surrounding area is popularly referred to. Reas's photograph—from a series that critically examines the British heritage industry—poses broader questions around the relationship between tourists' consumption of history and culture.[34]

Tourism, and particularly the photographic rituals that are interlinked with it, is an object of fascination for Martin Parr. His often garish and seldom flattering imagery extracts our sense of humor and highlights our absurd habits and tastes. Parr's *Small World* project darts from one major tourist destination on one side of the globe to another, showing often bemused-looking holidaymakers as they shuffle along guided tours and cram themselves around monuments and other "photo opportunities." The three figures repeat a familiar pose that is continually reproduced by observing the behavior of other tourists around them. What the three tourists are trying to achieve is a comic subversion of photographic perspective, to fake a photograph of them appearing to prevent the Tower from collapsing. (There are echoes here of the stereoscope's ocular subterfuge, tricking the eye into believing the picture is three dimensional.) However, by photographing the tourists at an angle, Parr reveals the process and subverts their ploy. As well as deriding this *photo ritual* (as opposed to photo opportunity, which implies something

Fig. 5.17
MARTIN PARR
Pisa, Italy, 1990* from the series *Small Worlds, 1995
Parr's photograph of tourists posing at the famous monument documents the ritualistic behavior of tourists and the role that photography plays in mediating their consumption. It would appear that too often photography defines how people engage with a new environment, leading us to recreate the views and perform the gestures of countless tourists who have gone before us. Irrespective of where all of these tourists have traveled, this performance is universally understood. Parr is perhaps more critical of the mechanism of tourism as he is disapproving of the tourists themselves, on several occasions turning the camera upon himself. Tourism is perhaps the most dominant subject of Parr's oeuvre, and the extent of his fascination can be seen in the dozen or so monographs that he has produced.

spontaneous or novel), Parr's photograph comments on the myopic nature of the "tourist's gaze."[35]

Another trick is at work in Banksy's irreverent text piece *This is not a photo opportunity*. The graffiti artist has spray painted this phrase across tourist attractions across numerous cities. Banksy's ironic statement is a call for us to consider the value of repeating the same views of the same landmarks and to take a second, more critical look at the object or scene in front of us, questioning the usefulness of taking yet another photograph of it. An alternative interpretation might be that by proclaiming the view in front of the text as not worthy of being photographed, it implies that it is simply a space, not a place that *should* be photographed. In this case, the photo opportunity is the Houses of Parliament in London, and such an order complements the anarchistic nature of much of his work. Banksy's order is, however, hard to disregard: it is cunningly provocative and elicits some kind of photographic response. His piece steals the privilege of the photo opportunity from the landmark, diverting the tourists' attention instead to Banksy's own graffiti and, like most tags, claims the territory for himself.

Fig. 5.18
JESSE ALEXANDER
London, 2002
Banksy's idiom has appeared in numerous cites across the world and has even been worn on the T-shirts of celebrities. The stencil work has, of course, been propagated by copycat sprayers, and the extent of its reaches can be seen on the *This is not a photo opportunity* Flickr page. There is irony in the fact that *This is not a photo opportunity*, which perhaps calls for a curb in the proliferation of photographs, predates the widespread use of digital photography, appearing in Banksy's 2002 book *Existencillism*. If this were an attempt to reduce the number of photographs in circulation, then it has fallen short.

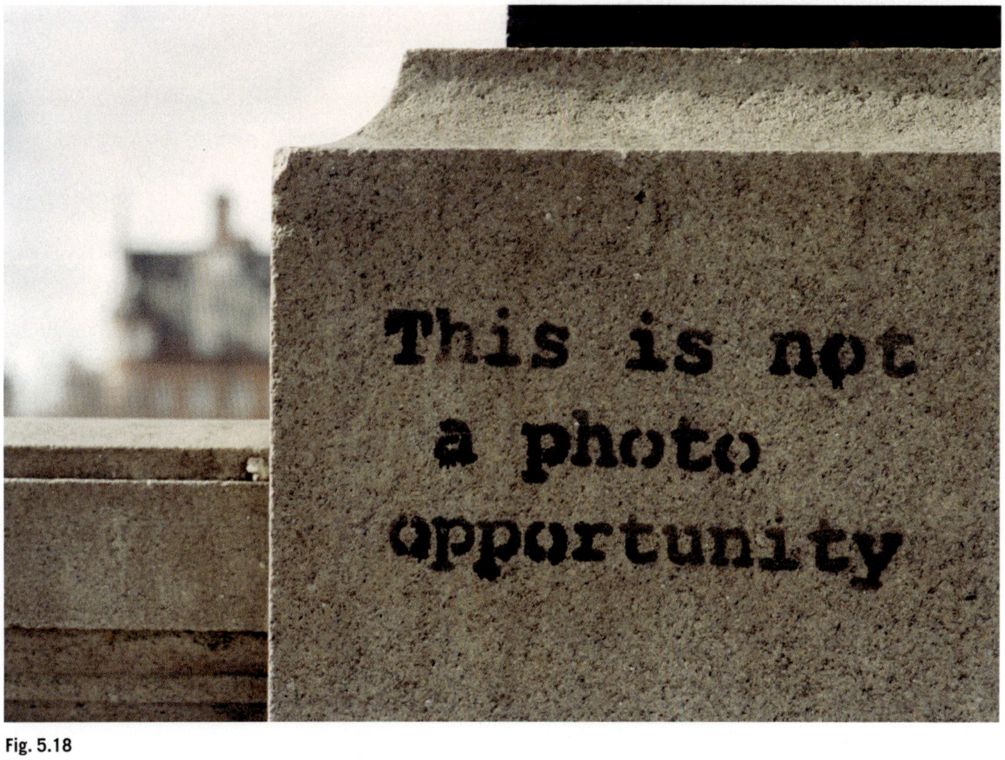

Fig. 5.18

1 A similar description exists in the Sumerian *Epic of Gilgamesh*, which dates from around the middle of the third millennium BC.

2 Merlin Coverley, *Utopia* (Harpenden: Pocket Essentials, 2010), 19–20.

3 Barry Cunliffe (ed.), *The Oxford Illustrated History of Prehistoric Europe* (Oxford: Oxford University Press, 1994), 79–136.

4 Coverley, *Utopia*, 27.

5 The photographs were taken from the archives of the Musée de l'Homme in Paris. Puranen's project can be seen in the context of critiques of the ethnographic use of photography by institutions during the nineteenth century. See Elizabeth Edwards, *Raw Histories: Photographs, Anthropology, and Museums* (Oxford: Berg Publishers, 2001).

6 As with the nineteenth-century U.S. Geological Survey photographs, John Szarkowski helped identify the artistic significance of some of these battlefield landscapes. In a famous essay, "Photography's Discursive Spaces: Landscape/View," critic Rosalind Krauss was skeptical of the attribution of these works, as well as those by Eugène Atget, as objects of art. *Art Journal*, 42, no. 4: 1982.

7 See Philip Knightley, *The First Casualty: The War Correspondent as Hero, Propagandist, and Myth-Maker from the Crimea to Iraq* (London: André Deutsch, 2003), 13.

8 Since Fenton's expedition predated the invention of the halftone process, which made it possible to render photographs in print media, his pictures were copied and reproduced from woodcut engravings in publications such as *The London Illustrated News*.

9 The location where the pictures were taken and the order in which they were taken have been researched extensively in Errol Morris, *Believing Is Seeing: Observations on the Mysteries of Photography* (New York: Penguin Press, 2011).

10 Susan Sontag, *Regarding the Pain of Others* (New York: Farrar, Straus & Giroux, 2003), 45.

11 See Malcolm Andrews, *Landscape and Western Art* (Oxford: Oxford University Press, 1999), 138–42.

12 Mark Durden notes that the bleached-out appearance of Seawright's photographs throughout the series "further distances them from the spectacle associated with the contemporary media representations [of Afghanistan]." Durden in Paul Seawright, *Hidden* (London: Imperial War Museum, 2003).

13 See Liz Wells, *Land Matters* (London: I.B. Tauris, 2011), 181–84.

14 David Campany, "Safety in Numbness: Some Remarks on the Problems of 'Late Photography,'" in David Green (ed.), *Where Is the Photograph?* (Brighton: Photoworks, 2003), 124.

15 Ibid.

16 Other more recent additions to that list are Hans-Christian Schink's photographs of devastation across Japan following the earthquake and tsunami in 2011.

17 Campany, "Safety in Numbness," 126.

18 This connection was first explored by Roland Barthes in his extremely influential book *Camera Lucida* (first published as *La Chambre Claire* in 1980), which is a eulogy to his *late* mother, narrated through a discussion of what he believed to be photography's intrinsic qualities.

19 David Campany, *Photography and Cinema* (London: Reaktion Books, 2008), 44.

20 Campany, "Safety in Numbers," 132.

21 Ibid., 127.

22 Since "Safety in Numbness" was written, the ways that news is gathered and disseminated have evolved dramatically, with social media playing a particularly dominant role to the extent that platforms such as Twitter have arguably succeeded the video cameras of news crews in terms of breaking the news.

23 Campany, *Photography and Cinema*, 44.

24 Evidence of the global financial crisis on architecture has been explored widely by practitioners including Edgar Martins (*This Is Not a House, 2008*), Richard Page (*The Blind Cartographer, 2012*), and Markel Redondo (*Economic Crisis in Spain, 2012*).

25 See Ian Walker, "Terrain Vague," in Paul Seawright, *Paul Seawright* (Salmanca: Ediciones Universidad Salamanca, 2000), 125.

26 For a convincing proposition of Atget's artistic credentials, see "Eugène Atget: A Photographer's Photographer," in Tod Papageorge, *Core Curriculum* (New York: Aperture, 2011).

27 Terrain Vague is discussed in depth in Ian Walker, *City Gorged with Dreams: Surrealism and Documentary Photography in Interwar Paris* (Manchester: Manchester University Press, 2002).

28 The film has been reinterpreted in David Bate's photographic project (2012) and Geoff Dyer's literary narrative (2012), both with the same title, *Zone.*

29 The long-term damage to the environment and human health of the Chernobyl disaster is far reaching, extending thousands of miles beyond the exclusion zone and including hundreds of farms in the UK.

30 Marc Augé, *Non-Places: Introduction to an Anthropology of Supermodernity* (London: Verso, 1995).

31 Graham Clark, *The Photograph* (Oxford: Oxford University Press, 1997), 149.

32 Wells, *Land Matters,* 56.

33 See W.J.T. Mitchell (ed.), *Landscape and Power* (2nd ed.) (Chicago: University of Chicago Press, 2002), 179.

34 See John Taylor, *A Dream of England* (Manchester & New York: University of Manchester Press, 1994), 247.

35 Phrase borrowed from the title of John Urry's book (2002).

ASSIGNMENT 5

A LONGER VIEW

PROJECT Create a series of photographs that engage with a previous narrative about a place or a landscape. These photographs could comprise an imaginary or mythological tale or something that took place near where you live—an urban myth perhaps. You may choose to take a forensic approach and rephotograph places where a particular event took place, or you may like to incorporate elements of performance into your series. Your project might focus around a very specific location, or you might like to retrace a journey or story.

Start thinking about a shooting strategy, and begin working on your project with some test shoots. Try to incorporate techniques and materials sympathetically to complement your ideas. How you do this will depend entirely upon your chosen narrative or conceptual approach. It may be pertinent to include text or other media or objects that relate to the narrative that you are investigating. Once you have made some preliminary progress, discuss your ideas and strategies with your peer group.

When you have developed your project, post your work onto your blog or show it to your peers along with a brief evaluation of your project. Refer to specific images and explain your working process.

Consider your audience and their prior knowledge of the narrative that your work addresses. You may need to supply additional information about the subject; however, this information should complement, not override, your photographs. Discuss the strengths and weaknesses of your project and how successfully you believe it addresses the themes that you set out to explore.

RESEARCH AND DISCUSSION Consider the following questions and write down your thoughts in your reflective learning journal or on your blog. You may find these questions helpful to develop your ideas for your project.

- How do you relate to landscapes depicting conflict, war zones, and atrocities? Do you think these are appropriate subject matter for contemporary photographers to pursue? Where do you think we should see this kind of imagery?
- What does "peripheral" mean to you? Describe areas around you that you think could be classified as peripheral or liminal. Or are there communities or groups of people that are assigned or "marginalized" to particular parts of the landscape near you?
- How do photographs contribute to the formation of places that are socially or culturally significant? Identify and discuss some examples.

CONCLUSION

The message of Banksy's graffiti might seem like a negative point to conclude a book that has attempted to inspire people to use photography to explore and engage with their surroundings. But the point that you should take away from this work is certainly not an order to pack away your camera but rather that you think about the subjects you are photographing *as you are shooting them* and, importantly, consider *why* you feel compelled to photograph them. At a time when reaching for one's camera phone at the sight of almost anything has become more of a reflex than an expression of creative intent, it has never been more important to think, if not before, then at least *while* you are making pictures.

The success of all of the photographers and artists discussed in this book is owed not to their having an eye for a picture but rather to their vision for an image, which in every case is underscored by an understanding of the subject matter. Mastering the techniques of photography will help you to realize your vision, but equally important is having a willingness to learn about your subject, as a greater understanding will aid the conceptual resolution of your photography. While there may be elements of spontaneity in many of the pictures discussed, none are the product of serendipity but rather all are the result of diligent practice, research, and thought. *Creating* opportunities, rather than keeping an optimistic eye out for them, will ultimately yield more rewarding photographs and increasingly thought-provoking projects and imagery. Do not be afraid to assert or challenge your ideas and preconceptions or your belief in your photography.

When you set foot in the landscape, try to remember that you are treading on ground that countless generations of your ancestors have walked on. It has been fought over, hunted upon, cultivated, worshipped, and used in myriad other ways. You are setting foot on it with the sum of your prejudices, memories, spiritual and philosophical beliefs, and hopes and expectations. Everything you know and have yet to discover about the place will be squeezed, in an instant, into your viewfinder. The possibilities for landscape subject matter are not limited to how far you can travel geographically, but rather by how much of yourself you are willing to invest in your photographs.

AESTHETIC Relating to feeling and sensory effect, or philosophy in the fine arts. In terms of the photograph, aesthetic tends to refer to the particular visual characteristics of the picture (style, such as application of photographic or postproduction technique) that have a bearing upon how the photograph is read. "Aesthetic" is often used to encompass visible characteristics and their philosophical underpinnings, such as *a picturesque aesthetic.*

ALLEGORY The exploration of ideological themes within a picture or other work, typically of a social or political nature. Often the author has a particular moral message, which is articulated through the course of a narrative and the fate of its protagonists.

APPROPRIATION The deliberate use of a work by another artist or author within someone's own practice. Appropriation is often seen in conceptual explorations of photography (e.g., Sherrie Levine and Richard Prince).

ARCADIAN Relating to Arcadia, the utopian setting described in Greek mythology and literature. "Arcadian" is frequently used to describe idealized landscape representations that appear to be idyllic or unaffected by mankind. The word "Edenic" is used to the same effect. See p. 156.

CHIAROSCURO Rendering a subject in three dimensions through use of light and dark tones. In photography and cinema, chiaroscuro tends to refer to images and sequences that are particularly contrasting in light, such as the use of "hard" light in low-light situations or the incorporation of long shadows.

CONTEXT The scenario in which a photograph appears or was taken. This may be the physical presentation of the image (e.g., within a gallery or in a newspaper), or it may be the social and historic environment. Context affects how meaning is constructed and how photographs are read.

CRITICISM The analytical evaluation of a subject, theme, or topic, or the use of a discipline as an analytical device (e.g., *Mitch Epstein's photographs critically examine the interrelationship between energy and political power*).

DISCOURSE The intellectual dialogue and debate surrounding a particular theme, subject, or philosophy (e.g., *the discourse of landscape photography*).

EARTHWORKS This is typically the large-scale landscaping of areas of land as practiced by artists such as Robert Smithson and Michael Heizer. This is often confused with Land Art, which still involves engaging with the landscape in a physical sense but on a smaller scale. Indeed, some practitioners, such as Richard Long and Hamish Fulton, deliberately distance themselves from the ostentatious proportions of some earthwork projects. Photography often plays a key role in these practices as a means of documenting these interventions, which have a connection with performance art that has developed since the 1960s.

GENRE The category to which a particular type of picture or methodological approach belongs, such as still life, tableau, social documentary, or fashion.

JUXTAPOSITION The creative or analytical effect of placing two or more elements, such as photographs, or combining materials, such as image and text. It can also refer to the relationship between elements within a single image, such as *the juxtaposition of the shark and the bather.*

MONTAGE The combination of several component parts to create a unified, single object, such as a photomontage. The term is also used in relation to editing sequences of moving images, particularly the quick succession of short clips.

NARRATIVE The story or message that is communicated within an image or across a sequence of images. Narratives may be linear, describing a sequence of events or suggesting a relationship between subjects within the frame, or it may be something nonlinear and abstract, referring to issues and events that are outside of the frame.

NATURALISTIC In accordance with nature. In photographic terms, naturalistic tends to relate to a comparison between the formal appearance of the image obtained from the camera's artificial lens and the image perceived by the human eye and brain.

OEUVRE The sum of a practitioner's work and the themes that he or she has explored through it (e.g., *Within Ansel Adams's oeuvre one can see an intense admiration for the drama of nature*).

PASTORAL Relating to agriculture. Usually a detail within a picture or text that tends to idealize rural lifestyles. Pastoral motifs have been used throughout art history and literature symbolically as means of delivering more complex meaning through an apparently simple lifestyle, such as within the poetic tradition of pastoral elegy. "Bucolic," meaning "cow herder," is sometimes used instead of "pastoral."

PICTORIALISM An approach to photography whereby the visual qualities and manipulation of the image are the primary expressive characteristics of a work. In the nineteenth century, the pictorial approach was the way that those who believed in the creative and artistic potential of the photograph separated themselves from the medium's scientific origins.

POSTMODERNISM The postmodern era describes the period from roughly the early 1970s to the present. Postmodernism is not an artistic movement as such but rather a collection of ideas and aesthetic values that amount to the "postmodern condition." Typical aspects of postmodern art and design are a rejection of Modernist aesthetics and values; the incorporation of previous texts or reinterpretation of existing works within new ones; embracing the "plurality" of interpretations of the meanings of a work or text; and promoting inclusivity of nonspecialist audiences.

PREVISUALIZATION The act of conceiving how the final photographic print of an object or a view will look *before* the picture is taken. Framing and understanding the limitations of the dynamic range of the film or digital camera is important to be able to accurately *previsualize* how a scene will be tonally distributed in the final image. The phrase was popularized by Ansel Adams, who also used the word "visualization" in the same way.

REALISM Relating to the accuracy or faithfulness of an impression or the narrative within a representation. In documentary photography for instance, "realism" tends to refer to works that reveal challenging aspects of society or are taboo.

TABLEAU *Tableaux vivants,* or "living pictures," were a form of nineteenth-century entertainment, whereby historic moments and scenes from works of art were recreated either professionally by actors and models or informally within the domestic parlor. In photography, tableau (plural: *tableaux*) usually refers to meticulously produced photographs that depict a carefully designed scene. These types of photographs tend to incorporate controlled lighting, prefabricated sets, and models. Narrative is an integral component of the tableau. Unstaged photographs (including landscapes) that have a particularly vivid sense of narrative are occasionally referred to as tableaux.

TOPOGRAPHY The physical features, both naturally occurring and man-made, of an area of land, such as hills, buildings, mountains, and rivers.

VERNACULAR Relating to the local or common use of something. In photography, the term refers to domestic photography or other applications that are not made for the sake of creative expression, such as forensic photography or the family album.

ADAMS, Ansel. *Examples: The Making of 40 Photographs.* Boston: Little, Brown & Co., 1983.

ADAMS, Robert. *Beauty in Photography.* New York: Aperture, 1996.

ANDREWS, Malcolm. *Landscape and Western Art.* Oxford: Oxford University Press, 1999.

AUGÉ, Marc. *Non-Places: Introduction to an Anthropology of Supermodernity.* London: Verso, 1995.

BARTHES, Roland. *Image—Music—Text.* London: Fontana Press, 1977.

BARTHES, Roland. *Camera Lucida.* London: Jonathan Cape, 1982.

BATE, David. *Photography: The Key Concepts.* London: Berg, 2009.

BURKE, Edmund. *A Philosophical Enquiry.* Oxford: Oxford University Press, 1990.

CAMPANY, David. *Art and Photography.* London: Phaidon Press, 2003.

CAMPANY, David. *Photography and Cinema.* London: Reaktion Books, 2008.

CLARK, Kenneth. *Landscape into Art* (2nd ed.). London: John Murray, 1976.

CLARKE, Graham. *The Photograph.* Oxford: Oxford University Press, 1997.

COTTON, Charlotte. *The Photograph as Contemporary Art.* London: Thames & Hudson, 2004.

DIMBLEBY, David (ed.). *A Picture of Britain.* London: Tate Publishing, 2005.

DOWLER, Lorraine (ed.). *Gender and Landscape: Renegotiating the Moral Landscape.* Abingdon: Routledge, 2005.

DURDEN, Mark (ed.). *Fifty Key Writers on Photography.* London: Routledge, 2012.

DYER, Geoff. *The Ongoing Moment.* London: Little Brown, 2005.

FARLEY, P., AND SYMMONS ROBERTS, M. *Edgelands: Journeys into England's True Wilderness.* London: Jonathan Cape, 2011.

FOSTER-RICE, G., AND ROHRBACH, J. (ed.). *Reframing the New Topographics.* Chicago: The Center for American Places at Columbia College Chicago, 2013.

GASKINS, Bill (ed.). *Perspectives on Landscape.* London: Arts Council of Great Britain, 1978.

GILBERT-ROLFE, Jeremy. *Beauty and the Contemporary Sublime.* New York: Allworth Press, 1999.

GILPIN, William. *Observations on the River Wye.* London: Pallas Athene, 2005.

HILL, Paul. *Approaching Photography* (2nd ed.). London: Photographers' Institute Press, 2004.

HILL, P., AND COOPER, T.J. *Dialogue with Photography.* London: Dewi Lewis, 2005.

HURN, D., AND JAY, B. *On Being a Photographer.* Anacortes: LensWork, 2009.

JEFFREY, Ian. *Photography: A Concise History.* London: Thames & Hudson, 1981.

JUSSIM, E., AND LINDQUIST-COCK, E. *Landscape as Photograph.* New Haven: Yale University Press, 1985.

LANGFORD, M., FOX, A., AND SAWDON SMITH, R. *Langford's Basic Photography* (9th ed.). Oxford: Focal Press, 2010.

MARKONISH, Denise (ed.). *Badlands: New Horizons in Landscape.* North Adams: Massachusetts Museum of Contemporary Art, 2008.

McCORMICK, John, *The Global Environmental Movement* (2nd ed.). Chichester: John Wiley & Sons, 1995.

MITCHELL, W.J.T. (ed.). *Landscape and Power* (2nd ed.). Chicago: University of Chicago Press, 2002.

PEELER, David. *The Illuminating Mind in American Photography: Stieglitz, Strand, Weston, Adams* Woodbridge & Rochester: The University of Rochester Press, 2001.

RITCHIN, Fred. *After Photography.* New York: W.W. Norton & Co., 2009.

RYAN, James R. *Photography and Exploration.* London: Reaktion Books, 2013.

SCHAMA, Simon. *Landscape and Memory.* London: Harper Collins, 1995.

SCHWARTZ, J.M., AND RYAN, J.R. (ed.). *Picturing Place: Photography and the Geographical Imagination.* London: I.B. Tauris, 2003.

SOLNIT, Rebecca. *As Eve Said to the Serpent: On Landscape, Gender & Art.* Athens: University of Georgia Press, 2003.

SOLNIT, Rebecca. *Motion Studies: Time, Space, and Eadweard Muybridge.* London: Bloomsbury, 2003.

SONTAG, Susan. *On Photography*. New York: Farr, Strauss & Giroux, 1977.

TAYLOR, John. *A Dream of England: Landscape, Photography, and the Tourist's Imagination.* Manchester & New York: University of Manchester Press, 1994.

TRACHTENBERG, Alan (ed.). *Classic Essays on Photography.* New Haven: Leete's Island Books, 1980.

URRY, John. *The Tourist Gaze* (2nd ed.). London: Sage, 2002.

WELLS, Liz (ed.). *Viewfindings: Women Photographers, Landscape, and Environment.* Tiverton: Available Light, 1994.

WELLS, Liz. *Land Matters: Landscape Photography, Culture and Identity.* London: I.B. Tauris, 2011.

WELLS, L., NEWTON K., AND FEHILY, C. (ed.). *Shifting Horizons: Women's Landscape Photography Now.* London: I.B. Taurus, 2000.

ONLINE RESOURCES

INSTITUTIONS & ORGANIZATIONS

Aperture Foundation
www.aperture.org
International Centre of Photography
www.icp.org
Land/Water Research Network
www.landwater-research.co.uk
Library of Congress
www.loc.gov
Musée de l'Elysée
www.elysee.ch
National Media Museum
www.nationalmediamuseum.org.uk
New York Museum of Modern Art
www.moma.org
Photoworks
www.photoworks.org.uk
The Photographer's Gallery
www.thephotographersgallery.org.uk
Tate Gallery
www.tate.org.uk
Victoria & Albert Museum
www.vam.ac.uk

MAGAZINES AND BLOGS

1000 Words Photography
www.1000wordsmag.com
American Suburb X
www.americansuburbx.com
The British Journal of Photography
www.bjp-online.com
Colin Pantall
www.colinpantall.blogspot.co.uk
Conscientious Photography Magazine
www.cphmag.com
Elizabeth Avedon
www.elizabethavedon.blogspot.co.uk
Foto8
www.foto8.com
Hotshoe International
www.hotshoeinternational.com
La Lettre de la Photographie
www.lalettredelaphotographie.com
Landscape Stories
www.landscapestories.net
New Landscape Photography
www.newlandscapephotography.com
On Landscape
www.onlandscape.co.uk
Photomonitor
www.photomonitor.co.uk
Photoparley
www.photoparley.com
Source Magazine
www.source.ie

ACKNOWLEDGMENTS My heartfelt gratitude extends, first and foremost, to the many photographers and artists who have contributed their pictures to this book. As well as their trust in me, their generous support has provided the raw material from which to map the various themes in this narrative, and I sincerely hope that I have represented their work accurately and fairly. Their contributions have made this book possible, and it has been a pleasure to rekindle previous connections and make new acquaintances throughout this lengthy yet rewarding process.

My understanding of landscape, and photography more generally, has developed with the aid of more people than it is possible to mention. My thanks go out to the many teachers, colleagues, and students who have tested my appreciation of what photography does and what it has the potential to be. My passion for the outdoors, and this attempt to examine our relationship to it, extends from the enthusiasm instilled in me by certain individuals much closer to me, and these people are ultimately responsible for sowing the seeds of my pursuit of a deeper understanding of landscape.

I would like to thank Lynsey Brough and Georgia Kennedy at Bloomsbury for their editorial support and management of this project—and for their patience! To those who have either officially or informally reviewed my synopsis and draft manuscripts, I am indebted to you all for your invaluable comments and suggestions, as well your words of encouragement. Finally, I would like to thank Paul Hill for writing such an insightful foreword and for so lucidly articulating some of the problems with how we tend to represent the land. I hope this book goes some way to help us overcome some of them and will expand the way we think about our relationship to place.

PICTURE CREDITS p9: ©Hans van der Meer; p11: Courtesy of the artist and Luhring Augustine, New York; p12: ©Gawain Barnard; p15: ©Jonathan Olley; p16: ©Jo Metson Scott & Nicola Yeoman; p18: ©Suzanne Mooney; p20: Plate 57 from *Geological exploration of the fortieth parallel*, Library of Congress Prints and Photographs Division Washington, D.C. 20540, LC-DIG-ppmsca-11836; p22: ©Thomas Joshua Cooper; p23: ©Dewald Bothal; p25: ©Massimo Vitali; p27: Henri Cartier-Bresson/Magnum Photos; p28: Library of Congress Prints and Photographs Division Washington, D.C. 20540, LC-DIG-ds-00274; p29: ©Paul Hill; p30: Library of Congress Prints and Photographs Division Washington, D.C. 20540, LC-USZ62-115228; p32: Fay Godwin/Collections Picture Library; p36: © Justin Quinnell; p37: ©Jesse Alexander; p39: Courtesy of the artist and Purdy Hicks Gallery [Unique Ilfochrome print 170 x 101.5cm]; p40: ©Martina Lindqvist; p42: ©Jesse Alexander; p43: Paul Fusco/Magnum Photos; p45: Library of Congress Prints and Photographs Division Washington, D.C. 20540, LC-DIG-pppprs-00244; p46: ©Jesse Alexander; p47: © Michal Iwanowski; p49: © John Davies; p50 courtesy of Getty Images; p52: © José Navarro/ Pangeafoto; p57: ©Noémie Goudal [Lightjet Print, 168x210cm]; p59: Courtesy RaebervonStenglin, Zurich and Peter Lav Gallery, Copenhagen; p60: Courtesy of the artist and Mark Moore Gallery; p62: ©Paul Hill; p63: © Keith Arnatt Estate and Maureen Paley, London / TATE Images; p65: courtesy of Getty Images; p66: ©Peter Kennard; p67: ©Suzanne Mooney; p68: ©David Moore; p71: courtesy of Getty Images; p73: courtesy of Getty Images; p74: © José Navarro/Pangeafoto; p75: ©Nadav Kander. Courtesy Flowers Gallery; p77: Library of Congress Prints and Photographs Division Washington, D.C. 20540, LC-DIG-ppmsca-10055; p78: Alec Soth/ Magnum Photos; p79: NASA/JPL/Cornell; p80: ©Paul Gaffney; p82: ©Chris Coekin; p83: ©Matt White [122 x 69cm digital C-type print]; p84: Mark Power/Magnum Photos; p89: ©Ilkka Haslo; p91: ©Richard Page; p93: ©Miklos Gaál; p95: ©Dan Holdsworth [C-type print 114.5 x 92.5cm]; p96: ©Paul Alexander Knox. All rights reserved; p99: Courtesy of the artist and Klompching Gallery; p100: ©Jesse Alexander; p102: courtesy of Special Collections & University Archives, Stanford University Libraries; p105: ©Raffaela Mariniello; p106: ©Edgar Martins (www.edgarmartins.com) / courtesy The Moth House (www.themothhouse.com); p107: ©Tim Simmons; p108: ©Michael Wolf. Courtesy of Bruce Silverstein Gallery; p109: ©Dan Holdsworth [C-type print, 186 x 246cm]; p110: courtesy of The Art Archive; p111: ©Joan Fontcuberta; p113: courtesy of Getty Images; p114: courtesy of Getty Images; p115: National Archives and Records Administration, Records of the National Park Service (79-AAG-1); p119: ©Black River Productions, Ltd. / Mitch Epstein. Courtesy of Sikkema Jenkins & Co., New York. Used with permission. All rights reserved; p120: courtesy of Getty Images; p122: ©Céline Clanet / Fondation Facim; p123: ©James Morris; p124: ©Suzanna Davison; p127: © Robert Adams, courtesy Fraenkel Gallery, San Francisco; p128: ©Lewis Baltz, courtesy Galerie Thomas Zander, Cologne; p129: ©Bernd Becher and Hilla Becher / courtesy of TATE Images; p131: ©John Darwell, 2001; p132: courtesy of NASA; p133: courtesy of Daniel Beltra / Getty Images; p135: ©Jonathan Olley [Chromogenic color print 60" x 50" C-type]; p137: ©Tom Stoddart Archive/Getty Images; p138: ©Penny Watson; p139: ©The Artist/ Aleksandra Mir; p140: ©Jo Spence and Terry Dennett; p141: © the Estate of Helen Chadwick, Courtesy Richard Saltoun Gallery; p142: courtesy of SSPL/Getty Images; p143: Farm Security Administration - Office of War Information Collection 11671-10, Library of Congress Prints and Photographs Division Washington, D.C. 20540, LC-DIG-fsac-1a33893; p144: ©Kate Kirkwood; p145: courtesy of Murray Close / Getty Images; p146: courtesy of Imperial War Museums/Getty Images; p147: ©Simon Roberts and courtesy of Flowers Gallery; p149: ©Peter Mansell; p154: Courtesy of Kerlin Gallery, Dublin; p158: ©Christopher Down 2014; p160: ©DACS 2013; p161: ©Michal Iwanowski; p163: Courtesy of the Roger Fenton Crimean War Photograph Collection, Library of Congress Prints and Photographs Division Washington, D.C. 2054, LC-DIG-ppmsca-35546, p164: courtesy of Gilman Collection, Museum Purchase, 2005 / The Metropolitan Museum of Art (www.metmuseum.org); Library of Congress Prints and Photographs Division Washington, D.C. 20540 USA, LC-DIG-ppmsca-12565; p165: ©Paul Graham, courtesy of Pace Gallery and Pace/MacGill Gallery, New York; p166: Courtesy of Kerlin Gallery, Dublin; p169: ©Joel Meyerowitz, courtesy of Harvard Greenberg Gallery; p170: ©Adam Broomberg and Oliver Chanarin [C-type print 19" x 23"]; p173: ©Hala Elkoussy; p175: ©Paul Alexander Knox, All rights reserved; p176: ©Anthony Hernandez; p177: ©Henk Wildschut; p179: p179: ©Paul Reas; p180: ©Martin Parr/Magnum Photos; p181: ©Jesse Alexander